THE NEXT
GREAT
PRESIDENT

Edward Thomas

ACCE Publishing LLC

Irvine, California

ACCE Publishing LLC

1 League, Unit 62422

Irvine, California 92602

Although every precaution has been taken to verify the accuracy of the information contained herein, the author and publisher assume no responsibility for any errors or omissions. No liability is assumed for damages that may result from the use of information contained within.

The Next Great President / Edward Thomas. —1st ed.

Library of Congress Control Number: 2020920957

ISBN 978-0-9983281-3-3 (Hardbound)

ISBN 978-0-9983281-4-0 (Paperback)

ISBN 978-0-9983281-5-7 (eBook)

Edited by Brooke C. Stoddard, AG, ASJA, NPC

Cover Design by JD&J Design LLC

CONTENTS

i

for AHT, AMS, DAT, EFT, and HKE

History never repeats, but it often rhymes.

—MARK TWAIN

Prologue

"History never repeats, but it often rhymes" is an aphorism attributed to Samuel Clemens (also known as Mark Twain). I am a believer in historical cycles, and that while the exact same situation and outcome do not recur, there are historical echoes that are reflections of the past. There is a natural flow and harmony to history, which is reflected in many things in nature and time-based relationships. I am good at recognizing patterns and believe these patterns exist in our everyday lives. They also exist in any time-based phenomena, which include the rise and fall of civilizations, empires, and even careers.

I was on a business trip to Washington, D. C., and visiting the monuments with a friend. We were admiring the WWII Memorial, which is on the Mall between the Washington Monument and the Lincoln Memorial, when it struck me. I said to my friend: "Three great presidents, three great wars." I reflected on a book I had read in 1998, which I had stumbled upon while writing a paper about the stock market for an MBA finance course.

The name of the book was *Generations* by Strauss and Howe. In this book, Strauss and Howe describe how the different generations of American civilization affect, or reflect, history. They also predicted a "great crisis" between 2004 and 2025, based on an 80-year cycle. I believe in this 80-year cycle (the secular crisis cycle), and that what has gone before will come again. History will repeat itself. We had the Revolutionary War in 1775-1783, the Civil War in 1861-1865, and World

War II in 1941-1945, and I expect the next War or major Crisis in U. S. history to occur sometime in the 2020s.

The curious thing about wars is they bring out the best in our country's leadership. Perhaps we were lucky to have the right people at the right time ascend to take the reins. Perhaps the worst of times brings out the best attributes of our country's leaders. Perhaps it is a combination of these things. Whatever the reason, it is my firm belief that our country's three greatest presidents to date are Washington, Lincoln, and Roosevelt, and that our next Great President will be elected in 2020, 2024, or 2028.

I am not a biographer. For a detailed biography on any of the three former presidents I discuss in this book, there are several available that are very good for each. One of my favorite biographers is Ron Chernow. He has an excellent biography of Washington, *A Life* (2010), which won the Pulitzer Prize for Biography in 2011, and I would also recommend his biographies of Hamilton and Rockefeller. I also liked Joseph Ellis' *His Excellency, George Washington* (2004). However, James Thomas Flexner's four-volume treatise (1965-72) and Douglas Southhall Freeman's seven-volume series (1948-57) are widely recognized as the definitive biographies of Washington.

Of the myriad of books on Abraham Lincoln and the Civil War, I particularly enjoyed *Team of Rivals* (2005), by Doris Kearns Goodwin. There are so many perspectives on President Lincoln and so many different ways his life has been analyzed, researched, and dissected that it is difficult to pick a single biography or biographer. I started with the biographies by Carl Sandberg and Benjamin Thomas (no relation). I also read David Herbert Donald's *Lincoln* (1995) and Ronald C. White, Jr.'s *A. Lincoln* (2009). For a single volume biography of Lincoln, I recommend White's book because of his thoroughness and chronological approach.

There is a considerable amount of material to consider when discussing Franklin Roosevelt's biography. Kenneth S.

Davis' multiple volume work (1972-2000) is in the mode of Flexner's or Freeman's treatment of Washington. Alonzo Hamby's *Man of Destiny* (2015) is a relatively recent biography of Franklin Roosevelt. *FDR* (2007) by Jean Edward Smith provides the kind of complete, chronological, and detailed biography in a single volume that most curious readers should enjoy. And Doris Kearns Goodwin's *No Ordinary Time* (1994) is a classic Pulitzer Prize winning portrait of Franklin and Eleanor Roosevelt during the war years.

My intent is not to provide an in-depth biography of these great presidents, but rather to show the parallels between them and whoever might fill a similar role in our history. My desire is to pique your interest. I hope you will enjoy these vignettes of our past presidents and, if you are intrigued, that you follow up this reading with an investigation into some of the more complete biographies of these great men. My purpose in writing this book is to raise awareness of the potential for a crisis in leadership in the coming years, and to prepare the public and potential voters of the coming singularity event in our country's future. I hope to convince people of the criticality of the coming election(s) so we can all make intelligent decisions, and hopefully put the right people in the right places to protect our future, our country, and our way of life.

Our First Great President

Our first Great President was George Washington. George Washington was unique. At no time in history, before or since, has a revolutionary leader _not_ become the dictator of the country/region/empire of which he has just led the insurrection. It has been said that King George of England, upon hearing that Mr. Washington was not becoming the King of the United States, stated that Washington must be the greatest man who ever lived.

George Washington was unique in other aspects. He was a person destined for greatness, and he knew this. His personal journals were written with an eye towards history. He seemed to self-edit the words and thoughts captured in those journals. He always seemed to do the right thing. Even the one criticism for which he has been persecuted, the fact that he owned slaves who worked his plantation in Virginia, is muted because he is viewed as being one of the more forward-thinking slave owners of his time for the fact that he freed his slaves in his will.

George Washington was a military man, a thinker, and a natural leader. At six foot three inches, he was extremely tall in his time. He was also extremely lucky. His battles on the field could have easily left him injured or incapacitated. In particular, there was an attack by Indians during the French and Indian War that could have ended in complete annihilation, but which Washington miraculously survived. The fact that he had several bullet holes in his jacket and none in his body almost suggested his invincibility.

George Washington surrounded himself with brilliant people. Alexander Hamilton was his personal secretary and is attributed to having written several of his correspondences about the war and what strategy should be undertaken. However, the final decisions were always Washington's. He seemed to have a conviction that the eyes of the world were on him and that he would be judged by history.

The first crisis of the nation, the war with England for independence, was George Washington's personal triumph through strength of will and perseverance. He led the forces of a fledgling nation against the greatest war machine the world to that time had ever known. The English hegemony was absolute and worldwide. England's naval armada was the most powerful in the world. The English Redcoats were the most highly trained and capable army in the world. For Washington and the Continental Army to defeat the British was to achieve the impossible. And he did.

George Washington was by no means a perfect man. He could be harsh and demanding, not only in the way he treated his soldiers, but also in the way he treated his slaves. But when one takes in the sheer span and scope of his decisions, how he handled himself in the face of overwhelming odds, and how prescient and precocious he was in performing his duties as both the commander of the Continental Army and as the first Commander in Chief of our nascent nation, it is amazing how well he got it right. He is and always should be the yardstick against which all future presidents and leaders should be measured.

CHAPTER 1

American Cincinnatus

Lucius Quinctius Cincinnatus was a Roman citizen and no-bleman who lived from 519 to 430BC, for those days an incred-ible life span of almost 90 years (most Romans of the time died before they turned 40). He became a Roman legend, because he famously retired from service three times, only to be called upon again when his country needed him. Each time he came back, and he did the right things at the right time to save his people. Then, when the crisis was over, he returned to his life on the farm and retired from the great scene of action. Each time, he sacrificed his personal finances, the welfare of his family, and his own interests. These sacrifices he made for the sake of honor, duty, and the glory of his country.[1]

Before Cincinnatus retired to his farm, he had been a suc-cessful and popular nobleman (patrician) and soldier, and the son of an important and well-known public official. He married young and came of age at the same time as the Roman Repub-lic. He and his wife Rascilla had four sons, the most famous of which was Caeso. This young man grew up to become a physi-cally imposing and intense character. He was well known for his military exploits and courage in battle, but he was seen as a boor and a bully by the public (plebeians). He was accused of attacking and killing a man while drunk, and that man's young-er brother brought the case before the Senate. Although de-fended by his military commanders, and by his father Cincinnatus, Caeso was put in jail. His bail was a pledge of

30,000 pounds of bronze, an enormous sum that took all of his father's and his father's friends' wealth to post. But when freed from jail on the pledge of bail Caeso fled to Etruria. Caeso lived, but Cincinnatus was ruined. Cincinnatus was honor and duty bound to the bail bond, so he sold all his belongings to pay the debt of the bail. After all of his friends and associates who helped him post the bail were repaid, Cincinnatus and his wife Rascilla retired in poverty to a small plot of farmland across the Tiber River from Rome to live out the rest of their days.[2]

The story of Cincinnatus was well known during the 18th-century Enlightenment, and it was common knowledge among the founding fathers of the United States. Benjamin Franklin, Thomas Jefferson, Alexander Hamilton, and others were well read in the classics of the Greek and Roman masters, as well as in biblical literature that was part of nearly every educated American's curriculum of the day. By the 1790s, the Cincinnatus reference as analogy was even used by newspapers for Washington's birthday celebration. Certainly, Washington was aware of the legend, and it seemed as if he modeled his life after that citizen-servant ideal.[3]

There are three instances of Washington's giving up power in the manner of Cincinnatus, which cemented his legacy as the father of our country. He was happily retired on his farm in Virginia when he was called upon to lead the Continental Army in our war for independence. At the end of the Revolutionary War, he gave up his title as General and Commander of the Continental Army and submitted his resignation to the Continental Congress. During his retirement from the war, he was called upon again to save his country. Because the fractious Congress was unable to pass laws to keep the country from the verge of collapse, Washington was brought out of retirement to lead the Constitutional Convention that wrote the supreme law of our nation. After his retirement from the Convention, he was brought back to lead us as the first president. And at the end of his second term as President of the United States he gave up his office, forsaking a third term. These three instances each show Washington's willingness to surrender power for the sake of his reputation and honor, and demonstrate his desire to live a life on his own terms.[4]

French and Indian War

The French and Indian War was George Washington's first introduction to the public spotlight. It was called the French and Indian War because the French colluded with different Indian tribes to fight the British colonials and the British army. The different Indian tribes of the region in dispute (the "Ohio country") deemed the French the lesser of two evils because they saw British colonials, and British colonial expansion, as the greater threat to their homelands and sovereignty. In addition, the French enjoyed a better relationship with the Indians owing to one of their commanders (Philip Thomas Joncaire) having been raised by Seneca Indians.[5] However, in the end the Indians would submit themselves to neither French nor English rule and decided to serve their best interests by aligning themselves with whomever they thought would win.

The Lieutenant Governor of Virginia, Robert Dinwiddie, commissioned Washington to scout the western lands of the Ohio country and discover the French intentions. It was rumored that the French had set up a string of Forts along the Ohio and Mississippi watersheds in an attempt to claim the central North American continent and halt British colonial expansion. It was this rumor that Dinwiddie wanted to assess. Washington volunteered for the mission of scouting the positions of the French forts in the Ohio country, and in October 1753 was commissioned by Dinwiddie for the task. That such an important mission was entrusted to such an inexperienced young man even surprised Washington, as he reflected in later life.[6]

Washington was provided a French interpreter (Jacob van Braam), a frontier guide (Christopher Gist), and four "servitors" to manage the horses and packs of provisions for the long trip through the northern Virginia and western Pennsylvania forest. On their month-long journey, they traveled across the Allegheny Mountains, down the Ohio River to pick up some Indian guides at an encampment called Logstown, through tree-filled forests to and up the Allegheny River, then up French Creek to Ft. Le Boeuf (at present day Waterford, Pennsylvania). On December 9, Washington delivered his message from Dinwiddie to the French commander, Jacques Legardeur de St. Pierre. For a few days, the French entreated Washington and his party, including three Indian chiefs they had brought along as additional guides, providing food and wine to the white men and bourbon to the Indians. The French even allowed Washington free access to the fort, whereupon he took detailed notes of the armament and dwellings. St. Pierre then told Washington that he would provide Dinwiddie's letter to his superiors but added he would not conform to its contents. He then supplied a response for Washington to take to Governor Dinwiddie.[7]

Washington tried to convince his Indian companions to return to the trail back down to the Allegheny, but the French continued to entertain the Indians – Washington was concerned that the French would turn the Indians against the British. After two days, however, the Washington party all boarded canoes supplied by the French and headed downriver. Travelling the rivers and trails through the wilderness in the dead of winter, Washington and his party survived a harrowing passage back down the Allegheny River, across the Allegheny Mountains, and eventually to Virginia. They endured treacherous terrain, bitter cold, and attempted murder by an Indian they met along the route. The French commander's message survived the journey also, even though Washington fell into the icy Allegheny and almost drowned. Upon greeting Washington on his return on January 16, Dinwiddie read the French commander's message, which stated France's intention of maintaining their frontier presence. This was the evidence Dinwiddie needed to raise an army and challenge the French occupation of the British-claimed territory. Dinwiddie asked Washington for a written account of the journey to be delivered the next day. Washington obliged and also provided detailed maps sketched with the hand of a surveyor (Washington's prior profession). Dinwiddie convinced Washington to publish a version of the papers, which became known as *The Journal of Major George Washington*; it was printed on both sides of the Atlantic and put Washington in the glare of public scrutiny. This document sowed the seeds of what was to become the French and Indian War.[8]

An Ignominious Defeat

Washington would have three more encounters with the French before the end of his first tour of duty as an army officer: the battle that ended up triggering a war; a subsequent defeat and surrender at Ft. Necessity; and defeat with honor at the Monongahela a year later. The first of these — Washington's encounter with the French in May 1754 — is thought to have provided the spark that ignited the French and Indian War, and in a larger context, the worldwide Seven Years War. Dinwiddie had sent Washington back into the Ohio country with as many soldiers as were available, and with instructions to kill or destroy any persons who attempt to obstruct or restrain British settlements there.[9]

An Indian force, commanded by a Seneca chief called Tanacharison, referred to as the Half King by the English, augmented Washington's army of about 150 troops. Half King was one of the three Indian chiefs who had accompanied Washington on his earlier trip to Ft. Le Boeuf.[10] Half King had been sent by the Iroquois Confederation to exert Six Nation authority over the inhabitants of the Ohio valley. The local Indians in Virginia had called Washington's great grandfather "Town Devourer." The sobriquet (in Indian, *Conotocarious*) was also bequeathed on George Washington when he became acquainted with Half King. This Seneca chief, believing that the French had murdered his father, was exceptional in his hatred of the French.[11]

Half King's presence among Washington's Virginia army caused an international incident. In late May, Indian scouts secretly discovered a French force of about 30 men camped in a clearing only a half mile from Washington's army. Washington ordered the Indians to move behind the French to block their escape then divided his forces into two columns to surround the clearing. As the French camp became aware of the British advance, they shouted an alarm and ran to their weapons. Washington commanded his troops to fire. The French fired on the exposed British lines and the Indians cut down the French from behind trees in the forest. The British and Indians killed or wounded a third of the French while suffering only minor casualties. Indians scalped the dead, and only the British presence kept the prisoners from being scalped as well. In a controversy that enflamed the passions of all of Europe, one of the dead Frenchmen was the commander, Joseph Coulon, Sieur de Jumonville, who was supposedly carrying diplomatic papers to deliver to the English. Half King is said to have personally butchered him either as he tried to surrender or after he was taken prisoner. Because this atrocity occurred under Washington's command, he was blamed for the entire affair.[12]

Some weeks later, in June 1754, French forces poured out of Fort Duquesne (at the river junction where Pittsburgh, Pennsylvania is today) and scoured the countryside in search of those who had killed Jumonville. They eventually caught up with Washington and his small army not far from the earlier skirmish. Washington had set up defenses and built fortifications out of some natural entrenchments in a clearing in the middle of the forest, and called it Fort Necessity. In addition, reinforcements of about 100 uniformed Colonials arrived to assist in the British-Colonial defense, led by a captain of British regulars named James Mackay. The French advanced about 600 troops, and in the inevitable clash the Virginians were surrounded and outnumbered. On the morning of July 3, the French rained down a relentless torrent of lead on the outgunned Virginians, cutting down humans, horses, and cattle where they stood. In the afternoon as the suffering wore on, a downpour of rain added to the misery. By evening, the French offered a parley, which Washington accepted. He surrendered the fort after signing terms of capitulation that allowed "honors of war," which meant the Virginians could leave with their possessions while flying their flag high. On July 4, Washington and his garrison were allowed to leave the field of battle with their wounded and their wounded pride.[13]

On July 17, Washington returned to Williamsburg and Dinwiddie to provide his report of the action. Dinwiddie treated Washington like a subordinate who has disappointed his superiors, and ordered him to report to Alexandria, Virginia, with the rest of his regiment. That fall, Washington traveled again to Williamsburg during the legislative session of the Assembly. There he learned British officers would be leading the colonists' military exploits, and that all of the Virginia colonial officers higher than captain would be demoted to captain, thereby to serve under their British counterparts. Rather than accept a demotion, Washington retired, and rented the Mount Vernon estate from the widow of his late brother.[14]

An Honorable Retreat

Over the next year, the French held onto the Ohio valley relatively unmolested, and the British planned their next move. The result of those plans was a major expedition led by British Regulars to expel the French from Fort Duquesne, and thus clear them out of that portion of the Ohio River watershed. Accordingly, British Major General Edward Braddock with two regiments of soldiers sailed across the Atlantic then up the Potomac, docked at Alexandria, Virginia, and began disgorging from their fleet cannons, artillery wagons, tents and soldiers. As the steady stream of ships made their way up the Potomac River, they were in full view of Washington at Mount Vernon. The fleet stamped a most congenial impression upon the young man, who wrote a congratulatory letter to the General upon his arrival. As the colonial officer most experienced with the area, Washington offered his services, and soon he became a member of Braddock's staff as a volunteer.[15]

Because he was serving Braddock in a voluntary position, Washington had an agreement that he could join the expedition after he had ironed out the management of his plantation at Mount Vernon. He was able to convince his brother Jack to manage the farm, over his mother's protestations, and Jack Washington would continue to render such service for the next three years. With his personal affairs thus resolved, Washington joined Braddock's army in May 1754. From May through June, Braddock's army slowly traversed the mountainous trail from Maryland to western Pennsylvania. By early July, the train of soldiers, horses, wagons and supplies were within a dozen miles of Fort Duquesne. But before they even reached the French fort, and after just having crossed the Monongahela River at a site now called Braddock, Pennsylvania, the British and colonial forces were ambushed by French and Indians.[16]

It was July 9, 1755 – a year and six days since Washington's disaster at Fort Necessity. Here came a rout of almost epic proportions. The vaunted British Redcoats, lining up as if for European-style open field combat, were methodically shot down by Indians using a guerilla fighting style of hiding behind trees and rocks. The fighting quickly turned to chaos as the British Regulars left their lines and ran back into guns and lines of the men behind them. Some of the British were even shooting down their own men in front of them in the confusion of the forest mêlée.[17]

Braddock was badly wounded in the battle, along with most of his staff and the other officers in the field. Washington alone remained unharmed and took it upon himself to roust the troops into an orderly retreat. Braddock ordered Washington to ride to the units still behind the theater of action and to bring them up to the battlefront so they could cover the army's retreat. When Washington arrived, he found that news of the disaster had preceded him and that the second division was already moving forward. Braddock decided to order a full retreat from the region and return to civilization. During the retreat, he died from his wounds and was buried on the road near the location of Washington's previous defeat at Fort Necessity.[18]

George Washington was commended for his gallantry during the murderous combat, and the blame for the disaster on the Monongahela went to Braddock. Credit for the successful retreat of Braddock's forces went to Washington, and he was celebrated as a hero upon his return to Virginia. In August 1755, he was commissioned by Dinwiddie as Colonel and Commander in Chief of all forces in Virginia. This was quite a turnabout from the previous year, when in light of the defeat at Fort Necessity, he was essentially dismissed by Dinwiddie and distanced from him.[19]

Fort Duquesne

George Washington was raised in an above average lifestyle – but given that the standard of living in those days was being able to feed and clothe yourself, it was a low average. He first attempted to find glory as a soldier in the British army. However, as a colonial colonel, he never quite got the credit or attention he felt he deserved. On numerous occasions, he proved his worth on the battlefield, only to be subsequently outranked by another British commander or colonial aristocrat sent by government bureaucrats. On his next assignment, he was hampered by having to submit to the commands of an inferior leader, a man named Captain John Dagworthy. Typically, a colonel outranks a captain; however, in this case Washington was a colonial colonel, while Dagworthy was a captain of the British Regulars. Nothing frustrated Washington more than having to suffer the pretensions of an incompetent officer. Washington complained bitterly to Dinwiddie about this turn of events, but to no avail. He considered retirement at one point but ended up suffering in service under Dagworthy.[20]

By the spring of 1758, Washington's fortunes were looking up, as a new commander was assigned to lead the British against the French and Indians. This was Brigadier General John Forbes, who was assigned by William Pitt to command new forces for a fresh campaign against Fort Duquesne. Washington mobilized his Virginia regiment in May near Winchester, Virginia, and joined the larger Forbes encampment in July near Raytown, Pennsylvania. The combined forces in Raytown numbered near 6000, over three times larger than the Braddock-led army Washington was a part of in 1755.[21]

Through the fall of 1758, Forbes' army cleared a path and built a road through the Pennsylvania wilderness over the Allegheny Mountains. When the British forces arrived within a few miles of their objective on Christmas Day, they found that the French had finally given up on Fort Duquesne (when the Indians deserted, they blew up what they could and torched the rest). George Washington knew that this spelled the end of Indian conflict in the region and possibly his opportunity to become an officer in the regular British Army. He announced to his superiors his intention to resign from the colonial forces and so informed his troops. The officers under his command all signed a letter thanking him for his service, commending him for his excellence as a leader, and begging him to stay on and lead them for one more year. Washington's written response on January 10 was also emotional and emphatic in his reply.

He thanked his men and expressed his happiness in receiving their declaration of approval in his conduct. He also said it had been "the greatest honor of his life" to have led them. Washington took his leave of the men and their command, and in January 1759, retired to his beloved Mount Vernon and Martha.[22]

Mount Vernon

Like an American Cincinnatus, Washington withdrew from his position as colonel and leader of the Virginia Regiment of colonial soldiers. This retirement is not widely recognized as a Cincinnatus-like act, because Washington risked little – and had much to gain – by retiring from his position in the Virginia Regiment. Indeed, Washington had threatened to resign multiple times, owing to his treatment by British authorities and his superiors during the previous several years. And for a year now he had been courting a rich widow, who was one of the most eligible women in Virginia. After the French abandoned and burned Fort Duquesne, he weighed his options and decided that resigning his commission was best. On January 6, he married Martha Dandridge Custis and began his life as a Virginia plantation farmer.[23]

Somewhat earlier, in 1758, while ensconced at Fort Cumberland awaiting the orders to march on Fort Duquesne, George Washington had been elected to the Virginia House of Burgesses. He was able to win the election in absence, because his friends and fellow officers had campaigned on his behalf. He won by over 75% of the vote (309 out of 396), which he attributed not only to his friends' part, but also to the generous libations they provided to the electorate.[24] This would become a learning opportunity, and, with his Virginia Regiment experience behind him, politics grew as a focus of his attention.

For seventeen years after his first retirement, George Washington played the part of the industrious Virginia plantation farmer. During this time, he also participated in Virginia politics as a Burgess. As such, he became attentive to issues that affected his community and sponsored a bill that would protect the area's drinking water from hog farms.[25] This experience exposed him to the inner workings of government; it was good training for his education in how to get things done politically. Washington did his best to faithfully represent the people of his district; indeed, he satisfied enough voters to retain his seat in the Virginia House of Burgesses for seventeen years. In Virginia government, he met people like George Mason, who schooled him in political theory.[26] He also met such other colonial political luminaries as like Thomas Jefferson, Patrick Henry, Peyton Randolph, and Richard Henry Lee.[27]

In 1761, Washington received a windfall from the death of his former sister-in-law; she died with no heirs so that the Mount Vernon property was transferred into his name per the will of his late brother Lawrence. But that year brought trouble, too; he suffered such a virulent cold – the only serious illness in his seventeen years on the farm – that he thought he was near death. The illness passed, though, and his health recovered.[28]

From 1763 to 1774, Washington also become a vestryman, a trustee, and a justice. He participated in, and tried to help resolve, the problems facing the people in his neighborhood, and lent money freely to friends and acquaintances, even though he was frequently not repaid. George was welcome, wherever he went, and never lacked a place to lodge wherever he travelled. In return, George and Martha Washington were gracious hosts, and never turned away a visitor, even total strangers. They frequently entertained guests several times a week, and some stayed for weeks on end. In one seven-year span, they entertained as many as 2,000 guests. Martha perfectly fit the role of the gracious hostess, and George played his part of the old war hero, living out his retirement in happy bliss.[29]

Cincinnatus' First Un-Retirement

Cincinnatus was living his humble and spartan life on the farm, happily married and enjoying his retirement with his wife Rascilla and their family, when he was abruptly called back to service by Roman officials to help them deal with a crisis. The city had been overrun by a neighboring enemy, the Sabines, who had come down from their mountain villages 30 miles north to plunder and capture the city. Their ruthless leader, Herdonius, was fomenting an overthrow of the existing Republican structure (the senate and consul governance), in order to wrest complete control of the city from the patricians (destruction of the Roman Republic from within, in addition to the external attack).[30]

While the city was under attack, a meeting of the Senate and one of the two governing consuls (Valerius) resulted in a law that would provide plebeians with representation in the government. With the law in place, Valerius was able to rouse the plebeian's efforts to provide a defense of Rome. He took control of these forces in support of the street-to-street fighting against Herdonius' troops, while Claudius, the other consul, commanded the forces protecting the city walls. In the violent hand-to-hand struggle that ensued, both Valerius and Herdonius were killed, but the Roman defenders prevailed.[31]

Because one of the two consuls had been killed in the battle, the remaining consul Claudius called a special election for a new consul to replace Valerius. They elected Cincinnatus; a patrician who was expected to be unsympathetic to the plebeians' cause. Cincinnatus received the government visitors at his farm outside of Rome, and immediately accepted the call to service. Upon arrival at the seat of government, he made a series of speeches that set the tone for his tenure as consul. He chastised the Senate for its recent behavior and not performing their duty to protect the city and the public from external threats. He overturned the new law providing plebeians a voice in the republic, saying that it was an ill-gotten gain and passed only because of the plebeians' threat of refusal to take up arms against the invaders. He also rebuked the tribunes for encouraging the plebeians to trade their honor and oath to protect the city for representation in the Senate.[32]

Cincinnatus reestablished the rule of law, and both he and Claudius ruled fairly and impartially over the cases that came before them. For the remainder of their term as joint consuls, they were widely appreciated by the citizenry for their just and humane reign. Cincinnatus' tenure as consul became legendary for its peaceful, contented time. At the end of the term, the Senate came to Cincinnatus with a proposal to re-elect him as consul. To this proposal he swiftly and strongly rebuked the senators for making laws and not following them – it was illegal to be reelected as a consul or tribune. When his term as consul drew to a close, he gave a speech to all the Roman citizenry, which chastised any tribune or consul who would attempt to stay in power beyond the legal tenure, and announced he would not accept reelection to the position. He then retired to his farm, content that he had fulfilled his duties honorably, faithfully, and to the best of his ability.[33]

A Call to War

A slowly boiling cauldron of passions was consuming the colonists in the New world as one event after another pushed the Americans toward impasse and eventual conflict with the mother country. In 1765, Parliament passed the Stamp Act, which collected a tax on every piece of paper used in the colonies, from official documents to newspapers and playing cards. In Virginia, the Burgesses registered their displeasure by declaring the Virginia Resolves, which challenged the constitutionality of the tax. One year later, the tax was repealed. In 1767, the Townshend Acts were implemented by Parliament to replace the Stamp Act. These Acts implemented import duties (effectively taxes) on different items imported by the colonists, such as lead, paint, glass, paper, and tea. This tax

caused extreme agitation in the colonies, and another response from the Virginia Assembly, which joined Massachusetts in a boycott of the taxed goods. When the Virginia
Burgesses met in 1769 to enact a complaint to King George III
regarding the taxes, and ask him to intercede in the colonies'
interest, the Governor of Virginia, Lord Botetourt, immediately
dissolved the assembly. The Burgesses, non-plussed, reconvened at a nearby tavern to continue their discussions, and
adopted a non-importation agreement proposed by Washington.[34]

On March 5, 1770, the same day as the Boston Massacre,
Parliament reduced the tax duty to tea only, an obvious coincidence in light of the time delay delivering communications
across the Atlantic Ocean. In 1771, the Virginia Assembly eliminated their import restrictions from all non-tea items, and later that year Washington was re-elected a Burgess. Some sense
of normalcy was returning to colonial life, at least in Virginia,
but it was like the calm before the storm. After Rhode Island
colonists attacked and burned the *Gaspee*, a British revenue
ship that had run aground near Warwick, Rhode Island, British
authorities threatened to deport the responsible parties to
England for trial. Virginia and other colonies agreed to convene
a committee for their mutual self-defense. This led to establishing the First Continental Congress, which met from September to October, 1774.[35]

Washington was one of the seven delegates voted by the
Virginia Assembly to attend the Continental Congress in Philadelphia, Pennsylvania. He was very active socially; he dined,
drank, or played cards with a great number of the delegates
from the other colonies. Although he was not a gifted speaker,
he had an ability that was rare and appreciated in this body of
political orators: he listened. He was also one of only two Virginia delegates who attended the entire 54-day meeting and
was in attendance when the final gavel struck on October 26.[36]

The Second Continental Congress convened on May 10, 1775, several weeks after Paul Revere's ride and the battles of Lexington and Concord. That same day, Fort Ticonderoga, a strategic stronghold on Lake Champlain – the invasion route from Canada into the American colonies – was captured by Benedict Arnold, Ethan Allen, and the Green Mountain Boys of the New Hampshire (subsequently Vermont) militia. Events were accelerating to a pace to launch a long-anticipated military conflict that would eventually change the world.[37]

His Legacy

In April 1783, eighteen months after its shocking defeat at Yorktown, Britain officially recognized the independence of the United States of America. Washington announced the peace treaty between the United States and Britain on April 18, exactly eight years from the date of the Battle of Lexington and the start of the war.[38] He wrote a document that would later become known as "Washington's Legacy," which was circulated to all of the states and would become his last official communication as the Commander in Chief of the Continental Army. This document would become his first act as Cincinnatus, as he laid out his plans for retirement from the Army, and provided his rationale for his return to plantation life.[39]

In November 1783, Washington made his way into New York City and was treated like a conquering hero as the British finally abandoned New York and American soil. At this point in the war, most of the soldiers had already been furloughed or sent home. Congress was afraid to allow a standing army of militia and career officers to maintain their arms and present a potential counterrevolutionary force to deal with. And it is with no small amount of grievance that the officers and men of the armed forces provided a challenge to civil order. Congress had failed to provide pay or even necessities like food and clothing to the Army for several years, because the national coffers had run dry.[40]

The Continental Congress had ceded all power to the states, to where the original members of Congress had long since fled. The original Articles of Confederation that were the basis of the Congress's authority were devoid of any ability to force the states to provide funding to the national government or to stand up a national army. This was intentional, because the people who had drafted those articles were afraid of a federal government that could do the same things they despised about the British government – namely taxes and an army to enforce the collection of those taxes.[41]

In December 1783, Washington surrendered his commission as Commander in Chief of the Army of the United States. He made a very deliberate and public return to Annapolis, Maryland (the temporary seat of the U. S. government owing to the British capture of Philadelphia during the war). Upon his arrival, he notified Congress and asked how its members wished him to hand over the reins of power. In the end, he attended a session of Congress and submitted his resignation in a very public display of his servitude to the public trust.[42]

Washington read a prepared statement to Congress, in a ceremony that was designed by Thomas Jefferson and others, to offer is resignation as the Commander in Chief of the Continental Army. Washington said, "Having now finished the work assigned me, I retire from the great theatre of Action, and, bidding an Affectionate farewell to this August body under whose orders I have so long acted, I here offer my Commission, and take my leave of all the employments of public life."[43]

This act of selflessness, of giving up the military power of an army that just defeated the British – the greatest army in the world – was unprecedented. And to give up that power, and turn over the reins to a fledgling civic government (of the people, by the people, for the people), was viewed as almost saint-like. It was an event of historic significance, and the echoes of that act reverberated throughout the halls of aristocratic power in Europe and elsewhere. Frances Hopkinson, a poet, stated, "had he lived in the lap of idolatry, he had been worshipped as a god."[44]

This was Washington's most famous incarnation as Cincinnatus – in the manner of the Roman legend he retired as a soldier and returned to his farm. Doing so should not have come as a shock to anyone who knew him. Washington had made a habit of voicing his resolve to leave the army for his farm in Virginia and thought that his retirement would be short because of the short life span of forebears in his family tree. His male ancestors rarely made it past the age of 50, and he was already 51. Little did he know then that he would twice more be called out of retirement to serve his country.[45]

Cincinnatus' Second Un-Retirement

Shortly after Cincinnatus' reign as consul, he was again called from his farm to protect the interests of Rome. The Romans had their hands full of enemies, as they were at war with both the Aequians, located in the hills to the northeast, and the Sabines, who were again approaching the city's walls. One consul, Lucius Mincius, had led an army to attack the Aequi, and the other consul, Gaius Nautius, led an army against the Sabines. Mincius had gotten his army surrounded by the Aequi and was at risk of being overrun. Nautius' army was too involved with the Sabines to help, and the Senate, desperate to find a savior, once again turned to Cincinnatus.[46]

A delegation of the Senate soon descended on Cincinnatus at work on his farm. He was plowing his fields when they asked him to stop to hear their urgent message. Rascilla went back to the house to fetch Cincinnatus' toga, and, once the man was properly dressed for the solemn occasion, the delegation asked that he come back to Rome to save the city. He accepted their call to duty and told his wife that they may have to go hungry in the service of Rome. Even though farming was his family's only means of subsistence, Cincinnatus left his home to save Rome from itself. He followed the Senate delegation back across the Tiber River to the city. Because most of the able-bodied men had been previously conscripted to one of the two armies already in the field, fear gripped the city. But Cincinnatus delivered a speech before friends, family, some members of Senate and the public that was inspirational and raised their spirits.[47]

The next morning at the Forum, Cincinnatus organized the citizenry for war: shops were closed, commanders were selected, and all available men from the very young to the very old were conscripted. In addition, women and children were given tasks, such as gathering supplies for the army being assembled. Everything that could be done to ensure the survival of Rome was instigated, and everything else was being laid aside for the duration of the emergency. As soon as they were ready, Cincinnatus marched his new troops 20 miles in half a day to the location where Mincius and his army were surrounded. Out of sight and sound of the Aequians, Cincinnatus positioned his army around the enemy to cut off their escape and resupply routes. Thus, Mincius was surrounded by the Aequians who were in turn were surrounded by Cincinnatus.[48]

Under cover of darkness, Cincinnatus had his army scream out their blood curdling war cries, surprising the Aequi. The Roman war cries were also heard by Mincius' army and Mincius rallied them to attack the Aequi. Caught between Cincinnatus' and Mincius' forces in an overnight battle that raged into the morning hours, the Aequi surrendered after Cincinnatus ordered a decisive charge. Cincinnatus marched back to Rome and a Senate-decreed victory celebration. The party was further enhanced by Nautius' glorious return after defeating the Sabines. Once the celebrations were over, and taking some time to clear up his affairs, Cincinnatus again gave up the reins of power and returned to his farm. Already a hero, this patriotic and republican act of virtue added to his legendary legacy and became a symbol of the Roman ideal from the early years of their Republic to the 18th-century Enlightenment age.[49]

Society of the Cincinnati

Near the end of the Revolutionary War, events would conspire to beget the establishment of a new organization dedicated to the men of the Revolutionary war effort who sacrificed so much for the sake of their country. This would be an organization to preserve the sense of comradeship these brothers in arms had enjoyed over the eight-year war, and also acknowledge, through some form of badge or medal, that they had fought in this great war for the liberty of their countrymen.[50]

The organization's notion is attributed to General Knox, who drafted the initial proposal in early 1783. The concept was for a national charter to include both national and state levels. The goals would be to recognize the members for their service, to provide a platform for charitable activities, and to serve as a union of common interest to remind the Continental Congress and the state governments of their fiduciary responsibility for back pay or the promised half pay for life to the members of the Continental Army.[51]

Thus, the former military officers from the Revolutionary War started a club called *The Society of the Cincinnati*, wherein membership was to be limited to the officers and their first-born sons (though it would also come to include "honorary" members). They offered Washington membership and the official presidency of the organization. Washington accepted the Society's presidency and did not see a conflict of interest in doing so. He was elected the Society's president on June 19, 1783. Because the organization was hereditary-based, critics believed it to be too much of an aristocratic organization for a nation born of revolutionary discontent. The hereditary component of the organization would become a lightning rod of controversy in the future and would eventually be removed from the organization.[52]

The hereditary nature of the Society raised concerns of sowing a "nobility" class into the American republic. Judge Aedanus Burke of South Carolina's state Supreme Court wrote a pamphlet condemning the organization as potentially spawning a Roman-like and eventually ruinous struggle of class warfare between commoners (plebeians) and nobility (patricians). As some newspapers and other anti-Society organizations began to reprint Burke's pamphlet, a storm of political protest against the Cincinnati began.[53]

As more and more newspapers and people came out, both for and against the Society, George Washington struggled with his involvement and commitment to the organization. Author Thomas Paine, poet John Trumbull, printer Noah Webster, the *Connecticut Courant,* and the *Boston Evening Post* supported the Society of the Cincinnati. The *Independent Chronicle*, the *New Hampshire Gazette*, some members of Congress, and Thomas Jefferson came out against the organization. With these events in mind, Washington attended the first convention of the Society of the Cincinnati at Philadelphia in May, 1784.[54]

At the opening of the convention, Washington expressed his concerns about continuing the organization in light of the current controversy regarding its existence. General Knox, Secretary *pro tem* for the organization, rose to add that if the institution would change its guidelines, then more people would be in favor of it. Washington took that opportunity to propose seven changes to the principles of the Society. These changes were discussed, then tabled for review by committee. When the final recommendations were provided by the committee, the institution's governance was amended by the following changes: 1) there would be no hereditary membership; 2) General (national) meetings would occur every three years instead of annually; 3) the annual state meetings would only be held to discuss charitable events and causes; 4) the donations received from its members would be entrusted to each state's legislature and only the interest therefrom would be used for charity; 5) each state chapter would request a charter from its state legislature; and 6) no donations would be accepted from foreign sources.[55]

Constitutional Calling

George Washington's second incarnation as Cincinnatus was his least recognized, at least at the time. Upon further review, Washington's participation in the Constitutional Convention was a Cincinnatus-like act. He had been happily retired on his farm in Virginia for the previous four years, attempting to turn his farm back to profitability after eight years of neglect during the war. Even before the war Washington had eliminated the pursuit of growing tobacco, because it was devastating to the soil, and had moved on to growing grains like wheat and corn. He was learning new farming techniques, including timing of crop rotation, and he had hired an English farming expert to help supervise his farms. He even traded seeds with Louis XVI of France and purchased seeds from China for use in experimentation or exposition in his botanical gardens.[56]

When James Madison requested Washington to attend the Constitutional Convention, he responded with a list of reasons for not going. One was his health, which had suffered recently from bouts of quinsy, severe headaches, constant tooth pain and rheumatism. Another reason, was that he had already rejected an invitation to attend the national meeting of the Society of the Cincinnati that was to be held in Philadelphia one week before the Constitutional Convention, due to personal reasons. But beyond that, he was conflicted and weighed political and historical ramifications of his decision.[57]

As notably documented in *Cincinnatus, George Washington and the Enlightenment* by Gary Willis, attendance and participation in the Constitutional Convention was actually an *unlawful* act. Washington's participation in that meeting could have been labeled as treason, because the Continental Congress and the original thirteen states were already operating under the Articles of Confederation, a constitution ratified in 1781. In addition, Washington would be risking his legacy – the act of giving up power after winning the Revolutionary War and retiring to his farm – by returning to power and the public scene as a member of this convention. In essence, Washington was risking his reputation and legendary legacy, making this decision the biggest gamble of his life.[58]

In December 1786, the Virginia Assembly named George Washington, James Madison, Edmund Randolph, Patrick Henry, George Mason, George Wythe, and John Blair to the Convention. Washington didn't commit to attending, but neither did he reject the nomination. By the end of that month, Pennsylvania had named Robert Morris, James Wilson, George Clymer, Thomas Mifflin, and later added Benjamin Franklin to their attendee list. By mid-February 1787, five more states had nominated attendees, and the momentum was moving towards an officially authorized gathering. When the Continental Congress met in March, they called for a convention specifically proposed to revise the Articles of Confederation and create a new Constitution. Immediately, five more states named their own delegates to the convention; the only hold-out was Rhode Island.[59]

With the legitimacy of the convention now resolved, Washington's friends John Jay, Henry Knox, and Edmund Randolph continued to try to convince him to attend the proceedings. In the end, it was the "call to duty" argument that worked best. At the end of March, Washington gave his commitment to attend, with a caveat: his health might cause his inability to honor that promise. But in May, with the other delegates on their way and feeling better than he had in months, he left his beloved farm for Philadelphia to fulfill his role in the creation of the living document that still serves us today, the Constitution of the United States of America. This was his second instance of performing the Cincinnatus role of fulfilling his duty to serve his country.[60]

Cincinnatus' Third Un-Retirement

Two decades after saving Rome for a second time, Cincinnatus was again looked upon to rescue the republic. Several years of drought and famine had brought starvation and disease to Rome. The poor were particularly devastated, some losing hope to the point of drowning themselves in the Tiber River. A new plebeian knight of recently inherited wealth, Spurius Maelius, took it upon himself to relieve the plebeians' plight by providing food for free or very low cost. This act of charity gained Maelius fame and worship by the public, but widespread distrust among the patricians and government. Many suspected a motive behind these altruistic actions, possibly one of aristocratic or dictatorial aspirations. Fearing an anti-state plot and potential overthrow of the government, one of the two ruling consuls, T. Quinctius Capitolinus, called on the Senate to recall Cincinnatus to duty.[61]

The Senate approved the request and sent another delegation across the Tiber River to Cincinnatus' farm. Cincinnatus was now over 80 years old, and understandably reticent to take on this heavy burden. But the delegation convinced him that his heroism and wisdom in resolving the two prior crises of Rome's history made him the right man for the job. Cincinnatus agreed to accept the assignment to serve as temporary ruler, but ordered complete secrecy until he returned to the city and the accused was brought to justice.[62]

Morning broke with Cincinnatus at his seat in the Forum, surprising the old who had not seen him in years and amazing the young who had only heard stories of the legendary hero. Cincinnatus ordered Maelius to be brought before the magistracy to defend himself against the charge of attempting a revolution. This duty fell upon the Master of the House, Servilius Ahala, and his guards. When Ahala came upon Maelius and served his summons to the Forum, Maelius was shocked and afraid. He first tried to escape to the safety of his followers, but Ahala pursued and a fight ensued. While inciting a riot and resisting arrest, Maelius was killed by Ahala.[63]

Ahala returned to the Forum and reported that Maelius had resisted the summons, started a mêlée, and was killed. Cincinnatus commended Ahala for performing his duty and defended him in the public outcry that ensued. Ahala was publicly ridiculed and chased out of the country for his involvement and actions in the affair. He was banished for life, but future generations of Romans would consider him a hero and savior of Rome. Cincinnatus ruled Maelius guilty of treason and sold all his possessions. He justified his actions as necessary to prevent the rise of a revolutionary and potential future king. Cincinnatus only stayed in power long enough to ensure a proper transition back to the prior authorities and retired back to his farm. Once there, he lived out the remainder of his days in peace and serenity, a simple contented life with his wife on the outskirts of Rome. Later generations of Romans, and republican advocates worldwide, would look to his example of a virtuous heroic life as a legendary example of greatness in a leader who gains power by giving it away. No other leader in world history would match that example, until George Washington.[64]

Presidential Calling

Washington's third incarnation as Cincinnatus is his true legacy, and his enduring gift to the American people and democratic governance. After the Constitutional Convention, Washington returned to Mount Vernon, but also did what he could to ensure that the new Constitution was ratified by the requisite number of states (a minimum of 9 of the 13 states). He was happily home, and had counted the days of his absence, while finding out that the year's harvest had been nearly destroyed by drought. Once again, in the manner of

Cincinnatus, Washington suffered personal loss in public service to his country.[65]

The Constitutional Convention had completed its work by the end of September 1787 and sent their document to Congress. By mid-January that next year, it had been adopted by five states, and within four more months, three additional states had approved the document. By the end of June, three more states voted for it, for a total of 11, ensuring ratification – only Rhode Island and North Carolina were hold-outs. Now that the Constitution was adopted, Washington knew he would be called upon to serve as the country's first President. And when that call came, he accepted. In those days, there was no popular vote, and the office of the president was voted on directly by the Electoral College, as defined in the newly ratified Constitution. On February 4, 1789, George Washington was unanimously elected President of the United States.[66]

Near the end of Washington's first term as President of the United States, his cabinet members were carrying on war amongst themselves. Thomas Jefferson, the Secretary of State and as leader of the Democratic-Republicans, was trying to implement an agenda of minimalist government, agrarian society, and no central bank. Alexander Hamilton, the Secretary of the Treasury and as leader of the Federalists, was trying to implement a strong national identity and federal authority (as opposed to state rights), with an industrial society and a strong central bank. The Jeffersonian and Hamiltonian factions would become the genesis of our two-party system of government.[67]

The schism in the cabinet was creating friction within the government and tearing apart Washington's team. It was causing Washington to resolve petty disputes between Jefferson and Hamilton. Washington was so frustrated by the conflict that he decided to ask James Madison to draft his resignation letter, stating his intent not to seek a second term as president. He also wanted to return to his farm and remove the yoke of responsibility for everything that was happening in the country. But when the time came for a decision, both Hamilton and Jefferson begged him to stay on. They argued that the country was too young to withstand the shock of his leaving, that he was the only thing keeping the country and its democratic experiment together. But that left Washington even more determined to step down at the earliest opportunity, and he considered retiring in the middle of his second term.[68]

His Farewell

By the time Washington was nearing the end of his second term as president, some things had changed. The country was a little more mature. Both Jefferson and Hamilton had left the cabinet to seek other fortunes – Jefferson had exposed himself as having provided secret information to the French, and Hamilton had quit over a perceived act of disrespect by Washington. But some things had not changed – namely, Washington's desire to retire from public life. Washington asked Hamilton to draft his resignation letter in May 1793 and sent him the original resignation letter from Madison during his first term, modified by Washington to reflect the changes that had occurred since then. Hamilton responded with two letters: an update to the Madison letter, and one that was completely rewritten with a more regal and lofty tone. Washington decided on using the new resignation letter from Hamilton, rewriting it in his own hand and editing it to conform to his own preferred phrasing and style.[69]

Before Washington completed his second term as President of the United States, he provided his farewell address to the nation. In this address, he plainly laid out his reasons and rationale for not seeking a third term as President and retiring to private life. He made clear his desire to retire after his first term as president, that his reason for not doing so was what he felt an obligation as leader and founder of the nation to hold it together until the country could continue without him. In his address he also wanted to make it clear to everyone that he wasn't "quitting" – just finally enacting a long-held desire to spend the remaining years of his life with his beloved wife Martha back on his farm in Virginia.[70]

Washington's *Farewell Address* of September 19, 1796, lays out his rationale for not seeking reelection, his gratitude for being selected for office, his hopes and vision for the future of the United States, and his thoughts on the Constitution. Washington was unique, in that he had the discipline and self-control to know when it was time to leave the stage, and he put in place the expectation that all future transitions will be as peaceful and effortless as his transition to the succeeding president. This is the standard to which all subsequent presidents were held – because Washington did not, no subsequent president dared stay in office longer than two terms (that is, until President Franklin Roosevelt was elected to four terms, and that act spawned the formal institutionalization of the Washington standard in the form of the 21st Amendment – a two-term limit on the presidency).[71]

In the manner of Cincinnatus, for the third and final time, George Washington freely gave up control and the reins of power to return to his beloved Mount Vernon farm. He lived the remainder of his years at Mount Vernon, writing letters, receiving and entertaining frequent guests, and maintaining the profitability of his farm – directing when and where to plant, what crops to raise, when to harvest and where to sell. He was always attentive to details and planned every aspect of the farm's output and the output's distribution. He maintained his strong work ethic, rising at dawn and making his rounds, preferring to show how he expected tasks to be done and otherwise leading by example. His meticulous and detail-oriented style of management was the hallmark of his legacy, and the foundation of his success.[72]

CHAPTER 2

The Revolutionary War

Washington loved the theatre, and Joseph Addison's *Cato* was his favorite play.[1] *Cato* is a tragedy about the last days of Cato the Younger, a senator during the end of the Roman Republic and before Julius Caesar became Dictator for Life. He led the resistance in the Senate against Caesar's civil war to become Dictator, the war between rivals Caesar and Pompey across the Mediterranean. As Caesar's legions were closing in on Cato's forces near Utica (present day Tunisia) in North Africa, Cato martyred himself by committing suicide rather than surrender to the despised future Dictator of the Roman Empire.[2]

Cato is a drama about the struggles of liberty versus tyranny, republicanism against totalitarianism, and virtue over lust for power. It was also the most popular play of the mid-1700s, and all the founding fathers were familiar with it. In fact, some of the most memorable quotes of the Revolution were modified lines from the play. Those of Patrick Henry ("Give me Liberty or give me Death") and Nathan Hale ("I only regret that I have but one life to lose for my country") are of particular note. Letters of Edmund Burke, Charles Thomson, Thomas Jefferson and George Washington to fellow revolutionaries also quoted passages from *Cato*.[3]

Like many of the founding fathers, Washington was a self-made man who owned a large personal library and was a lifelong learner. While he lacked the formal education of many of his contemporaries, he made up for it by reading, learning, and doing. For example, when it looked like he was going to be called upon to lead the Continental Army, one of the first things he did was to order several books on military procedures, strategy, and tactics. The last thing he wanted to do was to be embarrassed for want of knowledge in a time of need.[4]

Washington attended the Second Continental Congress as a representative of the Virginia Commonwealth. He was the only representative who attended dressed in full military uniform — which is probably the reason why he was eventually selected to lead the first Continental Army. He also looked like a leader, as he was the tallest person in the room. John Adams even nominated Washington over his fellow New Englander John Hancock, who as the chairman of the meeting expected to be rewarded with that plum assignment. However, it was clear to everyone in attendance that Washington was the logical choice, the only choice, to lead the rebellious cause to victory.[5]

During the Second Continental Congress, on May 25, ships arrived in Boston harbor, carrying a military presence intended to put down the rebellion. On June 14, 1775, Congress authorized raising troops from Maryland, Pennsylvania, and Virginia to march to Boston and support the local militia. The only question was, who would command what would become the Continental Army? Although many desired the position, responsibility, and authority, all were deemed flawed for the command for one reason or another. The only person who did not express any desire for the position, was the one who was unanimously voted by Congress as Commander of the Continental Army, George Washington. On June 18, having been called by his country to lead them out of a crisis, Washington left Philadelphia for Boston, and the beginning of his participation in the Revolutionary War.[6]

The Boston Siege

General Washington's first assignment was a tall order. All he had to do was rescue the city of Boston from a British occupation of 10,000 soldiers and a harbor full of ships from the greatest navy in the world at that time, the British Navy. No person in his right mind could have expected to win that battle, especially given the nature of the troops under his command (militia men), and their lack of training and discipline. They also lacked sufficient guns, gunpowder, and supplies.[7]

Washington and his army of 14,500 men surrounded the city and dug in along defensive lines less than a mile away from the British. Washington had to deal with colonial militia from different states that were more self-identified with their region or state than with the union. Additionally, their personalities and perspectives differed, leading to trouble. For example, the Massachusetts militia ridiculed the riflemen of the Virginia regiment for their appearance. Such territorial attitudes and contempt broke out into open hostility and fighting within the camp.[8]

Washington arrived at the Boston suburbs on July 3, 1775, but nothing happened between the warring armies for over six months. In fact, many of the enlistments of his original army expired at the end of 1775, and in January 1776 there was a tremendous turnover in the camp as the expired enlistments departed and new recruits and volunteers filed in. However, on January 17, 1776, Henry Knox arrived with 60 mortars and cannons from Lake Champlain's Fort Ticonderoga. This was treasure from the victory of Benedict Arnold who had captured that British fort. The fortuitous arrival of the mortars called for action, and Washington convened a council of war to discuss options.[9]

The council leaders decided on a night operation for seizing Dorchester Heights, which overlooked Boston and the harbor. This ground was unoccupied by either army but was a decidedly attractive target. From the Dorchester high ground and with the newly arrived mortars, the Continental Army could both bombard the British and repel an advance. The Americans pre-built ramparts and defenses to carry to the top of the hill, the point being to complete the operation in a single night. As darkness approached on March 4, 1776, the operation began with a bombardment of the city from other parts of the American lines, the better to drown out the sounds of the heavy cannons and equipment being dragged up Dorchester hill.[10]

On the morning of March 5, 1776, exactly six years after the Boston Massacre, the British saw the stunning result of the night's activity – a fortress of cannons, parapets, and defenses on the high ground overlooking their positions. Then the weather intervened – a torrent of rain. Instead of a battle, the next event was a decision by the British commander, General William Howe, to evacuate Boston and sail to Nova Scotia. On March 9, the British started a bombardment of the American lines to cover their retreat, and by March 17, they quit the city of Boston, never to return.[11]

New York

Washington did not spend much time reveling in his victory. In fact, he worried more about the potential for British treachery in doubling back and attacking some other coastal city. By early April, he had decided that the next most likely target of British aggression would be New York City – a place ideally suited to the British superiority in naval power, because the city then – Manhattan Island – was literally surrounded by water. On April 4, Washington led the American troops south to New York to intercept and engage the enemy.[12]

As successful as Washington's experience was in Boston, the opposite occurred in New York. Boston was a stronghold of revolutionary fervor while New York was a hotbed of Tory loyalist activity. Boston had been occupied by 10,000 Redcoats and the Continental Army had surrounded the town. At New York, the British Navy filled all the surrounding waterways with ships-of-the-line – thus Washington was attempting to defend an indefensible city. In Boston, Washington had played it safe and only acted when the odds and opportunity were in his favor. In New York, Washington played directly into the enemy's plans by providing them with an opportunity of delivering a crushing blow to the entire Continental Army and the revolutionary spirit itself.[13]

On April 13, General Washington and the Continental Army entered New York City. New York was indefensible, but Washington refused to give up so easily. He understood the political ramifications of surrendering the city to the British without a fight so early in the war. Then in May 1776, Congress summoned Washington to Philadelphia to discuss plans and political options. Washington used it as an opportunity to request changes to how the war was being handled administratively. Washington was able to get a Board of War committee set up to handle the concerns of the Army. He was also successful in overcoming Congress' objections to a longer-term or permanent Army with the implementation of three-year enlistments.[14]

In June 1776, Washington returned to New York to continue preparations for the expected British attack. On June 29, General Howe and British fleet arrived with over 50 ships and disembarked on Staten Island. Washington's instructions to the American forces were very specific with respect to what type of ammunition to load into their muskets (ball and buckshot), and that they were not to fire until the enemy was within easy targeting range among the grasses and small brush in front of their positions.[15]

On July 8, 1776, Washington received from Congress the text of the Declaration of Independence, and subsequently ordered the troops to gather on the parade grounds the next day. He had the Declaration read aloud at 6 p.m. on July 9 to all the soldiers on the parade grounds that evening. It was warmly received by the troops and caused enough of a stir that some men ran down Broadway to where a statue of King George III was located. They bowled the statue over, chopped off the head, and carried it around the city like a souvenir.[16]

Long Island

On July 12, 1776, Admiral Richard Howe, the brother of General William Howe, arrived with his fleet of over 400 ships and 30,000 troops. This was the largest projection of force by the British military in one location during the entire war. King George and his ministers had decided to "crush the rebellion" in a single blow, focusing on New York with a display of complete dominance. Washington and the Continental Army did not stand a chance, and over the next several weeks and months the British, with their total naval superiority, manpower superiority, and military experience, overpowered the Americans.[17]

The first clash was the Battle of Long Island. Washington had split his troops between Manhattan and Long Island because he wasn't sure where the British would attack. The British sent ships up the river to feign a naval engagement, then secretly landed over 10,000 troops on Long Island. This Long Island main force, commanded by General Howe took a circuitous route along Jamaica Road, which was inexplicably undefended. Two thousand Hessian (German mercenaries) took Flatbush Road, through the middle of the American outer defenses, and several thousand other British Redcoats attacked the American right flank near Gowanus Bay.[18]

The Americans retreated behind their fortifications on Brooklyn Heights, whereupon the British forces took up positions opposite. Washington sent for reinforcements from Manhattan and expected an imminent attack from the British. Meanwhile, General Howe did not want to repeat the experience of Bunker Hill. At that Massachusetts battle the British won but at such a high cost in lives lost that it was a hollow victory. Instead, Howe settled in for a long siege of the fortress-like heights.[19]

The next morning Washington awoke to a sea of white tents surrounding the American positions. As he assessed the situation, it became clear to him that the Americans must withdraw back across the East River to Manhattan. He later met with his officers, and they agreed with him. On the night of August 29, Washington and the Continental Army staged an incredible retreat across the river in the dead of night – over 10,000 men plus supplies and equipment were transported in rowboats, flatboats, sloops, and schooners.[20]

Washington kept the fires lit and sentries on post throughout the heights as the troops made their exit. The remaining guards were to stay at their posts until all the other men had been removed from Brooklyn. Finally, at daybreak the last of the American troops made it down to the water's edge, and Washington was the last man to board the ships headed back across the river to Manhattan. Incredibly, just in time a fog rolled in and protected the last of the Americans from the sight of the British invaders. About two weeks later, Washington decided that New York was indefensible, so he began moving most of his army north of the city to Harlem Heights though leaving a garrison of approximately 2,000 troops in what is now called Lower Manhattan.[21]

Harlem Heights

On September 15, the British bombarded Manhattan to soften up a beachhead for an amphibious assault. They landed 4,000 men at Kip's Bay, and barely had made it ashore when most of the American militiamen deserted their positions and ran in the direction of the main force at Harlem Heights. Of the few thousand men stationed in New York to defend the city, most made it up to Harlem Heights to fight with the remainder of the American troops. Hessian mercenaries ruthlessly gunned down the ones who didn't flee, even when they tried to surrender.[22]

Washington was astounded by the behavior of his own troops. As he rushed down with his officers to do battle with the British, the militia stampeded in the other direction with such velocity and force that even his attempt to block their path with his and the other officer's horses was of little avail. Without hesitation the men veered off the road and into the fields, running away from the enemy behind them. Then came an orderly march of Massachusetts's militia and Connecticut Continentals. Washington told them to take positions along the walls in the fields, but when the British came in sight, they also abandoned their positions and took flight.[23]

After all the troops made their way to the relative safety of Harlem Heights, Washington drew introspective. He could not conceive of winning a war when the tools for delivering a crushing blow to the mighty British Empire were so woefully inadequate. The Americans did not have the provisions, the weaponry, or the personnel to take this fight to the enemy. In particular, the militia was untrained, undisciplined, and unruly. They were nearly all on short-term enlistments of one year or less, and by the time they were sufficiently honed to useful instruments, they were released back to their farms and families. Washington's opinion was shared by General Knox, who blamed the debacle not so much on the militia, but on a failure in leadership of the men who were the officers of the troops. Both Washington and Knox shared the conclusion that an academy for military training was necessary to instill that leadership quality in officers.[24]

The subsequent Battle of Harlem Heights was not so much a battle as a skirmish. It occurred the morning after the Continental Army militia had so ingloriously retreated from the enemy. Washington had sent a scouting party of 120 New England rangers, who met with an advanced force of 300 British and fell back to the safety of Harlem Heights. The British sounded their bugles to the tune that is used when a fox is chased into his hole (at the end of the fox hunt), which was an attempt to embarrass and humiliate the Americans. Washington directed a group of soldiers to circle around the British, and then sent others toward the bugler to flush them out. The ensuing gunfight pushed the British back and the Americans gained some confidence from this small victory.[25]

On October 12, the British sent 150 ships up the East River and landed a force of 4,000 troops at Throggs Neck, east of Harlem Heights. This force was then augmented by reinforcements of another 7,000 men, so that Washington was now faced with the possibility of having his escape route from Manhattan Island cut off. When informed of the enemy's actions, Washington decided to retreat to White Plains, the closest defensible position. As the Americans retreated, he left a detachment at Fort Washington, a pentagon-shaped fort set atop the highest ground on the northwest portion of Manhattan Island, currently near the east end of the George Washington Bridge.[26]

White Plains

On October 26, the last of the retreating American troops arrived at White Plains. The main body of the Continental Army was now digging in and preparing for battle. Two days later the British, with their Hessian mercenaries, arrived by the thousands. The British charged Chatterton's Hill, overtook the position with relative ease, and then paused. Washington's troops kept digging in their positions and reinforcing their defenses. On Halloween night, Washington decided to withdraw his troops further into the hills, to retain the advantage of higher ground. The Americans successfully retreated to North Castle heights, while keeping a small rear guard below in White Plains. When the British advanced the next day on White Plains, the rear guard wreaked havoc on the British lines.[27]

The British defeated the Americans at White Plains, but it was a hollow victory because it achieved nothing of importance while costing 250 British and Hessian casualties. General William Howe considered his alternatives and decided to keep Washington, and the Continental Army, wondering where he would strike next. On November 5, the British army withdrew and marched back towards New York City. Some American officers rejoiced, saying that it meant Howe was retiring from the fight to set up winter quarters in New York. But Washington believed their next target was going to be Fort Washington (especially the few thousand American troops within its walls) or other fixed sites in the area. Additional possibilities were that the British would strike New Jersey, or the capital at Philadelphia. It is with these concerns that Washington made his next moves.[28]

Washington split his forces (something battle-experienced officers rarely, if ever, do), in order to provide flexibility for a response to General Howe's next target. Washington left 7,000 troops with General Lee in North Castle to protect the New England states. He sent 3,000 to 4,000 troops with General Heath to the Highlands (30 miles up the Hudson River) to protect the river route to Canada. And he left in place 3,000 to 4,000 troops (combined) in Ft. Washington and Ft. Lee (across the Hudson River from Ft. Washington on the New Jersey highlands) to hold the British Navy south of New York. Finally, Washington kept 2,000 troops with himself and planned to join up with 5,000 troops stationed at Flying Camp in New Jersey west of New York City; doing so would protect cities in New Jersey and Pennsylvania, including the capital of Philadelphia.[29]

On November 12, Washington led his force of 2,000 men across the Hudson River, then south along the river to Ft. Lee. There he met with General Green to discuss strategy. Washington thought Ft. Washington should be abandoned, but Green convinced the commander that another retreat would demoralize the troops. In any event, General Howe's plan for attack became evident within a few days. On the morning of November 16, Howe and 13,000 British and Hessian troops descended on Ft. Washington, and by 4 p.m. the garrison capitulated. Washington could only stand by and watch from his vantage at Ft. Lee as over 2,600 soldiers and over 200 officers surrendered to the enemy. This loss was devastating to the morale and esprit de corps of the Continental Army, and it had a melancholic effect on Washington.[30]

Trenton

However, Washington could not afford to wallow in self-pity, because four days later the British were scaling the walls of the cliffs around Ft. Lee and mounting a full-scale attack on the soldiers there. Washington knew that defending Ft. Lee was pointless because without Ft. Washington on the Manhattan side of the Hudson River, British ships would be able to navigate freely up and down the river. He decided to abandon the fort, and had to leave its 200 cannon, small arms, and supplies behind. Washington escaped from the British on a dreadful 16-day march across the New Jersey flatlands.[31]

On December 8, a few days after the Continental Army arrived in New Jersey, General Howe's army exchanged gunfire with the rebels. Howe had over 12,000 troops at his disposal and felt confident he could attack and destroy the American troops at will. At that point, General Howe decided to decamp to New York City and stay there for the winter. Washington had different ideas. He knew he had to strike a blow to get the hearts and minds of the Army and the American public back behind the rebel cause. In addition, hundreds of his militia volunteer commitments would expire at the end of the year, so he only had a few weeks of opportunity to do something.[32]

Washington met with his generals in a council of war to determine their next steps. It was Christmas Eve 1776. The Continental Army had just days before crossed the Delaware River from New Jersey into Pennsylvania, and the men were hungry, tired, and exposed to the elements. The result of the council of war was a decision to re-cross the Delaware back into New Jersey and attack the Hessian garrison at Trenton. They planned the operation to occur the next night, so that the battle would start in the morning on the day after Christmas. So began the famous Delaware Crossing.[33]

The main force of 2,400 men, including Washington, was to cross the Delaware River at McConkey's Ferry (now called Washington Crossing, Pennsylvania), nine miles north of Trenton. The river crossing operation started under cover of darkness and wasn't complete until three in the morning. About an hour later, Washington and his troops started their nine-mile march through a wicked ice, sleet, and snowstorm in total darkness. It took almost four hours to reach their destination; however, the surprise attack completely took the enemy off guard, and victory was assured. The Americans only lost two men in combat and four or five to exposure (froze to death). Over 900 Hessians were captured and over 100 were killed or injured.[34]

With the spoils of victory (the prisoners, captured ammunition, muskets, cannons, and swords), Washington and his army dashed back across the Delaware into Pennsylvania again to give his men a well-deserved rest. But they didn't get to rest for long. Washington, upon hearing that 1,800 American militia under the command of Colonel Cadwalader were in New Jersey attempting to mount a second offensive, decided to return to Trenton. Before he could attempt another battle, he had to convince hundreds of recruits to reenlist for an additional four to six weeks so the offensive could be sustained. Because these enlistments would expire on December 31, he was in danger of losing a large portion of his force. But the eligible men enlisted *en masse*, and Washington estimated that 1,000-1,400 agreed to stay.[35]

Princeton

The British General Cornwallis had 8,000 men at Princeton and marched most of his army to Trenton for attacking the Americans there. In the second Battle of Trenton, the Americans had a defensive position on Assunpink Creek. The British had brought 5,500 men and pushed the Americans back to a stone bridge over the creek. But here Washington held his ground and the British, after three attempts to take the bridge, decided to regroup and continue the battle in the morning. Washington had other plans. He was concerned about being encircled by the British and having his retreat route cut off, so he held another council of war. He and his senior officers decided to attempt another nighttime escape, and then attack the British forces at Princeton. Just as during their escape from New York, the rear guard kept up the ruse of an army digging in for assault with campfires burning and making entrenching tool noises, while the main body stealthily crept away.[36]

Washington and his Continental Army marched 12 miles at night in total darkness in the dead of winter and arrived after dawn just outside the town of Princeton. There the army split, with General Mercer taking Quaker Road over the Stony Brook Bridge, and Generals Green and Washington taking the Old Road to the village. Not long after the split, Washington heard a roar of small arms fire, and saw Mercer's men being driven back towards Old Road by hundreds of Redcoats who had gotten an early start on the march to Trenton where they expected to be aiding in the attack on the Assunpink Creek defenses. Washington rallied the troops and personally led the counterattack, riding on horseback in front of the marching army. He rode to within less than 30 yards of the enemy line and then commanded the Americans to fire at the British troops.[37]

Washington's courage under fire rallied the troops and turned the tide of the battle to the Americans. He was conspicuously front and center in the battle lines, spurring both his horse and the soldiers behind him to conquer their fear and their foes. This personal act of heroism defined Washington and his character. The British troops fell back on the town and sought refuge in the college building called Nassau Hall. The Americans brought up their artillery and started bombarding the structure, soon bringing about the British surrender. For the day, the British suffered 500 casualties, with 200 to 300 taken prisoner, while the Americans had only about 30-40 killed. The victory was complete, but the victors could not savor the moment – General Cornwallis and his troops from Trenton were on their way. So, Washington and the Continental Army moved on to Morristown, New Jersey, where they would camp for the winter.[38]

The greatest benefit these two victories over the British, at Trenton and Princeton, were to provide the Americans with some confidence that they could actually win the war. It also provided other European countries, notably France, with plausible rationale to support the American cause (the French were already natural enemies of the British). This caused a tremendous rush of contenders and pretenders to come to the American front, some with commissions from the official American representative in Paris, Silas Deane. Others arrived only with boasts of being generals in the European theatre, and therefore demanded general commissions in the American Army. Washington had to deal with all kinds of personalities and problems, but still was able to manage the situation. He was a consummate organizer and administrator, in addition to being a great leader.[39]

One of the most consequential French volunteers who came to America in support of the revolutionary cause was the Marquis de Lafayette. He was provided a letter of introduction by Benjamin Franklin, who was serving as an American diplomat in Paris with Deane, and upon his arrival in Philadelphia, Lafayette handed the letter to John Hancock. Lafayette was introduced to Washington in July 1977 and was provided a commission as Major General. In time, Washington and Lafayette would become enduring friends, and Washington would look upon and treat Lafayette like the son he never had.[40]

Philadelphia

On July 31, 1777, Washington was informed that the British fleet had just shown up on the Delaware River, and he quickly deduced the next target of General Howe – the capital of the American republic at Philadelphia. Washington marched his army from New Jersey, and they arrived in Philadelphia on August 24. In the same manner as the defense of New York City, Philadelphia's defense was a matter of psychological warfare. Washington felt that, because Congress was still housed in the city and functioning as the national government, he had to come to its defense. He marched the 12,000-man Continental Army through the city as a show of force and to be a source of strength and inspiration to the city's inhabitants.[41]

Washington then positioned his troops outside Philadelphia at Brandywine Creek, the better to challenge British troops as they came up from the Delaware Bay. However, General Howe had other plans. A spy had informed the British of two fords across the Brandywine upriver from the Americans defensive positions. Howe split his troops in two, one part to attack Washington at Chadds Ford, where the Continental Army was encamped, and the second larger part to cross the creek beyond Washington's left flank, then smash the Americans from behind in a pincer-like movement. On September 11, Howe's forces attacked and when the pincer closed, it took the Americans by surprise. The Americans retreated into the hills, and the British forces did not chase them. Washington regrouped his men at Chester, but the evidence was clear: Philadelphia was now likely to be overrun by the British. On September 18, Congress fled first to Trenton, then to Lancaster. On September 26, the British marched into Philadelphia.[42]

While the British moved into Philadelphia, they neverthe-less retained their main force in Germantown, six miles north-west of the city. Washington convened a war council on October 3, and expressed his belief that it was an opportunity too precious to waste. Washington designed an attack plan of four columns that would attack Germantown from different directions but synchronized to strike at dawn. The plan went awry. One problem was fog. Another was smoke owing to the British, having been warned of the impending American attack by a Tory spy, torching a nearby wheat field. In the confusion of battle and true "fog of war," the Americans lost several men to friendly fire, and because Loyalists had tipped off the British army, Washington's plans lost the element of surprise. Wash-ington remained convinced the plan would have worked if the weather would have cooperated, and he also felt that even though the English were not dislodged from the village, it was somewhat of a Continental Army moral victory.[43]

The American showing at Germantown also impressed French officials. The battle at Germantown occurred only about three weeks after the defeat at Brandywine, and it was considered a draw by outside observers. The French foreign minister, Vergennes, when discussing a possible alliance with American commissioners, stated that "nothing struck him so much as the Battle of Germantown."[44] The British eventually withdrew from Germantown to Philadelphia and dared the Americans to attack. Washington moved his army to Whitemarsh, within 12 miles striking distance of Philadelphia. He longed for a victory before winter, and had the French en-gineer Duportail survey the British fortifications around Phila-delphia for weaknesses – but Duportail reported that any attack would be suicide. All Washington could do was wait and contemplate his next move. Meanwhile, events were occurring to the north that would both inspire and confound the patri-ot's cause.[45]

Saratoga

Saratoga (current day Schuylerville, New York) is located on the west bank of the Hudson River, 190 miles north of New York City, about mid-way to Montreal, Canada. England's grand strategy was to send an army down from Montreal, through the waterways of Lake Champaign and the Hudson River, while a second army would drive north up the Hudson River from New York meeting the first army at Albany. They would both build forts along their paths from Canada to the Atlantic Ocean, thus cutting off New England, the head of the snake, from the rest of the American colonies. The leader of the army heading north from New York was expected to be General Howe. The leader of the army heading south from Canada was Lieutenant General Sir John Burgoyne.[46]

General Burgoyne, so confident in his abilities that he made a bet at Brooks Club that he would be victorious and back in London within a year, started out strong. In July 1777, Burgoyne was able to defeat the Americans at Fort Ticonderoga without firing a shot. Like the Americans at Dorchester Heights, he captured the high ground (Mount Defiance) overlooking the fort and aimed his cannons down onto it. The Americans immediately evacuated, and General Philip Schuyler, commander of the Northern Army, was removed from command by Congress for this disaster; he was replaced by General Horatio Gates.[47]

Horatio Gates arrived at the Northern Army camp near Saratoga on August 19. He was called "Granny Gates" by his men, because he had grey hair, walked hunched over, and wore his glasses at the end of his nose. His second-in-command was none other than Benedict Arnold, before his traitorous acts. Gates ordered the camp moved to higher ground, to an area called Bennis Heights overlooking the Hudson River that was more defensible. He had a fort built of logs and fallen trees that housed his 7,000-man army, then waited for the approach of Burgoyne. General Burgoyne's march through the woods of upstate New York wasn't as successful as his experience at Fort Ticonderoga. He lost 800 men near Bennington, New Hampshire (now Vermont), in a battle with an American force of armed farmers led by General John Stark.[48]

On September 19, Burgoyne's 6,000 remaining troops arrived at Freeman's Farm, a clearing in the woods of about fifteen acres located less than two miles from Bennis Heights. Gates had been informed by spies that the British had only about a month's worth of provisions and sent out raiding parties of infantry to harass their camp. Gates felt confident that his opponent would not miss an opportunity for direct action against an army in the field and patiently awaited an attack. On October 7, the attack came. General Burgoyne sent 1,500 men out to reconnoiter the American's position. From the high ground, General Gates could see exactly what the British were doing, and how exposed they were. He took the opportunity the enemy was providing and attacked the British from three sides: left, right, and center. Most of the British and their Hessian mercenaries were cut down in the fight, the remaining elements escaping pell-mell into the forest.[49]

General Burgoyne, in a scene reminiscent of Washington's retreat from Long Island, broke camp from Freeman's Farm in the dead of night while keeping his campfires lit. His men encamped on the high ground above Saratoga and dug in, awaiting the American's attack. Gates believed he held the upper hand, because he knew the British rations and supplies would not hold out for long. He surrounded the British camp and again waited patiently for Burgoyne's next move. On October 14, Burgoyne sent out an emissary with a truce flag to begin negotiations for surrender. Over the next few days, proposals passed back and forth, delayed by rumors of British forces, led by Sir Henry Clinton, arriving at Albany. In the end, Burgoyne's officers agreed that a rescue would not come soon enough to save them from starvation. On October 17, the British force of over 5,500 survivors, including lords, knights, and members of Parliament, surrendered to General Gates' Northern Army, one of the greatest American victories of the war.[50]

General Gates' victory went to his head – he no longer saw himself as subservient to George Washington. He did not advise Washington of his victory, but instead sent his aide James Wilkerson directly to Congress to advise them of the news regarding Saratoga. In an event historically referred to as the "Conway Cabal," General Gates, Thomas Mifflin, and General Conway were seen as colluding to make Washington look bad, in an attempt to supplant him with General Gates as commander in chief. Whether it was collusion or just the efforts of ambitious men to further their careers, the evidence is unclear. What is clear is that Washington was politically astute enough to stay above the fray and watch as their schemes failed.[51]

On October 30, Washington sent his aide Alexander Hamilton to General Gates in Albany to request a division of troops to support Washington's position in Philadelphia. Washington believed that, Burgoyne's army being no longer a threat and thus Gates having plenty of reserves, Gates could afford to reinforce Washington's troops in Philadelphia. When Hamilton arrived, Gates was outraged at the request, but Hamilton was able to negotiate two brigades to come to Washington's aid.[52]

On November 22, before the reinforcements from Gates arrived, British ships sailed up the Delaware River and dropped anchor at Philadelphia.[53] This dashed any hopes Washington had to mount an attack on Howe's troops and dislodge them from the American capital. By December 9, General Howe settled in for the winter in Philadelphia. Washington, who did not wish to burden nearby cities that were already housing patriots and personnel who had escaped Philadelphia before its capture, decided to search for a nearby clearing that would enable him to keep an eye on the British army and respond to threats or emergencies in an expeditious manner. The place he chose was 18 miles northwest of Philadelphia – Valley Forge.[54]

Valley Forge

Valley Forge is famous in the annals of American history for the sacrifices and the suffering that General Washington and the Continental Army endured. In order to set up a camp to survive the winter, the soldiers had to build their own quarters. Washington ordered that the barracks would be log cabins, fourteen feet by eighteen feet, with a fireplace and chimney built with clay. Each cabin would have an oak door and slat or turf roof and would house 12 men. The soldiers built their cabins, without the benefit of nails, while being threadbare and shoeless (over 70% of the men had no shoes and lacked adequate clothing). Amid the toil and drudgery, and on account of malnutrition and unsanitary conditions, disease spread through the camp – typhoid fever, dysentery, pneumonia and scurvy were common ailments, as was frostbite. In addition to this suffering, there was little food, no regular ration of meat, and few blankets.[55]

Christmas dinner at Valley Forge was "… a frugal collation of mutton, potatoes, cabbage, and crusts of bread, accompanied by water."[56] Washington was furious that Congress had not provided funding or procurement of the promised supplies to support the Army, and he was just as angry that American farmers in the area sold their goods to the British in Philadelphia for hard currency (gold and silver) while they refused to accept Continental notes. By the end of January 1778, Washington resorted to confiscating livestock and grain from the local farmers. It was truly a last resort, as he was also fighting a political battle, and was trying to keep the favor and goodwill of the general public. Even counting these confiscations, the army was barely fed, and hundreds of soldiers died that winter from disease, starvation, and the elements.[57]

At the end of February 1778, Washington's luck would change for the better with the arrival of a newcomer from Europe, Friedrich Wilhelm Ludolf Gerhard Agustin, Baron von Steuben. Baron von Steuben had been on the military staff of Fredrick the Great and had served as a Prussian captain during the Seven Years War. He was the perfect drillmaster for an American army that was nearly completely ignorant of military maneuvers – he taught them how to use their bayonet, which before his arrival they only used to cook their beefsteak over an open flame. He taught them how to march, move in formation, switch from line to column to line, and feu de joie (progressive fire with muskets), and he drilled them incessantly.[58]

About the same time as Baron von Steuben's arrival, the provisions situation started to improve. Washington decided he wanted to reward the army's steadfast dedication to the cause of liberty while enduring countless hardships. In April came word of an alliance with France, the cause for an all-out thanksgiving of sorts. By the time the official news reached Washington, it was May 5. The party was scheduled for the next day, and it turned into an all-day affair, from 9 a.m. to the evening.[59]

In May, there were also rumblings from the enemy quarter. The British magistrates in England recalled Sir William Howe and replaced him with Sir Henry Clinton as commander in charge. General Clinton was General Howe's top subordinate and had been commanding the garrison in New York. He moved to Howe's headquarters in Philadelphia to take command. By the middle of May, rumors out of Philadelphia were indicating that Clinton intended to leave Philadelphia for New York. These rumors were substantiated when about one hundred British ships sailed out of the Philadelphia harbor and down the Delaware River. The British army was still garrisoned in the American capital, but it was expected that they soon would also leave.[60]

Battle of Monmouth

On June 18, 1778, General Clinton and the British army departed Philadelphia for the march to New York. Having sent a small detachment of soldiers into Philadelphia to maintain law and order, Washington set out after them. The Continental Army paralleled the British movements as they tramped through New Jersey, although the British seemed in no hurry to get to their destination. By June 24, Washington held a council of war to decide if this was an opportunity to battle the enemy to a conclusive end of the war. General Lee argued against an attack, stating the Americans should wait until the French entered the war on the American side. Other generals disagreed, saying the current situation presented an opportunity. Washington decided on a middle course, wherein a small portion of the army was to attack the British flank in a harassing movement, and then to wait for an opportunity to attack the main body. Washington modified his decision when word came that the enemy was on its way to Monmouth Court House, because the Americans were within striking distance of the road they would have to travel to get there. What happened next is known as the Battle of Monmouth.[61]

On the evening of June 27, the advancing American forces reached within six miles of the British army. Washington ordered General Lee to attack the next morning, before the British got away. Washington would wait nearby with 6,000 men in case the main body of the enemy came into the fray. At noon on June 28, Washington advanced to Monmouth with his men, expecting to hear the sounds of battle. All he heard was the sounds of his own men clanking along in their march. He came upon some men walking through the fields and found that they had been ordered to retreat. Washington was livid! He raced up to Lee and demanded an explanation. Lee said he had encountered unexpected strength and resistance from the British forces and decided to save the army from an unnecessary action. He also said he thought the plan was a bad idea and undertaken against his opinion. Washington replied, "You ought not to have undertaken it unless you intended to go through with it."[62]

Washington ordered Lee to the rear and took over command of the battle. The British were advancing and would be upon the American positions in 15 minutes. He told General Anthony Wayne to hold the line with two regiments in a delaying action while he personally took charge of rallying the troops in retreat and set up defensive positions for General Stirling and General Greene. The troops graced themselves with their display of all the training Baron von Steuben had drilled into them. They formed lines with discipline and precision and withstood several charges by the British regulars. On this day they proved themselves equal to the greatest army in the world. As the sun went down on the daylong battle, American and British casualties were approximately equal, but one certain casualty was the notion that the American militia and members of the Continental Army were inferior in any way to the British army. Indeed, in some ways, they had proved superior.[63]

After the battle, the British slipped away in the middle of the night. Washington decided not to pursue. Instead, his orders for the next day commended the men for their bravery and their actions. General Lee, however, was court-martialed and found guilty of disobeying orders, permitting a disorderly retreat, and disrespecting the commander-in-chief. This was also to be General Washington's last action until the Battle of Yorktown three years later. In the intervening years, Washington would spend a significant amount of time planning a New York City invasion to take the city back from the British, and trying to get the French to employ their ships in battle against their British counterparts to wrestle sea superiority from the British. Both of those efforts were made in vain as neither would occur during the war.[64]

The French Alliance

In the three years between the Battle of Monmouth Court-house and the next battle that Washington would lead, there came a confluence of events that would turn the tide of the war. The French entered the conflict on the American's side, having recognized American Independence in April 1778. The French Atlantic Fleet was said to have departed the coast of France for the New World soon afterwards. A Gallic army of 4,000 men arrived in July 1778, headed by General Rocham-beau and delivered by a French fleet of 12 ships of the line and four frigates. However, this support was not enough to end the war. The Continental Army had been decimated by disease, desertions, and completion of planned enlistments (the long-est enlistments were three years, but those were expiring and the remaining soldiers were the ones who had signed up for the duration of the war).[65]

Between June 1778 and May 1781, most of the battles be-tween the British and the Continental Army occurred in Geor-gia and the Carolinas. General Clinton attacked the American army in Charleston, South Carolina, and with his naval superi-ority and thousands of Hessians and British regulars, captured the city. The American commander, General Lincoln, had been warned by Washington to withdraw to save his army, because he feared a repeat of the disaster of Ft. Washington. But his message arrived too late and the Americans lost 2,500 soldiers along with 2,000 militia. After the British victory, General Clin-ton returned to New York to protect his most important base and put General Cornwallis in charge of the southern opera-tions. With the loss of Charleston, most of the south lay bare to wanton pillaging by Cornwallis, until Washington sent Gen-eral Green with an army of about 2,000 men to counter the British threat.[66]

While Washington fretted and argued with Congress about the number of militia and soldiers in the Army, he also conferred with the French on likely targets of opportunity for their combined forces. The French General Rochambeau had received information that the French Navy in the West Indies under Admiral de Grasse was on its way north to support the American war efforts, and informed Washington of this news during their meeting in Wethersfield, Connecticut on May 21, 1781. This pleased Washington immensely, as he had been working since the beginning of the war on plans for a New York City siege as his ultimate goal.[67]

But by the time Washington requested that the French fleet sail to Sandy Hook in preparation for an attack on New York City, Rochambeau had already coordinated with de Grasse for an arrival at Chesapeake Bay. Rochambeau was intending to start a southern campaign, with the French Navy providing protection from possible British naval interference. Lucky for him and for the Revolutionary cause, General Clinton directed Cornwallis to take up a defensive position in Yorktown or Williamsburg in Virginia and wait for reinforcements. Dutifully, Cornwallis stationed his troops in Yorktown and Gloucester (across the waterway from Yorktown). As the plans came together, Washington gave up on his dream to recapture New York City. He eventually embraced the plan for an attack on Cornwallis and became an enthusiastic supporter.[68]

Yorktown

As the French and American armies raced southward overland from Morristown in New Jersey to surround Yorktown, Washington worried about Cornwallis escaping from the trap. He need not have worried, because Cornwallis dug in for battle, expecting the British fleet and Clinton's forces to come to his aid. The Franco-American plans come together perfectly, with de Grasse arriving in Williamsburg on September 5. By the end of September, the French and American forces had completely surrounded the British in Yorktown and Gloucester. From this moment, the battle's outcome was a *fait accompli.*

On October 9, Washington was ceremoniously given the honor of firing the first cannon shot in the battle.[69]

The bombardment lasted about a week, with the British cannon being systematically targeted and destroyed by the French siege tactics (they dug trenches in parallel lines to the British defenses large enough to bring up their cannons but below the line of targeting by the enemy's cannonade). By October 14, the French and American forces stormed the remaining two outer redoubts and turned the cannons around to face the British walls. On October 17, Cornwallis requested a truce to discuss the terms of his surrender. On October 19, 1781, the entire garrison of both outposts in Gloucester and Yorktown surrendered to Washington and Rochambeau. As the British troops marched out of the town to hand over their weapons and flags to the American and French conquering armies, their fife and drum musicians played the tune "The World Turned Upside Down."[70]

Yorktown was essentially the battle that defined the British defeat and ended the Revolutionary War. It resulted in the capture of over 8,000 British troops; about one fourth of the total the England had sent to snuff out the rebellion in the colonies. Even so, Washington knew that the remaining 26,000 (he estimated) British regulars were more than the strength of the Continental Army, and the English could always send more across the ocean. Even after the Yorktown victory, Washington wondered what the British would do next, and his thoughts and concerns were ever focused on the large contingent of British soldiers stationed in New York. What Washington didn't know was that back in England, the Lords and Ministry were arguing over the sanity of continuing a war, the expense of which was having an impact at home. By early 1782, Prime Minister Lord North's government would be toppled by anti-war sentiment. The British lost their will to continue the fight, and in the end, Washington's steady hand and perseverance won out.[71]

Newburgh

The battle of Yorktown occurred in October 1781, but it would be two full years of delays and negotiations before the British left America. During that time, Washington worried about several issues that continued to consume his time and thoughts: the constant incoming and outgoing of the militia volunteers (who typically signed up for one- or two-year enlistments); the pay and back pay of his army (for which the Continental Congress had trouble getting contributions from the individual states, this being before the taxing powers of the federal government); and the potential that the cessation of hostilities was actually a ploy by King George III and his generals to get the Continental Army to let their guard down in advance of a massive attack by the combined British Army and Navy.[72]

In August 1782, peace negotiations with the British had started in Paris. By November 1782, a preliminary peace treaty was signed. During this period, the Continental Army was in the throes of unending issues over supplies and back pay for the soldiers – the problem being that the states had refused to provide the promised funding to keep an army in the field and the Continental Congress being powerless to force them to capitulate. When a Congressional proposal to collect customs duties was rejected by Rhode Island (according to the Articles of Confederation, unanimity of all 13 states was required), it ended hope for a federal funding solution to adequately pay the army.[73]

In January 1783, a group of officers were selected to present their grievances to Congress. This committee of officers told Congress about their long-suffering issues: some soldiers had not been paid in five years, many had given up their personal businesses to fight in the war, and all had suffered the hardships of many years separated from their families. Washington worried that an armed and angry army in the field, with many grievances against the government, was dangerous. Some on the committee stated that they would not leave Congress until the issues were resolved.[74]

The issue came to a head within a couple of months. The members of the committee who had gone to Philadelphia to have their message heard by Congress had returned to Washington's military headquarters in Newburgh, New York, about 70 miles north of New York City on the Hudson River. A number of the officers were calling for an armed return to the capital, in effect threatening a mutiny or a junta takeover of civilian control of the government. A circular was published and passed around the camp for a meeting of the officers on March 11. Washington issued an order disapproving the illegally called meeting and requested a meeting of his own for March 15.[75]

Washington went to that gathering in Newburgh and started by making a short speech that thanked the officers and men of the Continental Army for their patriotic service. When he took out from his pocket some papers to read, he also pulled out some glasses, which nobody had ever seen him wear, and stated, "I have grown gray in your service and now find myself growing blind."[76] This bit of acting left no dry eye in the house, and took the wind from the sails of that potential military overthrow of our fledgling government. As James Flexner states in his biography of Washington, "Americans can never be adequately grateful that George Washington possessed the power and the will to intervene effectively in what may well have been the most dangerous hour the United States has ever known."[77]

CHAPTER 3

The First President

As the first President of the United States of America, George Washington had to be careful of his every action and every deed, because anything he did would potentially set a precedent for all presidents that would follow. His concern went so far as how the president would be addressed. The salutation had to be respectful but could not be interpreted as monarchical. A Senate committee was appointed to determine the appropriate address for the president, the office of which was eventually shortened by Congress to "The President of the United States." James Madison congratulated the President for the new moniker, and Washington found it much to his liking.[1]

One of Washington's initial issues as president was use of his time. He had so many visitors and people clamoring for his attention, including office seekers, that he could not do the more pressing work of the nation. Washington felt deeply obligated to republican ideals and thus allow himself to be visited by the public, but he did not want to let himself to be at the beck and call of every visitor. His solution for staying connected to the people while preserving time for the nation's business was creating a twice-weekly dinner for the public to attend. He announced in the local papers that every Tuesday and Friday at 2 p.m. he would accept visitors for an hour. Later, he revised this to a men's-only levee on Tuesday from 3-4 p.m. and men's and women's tea party with the First Lady on Friday evenings.[2]

Washington found it difficult to engage in small talk but performed his role beautifully by just staying silent and impressing others with his rectitude. Not everyone was happy with the manner in which Washington received his guests — some in the republican press denounced his behavior as being too aristocratic and monarchial. The reality was that Washington's manner was normally reserved. He was a man of actions and deeds, not words. And no matter how hard he tried, he was never going to be able to satisfy everyone's image as a president of the people, since no one had ever held that position before. William Maclay, a Senator from Pennsylvania and a constant critic of the President, was especially critical and caustic in his diary regarding Washington's manner at these public "levees." Maclay declared that Washington had, "a secret lust to be addressed as 'Your Majesty.'"[3]

The first year of Washington's presidency was relatively benign, which is exactly what he wanted. This initial level of marginal tranquility helped establish the initial protocols and expected behaviors of both the administration and the public. As the presiding official of the Constitutional Convention, Washington was well aware that the Constitution was more explicit about the "how" of the executive position — how it could be filled or unfilled (removed) — than the "what" it was all about in terms of defining what he could and could not do. As those points were fleshed out over the succeeding months and years, he carefully considered all options before making decisions and would use his cabinet to solicit advice as he had with his generals during the war. Initially, his cabinet was a stable of powerful influential thinkers: Jefferson as Secretary of State, Hamilton as Secretary of Treasury, Knox as Secretary of War, Randolph as Attorney General and Osgood as Postmaster General, but in time these thinkers began to war with each other. Although it was a critical health issue for a few days, another "benign" occurrence was a tumor that he had removed from his leg in June 1789.[4]

Touring the Northern States

About six months into his presidency, Washington decided to travel through the Northern states. His reasons were to get a better understanding of the state of the peoples in those regions, to get firsthand knowledge of the country's grip on the republican experiment, and to prove to his opponents that he was not a monarchist or king. Another benefit of the trip would be to strengthen the ties of local and state agencies to the federal government. Just before leaving, he signed a proclamation for a day of national Thanksgiving, to thank God for all of the blessings God had bestowed upon the country, and set the date of 26 November for that celebration.[5]

Washington's tour of the Northern states started in Connecticut (he was traveling from the temporary national capital in New York City) and went through Massachusetts and New Hampshire, before returning to New York. He did not visit Rhode Island, because as of that time it had not ratified the new Constitution (it eventually did in 1790). Washington began his trip on October 15, 1789, during the first recess after the first Congressional session under the Constitution. The first stop was New Haven, Connecticut, where he attempted to avoid the fanfare and arrive by an unexpected route ("the low road"). An unintended effect of this low-profile attempt at touring with his presidential entourage was that some inns turned them away, because they were so unexpected.[6] However, by the end of his trip he succumbed to the realization that everywhere he went, the public wanted to express their adulation and appreciation for him.[7]

When he arrived in Boston, the magnitude of the outpouring of love, respect, and appreciation for Washington's liberation of that city from British occupation touched him deeply. As he entered the city, church bells rang out and the French ships in Boston harbor shot off their cannons. In addition, the cannons at Dorchester Heights fired – an acknowledgement of

Washington's achievements by that battle. Washington rode his white horse wearing his old army uniform through the streets of Boston and stopped at the State house. There he was greeted with a wreath that said, "To the man who unites all hearts." When he appeared on a balcony the crowd gave a resounding roar of approval.[8]

Washington was also able to witness in his travel through the Northern states the progress of the industrial age and the use of (at that time) modern equipment for the manufacture of cloth and other textiles. His trip went as far north as Portsmouth, New Hampshire, where he went deep-sea fishing. Unfortunately, his luck would prove wanting – he was unable to catch a single fish. Washington was never very comfortable on the seas, and he was happy to conclude his travels with a pleasant dinner in Portsmouth. On his return trip to New York City, he made a detour to stop at Lexington, Massachusetts, the village where blood was first spilled in the Revolutionary War with Great Britain. Washington arrived in New York on November 13, 1789, almost exactly a month from his departure date from the capital.[9]

National Capital, National Debt

At the same time Washington had set out for his tour of the Northern states, Alexander Hamilton, the Secretary of the Treasury, had been given an assignment by Congress to come up with a plan to finance the national debt.[10] Hamilton's response was a proposal that eventually came to be called the "Assumption Bill." The name derived from the bill's object of having the federal government assume all the states' debts from the Revolutionary War, and then pay for that debt by levying new taxes that would finance the government. Washington's Secretary of State, Thomas Jefferson, wanted the United States Capital City to be located somewhere in the South, preferably in Virginia. Secretary of the Treasury Alexander Hamilton was keen to have his Assumption bill passed. In what has become known as the most influential (or infamous, depending on your political persuasion) dinner in U. S. history, Jefferson and Hamilton worked out a deal to help each other out. Jefferson would get Hamilton's support for a Capital City location on the Potomac (the new city would have to be planned, built, and populated) – in what became known as the Residence Act – in exchange for Jefferson's support to pass the Assumption bill in the Senate.[11]

After the passage of the Assumption bill (officially named the "Funding Act of 1790") and the Residence Act (signed by the President on July 16, 1790), Washington would have to move from New York City to the City of Brotherly Love, Philadelphia (named after a Greek city referenced in the Bible), in November 1790. The Residence Act set the new capital of the United States in Philadelphia for a period of 10 years, after which the capital would move to a site originally planned to be a square ten miles to a side (100 square miles in total area) astride the Potomac River; this would become Washington, D. C. (the District of Columbia).[12]

The exchange of favors for those two bills' passage was a rare example of cooperation between the two giants of Washington's cabinet. The rivalry between Hamilton's Federalist party (which included President Washington and Vice President John Adams) and Thomas Jefferson's Republican party (also known as the Democratic-Republican Party) was fierce. In addition, each party had its own advocacy press. The opposition press was Benjamin Franklin Bache's newspaper, and it was known to completely trivialize Washington's accomplishments and historical record while at the same time pushing the Democratic-Republican agenda. The Federalist papers were written by Hamilton, Madison (who switched allegiance to the Democratic-Republican camp), and John Jay (who negotiated the peace treaty with Britain) and became the platform for the Federalist party, which focused on a strong central government (versus states' rights), a permanent standing army to protect the country from invasion, and a semi-isolationist international political agenda to stay out of other country's wars.[13]

Washington restored American credit by not defaulting on debts to England and other countries at the beginning of his administration, as some had recommended he do. He also presided over the creation of the United States' federal debt, and he expected the nation and the merchants who owed money to businesses in other countries to pay their debts. Washington was a meticulous writer and documented in detail all his debts and payments. He was a man of honor and expected those around him to be likewise. Washington insisted that the citizens and business of this country fulfill their commitments and repay their obligations to the businesses and citizens of England, even after we defeated them. He also tried to instill a habit of prompt payment of the national debt and he stated so as a priority in his Farewell Address. The prompt payment of the national debt, and never defaulting on our debt, resulted in the perception that U. S. treasury bonds are among the safest investments in the world.

Touring the Remaining States

Before Washington's trip through the Northern states, James Madison had written the first 12 proposed amendments to the Constitution. What came out of the contentious debates during the state conventions held to ratify – or not – the United States Constitution was an effort to address issues brought up by anti-Federalists delegates. Madison's efforts to push the amendment articles through Congress was facing an uphill battle, so he asked for help from the President. Washington wrote a note to Congress expressing hope that the articles would be passed by both houses. In September 1789, the 12 articles passed Congress. In December 1791, ten of the twelve articles were ratified by the states, and those ten articles became the first ten amendments to the Constitution. These amendments became known as the United States Bill of Rights. These amendments having been passed, the remaining two states (Rhode Island and North Carolina) adopted the Constitution, and in May 1790, the United States reunited as the original 13 states of the union.[14]

Another success of the summer of 1790 was the Treaty of New York. Washington hosted the Creek Indian leader Alexander McGillivray and his party, escorted by Secretary of War Knox, at Washington's presidential mansion at 39 Broadway in New York City. The Treaty of New York was a treaty between the Creek, Chickasaw, and Choctaws Indians of Georgia and the United States. The treaty paid the Indians for the land north and east of the Oconee River; the Creek nation and their heirs and descendants were to relinquish and quit claim title to these lands. In addition, the treaty guaranteed legitimacy to the Creek Nation west and south of that boundary. There were also two secret agreements in the treaty: the first committed the United States to a trading relationship with the Creeks worth $60,000 of duty free merchandise a year, and in the second, McGillivray would receive an annual stipend of $1,200 as a commissioned officer in the U. S. Army (other chiefs would also receive annuities).[15] On August 7, the Senate approved the treaty, and in a ceremony at Federal Hall on August 13, Washington signed the treaty in the presence of Congress, Knox, McGillivray, and Indian chiefs and warriors.[16]

Washington had avoided visiting Rhode Island in his first tour of the Northern states because it had not yet ratified the Constitution. But by May 1790, Rhode Island had ratified, so Washington wanted to tour that state also. So, in mid-August, Washington, Jefferson, and New York governor George Clinton, decided to visit Rhode Island. Washington spent a week traveling to Rhode Island's capital (Providence) and college (which later became Brown University). He returned to New York in time to prepare for the move of the federal government to Philadelphia.[17]

Life in Philadelphia was a welcome change for the President and Mrs. Washington. Its broad streets and beautiful, large brick buildings were well aligned to Washington's need for structure and order. At the time, Philadelphia was the largest city in the United States (population 45,000) and provided a rich cultural and intellectual experience. It was home to two organizations founded by Benjamin Franklin: the American Philosophical Society and the Library Company. It also fostered an array of theaters supported by wealthy merchants, in addition to a lively soiree circuit. President Washington enjoyed attending plays at the South Street Theatre and spent so much time there he received his own box. As for Mrs. Washington, she also enjoyed the change of scenery, as it allowed her to visit her friends, while still performing her duties as First Lady.[18]

At the end of the first session of Congress in the new capital, Washington decided to take a tour of the Southern states, as he had done for the Northern states in the prior year. He wanted to take the pulse of the Southern states of the union and get acquainted with how this self-governing experiment was working in the South. Among the states, Washington had never been further south than Virginia in his life – the Revolutionary War kept him battling the British in the Northern states. As part of his preparations, he provided a detailed itinerary to his cabinet members, with detailed instructions on how to handle government business while he was traveling, and how to call him back to Philadelphia in case of emergency.[19]

Washington asked for advice from congressmen and others for planning purposes and detailed out his Southern tour like a military campaign. He spent two months on the road visiting North Carolina, South Carolina, and Georgia. He started his journey on April 7, 1791, and went through Halifax, Newbern, Wilmington, Charleston, and Savannah. His southern travels surprised him with how sparsely populated the region was in stark contrast to his northern route. He was most impressed by his visit in Charleston, where the brick and wood houses, tree-lined streets, and gardens of the residences pleased his discerning eye. His return route to Philadelphia took him through Augusta, Camden, Salisbury, and Winston-Salem. He arrived back in Philadelphia on July 6, almost exactly three months after he left.[20]

The Northwest Frontier

Toward the end of 1791, Washington was informed of two major events. The first – via Jefferson then in Paris – was that Lafayette had placed Louis XVI and Marie Antionette under arrest, the two having attempted to flee the French Revolution and join Prussian and Austrian armies in an invasion of France. The second was the massacre of nearly 1,000 troops who had been sent to the Ohio country to protect settlers from Indian uprisings. General Arthur St. Clair's army was decisively routed by the Miami Indians in what was the greatest defeat of the U.S. Army by Indians.[21]

St. Clair was the Governor of the Northwest Territories, a region between the Ohio and Mississippi rivers encompassing the current states of Ohio, Indiana, Illinois, Michigan, Wisconsin, and parts of Minnesota. The Northwest Territories were surrendered by the British to the Americans as part of the Treaty of Paris, which ended the Revolutionary War; however, the British never vacated their forts in that region as the Treaty had promised they would. These forts controlled the waterways of the region from the Great Lakes to the St. Lawrence River and were used as the trade routes for the North American fur trade.[22]

Washington pressed St. Clair to urgently send his army of roughly 1,400 men out from Fort Washington (present day Cincinnati) to the outskirts of the Miami Indian territory, near present day Ft. Wayne, Indiana. The intent of this show of force was to deter the number and severity of Indian raids on the frontier peoples living in the area. It would also put the British on notice of an American presence in the region and help to ease the embarrassment of British occupation of forts in the area. St. Clair notified the British of his planned presence, perhaps to avoid an international incident of a confrontation, by letting them know he was not there to attack them. If the British informed the Indians of the coming army, it is not known, but in December 1791, St. Clair's troops were ambushed by Shawnees and suffered 950 casualties, including 35 officers.[23]

St. Clair's infamous defeat at the hands of the Indians caused the Congress to initiate an investigation. They requested from President Washington all material information regarding the matter, which caused Washington to pause and consider the precedent-setting effects. He canvassed the cabinet members for their opinions, and eventually decided to provide the documents. The resulting analysis revealed the unpreparedness of the untrained militia in battling the Indians, and resulted in President Washington's long sought goal, the recommendation by Congress for a "federally supervised militia" – in other words, a standing U. S. Army.[24]

Until that army was established, the northwest frontier would be vulnerable to repeated attacks by Indian tribes throughout the region. Recognizing this predicament, Washington responded by seeking reconciliation and negotiation with those tribes. In June 1792, he invited to Philadelphia representatives of the Six Nations of the Iroquois Confederacy to promote peace in the area. The conference was so successful that the representatives of the Indian tribes promised to pass the message to other hostile tribes, and there was an eventual reduction in the number of raids by the Indians in the area.[25]

Government Transition

In addition to being an election year, 1792 was difficult for Washington personally. Although it was Washington's earnest desire to retire to Mount Vernon at the end of his first term, national and international events conspired to eliminate that possibility. As Washington's first term waned, two factions within his own cabinet created forces that could potentially tear his establishment, and possibly the nation, apart. Alexander Hamilton, the leader of the Federalists (also known as the "Hamiltonians"), had put in place fiscal policies and economic instruments (via the assumption of the states' debts for the Revolutionary War, capitalization of the national debt at full value, and creation of the Bank of the United States) necessary for a strong national government. Thomas Jefferson, the leader of the Democrat-Republicans or sometimes just Republicans (and also known as the "Jeffersonians"), strongly backed states' rights and tried to protect the government from falling into monarchial tendencies (he strongly backed the French Revolution, even though it would become the epitome of class warfare and mob rule).[26]

By the end of Washington's first term as president, his two greatest cabinet members, Alexander Hamilton and Thomas Jefferson, were both threatening to resign. What was so ironic about that was that Washington himself had desires to retire to his beloved Mount Vernon; however, retirement was not in the cards for him. He was destined to serve another four-year term as president. Even with his Secretary of the Treasury and his Secretary of State constantly at each other's throats, the *one* thing they both agreed upon was the need for President Washington to continue to provide a guiding hand to get the country through the tough times ahead. Reluctantly, Washington agreed to put his dreams away, and once again sacrificed his own preferences to do his duty and calling to lead the country for another four years.[27]

Washington's second term as president was as difficult and politically challenging as his first, and in many ways even more so. He had to deal with international disputes that threatened to pull the new nation into a pan-European war – the aftermath of the French Revolution. He had to deal with domestic disputes of Northern mercantilism and industrialism versus Southern agrarianism, and with Eastern populism versus Western expansionism. He also had to deal with political intrigue and disputes within his own cabinet of Jefferson versus Hamilton and the creation of the first political parties – the Democratic-Republicans (Jeffersonians) versus the Federalists (Hamiltonians).[28]

One of Washington's first acts during his second term as president was to issue the Neutrality Proclamation in April 1793. The proclamation's purpose was to explain to the American public the reasons and rationale for not entering on either side the recent war between England and France. Washington wanted to ensure the new nation's health and worried that another drawn-out war would be financially disastrous for his country that was still recovering from and paying off debt from the Revolutionary War. Also, it was Washington's personal belief that nations acted and should act only in their own self-interest. This decision for neutrality was completely at odds with Thomas Jefferson's belief (and that of many of his countrymen) that we were indebted to the French for their support to us during the Revolutionary War.[29]

Citizen Genet

The publication of the Neutrality Proclamation "elicited howls of rage from the republican press,"[30] and caused Washington considerable consternation. One paper was extremely hostile in their attacks on Washington's administration. Philip Freneau, who was hired by Jefferson in the State Department, was editor of the *National Gazette*, a newspaper that took sadistic pride in attacking Washington and his policies. In addition, Freneau had three copies of the *Gazette* delivered daily to Washington's doorstep, which further infuriated the President.[31]

About the same time that Washington declared the United States neutral in the war between England and France, the new French ambassador arrived. His name was Edmond Charles Genet (referred to often as "Citizen Genet"), and he arrived in Charleston, South Carolina on the French frigate *Embuscade*. He was greeted with cheering crowds of pro-French citizens, and he became emboldened with their adoration. He spent a month in the South, hiring privateers (mercenary sailors on merchant ships) to capture British merchant shipping vessels and take them and their cargo to U. S. ports. He also recruited American citizens to infiltrate the British and Spanish possessions north and south of the United States to foment dissent and foster uprisings.[32]

Genet finally made his way to Philadelphia in May 1793. He entered Philadelphia to resounding cheers and pro-French sentiment. And when he finally made his way to visit President Washington and his cabinet, Thomas Jefferson practically fawned over him. Jefferson recounted Genet's speech to James Madison, saying said that Genet did not ask for anything in their conflict with the British while offering only support to the American cause. Jefferson looked upon Genet with rapture for the man and his mission. To Jefferson, Genet was the embodiment of the republican cause. Moreover, he believed not only that the United States owed a debt of gratitude to the French for their support of America's independence but also that we should reciprocate that support to France. Washington was not so impressed but was concerned that Genet could be a treacherous diplomat with hidden motives.[33]

At that time in our history, the nation's popular opinion was that the British, having been our colonial oppressor and enemy in our struggle for independence, was still our enemy, while France, having helped us win independence from Britain, was our friend. However, much had changed in the ten years since the end of the war. The United States had inspired in France a similar revolution, which had taken hold as a fight for freedom from the monarchy but had devolved into a dark and sinister insurrection. Moreover, the American public was not receiving complete knowledge of what was really happening in France, but President Washington was getting information directly from his minister to France, Gouverneur Morris. Gouverneur gave Washington first-hand reports on the atrocities being meted out in the name of democracy and freedom.[34]

In France, the radical Jacobins had taken over from the more moderate Girodins, and there were grisly massacres all over the country; thousands of aristocrats and people of noble blood lost their heads to the guillotine. French mobs roamed the streets of Paris looking for excuses to spill blood, and the Jacobins worked to squash any attempts at counter-revolution. When the Girondin Charlotte Corday assassinated the Jacobin Jean-Paul Marat, the Jacobins unleashed the Reign of Terror, which was in effect a purge of all threats to their power. Estimates range between 18,000 and 40,000 people were executed during the Terror.[35] In a testament to the passions of the times and the irony of history, it would only be a matter of time before the Jacobins would be demanding the heads of both Citizen Genet and Gouverneur Morris.[36]

Genet's behavior after meeting the President was not mollified; if anything, it was even more self-delusional and extreme. Genet seemed to think he had the American people eating out of the palm of his hand. He also held private conversations with Jefferson, during which the Secretary of State divulged inside information concerning President Washington, the cabinet, and the political struggle between the Federalists and the Democratic-Republicans. Jefferson's behavior in this affair can only be described as delusional and possibly traitorous. For Genet's part, he was strengthened in his resolve and belief that he could take the question directly to the people – the question was of the legality of the Neutrality Proclamation and of the United States' responsibility toward their political ally and fellow republic, France.[37]

Genet's Mistake

Genet was successful in promulgating the French cause, and soon came an episode with the potential for sparking a negative British reaction and bringing the United States into the war. A British merchant ship *Little Sarah* was captured by the French, then was armed and outfitted in Philadelphia and renamed *La Petit Democrate*. The arming and outfitting in U. S. waters was in direct conflict with the commitment of the Neutrality Proclamation. Thomas Jefferson called upon Genet to keep the ship from sailing out of Philadelphia to the open sea. Genet told Jefferson it was not ready to sail, but that he would not keep it moored when it was.[38]

But Genet sent the ship to sea anyway and asked Jefferson for an audience with Washington to explain himself. Genet presented to Washington his interpretation of the will of the American people to side with the French. He also stated that he considered the Neutrality Proclamation an annulment of the peace treaty between the United States and France. Washington politely listened and exhibited no external emotion or reaction. He then showed Genet the door. Washington's strength of resolve and command of his composure is exquisitely demonstrated by this incident. A lesser man would have had a strong negative reaction to Genet's insulting and presumptuous manner.[39]

The extent of the public's affection for France and their desire for war with England was not a minor thing. Philadelphia was a hotbed of activity and Anglophobe antagonism. The streets swelled with swarms of men looking for excuses to express their anger at a government that refused to side with France. In his old age, John Adams confessed his fear that Genet had excited the street mobs in Philadelphia to such a state that they would drag Washington out of his house, start a revolution, and declare war on England.[40]

On August 1, 1793, Washington held an all-day cabinet meeting for the express purpose of reaching an agreement on what to do about the Genet issue. In previous meetings on this subject, a decision always had to be deferred, because the discussions would become so agitated between Hamilton and Jefferson that nothing would come of the meeting. This time Washington planned to have an all-day affair, from 9 a.m. until 4 p.m. to be followed by a "family" style dinner. At this particular meeting, Washington was the one who would become volatile and cut the meeting short. In the end, Washington decided once again to delay a decision until events unfolded to require it.[41]

On that same day in August, the residents of New York were treated to a naval battle off the coast of Sandy Hook. The French ship *Embuscade* defeated the British frigate *Boston* and then a French fleet of fifteen warships sailed into New York harbor. Upon hearing this news, Genet traveled from Philadelphia to New York where the Republicans were planning a welcoming party for him and the French victors. The Federalists in New York had other plans, however, and published in newspapers what Washington and his cabinet had been struggling with all along – an accounting of Genet's behavior.[42]

On August 12, 1793, an open letter signed by Chief Justice John Jay and New York Senator Rufus King disclosed Genet's threat to take his case to the American public. In Genet's public response (in an open letter to President Washington), he managed not only to insult the President, but to also appeal directly to the people while stating that he was not going to do so. The public outcry from this letter by Genet effectively eliminated him as a threat, and at the same time cooled the flames of the passionate Republicans who were demanding that the United States go to war with England.[43]

Yellow Fever

The next event in the history of the United States would do even more to douse the flames of Republican war-mongering than any letter or publication in the press – the Philadelphia Yellow Fever epidemic of 1793. It started in the summer on the wharves of Philadelphia and by August 19, Dr. Benjamin Rush (the President's doctor) declared an epidemic. Thousands died from the disease; at the epidemic's peak the daily death toll was in the hundreds. By early September, the nation's capital had become a ghost town, both from the high number of deaths, and from the flight of people trying to avoid infection. On September 6, Washington heard that Hamilton had contracted the disease. Hamilton recovered and convalesced in Albany, New York. On September 10, the President decided to leave Philadelphia and travel to Mount Vernon.[44]

By mid-October, ten percent of the population of Philadelphia had died from the disease.[45] The capital was largely deserted. Washington called a special cabinet session to be held in Germantown, six miles northwest of Philadelphia, on November 1. At this meeting, the cabinet agreed to publish all the correspondence regarding Genet and would officially request his recall by the French government. The cabinet then discussed what Washington would say in his next State of the Union address. They agreed that the President should explain his stance on the Neutrality Proclamation. As cooler weather returned, so did Philadelphia's populace. In late November and early December, members of Congress started returning to the city for the coming session. When Washington delivered his next annual message on December 3, it was met with almost universal acclaim.[46]

But as the waters with France were calming, things with the British were again heating up. The British government had still not honored its agreement at the end of the Revolutionary War to close their posts and forts on the Great Lakes and hand them over to the United States. In addition, British ships were capturing neutral ships loaded with any cargo bound for French ports. The British were also continuing their policy of turning American seamen from captured cargo vessels into British navy personnel. By the end of 1793, the British also allowed the Portuguese (their ally in the war with France) to stop patrolling the Mediterranean Sea, which loosed Algerian pirates on American shipping.[47]

Pirates based in the North African seaports around Algiers, Tripoli, and Tunisia increasingly raided U.S. vessels in the Mediterranean and required payment to get the ships and hostages back. In March 1794, Washington worked with Congress to build six frigates for overseas protection of American shipping. This act in effect was the cause and creation of the United States Navy, although it would take another four years to officially designate a Department of the Navy. Federalist leaders also requested the creation of a 25,000-man standing army to protect the domestic population from Indians and foreign governments, but the Republican opposition in Congress, always suspicious of a military establishment, pushed back.[48]

A Tax Revolt

The next conflict involved defending the country not from external enemies but from internal foes. The federal government from its very first days always seemed to struggle with providing enough funding to keep the government working. But that was before the Tariff Act of 1789 started generating federal income from customs duties. As Secretary of the Treasury, Alexander Hamilton based his financing of the government on a tax system similar to that of the British government. Taxes and collection of duties from the importing of goods was initially the basis of the U. S. system. The Tariff Act of 1790 provided further funding of the government through increased customs and duties on specific items. But with the Assumption Bill, which called for all of the states' debts from the Revolutionary War being assumed by the federal government, there was the need for additional tax revenue to make payments on the debt. Hamilton believed that he had already increased customs duties about as high as they could go. So, he investigated potential means for a domestic tax. One of these was the Whiskey Tax. This tax would be collected from the makers of whiskey at the source, which were usually farmers who were distilling their own grain.[49]

Hamilton had originally proposed a tax on distilled spirits in his *Report on Public Credit* in January 1790, but now there was a need to put such a tax into action.[50] Congress enacted an enabling act, which was called the Excise Whiskey Tax, or *"An Act repealing, after the last day of June next, the duties heretofore laid upon Distilled Spirits imported from abroad, and laying others in their stead; and also upon Spirits distilled within the United States, and for appropriating the same."*[51]

Washington signed the bill into law on March 3, 1791. By late 1792, Hamilton put Washington on notice that lax enforcement of the excise tax was a concern, and he requested that the President sign a proclamation requiring enforcement of the law. The President issued the proclamation, and the matter appeared to have been resolved. Washington addressed the topic briefly in his fourth State of the Union address: "The prosperous state of our revenue has been intimated. This would be still more the case, were it not for the impediments which, in some places, continue to embarrass the collection of the duties on spirits distilled within the United States."[52]

The "some places" Washington was referring to were four counties in western Pennsylvania, around what is now Pittsburgh. In these areas, the local citizens had taken it upon themselves to scoff the whiskey tax, and even tarred and feathered the local tax collector. They went so far as to destroy the stills of anyone who had paid the tax, burned the barns of anyone who supported the government, and ceased to obey any laws. What concerned Washington was not so much the destruction of property as the destruction of the principle upon which the government was based – the idea of a government of the people, for the people, and by the people could be ignored or overruled. He abhorred the concept that a small minority could dictate to the majority how things would be handled. Washington saw in this the potential for the destruction of the concept of republican government, and that the ability to ignore the federal government could lead to the secession of an area from the Union.[53]

By the summer of 1794, the situation in western Pennsylvania was critical. On August 2, Washington convened a session of his cabinet to decide how to handle the issue. The vote was split regarding taking military action to suppress the rebellion, so Washington requested an opinion from Justice James Wilson. Wilson's opinion authorized the use of force, but Washington made one more attempt at diplomacy, and sent a three-man commission to the area to negotiate.[54]

Whiskey Rebellion

The commission was headed by Attorney General William Bradford, and included James Ross, a Pennsylvania Senator, and Justice Jasper Yeates, a judge on the Pennsylvania Supreme Court. The commission was authorized to provide amnesty to those willing to support the implementation and execution of the laws of the nation. However, when they arrived, they found the area of western Pennsylvania in complete disarray. There was no rule of law, local government officials were terrorized, and someone had built a guillotine (a la the French Revolution). Some of the leaders of the rebellion were even advocating succession from the Union.[55]

In response to the crisis, Washington requested the governments of four states (Pennsylvania, New Jersey, Virginia, and Maryland) to provide volunteer militia of 13,000 men. The reaction was overwhelming and Washington received more than enough volunteers to fill the quotas. Washington also issued a proclamation that the insurgents must lay down their arms and go home by September 1. They did not. Washington issued another warning to the Pennsylvanians on September 25, though he expected and received no reply. Thus, Washington prepared for battle; he packed a new tailored uniform modeled after the one he had worn during the Revolutionary War. At the end of September, he departed Philadelphia by carriage for Carlisle, Pennsylvania, to meet up with the Pennsylvania and New Jersey militias.[56]

On October 4, Washington reached Carlisle, and on the outskirts of town he exited the carriage to mount his horse for a review of the troops. Upon his arrival at the camp, the sight of Washington on his horse put the men into a sudden reverence and silence as he reviewed the men standing at attention. Captain Ford of the New Jersey militia wrote that the men were awestruck by Washington and that, "As he passed our troop, he pulled off his hat, and in the most respectful manner, bowed to the officers and men and in this manner passed the line."[57]

Washington accompanied the troops on their march to Fort Cumberland in Maryland to meet up with the Maryland and Virginia militia. Virginia's Governor Lee was a former general during the Revolutionary War and was in charge of the Virginia militia. The combined forces then marched over the Blue Ridge Mountains to Bedford. At the Bedford encampment in Pennsylvania, Washington met with Hamilton, Lee, and the other leaders to plan the operations in western Pennsylvania. It was decided that they would leave Bedford in two columns, one led by Lee and the other led by Hamilton, for the 100-mile trek to Pittsburgh. In his farewell speech to the troops at Bedford, Washington stressed the militia's sacred duty to uphold the law and to be accountable to the civic leaders. He said, "The essential principals of a free government confine the provinces of the military to these two objectives: first, to combat and subdue all who may be found in arms in opposition to the national will and authority; 2nd, to aid and support the civil magistrate in bringing offenders to justice. The dispensation of this justice belongs to the civil magistrate and let it ever be our pride and our glory to leave the sacred deposit there unviolated."[58]

The two columns of militia marched through western Pennsylvania without opposition, and the Whiskey Rebellion leaders were rounded up peacefully. The two leaders of the rebellion were charged with treason and sentenced to death; however, Washington eventually used his presidential powers to pardon those two individuals. In the meantime, Washington left Bedford for the over 200-mile journey back to Philadelphia and made it back just in time to submit his sixth State of the Union address to the new congressional session that opened on November 3, 1794.[59]

Democratic Societies

Democratic Societies were partisan organizations that originated in Philadelphia in 1793 and were usually aligned with Jeffersonian policies (pro-French, anti-British, and anti-monarchial). These organizations were also anti-Federal, opposed taxation and, in general, were against the policies of Washington's administration. The Citizen Genet affair had greatly increased the number of Democratic Societies throughout the country, and Washington believed that the revolt and anarchy fomented by the leaders of the Whiskey Rebellion was a direct result of those organizations.[60]

Washington delivered his Sixth Annual Address to Congress on November 19. In this address he explained his response to the Whiskey Rebellion, and the government's efforts to address the issues at the source of the conflict. Washington spent 20 minutes describing the situation, the actions he took, and the outcome of the events. A review of the text of this address reveals that about three quarters of the speech dealt with the rebellion and his response to it. The remainder dealt with the militia, the success of General Wayne in fighting the Indians in the Northwest Territories, and the state of the government finances, including the need to reduce the public debt.[61]

Although he did not mention them by name, Washington felt the Democratic Societies that had sprung up as a result of the French Revolution, and that had tripled in number in the heyday of Citizen Genet's frenzied activities, were at least partially at fault for the behavior of the western Pennsylvanian citizens. To him, they seemed to be fomenting anarchy and revolution, and that no government was their preference to republican government. By making slight mention to "certain self-created societies" and "associations of men" as being the cause of the insurrection in his address, Washington managed to shine a light on the dark "machinations of the wicked" the better to eliminate the causes of "internal sedition." In 1794 there were 35 documented Democratic Societies, but by 1795 only three.[62]

In January 1795, Washington had to replace two more of his cabinet members. Treasury Secretary Alexander Hamilton, whose wife had a miscarriage while he was away fighting the Whiskey Rebellion, turned in his resignation in December 1794 but promised to stay until the end of January. The comptroller of the treasury, Oliver Wolcott, Jr, replaced Hamilton. Wolcott had also previously served as the auditor of the Treasury Department. The Secretary of War, Henry Knox, had disappointed Washington by taking a leave of absence before and during the Whiskey Rebellion, and resigned at the end of December 1794. He was replaced by Timothy Pickering, who had previously served as postmaster general, and had served as an adjutant general during the Revolutionary War.[63]

The Jay Treaty

Just before the end of the session of Congress in early March 1795, Washington announced he would bring the results of Chief Justice John Jay's negotiations with the British before Congress in June. Jay had been appointed "special envoy" to England about a year before and, communications being what they were in the late 1700s, he had actually signed the Treaty of London (also known as the Jay Treaty) on November 19, 1794. The first Washington had heard of the specifics of the negotiations was the treaty he held in his hands on March 7, 1795. He was surprised, almost shocked, at the lack of American interests being supported by the treaty, but after careful review he decided that on the whole it was probably the best treaty the United States could have negotiated at that time.[64]

Washington presented the treaty to Congress on June 8, 1795. Congress debated the treaty for about two and a half weeks, and then they approved it by exactly the two thirds majority required. Now that Congress had ratified the treaty (with a concern regarding Article XII), the President had to decide to sign it or not. Washington consulted his cabinet, and requested written responses to the question: Should the treaty be signed? He also wondered if it should be released to the public, but that question was answered when an opposition senator supplied it to the anti-government publisher Benjamin F. Bache.[65]

The general public did not have as favorable of a view of the Jay Treaty as Washington did. Public sentiment was that Jay had negotiated a bad deal, and they were extremely upset about it. When John Jay finally made it back to the United States after crossing the Atlantic, he said that he could have traveled at night and found his way home by the light of the burning effigies of his likeness. With all the public controversy, Washington was now concerned about signing the treaty, and consulted the retired Alexander Hamilton for his opinion. Hamilton provided a 41-page analytical response that found fault with Article XII, but generally approved of the treaty. After much consternation Washington finally approved and signed the treaty on August 18, 1795.[66]

Over that same period, another significant negotiation was going on. This was with the Spanish. As a result of their involvement in the French and British war, the Spanish were suffering financially. In addition, they had suffered naval losses in Europe and the Caribbean that forced them to reconsider their strategy. And the fact that the United States had just completed negotiations with the British made them concerned about a possible U.S.-British push through North America. The Spanish King Charles IV requested that Washington send an envoy authorized to negotiate a treaty. Washington assigned Thomas Pinckney to this task, and Pinckney arrived in Spain in June 1795.[67]

Treaty of San Lorenzo

Prior to the treaty, the Spanish had kept the southern part of the Mississippi River closed to American shipping. This kept the western United States (including Tennessee and Kentucky) from being able to use the Ohio and Mississippi rivers for transport of their products to sell in New Orleans. Kentucky residents were so upset about it that they were threatening to secede from the Union. This was another reason why Washington wanted to negotiate with the Spanish. However, he had no idea that Pinckney would be so successful.[68]

The treaty that Pinckney was able to negotiate, known as the Treaty of San Lorenzo (also known as Pinckney's Treaty) defined the Mississippi River as the western border of the United States and Florida's northern border as the 31st parallel (Florida was still owned by the Spanish). It also allowed American ships full use of the Mississippi River, with no duties on American products being sold in New Orleans (also owned by the Spanish). The treaty was signed on October 27, 1795 and was an immediate success. This new definition of the western border allowed expansion of the population, and the duty-free commerce in New Orleans made selling American products a profitable venture. The treaty also helped the Federalist Party gain popularity in the South and West and offset to a large extent the disaffection of the population owing to the Jay Treaty.[69]

At noon on December 8, 1795, Washington delivered his annual address (State of the Union) to Congress. He talked about the victory by General Wayne in the Northwest Territories and the subsequent treaty that the General had negotiated with the Indian tribes there. He talked about the Barbary pirates, and how the new Emperor of Morocco had recognized the treaty that the United States had made with his father. He also talked about the potential of a truce with Algiers. Washington then moved on to the progress being made by Thomas Pinckney, who was negotiating a treaty in Madrid with the Spanish King (communication being what it was in those days, Washington did not yet know the details of the agreements). He finally discussed the Jay Treaty, and how it had been approved by the Senate and then signed by the President. He further stated that the Jay Treaty would be brought before Congress for ratification.[70]

Washington then attributed the peace and prosperity of the United States to the effect of these treaties and to the course of neutrality that the country had steered through: " . . . our favored country, happy in a striking contrast, has enjoyed general tranquility – a tranquility the more satisfactory, because maintained at the expense of no duty. Faithful to ourselves, we have violated no obligation to others."[71] Although being buffeted by a public outcry over the Jay Treaty, and being mercilessly skewered by the Republican (anti-Federalist, anti-government) press, Washington managed to turn the tables on the opposition. Washington had successfully argued that his Neutrality Proclamation and adherence to a policy of independence from entanglements with other governments had provided the country with unprecedented peace, prosperity, and security. Washington would take those thoughts further in his famous Farewell Address.

The Farewell Address

Washington's Farewell Address is one of the most inspiring and noble public documents of our nation. It stands shoulder to shoulder with the Declaration of Independence and the Gettysburg Address in its poignancy and effect. Washington had struggled with balancing his obligation to public duty and his desire to return to a private life for the entire eight years of his Presidency. He had originally expected and attempted to retire at the end of his first term but was pressured by both Jefferson and Hamilton to serve a second term. Washington had initially intended to include the text of his first farewell address, which was written by James Madison, to prove to the public that he had never intended to fall for the trappings of an aristocracy or a monarchy. He also did not want to let his detractors get the satisfaction of thinking they had run him out of office. However, in the end none of Madison's writings made it into the final version.[72]

In May 1796, Washington sent his first draft of the address to Alexander Hamilton and asked for his review. In his usual mode of attention to detail and strategic thinking, Hamilton rewrote the address to provide the wording and flow of a more permanent and lasting document. Hamilton provided this new draft to Washington at the end of July. Washington's initial reaction was a concern regarding its length, because he was uncertain that the papers would print such a long document. Subsequent to delivering his initial response, Hamilton provided a response to Washington's request that was more of an edited version of Washington's original text. After a careful review of both documents, Washington decided on working with Hamilton's rewrite (first) version.[73]

Washington rewrote the address in his own handwriting and in his own voice (the terminology and verbiage he was more accustomed to). Washington then deleted whole sections he did not agree with and added paragraphs from Hamilton's second version of the document. Washington also added whole sections, including a new section on the need for a National University (which Hamilton later recommended be removed and included in Washington's next annual address to Congress).[74]

Washington's Farewell Address was published on September 19, 1796, in the *Daily American Advertiser*. It started with his decision to retire and his rationale for the timing of that decision. It continued with his gratitude for the opportunity to serve the country and his sincere wishes for the continued welfare of the nation. Washington expressed his desire that the country unite in a common cause for liberty and the principles of representative government, North and South, East and West, and a repudiation of the geographical discriminations that cause a local view to misrepresent the facts and cause disaffection. He professed his faith in the new Constitution and the duty of all citizens to obey the laws and principles of the government.[75]

The address continued with an admonition that the government should preserve its public credit by using it wisely and repaying it promptly. It went on to state that government revenue was required in the execution of its functions, and that taxation was a required element of government. However, the majority of the address, and the biggest lasting impact of its message, regarded public policy with foreign nations. He explained that the country should attempt to have peace and harmony with all nations, and not allow passions of imaginary attachments to certain nations embroil the United States into alliances and wars that do not serve the best interests of this country. The Neutrality Proclamation successfully avoided a war with Europe, the Address declared, and was the reason why the nation's economy was so strong. This final message was Washington's personal opinion regarding the behavior of nations and one of the address's crowning achievements. It is also one of Washington's lasting legacies.[76]

CHAPTER 4

Washington's Legacy

President Washington's legacy is a surprisingly long shadow, considering that he served as our founding president over 230 years ago. Even through the ages, his legacy lives on because as the first President of the United States, everything he said, wrote, and did became a precedent for all subsequent presidents. Washington wrote, "...I walk on untrodden ground. There is scarcely any part of my conduct which may not hereafter be drawn into precedent."[1] He was constantly performing self-examination of his conduct, to make sure he was not violating the letter of the Constitution, or creating a potential future issue with his decisions. Those internal debates started as early as the Inaugural Address, which wasn't specifically called for in the Constitution, but is now a tradition that has continued for every subsequent president to this day. In one of his first acts as president that is also with us today, Washington called for a day of Thanksgiving, on Thursday, November 26, 1789, a proclamation to thank God for the many blessings God bestowed upon our nation.[2]

As president of the Constitutional Convention, Washington served as the ultimate arbitrator for how the government was to be reformed after the Americans expelled the British in the War of Independence. He observed much and said little during the lively discussions between the founding fathers. He played that patriarchal role like a proud father overseeing the progress of his children. Then, nearing the close of the convention, he provided one of the most nuanced final touches on the Constitution when he decreased the population equation ratio per representative from 40,000 to 30,000 people.[3] He explained that he felt that 40,000 people were too many for one person to represent and properly defend their rights and interests. In this and other acts he performed both before and during his presidency, Washington was seen and celebrated as the Father of the Nation.

As Commander of the Continental Army, Washington achieved the nearly impossible, by defeating the most powerful armed forces in the world at the time, the combined might of the British Redcoats and Royal Navy. He achieved this astonishing feat with patience, ingenuity, and daring. Throughout the conflict he maintained his poise, even in the face of incredible challenges: his troops were untrained, unfed, unfit, and unpaid. The constant turnover in the militia forces – because of their short commitments to the cause of six months to a year – forced him to have to repeatedly train new recruits. And because the Continental Army was a collection of militias from across the fledgling country, their allegiances tended toward their home states rather than to the Army, a circumstance that caused infighting and dissention. Washington not only had to deal with upheaval within the ranks but also with intrigue among the officers, as proven by several attempts by other generals of the Army to gain support within factions of Congress to replace Washington with themselves or other power-hungry men.

Washington's legacy is preeminent not only because of what he did but also because of how he achieved that pinnacle. His record represents a standard of excellence that all leaders should try to replicate. Washington succeeded precisely because of who he was, a man of principle, guided by his own internal compass of ambition mastered by restraint, and a desire to always do the right thing. He is the father of our country and the greatest president in our history.

The Cabinet

Washington's style of leadership created the cabinet system, wherein the president named the Secretary of the Treasury, the Secretary of State, the Secretary of War, the Attorney General, and the Postmaster General. In Washington's leadership system, which derived from his experience in leading the Continental Army during the American Revolution, he would ask for advice and input from his cabinet, akin to a Counsel of Generals (or a Council of War), to aid in his decision-making. Congress, trying to define the ambiguous separation of powers between the legislative and executive branches of the government as defined in the Constitution, attempted to make the hiring and firing of all executive appointments be confirmed by the legislature and passed legislation in the House to that effect. But in the Senate, this bill for limiting the executive power was defeated by Vice President Adams' tiebreaking vote. Subsequently, the Senate successfully blocked one of Washington's first appointments, that of Benjamin Fishbourn to be collector for the Port of Savannah. This set the precedent that the executive branch would make appointments without the interference of Congress, but that after the appointments were made, they were presented to the Senate for approval (confirmation) or rejection by simple majority.[4]

Washington's cabinet members could also be said to have set the bar for the quality of the personnel Washington chose to lead. Alexander Hamilton is arguably the greatest Secretary of the Treasury the United States has ever had. Thomas Jefferson, while at times working against President Washington's desires and intents as his Secretary of State, may be one of the best ever at his position. Henry Knox was famous for his leadership and courage during the Revolutionary War and was a very able Washington confidant and Secretary of War. Attorney General Edmund Randolph was a member of the Constitution convention, a former governor of the state of Virginia, and later served as the Secretary of State after Jefferson resigned. In some ways, Washington's cabinet was as much a "Team of Rivals" as Lincoln's cabinet. However, the significant rivalry was between Jefferson and Hamilton, and this created the first political parties.[5]

For better or for worse, another legacy of the Washington administration was the creation of the first political parties and the two-party system of government in the United States, as much as Washington himself pushed against it and tried to steer clear of party politics. However, as Jefferson became more militant against the administration's policies, and hired a newspaper publisher in an attempt to sway the public, the rhetoric in the newspapers on both sides of the Federalist vs. Democratic-Republican debate intensified. The newspapers of the late 1700s were not balanced by any means; they were political tools that were either interpreting or debating the subjects along clear party lines. Washington tried his best to communicate his message directly to the people by publicly providing his annual address to Congress, and therein state in his own words the rationale and justification for his decisions and actions.

The cabinet system still exists today, although it is now expanded to consist of 15 executive departments and the vice president. Initially, Washington didn't hold cabinet meetings until the end of his first term, and he didn't even use the term "cabinet" until his second term in office. Washington's preference was to gather information and inputs from his top advisors individually, preferentially in a letter or memo form, and then to come to his own conclusions as to the path forward. On matters of grave importance, he would hold a conference, but that would be the exception. Washington did see to it that correspondence to the cabinet members would also be forwarded to him for his cognizance, and responses would also be approved (if no comment) or commented on for questions or suggestions.[6]

Negotiation of Treaties

Washington tried as best he could to adhere to the letter of the Constitution. One example is the Senate's review of U. S. treaties. Washington's first act as president (in August 1789) was to attempt to bring to the Senate some proposals for Indian treaties, in order to get its opinion. He was dutifully trying to stay within the letter of the Constitution, which states in Article II, Section 2, clause 3, that the president has the power to make treaties "with the Advice and Consent of the Senate."[7] When the discussion in the Senate degenerated into a shouting match over questions of procedure, Washington abruptly left the Senate floor, stating, "This defeats every purpose of my coming here."[8] He never again visited the Senate for such "advice," and by default created the precedent of the executive branch having total control over the negotiation of treaties with foreign entities (the Senate still having final approval authority of treaties).

Washington's first significant treaty success was the Treaty of New York, which established the precedence of the executive branch having power over the states in dealing with the multiple Indian tribes around the region. This treaty negotiated lands in the state of Georgia to be defined as Indian territory and paid the Indians for other lands round about. Although the treaty was ratified by Congress and signed by the President and leaders of the Indian tribes in Federal Hall in the presence of the legislature, the treaty was never implemented. This was because a multitude of other factions – the British, the Spanish, Georgia politicians and citizens, and other Indian chiefs and tribes – all fought to thwart the treaty going into effect. However, the result did not keep the precedence from being established, which unequivocally set the standard that the responsibility and power to negotiate treaties with other nations was exclusively the purview of the executive branch.[9]

Washington sought and maintained peace at home and abroad; he negotiated treaties with the British, the Spanish, and several Indian tribes during his two terms as president. Washington also recognized the fragility of the country in its embryonic state – he did not wish the country to be stillborn in its weakness. He had to deftly negotiate the country through troubled waters as the Hamiltonians attempted to retain a beneficial trade relationship with the British and stay on friendly terms, while the Jeffersonians tried to stay true to the revolutionary cause and support the French who had come to America's aid. This caused a significant rift in Washington's cabinet, and also caused Washington's affront and embarrassment owing to the Citizen Genet affair.

In his second term, Washington declared the Neutrality Proclamation – this act engendered a century and more of American isolationism and was a cornerstone of American diplomatic strategy and behavior. Except for the War of 1812 (against the British), American hegemony was contained to the North American continent. Furthermore, President James Monroe's "Monroe Doctrine" (in 1823) declared that the Americas were separate from European systems and not subject to European colonization, but also that the United States would not interfere with existing European colonies. Not until America's second century would the United States became a player on the world stage, with the start of the Spanish-American War in 1898.

Annual Message

Washington initiated the "State of the Union" address, because of how he interpreted phrasing in Article II, Section 3, clause 1 of the Constitution: "[The president] shall from time to time give to the Congress Information on the State of the Union, and recommend to their Consideration such Measures as he shall judge necessary and expedient."[10] He decided he would provide what he called his "Annual Message" to Congress each autumn at the beginning of the Congressional session for that year. It would not be officially called the "State of the Union Address" until 1947.[11] Washington, in his first annual message of his presidency, provided the shortest message on record, just over one thousand words.[12]

In the first annual message, after congratulating the legislature for its achievements to date, Washington said that in order to avoid war one must be prepared for war, and this called for development of domestic manufacturing capabilities, especially for supplies that would enable the country to defend itself from outside attack. He also promoted the advancement of agriculture, commerce, science, and literature as the path toward our pursuit of happiness. He implored the establishment of a National University as a means to achieve these objectives and laid it upon Congress to deliberate as to how to affect these goals.[13]

Washington always provided his annual message in person, in the presence of Congress, as a speech. This continued with John Adam's presidency, but was discontinued by Thomas Jefferson, and then not reestablished as the norm until 1913 under President Wilson, over 100 years later.[14] Every year, Washington provided his message dutifully to the opening session of Congress, and gave what reads like a report on the prior year's events. Washington provided eight of these messages in all, but there were some recurring themes. He talked about the "prosperity" of the country in seven of the eight annual addresses, and in the only exception (the second address), he put it in terms of the many blessings of our country due to commerce and public credit: "The abundant fruits of another year have blessed our country with plenty and with the means of a flourishing commerce."[15]

Washington also talked about the public credit – established via Hamilton's Assumption Bill that collected the states' Revolutionary War debt into the national debt – six times (including the second address) as a positive effect on the economy as long as the nation continued prompt payment and pay-off. Another topic, related to prosperity and the economy, was the establishment of a mint to produce coinage, discussed in five of the addresses. A last major theme brought up in every address one way or another was the militia and national defense. The words military, militia, and war are mentioned over 40 times in the eight addresses, an average of over five times per address. Washington's mantra, stated in the third paragraph of the very first address, is: "To be prepared for war is one of the most effectual means of preserving peace."[16]

Commander-in-Chief

The current expectation of the president as Commander in Chief of all of the combined armed forces of the nation is a vision that Washington embodied and fulfilled. As stated in the Constitution, Article 2, Section 2, Clause 1: "The President shall be Commander in Chief of the Army and Navy of the United States,"[17] and Washington was the embodiment of the phrase to "preserve, protect, and defend"[18] the Constitution and the United States. He avoided war with the British, because he knew the United States was unprepared and unsuited to fight a battle with our foremost trading partner. He refused to be drawn into an agreement or treaty with the French that would have involved the country in an international conflict, and instead declared a Neutrality Proclamation. Washington also defended the country from raids by Indians in the Northwest Territories by sending an army to defend the frontiersmen and settlers in the Ohio country. Additionally, he agreed to several treaties with the Indians in an attempt to create and maintain a peaceful coexistence with the Native Americans. He set a standard of executive command and leadership that was the gold standard for all future presidents to follow.

Washington was the only president to lead troops in a combat situation, when he led 13,000 militia against the Whiskey Rebellion in western Pennsylvania. He left Philadelphia in late

September to join the militia in Carlisle in the beginning of October, 1794. Although he didn't personally lead the charge, he
was in the field organizing the troops and providing the leadership one would expect from a president. He reviewed the
troops in Carlisle and joined them on their march to Ft. Cumberland as they prepared for battle, and he provided guidance
and strict instructions on how they were to conduct themselves. He then provided a farewell speech at Bedford, where
the combined militia forces organized before the final push to
Pittsburgh. When Washington assessed the situation as being
under control, and not necessitating his direct command, he
decided to rush back to the capital in Philadelphia so he could
deliver his next "Annual Address" to Congress.[19]

In his sixth annual address to Congress, Washington discussed the situation regarding the insurrection in western
Pennsylvania, and his disappointment thereof. He went
through the legal processes that had been attempted to rectify
the situation and, those processes having failed, the need to
raise a militia to enforce the laws of the United States. He further described his actions as Commander in Chief to gather the
army of 15,000 men and their march of 300 miles to put down
the revolt. Having set the army on its path to action and left
command in the hands of the Governor of Virginia, he returned to the capital. These actions he took to preserve, protect, and defend the Constitution and fulfill his oath as
president and Commander-in-Chief.[20]

Washington led by example and demanded that his officers
to do the same. In war, he wouldn't expect to ask the troops to
sacrifice and do things that he wouldn't be willing to do himself. He led charges on several occasions and would put himself in harm's way in nearly every battle of which he was a
participant. Washington's bravery and near-invincibility in battle was famous and documented by several of his commanders
in their own memoirs and letters. He had high expectations for
his officers, and they tried very hard to live up to those expec-

tations (with some exceptions). Washington dealt with multiple challenges to his authority by other generals who considered themselves superior to him, but were eventually disproved by their behavior or performance. Generals Lee, Gates, and Arnold, all thought they could outsmart Washington, to their eventual demise: Lee was court-martialed after the Battle of Monmouth Courthouse, Gates was demoted after the Battle of Camden, and Arnold was exposed in a plot to surrender West Point and defected to the British Army (and his name would forever be synonymous with treason). He inspired his troops to achieve the improbable – defeating the English Redcoats in battle – and he continued to inspire a new nation as president.[21]

The Army

A standing army was something the founding fathers had difficulty with on account of the unsavory taste that remained from occupation by the British army in the colonial states during the pre-Revolutionary days. Thus, the concept of and preference for a volunteer militia – rather than a standing army – was born. However, President Washington had a different perspective. As the supreme commander of the Continental Army during the Revolutionary War, he was constantly hamstrung by the revolving door of expiring commitments and being forced to retrain his soldiers. He understood on a personal level the need to defend the country with a professional army.[22]

Washington's lengthy letter to the President of Congress on September 24, 1776, contains an early example of an oft repeated complaint that the temporary and undisciplined nature of the short-termed militia was not only difficult, but also could in the end be the patriots' undoing and result in a lost cause. Washington wrote, "To place any dependence upon Militia, is, assuredly, resting upon a broken staff. Men just dragged from the tender Scenes of domestick [sic] life ... makes them timid, and ready to fly from their own shadows."[23]

This letter was written after the debacle at Harlem Heights, when the British invasion at Kip's Bay scattered the American troops, and Washington was appalled and embarrassed by their behavior, even days afterward when his anger had passed. He wrote a week later to his cousin Lund Washington, and again expressed both his frustration with the militia and his desire for a standing army.[24]

Washington's annual addresses to Congress are littered with references to the militia and the need for a standing army. I have already stated in the Annual Message section how Washington advocated peace through strength in the first address. In the second address, he stated that we should not overlook military preparedness, doing so being an act of independence from other nations. In the third address, Washington expressed the need for the defense and security of our western borders and recommended the building of arsenals and forts to support those efforts. In the fourth address, he described the continuing hostilities with Indians in the Northwest territories (current Midwestern states) and the need for raising troops to deal with those contingencies. In the fifth address, Washington discussed world events and the potential for those events to affect the peace and security of the United States, concluding that we could not neglect our preparedness for war and must maintain a condition and posture of defense. In the sixth address, he described how the militia was used to put down an internal insurrection. In the seventh address, Washington reported with satisfaction the end of hostilities with the Indians in the Northwest, and the agreement to a treaty with the rulers in the Barbary States for the return of our sailors, but also that the time was at hand for the establishment of an army to ensure our domestic tranquility.[25]

In his eighth and final address to Congress, Washington stated, "My solicitude to see the militia of the United States placed on an efficient establishment has been so often and so ardently expressed . . . ,"[26] thus repeating for the last time his desire for a professional army. He pushed for a strong military because of his experience as Commander in Chief of the Continental Army. The inadequacy of the Congress to provide enough provisions and pay to keep the Army fed and clothed was something that Washington wanted to ensure was not repeated. When he was President of the United States, he wanted to make sure it was something that a future Commander in Chief would not have to endure. As he left office, he left a legacy of the importance of a standing army to defend our hard-won liberty, a legacy of peace through strength, and a willingness to defend that liberty against all enemies, foreign and domestic.

The Customs Service

Washington was an excellent judge of talent, and a prime example of this was his choice for Secretary of the Treasury, Alexander Hamilton. That the United States Treasury Department is much the same as Hamilton designed over 200 years ago is a testament to his intelligence and forethought. Hamilton also implemented the first accounting, tax, and budgetary procedures for the nation. Hamilton managed the customs service to collect duties as a source of income for the country, and he created the Coast Guard to help collect those duties from the merchant ships transporting goods to and from the nation's ports. All of Hamilton's programs were like an interlocking mesh of pieces that laid the foundation for the prosperity of the nation. Washington fully supported these plans and programs, and helped Hamilton see them through to fruition.

In July 1789, Congress passed three acts to establish the Customs Service. The Tariff Act of 1789 provided the first opportunity to seek revenue for the nascent country through taxation of imported products, by requiring duties on imported goods, wares, and merchandise. This act defined specific duties per unit of product to be collected to fund the government. The second act established additional tariffs by taxing the tonnage of imported material at ports of entry. The third act named and defined the organization that would collect these duties: a Collector of Customs who would collect the tariffs in the legal ports of entry in 59 customs districts for all of the states that had ratified the Constitution.[27]

The ninth act of the First Congress of the United States created the Lighthouse Service, which was to transfer ownership of the country's lighthouses to the federal government. It would also put repair, maintenance, and management of the lighthouses under the Collector of Customs administration and specified payment to be made by the U. S. Treasury. Furthermore, it proposed that a lighthouse would be built at the entrance of Chesapeake Bay, which would be contracted for by the Secretary of the Treasury, and by whom the operation, repair, and maintenance would be provided under his auspices. Upon taking over as Secretary of the Treasury, Hamilton delved into the details of lighthouse construction, technology, repair, location, manning, and every imaginable nuance of this maritime navigation aid.[28]

The eleventh Act of the First Congress created the Department of the Treasury and was signed by Washington on September 2, 1789. Nine days later, Alexander Hamilton was nominated as Secretary of the Treasury, and his nomination was confirmed that same day. He would be responsible for the country's finances, including all the revenues generated by the Customs Service through their collection of tariffs. By means of his magnum opus *Report on Public Credit*, Hamilton explained the "blessing" of debt obtained for the purpose of liberty, and that such debt must be by honor repaid. This would lead to the Tariff Act of 1790.[29]

The Coast Guard

On August 4, Washington signed the Tariff Act of 1790, which authorized the building of ten ships to be used by revenue enforcers of the previously defined tariff laws to collect funds on behalf of the country. Called the Revenue-Marine, it would eventually become known as the U. S. Coast Guard, one of the five armed services of the U. S. government. At the time it was created, it comprised the only naval force of the United States and would succumb that role when the Department of the Navy was established in 1798.[30]

This Act would increase the number of collections districts to 67 and define their locations to include Rhode Island and North Carolina (the two states that had not been included in the Tariff Act of 1789). It provided a myriad of directions and instructions on the duties of the collections officers, the un-loading goods without a permit, and the requirements for maintaining a manifest, fees, rates, and ad valorem charges. Of the ships to be provided, the act also specified the number of officers on each ship and their pay, their duties onboard the ships, penalties for accepting a bribe or making false entries, and punishments for conviction. The act also empowered the president to define the number of cutters to be built (up to ten), and enabled the president to appoint the officers for each ship.[31]

In a political precedent, Hamilton recommended to Washington that the contracts and locations of where the cutters would be built be spread around the country, thus to avoid favoritism and to promote economic growth. This approach would be followed by Washington when six frigates would be built, in response to the Mediterranean crisis later in his second term. Hamilton provided detailed instructions to his revenue cutter captains, demanding the utmost attention to detail and above-reproach behavior. Because U. S. citizens were free men, in Hamilton's view they would respond more favorably to the concepts of respect, even-handedness and a sense of fair play than they would if the revenue cutter captains imitated the arrogance and haughtiness of British captains. This resulted in Hamilton's directives being employed and used for over 150 years.[32]

The Revenue-Marine (Coast Guard) service was critical to the function on the federal government because at the time customs duties accounted for 90 percent of the revenue of the country. If the customs could not be collected due to some perceived weakness on the part of the government by lack of enforcement, then the government would not and could not function. In what had become sport for Americans during their objection to British rule before the Revolutionary War, merchant marines had become very adept at avoiding customs collectors. Now it was up to the Revenue-Marine to keep America's coffers full. In addition, with British merchant ships providing 75% of the tariff revenue due to their position as America's premier trading partner, the shoe was on the other foot, with respect to ensuring customs duties were being paid.[33]

With the approval of the Jay Treaty, which resolved the remaining issues between the United States and England regarding impressment of American sailors on the open seas and evacuation of forts in the American northwest frontier agreed to at the Treaty of Paris, a new conflict arose – the Quasi-War with France. The French Directory, upset with the United States apparent alliance with England (owing to the Jay Treaty favored-nation trading status), authorized French privateers to seize American shipping in an undeclared war on U. S. commerce. With no navy to challenge the French privateers, the Revenue-Marine cutters were pressed into service to protect and defend American interests on the seas, until the creation of the U. S. Navy.[34]

National Capital

The planned city that graces his name, Washington, D. C., is another legacy of our first president. The agreement of the final location of the capital (owing to the Residence Act, passed in July, 1790) was the first half of the bargain that Hamilton made with Jefferson to get his Assumption Bill through Congress (the Funding Act, passed in August 1790). The bargain was struck between Hamilton, Jefferson, and Madison at a dinner meeting in June. In July, the Residence Act provided Washington the authority to choose the site of the new capital anywhere along a 65-mile stretch of the Potomac River. It also provided him the power to supervise and oversee the development of the district, including the appointment of commissioners and surveyors for the design and development of the city.[35]

Washington was extremely involved in the planning and building of the capital. For the architect of the city, he selected Pierre-Charles L'Enfant, a former French volunteer in the Continental Army who had designed Federal Hall in New York City. In the early months of 1791, L'Enfant reviewed the city site to determine locations for the federal buildings and sketch a rough plan. At the end of March, he met with Washington to lay out his vision for the federal city. L'Enfant showed Washington sketches of a city layout that put the Congress House on a hill, with diagonal streets radiating outwards from it. The beauty of the design was that the city would be able to grow with the size and the wealth of the nation. Washington appreciated and approved the design, aside from the elimination of a few of the diagonal streets.[36]

In July, Washington toured the federal district with L'Enfant to see the sites for the proposed locations of the federal buildings. He approved the location of the Congress House but revised the site for the Executive Mansion to an elevation that was on par with that of Congress, slightly west and with a view of the Potomac. In September, the President learned that the federal city commissioners had named the city Washington, and the 100-square-mile area on which it stood Columbia. This has transformed over time to become Washington, District of Columbia (D.C.).[37]

Washington had a hand in all the significant decisions regarding the federal city. He approved the design by Dr. William Thornton for a Congress House that offered a combination of Greek and modern architecture thus providing a feeling of timeless permanence from the ancient to the present. Thomas Jefferson was enthralled with the design, and enthusiastically renamed the structure the Capitol building. Washington also approved the design by James Hoban, an Irish architect, for the Executive Mansion. In October 1792, the cornerstone of the Executive Mansion was laid down. At the time it was called the President's House, but it would later become known as the White House. In September 1793, Washington performed a Masonic ritual for the laying of the cornerstone for the Capitol building, overseen by the local lodge in Alexandria and the Grand Lodge of Maryland. After a ceremonial dab of cement, Washington poured oil, corn, and wine over the cornerstone in a blessing of this foundation for our democracy, and a prayer for its continued success.[38]

National Mint

A National Mint was something that Washington raised as a need in his second annual message.[39] It was a grave concern to the public and government as well, because the existing system of individual states and foreign coinage was inconsistent and ill defined. The varied coinage also served as an embarrassment to the national government, because it was a vestige of the Continental Congress via the Articles of Confederation that allowed individual states to mint their own coins. The U. S. Constitution crafted by the Constitutional convention, specifically prohibited individual states from coining their own money.[40]

Alexander Hamilton, as Secretary of the Treasury, described and designed the United States Mint, and defined the nation's coinage from a gold ten-dollar piece and the silver dollar down to the copper penny and half cent. These recommendations were made in a report to Congress, called *Report on the Estab-lishment of a Mint*, and submitted on January 28, 1791. In this report, Hamilton provided recommendations concerning the monetary unit of the United States, the proportion between gold and silver coins, the composition of alloys in those coins, the payment for the cost of minting those coins, the number, denomination, and size of the coins, and whether or not foreign coins should continue to be used. He even proposed how the mint should be organized, its officers, staff, and positions.[41]

The U. S. Congress adopted most of Hamilton's suggestions and modified some others, and these were implemented as the Coinage Act of 1792. This act created the U. S. Mint and was signed into law by Washington on April 2, 1792. The Coinage Act named Philadelphia as the location of the first U. S. Mint, because at that time it was the seat of the U. S. government. The Act defined the officers of the mint as: a Director, an assayer, a chief coiner, an engraver, and a treasurer, and also specified their salaries. It also defined the types and values of the coins to be minted: a gold Eagle ($10), a gold Half-Eagle ($5), a gold Quarter-Eagle ($2.50), a silver Dollar ($1), a silver Half-Dollar ($0.50), a silver Quarter-Dollar ($0.25), a silver Disme (now called a dime – $0.10), a silver Half-Disme ($0.05), a copper Cent ($0.01), and a copper Half-Cent ($0.005).[42]

Washington appointed as the Mint's first director David Rittenhouse, who purchased the ground plots where the Mint would be located, and proposed a three-story building to house the facility. It would become the first building constructed under the auspices of the U. S. Constitution. On March 1, 1793, the Mint produced its first coins: 11,178 copper Cents – and the Half-Cent followed. In 1794, the Mint started producing Half-Dimes, Half-Dollars, and Dollars. In 1795, the Mint started producing Half-Eagles and Eagles. Finally, in 1796, the Mint completed the planned coinage line-up, and began producing Dimes, Quarter-Dollars, and Quarter-Eagles.[43]

In an interesting side note, during construction of the new facility for the Mint, a nearby building was used to make uncirculated Half-Dimes. The silver used to create these ceremonial coins given out to friends and dignitaries was purportedly to have come from the smelting of silverware provided by Washington. It can certainly be said that he was not only the father of our country, but also the father of the U. S. Mint.[44]

The Navy

Although the official birthdate celebrated by the U. S. Navy is October 13, 1775, and although John Adams is sometimes referred to as the "Father of the Navy," because Washington was a vocal proponent of an American fleet during the Revolutionary War and president when the Department of the Navy was established, Washington should get credit for the creation of the Navy. It is true that the Continental Congress voted in 1775 to employ two sailing ships of ten guns each to harass British transports and interfere with their supply lines, but it was the reading of an announcement by General Washington that he had commandeered three schooners to interdict British shipping off Massachusetts which led to the approval. Over the course of the War of Independence, the Continental Navy grew to a fleet of 50 ships; however, at the end of the conflict, those ships were sold off, and the officers and crews were disbanded.[45]

When the government was reconstituted under the U. S. Constitution, and the new president took charge of the Army and Navy as prescribed under the auspices of that document, there was no navy to take charge of. The closest thing to a navy that existed in the government were the revenue cutters of the Customs Service (Coast Guard), which was created in 1790 after Washington was in office for a year. However, those ten ships were designed and intended to defend and patrol the coast and ports of the United States; they were not warships intended to project power or an international presence. As such, American merchant ships in foreign seas were subject to piracy and ransom of their crews. Pirates based in the North African seaport towns around Algiers, Tripoli, and Tunisia were raiding U.S. vessels in the Mediterranean and requiring payment to get the ships and hostages back. Washington was distressed about the ransoms and determined to change the situation. While negotiating with the pirates and paying for the release of the American prisoners, he also attempted to negotiate a treaty with the Barbary Coast city-states. But ultimately, Washington desired an alternative that would allow the United States to negotiate from a position of strength.[46]

In his fifth annual message delivered on December 3, 1793, Washington called for the building of several frigates by the federal government in order to battle the corsairs of the pirates in North Africa. In March 1794, Congress replied with an act to provide a Naval Armament. This act reestablished the United States Navy; although, the Navy was not an official department of the government until four years later (made so in 1798 during President Adam's administration), and until then it operated under the Department of War. The act called for the building of four 44-gun frigates and two 36-gun frigates, and defined the number and types of officers for the ships, their pay and their rations.[47]

These ships would become the USS *United States* (44-guns, launched 1797, Philadelphia, Pa.), the USS *Constellation* (38-guns, launched 1797, Baltimore, Md.), the USS *Constitution,* also known as "Old Ironsides" (44-guns, launched 1797, Boston, Mass.), the USS *Congress* (38-guns, launched 1799, Portsmouth, N.H.), the USS *Chesapeake* (38-guns, launched 1799, Norfolk, Va.), and the USS *President* (44-guns, launched 1800, New York, N.Y.). These ships would play a crucial role in the future of the United States, all of them serving during the War of 1812 against the British, and the USS *Constitution* serving as the longest tenured ship in the U. S. Navy. In fact, the USS *Constitution* is still serving as a Ship of State for the U. S. Navy.[48]

West Point

It is ironic that Thomas Jefferson should get credit for establishment of the Military Academy at West Point.[49] As one of the founding fathers, and the author of the Declaration of Independence, he was an ardent opponent of an established military or a military academy. Even as a member of Washington's cabinet, Jefferson opposed the military for fear of an authoritarian state, and the use of that body for implementation of a monarchy or aristocracy. He argued with Washington against the establishment of a military academy, on the basis that it was not expressly authorized by the Constitution. Helping to found the military academy was so incongruous to Jefferson's character and inconsequential to his legacy as to barely merit a mention in his biographies.[50]

The true force behind the eventual establishment of a military academy was Washington. On many occasions he argued and proposed a need for the army to have proper training for the officers so that they might be more effective in the execution of their duties. The constant turnover and lack of training of the militia was a repeated and tired complaint in Washington's letters to Congress, and to his friends and associates, as the Commander in Chief of the Continental Army. He continued this mantra after he became president. In his fifth annual address, Washington discussed the militia, and the need for additional study of the branches of the military arts that cannot be practiced. In his eighth and final annual address, Washington implored Congress to consider the establishment of a military academy for the reason that adequate knowledge and study in the art of war is an imperative for all nations for their own security owing to the fact that other nations regularly employ such study and the perfection of expertise in it.[51]

Washington's repeated refrain had some effect. In May 1792, Congress enacted a bill to establish a consistent militia across America to ensure the country's defense. However, that bill did not include instruction in the military arts. Two years later, in response to Washington's fifth annual address, Congress enacted a bill related to military training, to provide an army corps of engineers and artillerists to receive this instruction and held the Secretary of War responsible for procuring all the training material, instrumentation and equipment to perform this training. Unfortunately, these acts did not establish a military academy during Washington's presidency. [52]

Under the auspices of President John Adams, continued efforts by Secretary of War James McHenry for the establishment of a military academy made headway. In April 1798, Congress enacted authorization for a number of engineers and artillery specialists to augment the army, but again did not approve additional training. Secretary McHenry responded by complaining to the Committee of Defence, that the additional artillerists and engineers would need instruction in the arts and science of required subjects. This resulted in an act passed on July 16 of that year to authorize the president to appoint four instructors to provide the necessary training and education for the additional specialists.[53]

Finally, in March 1802, Congress passed an act establishing a Military Academy at West Point, New York. The only contribution to said act by President Jefferson was the requirement that the candidates for this military training would be "representative of a democratic society."[54] This is where the requirement for a Congressional nomination (by your Congressional Representative or one of your state's two Senators) came from. That the military academy was established at West Point is another nod to Washington, because during his tenure as Commander of the Continental Army, he considered West Point, and its position at a critical bend in Hudson River, to be the most strategic location in the United States. West

Point's fortifications were designed in 1778 by Thaddeus Kosciuszko, a Polish engineer, at the direction of Washington, and Washington's headquarters were transferred to West Point in 1779. Since the occupation of those fortifications in 1778, the U. S. military has never left, making West Point the oldest continuous military location in the United States.[55]

Adherence to the Constitution

Washington was a critical leader and member of the Constitutional Convention. Without his attendance and chairmanship of the convention, the Constitution as we know it today may never have been born. The fact that he lent his name to the endeavor, even though it risked his reputation in doing so, showed his commitment to the creation of a document that would result in a better form of government. He was well acquainted with the document, having been the presiding member of the convention, and even lent his own vision of the future of America in determining the minimum population for representation in the House of Representatives. Examples of his following the Constitution, not just considering it a guiding instrument to his responsibilities but also holding to the letter of the law, are found in the examples above with respect to negotiation of treaties, the annual address to Congress and the Commander-in-Chief's role within the executive branch of government.

Washington felt so duty bound to the Constitution that he let his adopted son Lafayette sit in a jail in Austria rather than risk an international incident by attempting to use his position as president to get him released. It was after the Revolutionary War, when Washington had first met Lafayette and had grown to love and cherish him as the son he never had, that the French Revolution caused Washington great pains and heartache. Lafayette had returned to his native France, to help usher in a patriotic revolution similar to what he had seen in America – but somehow everything had gone wrong. Lafayette originally was one of the men who had charged the French King and Queen with treason and put them under arrest. When the revolution started going awry, with the Jacobins radicalizing the revolution, Lafayette ended up on the outside looking in. He was in charge of the National Guard and responsible for the King's custody. When a plot for the King's escape (the "Flight to Varennes") was discovered, Lafayette was charged with attempting to free the King and was thrown in jail.[56]

Lafayette's wife sent a heartfelt letter, begging Washington's help for his release. Then, when Washington did not respond, Lafayette's son arrived in the United States with a letter addressed to his godfather, George Washington. Unfortunately, Washington was so deeply mired in the national debate of the European war between England and France that he could not afford to be seen with Lafayette's son or to be found helping Lafayette obtain release from prison. Washington was concerned that any action on his part to get Lafayette released would anger the current French government. He was so distraught by this conflict of national versus personal interests that he sought advice and help from both Hamilton and Federalist Senator George Cabot.[57]

Hamilton responded that Lafayette's son – George Washington Lafayette – was living with him for the winter, and that Washington should invite the boy to visit him. Washington then asked James Madison his opinion of how the situation should be handled. Ultimately, Washington decided to send for the boy and his tutor, and they both traveled to Philadelphia in April 1796. When Washington met the young Lafayette, his namesake and godson, and heard the whole story about how his father was being treated in prison, he decided to send a personal letter to the Austrian emperor to request the older Lafayette's release. Young Lafayette and his tutor remained as guests of Washington for a year and a half, until in October 1797 they received word of his father's release from prison.

Lafayette and his tutor then returned to Europe to reunite with his family; however, they never returned to America.[58]

Two-Term Limit

George Washington is the only president to have been elected unanimously. And he not only did it once, but for both his terms as president. For his first term, the Electoral College made him the unanimous choice as president on February 4, 1789. For vice president, they selected John Adams. However, these selections could not be announced until the Electoral College met with Congress and counted the votes in front of them. Due to the lack of a quorum of Senators and Representatives, it wasn't until April 1789 that the votes were actually counted in Congress. For his second term, the Electoral College made Washington the unanimous choice for president on February 13, 1793. For vice president, they again selected John Adams. This time, Congress reconvened on March 1, 1793, and Washington was not made to wait to hear about his fate. Washington retired before a third term was offered to him, but it is said that he probably would have repeated the unanimous decision a third time.[59]

Before anyone had even the slightest chance to nominate him for a third term, Washington made his intentions known by publishing his Farewell Address. This document is epic in its originality and scope and laid out Washington's future vision for the United States of America. His decision to not seek a third term was not only unexpected, it was also unique in all history. Once politicians taste power, they usually are loathe to give it up. History is littered with the names of revolutionaries who were seemingly intent on just doing what was best for their country, but ended up doing what was best for themselves: Julius Caesar, Oliver Cromwell, Napoleon Bonaparte, Vladimir Lenin, Mao Zedong, and others were all corrupted by power, and absolutely could not let go. Current examples of foreign leaders who have now made themselves leaders for life are Xi Jinping of China and Vladimir Putin of Russia. Washington set a precedent which was religiously followed in the United States for over 140 years. And after someone dared to not follow this example to the letter, a change to the Constitution remedied that situation permanently.[60]

Washington lived the life of the Roman Citizen-Servant Ideal, and when the time came, like Cincinnatus, he retired from the great scene of action to his beloved farm and home at Mount Vernon. Does the man make the time or does time make the man? In other words, if Washington had lived in a different era, would he have made the same decisions, and would we have had the same results? Did the period of the 18th-century enlightenment with its emphasis on the revival of classical Greek and Roman attitudes and opinions regarding republicanism, liberty, self-determinism, and morality provide the framework for Washington's behavior and decision-making? Or would he have made those same decisions and held those same beliefs if he had been raised of lived in a different era?

We may never know the answers to these questions, but there is one thing we can be fairly certain of – without Washington, there would not be a United States of America, at least not the country we know and love today. In its embryonic state, our government balanced on the edge of a knife, and any unbalanced move could have pushed to one side or the other. By the strength of his will and the magnitude of his persona, he kept the country together. Then when the right time came, he let go, and watched our democratic experiment move forward, like a father teaching his children how to ride a bicycle.

Transfer of Power

One of Washington's greatest legacies and his gift to all future generations of Americans was his peaceful transfer of power. He graciously and gladly handed over the reins of the most powerful office in the United States to his successor, and in so doing, made that transition a peaceful moment for all subsequent transitions. Regardless of the acrimony and distrust between conflicting political parties, particularly in the case where a Democrat replaces a Republican or a Republican replaces a Democrat in the White House, this transition is always a voluntary act. Because Washington became a modern Cincinnatus, all subsequent transitions of power from one president to the next has had the quality of a former president moving on to the next phase of his life (with the exception of those presidents who died in office).

John Adams was selected the second President of the United States and was the first in a long line of men who played the President-Elect role. As such, who would have a better view of the transition in power from one president to another? He had played the role of the understudy, having been the vice president to Washington for eight years. It was a role that chafed at his pride and ambition. He saw himself superior in intelligence and political savvy to Washington, and even felt that he had, a very long time previous, played a part in making the man who would become the myth and the legend on account of having recommended Washington for the role of Commander in Chief of the Continental Army at the Second Continental Congress.

Now that he would finally be out of Washington's shadow, it was with a jaundiced eye that he observed the praise and devotion being heaped upon Washington as Adam's inauguration day drew near. When they met at the inauguration, Adams felt that Washington, instead of having a somber mood at the solemnness of the occasion, was enjoying himself almost to the point of elation. That the out-going president was so triumphant in this transition to the incoming president was a complete surprise to Adams. In a letter he wrote to his wife Abagail, John Adams said he thought he heard Washington say, "I'm fairly out and you are fairly in. See which of us will be happiest."[61]

Where would we be if George Washington had not been our first president? In all likelihood, we would not be a nation, we would more likely be a collection of states, or worse, separate nations altogether. Washington kept the country together when the factions within our country were tearing us apart. He had every opportunity to take advantage of the situation and become a dictator or supreme ruler, but he did not. Washington was the perfect man in the perfect place at the perfect time to ensure the "republican experiment" did not go awry. One only has to look at the French Revolution to see what could have happened, but didn't. And during that time in our history, there were those in the country and in the government, who actually thought the spillage of innocent blood in the name of revolution was an unfortunate but necessary act.[62]

Washington established and maintained the executive branch of the United States, and in so doing, he shaped the future of our country and of how all future presidents would be expected to behave. Washington is the gold standard of presidents, and as Congressman Henry Lee (also the ninth Governor of Virginia) so eloquently stated at Washington's eulogy, he was "First in war, first in peace, and first in the hearts of his countrymen."[63]

Our Second Great President

O ur second Great President was Abraham Lincoln. He seemed to be larger than life. He was a great thinker and speaker, and he told great stories. He was able to communicate his thoughts and ideas better than any president before or since. His speeches were legendary, and his most famous speech was only 271 words long. His eloquence was polished on the Illinois Court Circuit, where he practiced law and sharpened his wit and skills at verbal jousting.

Abraham Lincoln was a deep and complex man, and his legacy reigns supreme. In fact, most rankings of the greatest presidents in history place Lincoln at the top of the list. Primarily, I rank him second to Washington because without George Washington serving as our first president, I seriously doubt we would have had a second. Lincoln's greatness comes from not only being able to wield great power for the good of the people, but to also have the compassion and humanity to understand its consequences. He felt deeply the gravity of the decisions he was making and struggled to reconcile his desires for the country with the forces of politics and temperament of political reality.

Abraham Lincoln became president at a time in our country when things were bad and getting worse. The nation was founded on a great compromise. That compromise was between the large agrarian landholder states of the South and the smaller manufacturing and business states of the North. The compromise was that the national legislature would be composed of two houses: a Senate, with two representatives from each state (to allow the less populous Southern states to have an equal voice with the Northern states), and a House of Representatives, with the number of a state's Representatives determined by the population of that state. In addition, slaves would be counted as 3/5ths of a person – another compromise with the Southern states.

By the time Lincoln came to office, that great compromise was about to tear the country in two. The Southern states wanted each new state entering the union to be a slave state while the Northern states wanted each new state to be a free state. This eventually led to the Kansas-Nebraska Act, by which it was agreed that each state would be able to choose for itself whether to be a slave state or a free state. Unfortunately, this became a flash point that drove the behavior of the Southern states and the reaction of the Northern states. As each new state entered the union, more and more pressure was applied to the case for each side and caused the stakes to go higher and higher.

Before Lincoln's term in office, the nation had seen several single-term Presidents come and go. Presidents Van Buren, Harrison, Tyler, Polk, Taylor, Fillmore, Pierce, and Buchanan were all single-term presidents (Tyler and Fillmore were elected as Vice Presidents, but took over upon Harrison's and Taylor's death, respectively, in office), and all but President James K. Polk are ranked at or near the bottom of the listings of the greatest presidents of our nation. Each of these presidents is viewed negatively because of his inability to deal with the slavery issue or to avert the coming Civil War. Each of these had the slavery issue staring him in the face, and blinked, and lost the opportunity to have his name become as revered as Lincoln's.

CHAPTER 5

Training Grounds

Abraham Lincoln got his start in business and politics as a storekeeper and postal worker in rural Illinois. The Lincoln family had begun in Kentucky, then moved to Indiana, and ended up in Illinois. Abraham's father, Thomas Lincoln, was brought up in Kentucky in the late 1700s, when the area was the definition of wilderness, as bears and panthers stalked at night, and Indian attacks in broad daylight were a threat. Thomas Lincoln's father, also named Abraham, was killed by one such Indian attack in 1784. When Abraham was born on February 12, 1809, he was named after his grandfather.[1]

In 1816, slavery was on the rise in Kentucky, which was something that Thomas Lincoln couldn't abide by, so in December 1816, he moved his whole family to Indiana. In October 1818, Abraham's mother, Nancy Hanks Lincoln, passed away from "milk sick" — believed to be caused by the cows eating poisonous white snakeroot in the fields of the area. Thomas Lincoln remarried in December 1819, to a widow with three children, a kind woman by the name of Sarah Bush Lincoln. After ten years of trying to make a living on farms in Indiana, Thomas Lincoln decided to move again, this time to Illinois. On March 1, 1830, the whole Lincoln family moved to Macon County, Illinois, to a site on the Sangamon River about ten miles south of Decatur.[2]

At age 22, young Abraham decided to try to make his own way and landed in New Salem, Illinois in July 1831. He was employed as a clerk for the local general goods store and was known for his honesty. Lincoln was also known for his physical strength, and the storeowner bragged about him around town. Lincoln was subsequently challenged by the local bully and asked to fight. He fought the bully and won, and immediately gained the friendship and respect of both the bully (Jack Armstrong) and his gang (the Clary's Grove Boys). That winter he also joined the New Salem debating society, and by all accounts he seemed to be a natural public speaker, but the opportunity to speak twice a month on a variety of current topics would improve that talent.[3]

During the Black Hawk war of 1832 with the Sauk and Fox Indians (Black Hawk was their leader), Lincoln enlisted with a company of militia from New Salem and was elected their captain. His company eventually joined a detachment of U. S. regulars under the command of Colonel Zachary Taylor (the future President of the United States). In all, Lincoln's service in the army was less than 90 days. He had no prior military service or experience, so his tour of duty as an army captain in the militia was not particularly noteworthy, other than the fact that he was elected captain by his peers (which he would later reminisce as one of the proudest moments of his life). However, he did learn a lot about military life, particularly the camaraderie, morale, and discipline of the troops. In the future, this experience would serve him well, notably in terms of the memories and anecdotes it would add to his litany of stories.[4]

When Lincoln returned to New Salem from his war duty, he had made acquaintances and new friends with many of the future movers and shakers in Illinois politics, all of whom had some level of experience in the military during the Black Hawk war. Lincoln's return was in July 1832, two weeks ahead of the mid-term election. He campaigned resourcefully for the state legislature, but was a relative unknown and wound up eighth in a field of thirteen. Eventually, he was offered and accepted the position of Postmaster of New Salem. As Postmaster, he would receive a salary and would further his political ambitions. However, his salary as Postmaster did not cover his expenses, so he took odd jobs to make ends meet. He worked as a rail-splitter, mill operator, farmer, newspaper agent, election clerk, and surveyor during those years, and bided his time while preparing for his next opportunity. That next opportunity would not keep him waiting long.[5]

Illinois Legislature

In 1834, Lincoln decided to run again for office as an assemblyman in the Illinois state legislature. This time he won handily and, in the process, made a new political friend, John T. Stuart. Stuart also won, and was a companion delegate. Stuart supported Lincoln's desire to become a lawyer, and provided several books and legal forms. Lincoln soaked up the knowledge and studied at every opportunity. Then, when it came time to travel to the state capital for that year's congressional session, Lincoln borrowed money for a suit, and joined his companions for a stagecoach ride to Vandalia, the Illinois state capital.[6]

Lincoln jumped into his role as legislator for his district with enthusiasm. His friend and mentor, John Stuart, was the de facto Whig leader for the State House of Representatives. And whenever Stuart was busy, Lincoln stepped in and assumed that role. They worked as a team, and would strategize over Whig policies and plans on how to implement them. They also strategized over Democrat policies and plans on how to defeat them. Two of the most significant bills during Lincoln's first session as an Illinois state legislator were the Illinois-Michigan canal and the charter for the first Illinois state bank.[7]

After his first session in the Illinois legislature, Lincoln returned home to New Salem. He spent the spring and summer of 1835 in the Post Office, and when he wasn't delivering mail filled his time reading law books. He also performed surveying jobs for local farmers and businessmen – while the wives of his circle of friends attempted to find him a mate. Many prospects were suggested to Lincoln by the matchmakers, but none were to his liking. Instead, he focused his attention on the daughter of the local tavern owner. Her name was Ann Routledge; she was short, but very pretty. Lincoln was not the only man in town with eyes for Ann. A year earlier, Ann had become engaged to the local storekeeper, John McNamar. Afterwards, John told Ann he needed to travel to New York and bring the rest of his family back with him.[8]

As time wore on, Lincoln the Postmaster noticed that the numbers of letters between the betrothed couple dwindled. It appeared that John might not return from New York. Lincoln had maintained his friendship with Ann, and the fact that she was unavailable had made it easier for him to talk to her. That summer in Illinois was one of the hottest on record, with rains that caused the roads to turn into rivers. In August, Ann became sick and was recommended complete rest, but she ignored that prescription and continued to see Lincoln. On August 25, she passed away, possibly from typhoid fever. Lincoln fell into a depression, which only deepened after the funeral and the rains returned. His friends were anxious about his state of mind, and recommended he leave town for a few days to rest. He visited a friend named Bowling Green who lived a mile away, and by the end of September was back to his surveying work. But he never forgot Ann.[9]

Lincoln attended his second session in the state legislature in December 1835. This session was unusually productive in terms of the volume of bills enacted; however, no bill was as significant as the canal bill or bank bill that he had worked on during his first session. Lincoln's third session in the legislature started in December 1836, and he was swept into office in a landslide of support. This time, the Whig Party had considerable public popularity, and nine Whig legislators (two senators and seven assemblymen) were elected from the same county. They were called the "Long Nine" – because they were all over six feet tall. The primary objective of this group was to move the state capital from Vandalia to Springfield. In his letter to Mary Owen, a woman he was courting, Lincoln stated he felt confident that he could get the capital moved: "Our chance to take the seat of Government to Springfield is better than I expected."[10]

The Long Nine

The other significant activity for Lincoln and the Long Nine was the proposal and negotiations to pass a bill for proposed Illinois internal improvements. The bill would eventually grow to the staggering sum of $10,000,000 in 1836 dollars. The improvement program would include railway lines (two major trunks plus spar lines), canals, river dredging, new roads, and other "pork barrel" projects to help keep the state capital move to Springfield a guaranteed outcome. The bill was approved at a time when the state income was just under $60,000 for the year and the state expenses were just over $55,000.[11]

Once the state improvements bill was passed, the Long Nine were able to focus their attention on the location of the state capital. Lincoln nearly met his match in the opposition to move the capital from a man who represented Fayette County (for Vandalia), John Dement. Dement was a skillful tactician and parliamentarian, and countered every move of the Long Nine. After the Long Nine proposed that any city that wanted to host the capital had to donate $50,000 and two acres of land, Dement tried to get the proposal tabled until July 4, a date after the current session of the legislature. Dement's motion passed by one vote; however, Lincoln was able to nullify the motion by rounding up every representative and having them vote again on the measure. Then the whole group voted on several ballots regarding which town or city to which the capital would relocate. By the fourth ballot, Springfield finally received enough votes to become the future home of the Illinois state capital.[12]

With his agenda for the current session successfully completed, Lincoln decided to make public his personal stance about slavery. Just before the end of the legislative session, Lincoln wrote an opinion about the resolutions that had passed earlier in the session. He protested the resolutions the Illinois state legislature had passed six weeks earlier that had condemned abolitionists for agitating the states where slavery was practiced. The resolution also stated that the Constitution allowed slavery and protected the rights of slave owners. Lincoln stated that slavery was "...founded on both injustice and bad policy"[13] and that the Constitution did not prohibit Congress from abolishing slavery in the District of Columbia.

This was and would continue to be his position – that slavery was immoral and that the spread of its practice should be stopped. However, then and later he would stop short of stating that he thought it should be eradicated. In fact, he believed at that time that the Southern states were within their rights to continue the practice. At the conclusion of his third session as a legislator, Lincoln also satisfied his final requirement for becoming a full-fledged lawyer when the state Supreme Court enrolled his name as an attorney.[14]

Becoming a Lawyer

In April, 1837, Lincoln moved to Springfield, Illinois, and he became partners with John Todd Stuart. Stuart had previously been partners in a firm with Henry E. Dummer from 1833 to 1837. The firm was well established, and since he was taking the place of Dummer, Lincoln would not have to find his own new clients. Stuart was also a politician, and he had served as a major in the Black Hawk war, where he and Lincoln had met. Stuart was an early influence in Lincoln's career, and was the person who originally turned Lincoln on to the law as a profession. Stuart won election to the U. S. House of Representatives in 1838 and 1840. During the time Stuart was campaigning for office, Lincoln handled a majority of the partnership's work. Stuart was also a favorite cousin of Mary Todd, who would eventually become Lincoln's wife.[15]

Martin Van Buren was inaugurated as the eighth President of the United States in March 1837, succeeding Andrew Jackson. Van Buren was in office only five weeks before the Panic of 1837 struck. The panic started a chain of events that would eventually cause banks to fail, bond and loans to default, and thousands of people to lose their jobs. It also spelled doom for the grand public infrastructure improvements programs that Lincoln and the Illinois representatives had proposed and financed with bonds and state debt. In his first year as a bonified lawyer in Springfield, Lincoln's cases reflected the harshness of the times: collecting damages, reclaiming small debts, and clearing land titles.[16]

Lincoln was re-elected in August 1838 to a third term in the Illinois legislature. He would seek, but lose, the position of speaker of the House of Representatives. However, he remained an influential member of the House, and during the 1838-1839 legislative session, he was a member of 14 committees. He was a member of the finance committee, and pushed to save as much of the internal improvements programs as he could for the locality of Sangamon (which encompassed Springfield) and the rest of the state, but it was an uphill battle owing to the Panic of 1837 and the collapse of the bond market. Lincoln proposed to purchase Illinois land from the federal government and resell it to finance the improvements program. That proposal failed when the federal government never responded to the land purchase request. Frustrated, Lincoln then proposed a graduated tax on land that would most heavily affect the wealthy, but his efforts again were in vain, and Illinois eventually defaulted on its bonds and loans.[17]

In August 1840, Lincoln was re-elected to a fourth term in the Illinois legislature. In December 1840, Lincoln's other favorite piece of legislation, the Bank bill, was also in trouble. The State Bank of Illinois, located in Springfield, had survived repeated attempts by the Democrats to kill it. Just like former President Andrew Jackson's administration, the Democratic representatives in Illinois were opposed to banks on general principle. Jackson felt that the National Bank was a tool of the rich and powerful, and rejected its request for the renewal of its charter. In Illinois, the Democrats tried to have the state bank investigated, looked into its solvency, and tried to legislate it out of existence. They also had allowed the bank to suspend its specie (hard money versus paper) payments only until the end of the current legislative session. As the Democrats tried to adjourn the legislative session, the Whigs attempted to avoid the roll call so as not to provide enough votes for a quorum. Lincoln and his fellow Whigs amused themselves with the proceedings but accidentally got caught in session. When the next roll call occurred, Lincoln and two others tried to jump out the window to keep from being counted in the quorum vote. They were unsuccessful in avoiding being counted, and for several years later were ridiculed for their gymnastics in the legislature.[18]

A New Partnership

In April 1841, Lincoln entered into a new law partnership with Stephen T. Logan. His previous partnership with John Stuart was a blessing initially, because it came with built-in clientele and friendship. But both Stuart and Lincoln were too interested in politics as a career, and they eventually realized that one of them had to take care of the business end of the partnership. They separated amicably, and Lincoln moved on to a partnership that would provide him the discipline and expectations that would drive him to hone his craft, and become one of the best lawyers in the state.[19]

Lincoln completed his fourth term in the Illinois state legislature in early 1841 and decided not to seek a fifth term. Instead of reelection to the state legislature, he campaigned to regain his senses from the burden of a heavy heart. Lincoln had become engaged to Mary Todd in 1840, and they were supposed to wed on New Year's Day the following year. Instead, he told her he didn't love her and called it all off. He spent the next several months beating himself up for hurting her, and for making the mistake of getting engaged. Lincoln had been living in a room above the grocery store of his best friend, Joshua Speed. Speed sold his store and moved to Kentucky in April 1841, so at his first opportunity, Lincoln joined him in August to clear his mind and help him sort out his love confusion. Speed had moved back home with his parents, and Lincoln stayed with them for three weeks. Lincoln convalesced with the help of Speed's mother, who gave him a Bible, and Lincoln gradually recovered.[20]

Between April and August while Speed had been away from Lincoln, he had gotten engaged to Fanny Henning. As the wedding date approached, Speed started to get cold feet. He told Lincoln he was going to tell his bride-to-be that he didn't love her and he was going to call the wedding off. This time it was Lincoln's turn to play the therapist. He wrote a long letter explaining to Speed why he should go through with the wedding and why he thought Speed was going through those feelings of doubt and foreboding. Lincoln had just experienced the same feelings with his engagement to Mary and could express in words what Speed was experiencing in thoughts and feelings. When the fateful day came, the event occurred without a hitch and Joshua Speed and Fanny Henning were married. Some time later, Speed wrote to Lincoln to share his feelings of wedding bliss. Lincoln responded by saying how happy he was for the both of them, but that he also sorely missed his friends.[21]

Meanwhile, events were unfolding in Springfield to conspire to bring Mary Todd and Abraham Lincoln back together. Mrs. Simeon Frances had invited both to a party at her house, so she could play matchmaker to what she and her husband, the editor of the local paper, believed to be a political match made in heaven. Lincoln and Mary did start seeing each other again, but kept it a quiet and closely guarded secret. During this time, Lincoln also became involved in an escalating political satire of the state auditor, James Shields. As this satire played out in the newspaper, Shields confronted the editor to find out who the real author was. When he was told the author was Abraham Lincoln, he challenged Lincoln to a duel. The truth was that Lincoln, Mary and Mary's friend Julia Jayne were the authors of most of the articles, but the chivalrous Lincoln took credit for all of the articles so the women would not get into trouble.[22]

The Duel and Marriage

Because dueling was illegal in Illinois, Lincoln and Shields had to go Missouri to execute the procedure. The site they chose was across the Mississippi River from the town of Alton, Illinois, about 50 miles southwest of Springfield. Since Shields had issued the challenge, Lincoln was allowed to choose the weapon, and he chose cavalry broadswords. This weapon of choice gave Lincoln the clear advantage, because he was much taller than his opponent and had a much greater reach. In addition, the broadsword was not unlike an axe – the instrument by which Lincoln had made his living in his younger years.[23]

In September 1842, the combatants travelled to Alton, and then across the river to the dueling grounds in Missouri. As the two sides prepared to fight, their seconds, friends, and others discussed the contest. Soon enough, an agreement was reached that would save face by both sides, and bloodshed was averted. But the experience left a permanent mark on Lincoln; he considered it an embarrassing and shameful event in his life and he never discussed it with anyone. It also taught him a life-long lesson on the power of the written word, and the care by which those words should be used.[24]

In October, Lincoln wrote to his friend Speed to ask of his state of mind now that he had been married for eight months. He requested his friend's indulgence on the matter and wanted to know if he was happier now and glad he had gone through with it. Speed responded in the affirmative. A few weeks later, on November 4, Abraham Lincoln took Mary Todd as his bride. It was a quaint ceremony, held in the house of the Edwards family and it was necessarily small, as both Lincoln and Todd had told few people of the event. Even the Edwards were only told the day of the ceremony and had little time to prepare. One may surmise that Lincoln feared that, given a longer period of time between commitment and occurrence, he may have again gotten cold feet and left Mary standing at the altar. As it was, friends who witnessed the wedding later said that Lincoln looked more like he was going to a funeral than entering into wedding bliss.[25]

His new law partnership with Stephen Logan began to pay dividends, because Logan had a much higher expectation in performance and professionalism. Logan demanded preparedness and thoroughness in Lincoln's briefs and presentations, and taught Lincoln life-long lessons on research and the law. However, there were no immediate dividends in his financial situation, because the partnership, owing to his agreement with Logan, only provided Lincoln with one third of the income they brought in.[26]

Marriage suited both of the Lincolns, as Mary soon became pregnant and Abe became much more focused on being a provider for the family and on dedicating himself to the law profession. After the wedding, the Lincolns moved into a small room in the local hotel named the Globe Tavern. Almost exactly nine months after they were married, the Lincoln's first child was born. Robert Todd Lincoln was named after Mary's father. With the new addition, they decided they could no longer live in the hotel room. In late 1843, they moved to a small house in Springfield on Fourth Street. Mary's father, Robert Todd, visited the new family and took a liking to Lincoln, who was representing Todd on a case regarding some land transactions being tried at the Illinois Supreme Court. Eventually, in 1844 Lincoln was able to buy a small house on Eighth Street for $1200 cash and an additional lot nearby (for an estimated total cost of $1500).[27]

The Law Office

For the next few years, Lincoln worked hard to be a provider to his new wife and family. He took on all kinds of cases, large and small. He had lots of bankruptcy cases, due to a Bankruptcy Act that had gone into effect on February 1, 1842. However, he made most of his money by performing ordinary tasks for clients, such as handling wills, petitions, and petty suits. With the dedication and resolve of a man trying to create a better life for his growing family, the business grew so much that they had to find a larger office for the partnership. The new location of their business would be in the same building as the Springfield Post Office and the U. S. District Court. It overlooked the city square across which they could view the state capitol building and the county courthouse.[28]

In 1843, Lincoln's friend and former law partner, John Stuart, announced he would not seek reelection for his seat as a Representative from Illinois to the United States Congress. In addition, due to a significant increase in the population of the state from immigration, Congress was adding another representative, increasing the total number of Illinois Congressmen to seven. The new 7th district was going to encompass 11 counties, of which the most populous would be Sangamon, Lincoln's county. This Congressional opportunity piqued the interest of two of Lincoln's lawyer friends, Edward Baker and John J. Hardin, who were also Whig candidates. Baker was such a good friend that Lincoln would later name his second son after him, Edward Baker Lincoln.[29]

The three candidates made their way to the statehouse in Springfield to start the nomination process on March 20, 1843. Baker's supporters outflanked the Lincoln team, and Lincoln wound up as the chairman of the Sangamon County delegation for Baker. The Whig candidate convention was held on May 1, 1843, at the Tazewell County Courthouse in Pekin, Illinois. John Hardin won the nomination, and eventually the election. At the convention, Lincoln proposed that the candidates consider a rotation program, where each would serve only a single term. This would ensure Lincoln's candidacy after Baker followed Hardin. The rotation proposal did not suit Hardin, and they left the convention on less than amicable terms. However, both Hardin and Baker would fulfill their commitments and served single terms in Congress.[30]

In the intervening years between his last term in the Illinois Legislature and his next political opportunity, Lincoln focused on two things: his law practice and his family. The house he purchased in 1844 would be his family stronghold for the next 17 years. He and Mary would raise their four sons there. Lincoln also ended one law partnership and started another. His partnership with Stephen Logan ended when Logan told Lincoln he wanted to take on his son as a partner, to which Lincoln quickly agreed. By the end of 1844, Lincoln started a new legal partnership with William Herndon. Billy Herndon was the son of one of Lincoln's colleagues in the Illinois legislature and had served as a student in Lincoln's partnership firm with Logan.[31]

U. S. Congress

The next viable opportunity for Lincoln to become a Congressman representing the 7th district of Illinois wouldn't come until the 1846 elections, but toward the end of 1845 Lincoln started laying the groundwork. First, he contacted Baker to make sure he would not run for a second term. Once that assurance was received, he contacted Hardin to find out if he would run. Hardin indicated he did not agree with the principle of taking turns for office, and that he wanted to eliminate the convention system. Lincoln reminded Hardin that it was good enough for him and Baker to be sequentially elected, so why change it now? Lincoln left nothing to chance and tried to meet with every Whig delegate in the district to remind all of them that turnabout was fair play. Lincoln's behind the scenes efforts paid off, and in May 1846 he was nominated as the Whig delegate for the upcoming election.[32]

In August 1846, Lincoln was elected to the United States Congress. He would serve in the 30th Congress, and he would only serve a single term. As was customary, that term would start on the first Monday in December 1847. He moved himself and his family from Springfield, Illinois to Washington, D.C. However, after three months, Mrs. Lincoln decided she did not like living there, so she moved with their two children to Lexington, Kentucky to live with her father. Washington, D. C.'s social life did not exactly suit Mr. Lincoln either; however, he dedicated himself to becoming a much better prepared speaker and legislator. Lincoln was also a temperate drinker (he drank little, if at all), and the watering holes of the politicians where business gets done were not places where he was comfortable, so he was at somewhat of a disadvantage. While he was in Washington, Lincoln did take advantage of every opportunity to tell stories and share his witticisms.[33]

While in Congress, Lincoln made much of the debate regarding the nature of the cause of the start of the Mexican War (1846-1848), which was winding down by the time Lincoln took office in Congress. In speeches on the floor of the House, Lincoln challenged President Polk to specify the "spot" upon which the first American blood was spilled, in order to prove it was on American soil and not an unjust war waged for land and political capital. Later upon his return to his home state, Lincoln would suffer derision and a political backlash for not supporting a popular war and for challenging the President during the crisis. Democrats in Illinois would take to calling him "Spotty" and would challenge his patriotism; the nickname would follow him for many years.[34]

The other major effort Lincoln took on behalf of the Whig party was to promote General Zachary Taylor as the next presidential candidate in the 1848 general election. Mary and their two sons had returned to Washington from Kentucky by the end of July 1848. When Congress adjourned for the summer on August 13, Lincoln joined Taylor's election campaign. By September, the Lincoln family was on the road to New England to stump for Zachary Taylor. He made many speeches throughout the Massachusetts area, and then concluded the tour in Boston. In Boston, Lincoln met William Seward, who would become Lincoln's Secretary of State in 1861, but for now he was known as a former governor of New York and an anti-slavery speaker. After the campaign trail was completed, the Lincolns traveled to Albany, New York to meet the future vice president Millard Fillmore. From Albany, the Lincolns traveled to Buffalo to visit Niagara Falls, then took a steamer to Chicago. They arrived in Springfield in October, and in November Lincoln witnessed the fruits of his labor when Taylor was elected President.[35]

The Compromise of 1850

Lincoln returned to Washington for the final sessions of the 30th Congress in December 1848, when the biggest topic and subject of debate was slavery. With the annexation of the California and New Mexico territories as part of the Treaty of Guadalupe Hidalgo to end the Mexican-American War, Congress and the rest of the nation was arguing whether these territories would become free or slave states. In addition, the fact that Washington D. C. was a slavery permitted area was an affront to nearly every Northerner who did business in the capital. At this time, Lincoln stated his intent to introduce to Congress a bill that would provide a compromise – it would allow slave-owning Congressmen to bring their slaves to Washington and it would enforce the fugitive slave laws, but would also eradicate the practice of slavery within the District of Columbia. However, support for the bill dried up and so did Lincoln's hopes of introducing it.[36]

When Lincoln's Congressional term as Representative of the 7th District of Illinois ended, he retired from politics and focused on his legal practice. However, he did continue his thorough absorption of the local and national newspapers and followed current events closely. His law acquaintances noticed his becoming more circumspect and analytical. This was a time of great personal growth and internal change for Lincoln. He absorbed more, thought more, and internalized more than he ever had before.[37]

As Lincoln deepened his knowledge and thinking, he became a better lawyer and started to grow a significant reputation. A local paper placed him at the top of the list as a practicing lawyer in the state of Illinois. He was well known as a peacemaker, mediator, and compromiser. He knew well how the people of the small towns he visited in his travels on the Eighth Judicial Circuit of Illinois were integrated into the communities in which they lived, and as such had to remain in close quarters and live together – both the winners and losers – after a judgment of the court. Thus, he favored conciliation and compromise in almost all matters he undertook.[38]

Personal tragedy struck the Lincoln family in 1850 with the death of their son Eddie on February 1. He was only three years old when he died of pulmonary tuberculosis, and his death devastated both Mary and Abe. Subsequently, Lincoln was afflicted with a kind of permanent sadness. As his law partner Herndon once said, "Melancholy dripped from him as he walked,"[39] and Lincoln himself wrote that he and Mary dearly missed Eddie. Within weeks of losing Eddie, Mary again became pregnant. William (Willie) Wallace Lincoln was born on December 21, 1850.[40]

Congress passed the Compromise of 1850 in September, and Lincoln saw it as a good thing. He admired the efforts by his fellow Whig politicians, and especially Senator Henry Clay, to find common ground between the abolitionists in the North and the Southern secessionists. The Compromise was actually a collection of five separate bills that provided the following resolutions: organized the new territories of Utah and New Mexico (gained from Mexico after the Mexican-American War) without determining the slavery issue in either territory; admitted California as a free state (also gained from Mexico); established the boundary of Texas at its current extent (after absorbing Texas' state debt of $10,000,000 into the national debt); abolished slavery in the District of Columbia (but allowed Congressmen to travel there with their slaves); and enabled the Federal courts to gain jurisdiction regarding fugitive slaves cases (strengthening the Fugitive Slave Law).[41]

At the end of 1850, Lincoln received a letter from his stepbrother informing him of his father's failing health. Lincoln replied that both his work and his home situations would not permit his travel to his father's farm in southeastern Illinois. Lincoln had received other letters from his stepbrother at his father's "deathbed" – in May 1849 a similar situation had occurred, and at that time he immediately traveled to his father's bedside. On that prior occasion, he arrived to find his father in fine health at a time when Lincoln was trying to obtain a position in President Taylor's administration in the Land Office – Lincoln's absence from Washington probably cost him the appointment. When Lincoln's father died on January 17, 1851, he didn't attend the funeral, but Lincoln's next son, born on April 4, 1853, was named Thomas, after his grandfather.[42]

The Kansas-Nebraska Act

For the first half of the 1850s, Lincoln focused almost exclusively on his law practice. In 1850, Lincoln's partnership with Herndon handled 18 percent of the case load in the Sangamon

County Circuit Court, and in three years they had almost doubled that number. In Springfield, the capital of the state of Illinois and a growing city of 6,000 inhabitants with a multitude of other capable lawyers, they were rated as one of the top law firms. This was no small feat, and it reflects the personal and professional growth that Lincoln was going through during this period.[43]

During the 1852 presidential campaign, Lincoln was named the Whig national committeeman for the state of Illinois. The Whig Party had decided to back General Winfield Scott as their candidate for President, their third military commander as presidential candidate in four elections – the other two being William Henry Harrison in 1840 (won) and Zachary Taylor in 1848 (won). Senator Henry Clay, the Whig candidate in 1844, was a lawyer and career politician who lost to Democrat James Polk. In 1852, the Whig political machine went back to choosing a military leader as their man, because they thought it provided their best opportunity to win. Lincoln was not particularly enamored with Scott as the Whig candidate and did not or could not bring himself to fully commit to supporting his candidacy for president.[44]

When Senator Henry Clay died on June 29, 1852, it was a day of national mourning. In Springfield, citizens memorialized his passing by closing all businesses on July 6, and holding two memorial services. One service was held at the state capital, and the eulogy was delivered by Abraham Lincoln. To Lincoln, Clay was not just a fellow Whig but also the embodiment of Whig principles and his personal beliefs. He eulogized Clay as a man who was fighting the good fight against slavery, but in a measured and masterful way that would achieve the results he wanted (an end to slavery) without tearing the country apart. Lincoln admitted that Clay was a slaveholder, but stated Clay was on the forefront of the opposition to slavery in his home state of Kentucky and in the Senate chambers of Congress. In addition, upon his death Clay (like Washington before him) emancipated his slaves in his will.[45]

During the 1852-1853 Congressional session, events were occurring that would change the national political landscape forever. In 1820, a political bargain had been struck between the Southern slave states and the Northern free states that was called the Missouri Compromise. It was a law proposed by Senator Henry Clay to prohibit slavery in the states created from the Louisiana Territory north of the 36th parallel (the southern boundary of Missouri). In addition, the new state of Maine was incorporated as a free state. In compensation for this agreement, Missouri was admitted to the Union as a slave state. During the end of the Congressional session in 1853, the House passed a bill for the organization of the new Nebraska Territory. This bill then went to the Senate Committee on Territories, headed by Senator Stephen A. Douglas. When the bill came out of the committee, it included a new section on "popular sovereignty" – which would allow the white male occupants/citizens of the territory to determine for themselves if they wanted to be a free or a slave state. This section effectively repealed the Missouri Compromise. The new bill was reported to the Senate in January 1854.[46]

The new version of the Nebraska bill also included the organization of the Kansas Territory, and hence the bill became known as the Kansas-Nebraska Act. It allowed the citizens of both territories to self-determine their free state/slave state status. The Act was passed by the Senate in March 1854 and was ratified by the House in May. President Franklin Pierce signed the Kansas-Nebraska Act into law on May 30, 1854. This event caused a seismic shift in the national debate on slavery and awakened a sleeping giant. Regarding the passage of the Act, Lincoln reflected the bitter reaction Whigs and abolitionists felt toward its passage when he said: "We were thunderstruck and stunned; and we reeled and fell in utter confusion."[47]

After passage of the Kansas-Nebraska Act, Lincoln reengaged in the Whig political scene. His intent was only to stump on the political trail for his fellow Whig, Richard Yates, who was the current Representative for the Illinois 7th district. But by the end of August, he decided to run for a seat in the Illinois state legislature, along with his friend Stephen Logan. Lincoln was extremely troubled by the Kansas-Nebraska Act, and spoke out against the Act in speeches on the campaign trail. His speeches drew larger and larger audiences, and he was beginning to garner some national attention. This brought about his reengagement to the national political scene.[48]

Political Reengagement

In November 1854, Lincoln and Logan both won their races for the state legislature, while Yates lost his reelection to Congress. Because a number of anti-Democrat candidates had been elected to the state legislature (owing to the statewide reaction to the Kansas-Nebraska Act), it was likely that the chamber would elect a new Senator to represent Illinois in Congress (ultimate election of a U. S. Senator being a choice of the state legislatures rather than of the public at that time). Lincoln wanted to be that Senator. Because Illinois state representatives were prohibited from electing one of their members to the Senate, Lincoln resigned his newly won position in the state legislature.[49]

Lincoln immediately began campaigning for the Senate position by writing letters to friends and political contacts requesting support. In December, his behind the scenes campaigning went into full swing. He compiled a list of the members of the legislature and annotated each name with notation of which members were Whig, Democrat, and Anti-Nebraska Democrat. He concluded that his chances were good. The joint session of the legislature to determine the Illinois Senator was held on February 8, 1855. Although Lincoln garnered the most votes on the first ballot, they were not enough to win, and on each succeeding ballot he received fewer and fewer votes. Finally, after the 9th ballot he recommended that his supporters vote for Lyman Trumbull, an Anti-Nebraska Democrat. Trumbull won on the 10th ballot.[50]

After Lincoln lost the election to Trumbull, he again returned to his law practice. Only this time he would remain engaged with the political scene. In addition, these next five years (1855 to 1860) would be his most profitable as a lawyer. The transportation and improvement vision Lincoln had as a young Illinois legislator was coming to fruition, as different railroads and other improvements crisscrossed the state. A majority of his workload was now involving cases either representing the railroad companies or individuals and municipalities against the railroad companies. His largest payment came from a case representing a railroad company, for which he was eventually paid $5000 – a tremendous sum in those days. And he had to sue the railroad to be paid.[51]

Since 1856 was a presidential election year, Lincoln was once again swept up in local and national politics. This was a key time that would redefine his political future. His partner Herndon was helping set up an anti-Nebraska convention in Bloomington and submitted Lincoln's name on the list of delegates to the convention without Lincoln's approval. After the list was published in the paper, Lincoln's conservative friends were surprised and concerned about the development, but when Herndon finally asked Lincoln about it, he indicated he would attend the convention with the rest of the radicals.[52]

Lincoln attended what was subsequently called the first Republican convention in Illinois. Owing to some conservatives in attendance, the platform was not as radical as some people expected. With a platform he believed in, and a mission to accomplish, on the last day of the convention Lincoln delivered what some say was his greatest speech. In fact, it was so good that even the newspapermen who had come to cover the convention were so spellbound that they didn't write down what

Lincoln said. There is no formal documentation of that speech, and as such it has become known as Lincoln's Lost Speech.[53]

The Dred Scott Decision

With the launch of the Republican Party as a national entity, Lincoln put his usual enthusiastic effort into supporting the party, its platform, and its candidates. For the national presidential election, the Republicans chose John C. Fremont, a famous western explorer and writer, and a platform that proposed prohibition of slavery and polygamy in the territories.[54]

Lincoln stumped throughout Illinois on Fremont's behalf and on behalf of the Republican Party. He also received numerous requests to speak at venues in other states, including Indiana, Wisconsin, Iowa, and Michigan; however, the Michigan gathering is the only offer he accepted. This is an indication of how Lincoln was beginning to be perceived at the national level – that of a significant force in Republican politics. After four months on the campaign trail, Lincoln returned home to anxiously await the fruits of his labor. The November election results revealed a strong showing for the new party, but it fell short of winning the presidential election.[55]

On March 4, 1857, Democrat James Buchanan was inaugurated as the 15th President of the United States. Two days later, the Supreme Court announced its Dred Scott decision. Dred Scott was a slave who had traveled with his master from Missouri (a slave state) to Illinois (a free state) and then later to the northern part of the Louisiana Territory (present day Minnesota). Upon the death of his master, Scott sued in court that he should be free on account of having lived for several years in a free state. Upon appeal, the case eventually made its way to the Supreme Court. The Court's decision was that slaves were not citizens of any state, so therefore they were not citizens of the United States. Thus, the case was dismissed because Scott, not being a citizen, had no right to sue in court.[56]

The announcement of the Dred Scott decision caused a fire-storm of reaction across the Northern states. Abolitionists were calling for cessation from the Union. The *Chicago Tribune* was predicting that slavery would be extended to the free states, while the *New York Herald* expected full-blown rebellion.[57] U.S. Senator for Illinois Stephen A. Douglas, who agreed with the decision, addressed the topic at the U.S. District Court in Springfield on June 7. Lincoln attended the session and provided his response about three weeks later.

Lincoln's response was thoroughly researched in the District Court library and analyzed both the decision of the Court and Douglas's reflections on it. Lincoln's speech was devoid of emotional rhetoric, and calmly walked the attendees through the logic of his position, which reiterated that, as written in the Declaration of Independence, all men are created equal. He recognized that all men did not have the same intelligence, or morality, or other distinctions, but Lincoln stated that all men were equal in the rights described in the Declaration of Independence. This was Lincoln's only political speech of 1857, and he went back to his law practice in Springfield. But he did look forward to the following year, which would hold mid-term reelections. It was an opportunity to face his rival Stephen Douglas for his Senate seat in Congress. Lincoln felt he was the obvious choice as the Republican candidate and looked forward for the chance to return to Congress.[58]

A House Divided

A Republican convention for the election of a state's U. S. Senator was a rare event. Only one such convention was held before June 1858. To witness and participate in such a spectacle brought people to Springfield by the thousands. Lincoln was ready. He had prepared his acceptance speech before the first meeting took place or the first vote was cast. This one-day event ended with an evening address by the Republican nominee for the U. S. Senator seat, Abraham Lincoln. For his acceptance of the nomination, Lincoln delivered his now famous "house divided" speech. "A house divided against itself cannot stand,"[59] Lincoln said, and warned that the country would eventually become either all free or all slave states. With this opening salvo, the battle with Stephen Douglas for his job in Washington began.[60]

Stephen Douglas returned to Illinois from Washington like a Roman general after the conquest of a faraway country. As his train pulled into Chicago, he was met with welcome banners, a 150-gun salute, and cheering crowds. Douglas was prepared to do battle toe-to-toe, *mano a mano*, until only he or Lincoln was left standing. This was what he excelled at. He was naturally combative and enjoyed the dance. He knew that Lincoln was an able challenger, and he invited Lincoln to his opening campaign speech in Chicago on July 9, 1858. Douglas addressed the crowd and then asked of Lincoln a series of questions, intending to paint his rival into a corner. The next day, Lincoln responded with a speech defending his "house divided" speech and quoting the Declaration of Independence.[61]

Douglas traveled by a special train that housed his family and entourage and included a special flat car that carried a small cannon, operated by two young men in semi-military dress. The cannon would be fired as the train neared each town to announce Douglas's arrival. Sometimes Lincoln would be a passenger on the very train taking Douglas to his next stop. As recommended by his campaign advisors, Lincoln followed Douglas to several towns to speak in response to Douglas's comments. The Douglas camp complained that Lincoln could not command the large crowds without Douglas' being there, and that Lincoln was benefiting from their publicity efforts. In response to that accusation, Lincoln proposed that the candidates have a series of debates. Douglas's advisors agreed to seven debates, one in each district and excluding the two where both had already talked. Lincoln agreed. The debates crisscrossed the state of Illinois from north to south and east to west, and each debate attracted thousands or tens of thousands of people.[62]

These debates garnered national attention, as reporters covered both candidates and printed their speeches as news. In the 1850s, newspapers were extraordinarily politicized, and typically took a completely biased position. They were either pro-slavery or pro-free, Democrat or Republican, Douglas or Lincoln. However, whether for or against Lincoln, his name was almost becoming a household word – which was new for Lincoln – whereas the incumbent Douglas was already a public figure. The other major effect the debates had was to anneal and hone the malleable Lincoln through the blunt force of Douglas's savage verbal barrage, like the hammer and anvil to a steel blade. Lincoln emerged from the debates more focused, with a sharper mind and a clearer vision.

A New Beginning

Lincoln returned to Springfield in late October 1858, in time for Election Day on November 2. Lincoln won the popular election by more than 4,000 votes, but it was the state legislatures that voted U. S. Senators into office. Because Illinois Democrats won the most seats in the election, they also had the power to name the Senator, which they did in January 1859 – it was Douglas. Although Lincoln had lost the election for Senator, he did not act or feel like a loser. The experience actually whetted his appetite for a political re-engagement and his thirst for achievement. This was not a failure, and it was not an end. It was a new beginning.[63]

As soon as the election was over and despite Lincoln having lost the Senate seat, newspapers across Illinois and the northern states were proposing Lincoln as the Republican candidate for the presidency in 1860. However, Lincoln at first was not so sure. His first tendency was self-depreciation and modesty. But as more and more friends, acquaintances, and even outright strangers openly discussed the topic with him, he became enamored of the idea. When speaking publicly, he denied he was seeking the position, and dissuaded others of that impression. It turned out to be a great strategy, because as the obvious Republican candidates negotiated and bartered over the location for the Republican National Convention — Buffalo for former New York Governor William H. Seward, Cleveland or Columbus for Ohio Senator Salmon P. Chase, Harrisburg for Pennsylvania Senator Simon Cameron, and St. Louis for former U. S. Representative from Missouri Edward G. Bates — Lincoln's associates argued for Chicago as the location, because it would be a neutral site (at that time Lincoln was not yet in the running).[64]

In 1859, Lincoln made speeches throughout the Midwest, including Wisconsin, Ohio, Indiana, Iowa, and Kansas (in addition to Illinois) in support of the Republican platform and Republican candidates prior to the 1859 elections. In October, Lincoln received a request to speak in New York City at Reverend Henry Ward Beecher's church in Brooklyn. Beecher was the most famous minister of the age, and Lincoln was very excited and happy to oblige. The offer also included payment of $200 for the speech, an extremely large engagement fee at that time. Lincoln accepted the offer, and requested the event be delayed until February, so as not to conflict with his schedule.[65]

It is possible that the Cooper Union speech, as it is known today, may have tipped the scales in favor of Lincoln winning the nomination of the Republican Party and eventually the Presidential election. Because of strong interest in the speaker, the location was moved from Beecher's church to Manhattan's Cooper Union, a school with a basement auditorium that could seat 1,800 people (1,500 would attend). Lincoln's speech was on the question of the meaning and intent of the words in the Constitution regarding the federal government's authority on the question of slavery. This was in response to a speech by Stephen Douglas that implied that the founding fathers (and the Constitution) favored local rights over federal control with respect to the question of slavery in the territories. Lincoln laid out his reply to Douglas's thesis in a methodical approach. He offered the position of the Constitution's signers regarding this question by examining how they acted in their official capacities from 1787 to 1820, showing that the majority were for federal control. His speech was electrifying and kept the audience spellbound. Lincoln then provided a message to the Southern people, reminding them of their rights as defined in the Constitution, and that the words slave, slavery, and property (with respect to slaves or slavery) are not in that document. He continued with a call upon all Republicans that it was their duty to keep slavery out of the territories, thereby keeping it out of the free states. Lincoln finished with the statement "Let us have faith that right makes might, and in that faith, let us, to the end, dare to do our duty as we understand it."[66]

At the conclusion, the audience showered Lincoln with waves of applause. The newspapers carried the full text of his speech, and he received numerous requests to speak at other venues in the New England and New York area. Lincoln proceeded to deliver speeches in several New England states before visiting his son Robert, who was attending Phillips Exeter Academy in Exeter, New Hampshire. These speaking engagements throughout the northeast provided Lincoln's political aspirations with momentum and propelled him to the Republication National Convention.[67]

Republican Nomination

In March 1860, Lincoln returned to Springfield. He may have had doubts when he left for New York a month prior, but he arrived back in Illinois a believer. He had been so well received in New York and New England that he started to believe in himself, and with that he even started to believe he could win. With the success of his speaking tour, he also received more support and more offers for advice and help. This effort netted

Lincoln new friends from the East Coast who would help secure votes. The Republican national convention was moved up
a month from June to May, and that may have also worked in
Lincoln's favor, because his popularity was peaking at the right
time. At the Illinois state Republican convention in early May,
Lincoln was nominated as a candidate for President of the
United States, and his star was shining brighter than ever.[68]

The national convention started on May 16 in Chicago, and
the first item on the agenda was to organize and staff the
committees. The second day focused on development and
agreement of the party platform, which beyond the anti-
slavery plank included federal support for the Homestead Act,
a transcontinental railroad, a protective tariff, and infrastructure improvements for rivers and harbors. The delegates also
voted for a simple majority process for the Presidential nomination, as opposed to a two-thirds rule. The third day started
the balloting process, which would continue until a candidate
had a majority of the delegates committed to his nomination.
The first ballot came back with Senator Seward solidly in the
lead. Lincoln was surprisingly in second place, with over a hundred votes of the delegates. A total of 233 votes would win the
nomination. Lincoln's staff was feverishly working with the
delegates of each state, trying to get him nominated as their
second choice if their first choice was not going to win. On the
second ballot, Lincoln had 181 votes. As was the tradition in
those days, the candidates did not attend the convention. Lincoln was back in Springfield, anxiously awaiting the results. On
the third vote, Lincoln won the Republican nomination.[69]

Back in the 1800s, the time-honored tradition was that
presidential candidates did not "beg" for votes, but let their
friends, their associates, and their record to speak for them.
Lincoln observed this tradition faithfully and gave no speeches
prior to the convention's election. In another difference between those days and today, state elections were held
throughout the year. As such, Lincoln received an early indica-

tion of his potential success when the Republicans won both Maine and Vermont. This was further strengthened by October victories in Pennsylvania, Indiana, and Ohio. Finally, on Election Day in November, New York and the remaining Northern states (except New Jersey) went for Lincoln. Lincoln did not receive a single vote in the South, but that did not matter, because the Democrats had nominated two candidates. Stephen Douglas was the Northern Democrat candidate, and John Breckenridge was the Southern Democrat leader. Aided by the split in the Democratic Party, Lincoln was elected President on Tuesday, November 6, 1860.[70]

After the election, events were taking shape that would put the North and the South on a collision course. Lincoln was under the misguided impression that his heritage as a son of the border "southern" state of Kentucky gave him insight into the minds and hearts of the deep-South Southerners. He felt that the secessionists of the Southern states were minority fringe troublemakers, and that the Southern Unionists and the common sense of the people would overrule them. He was quickly proven wrong.

On December 20, South Carolina seceded from the Union. Then six more states – Alabama, Florida, Georgia, Louisiana, Mississippi, and Texas – seceded between January 9 and February 1. These states took over Federal forts and arsenals and replaced the national flag with state flags. As the inauguration approached, Lincoln made decisions and selections to fill his cabinet, surrounding himself with experienced leaders from throughout the Republican Party. They were all his rivals from the Republican national convention, yet they were all included in his Presidential cabinet, and represented factions with intentions potentially hostile to his own. Lincoln made a farewell speech before he left Springfield and arrived in Washington on February 23. Abraham Lincoln was sworn in as the 16th President of the United States on March 4, 1861. A little more than a month later, the country would be at war.[71]

CHAPTER 6

The Civil War

Fewer than 40 days after Abraham Lincoln took the oath of the office of the President of the United States, the war to preserve the Union and our democratic institution would begin. The Civil War started on April 12, 1861 at 4:30 am, as the Confederate cannons that surrounded Ft. Sumter in the middle of the Charleston, South Carolina harbor opened fire. For over 30 hours straight they bombarded the Union garrison, and with supplies almost gone and fires in the armory, the defenders' chances didn't look good. Then an unauthorized Confederate negotiator, "Colonel" Wigfall, arrived by his own boat. He attached a white flag to his saber and demanded to see the commander to ask for terms of surrender.[1]

The Union commander, Major Robert Anderson, defined terms that would allow full military honors, to leave with colors flying and heads held high. Wigfall accepted the terms and returned to the Confederate side. Anderson hoisted the white flag. Then the Confederate commander, General Beauregard, sent officers to negotiate terms of surrender. When they found that Wigfall had already offered terms, they returned to Beauregard. Beauregard accepted the terms, and the Union forces surrendered the fort. They were not taken prisoner, but were allowed to evacuate to the *Baltic*, a Union ship waiting nearby with supplies and reinforcements, and sailed back to the North.[2]

In response to the South's military action, Lincoln called for 75,000 volunteers and a 90-day enlistment. This was back in the day when the United States had a very small army and used the militia – state-organized volunteer brigades – as the reserves to help defend the nation. The militia dates back to the Revolutionary War and was a response to how the public felt about King George's Redcoats – they didn't trust the government enough to fund a standing army to which they might potentially submit their independence. Lincoln was fortunate in that his call to arms was more than answered.

The public reaction and outcry to the South's unprovoked attack on Ft. Sumter was swift and strong. State militia units across the North would answer the call: Minnesota, Maine, Massachusetts, New York, Michigan, Ohio, and Indiana all promised thousands of troops. But throughout the border states of Delaware, Kentucky, and Missouri, the citizens and governors were indignant, saying they couldn't and shouldn't raise arms against their brothers. Over the next 60 days, four more states (Arkansas, North Carolina, Tennessee, and Virginia) would join the Deep South's seven-state Confederacy, and the Confederate capital would move from Montgomery, Alabama to Richmond, Virginia.[3]

Pro-slavery rabble rousers in Baltimore and throughout Maryland had cut telegraph lines, burned bridges, and destroyed rail lines connecting Washington and the surrounding area in order to cripple communications between the capital and the Northern states. Due to this interference, Lincoln suspended the writ of habeas corpus between Philadelphia and Baltimore (and in Washington). This allowed the military to arrest and hold suspected Southern sympathizers without having to formally charge them with a crime or releasing them if there wasn't enough suitable evidence to obtain a conviction. Lincoln's law background allowed him to use the Constitution's Article 1, Section 9, describing the conditions under which habeas corpus could be suspended as the legal authority for his action.[4]

Military Buildup

As Lincoln waited for militia to arrive to protect the nation's capital, news and rumors swirled about Confederate forces marching on Washington. There were reports of thousands of Confederate troops in Alexandria, Virginia. The Federal City was vulnerable and unprotected, and people were leaving like rats off a sinking ship. Stores were closed, hotels were nearly empty, and the empty streets made the city look like a ghost town. Meanwhile, in nearby Pennsylvania, about 200 light infantry and artillery gathered in Pottsville for the train ride to Washington. These "First Defenders" arrived in Washington at about 7 p.m. on April 17.[5]

A few days later, a Massachusetts infantry unit of about 700 soldiers arrived. Not only did they make the trek of over 400 miles in less than a week, but they also had to overcome a riot in Baltimore to get there. About a dozen of the rioters were killed, while four of the Sixth Massachusetts Volunteer Infantry were killed along with 36 wounded.[6]

As a Southern "border state," Maryland was home to a significant pro-slavery movement, and since it completely surrounded Washington, the capital was extremely vulnerable. About two weeks after the Ft. Sumter attack, the first significant number of troops arrived in Washington. General Benjamin F. Butler and thousands of the New York Seventh Regiment arrived on April 25 by train, having sailed to Annapolis and then rebuilding destroyed railroad tracks on the route to Washington. Upon the arrival of the Seventh Regiment, confidence was restored to a people feeling the weight of impending doom, and men, women, and children standing in doorways and some on rooftops all cheered and shouted their appreciation.[7]

The unprovoked attack of Ft. Sumpter kicked off a buildup of men, material, and supplies converging on the nation's capital, as militia units from nearly every Northern state were sent to Washington. In fact, both sides of the Potomac experienced a military buildup like never before. As thousands of volunteers from the Northern states descended on the capital, likewise thousands of Confederate soldiers amassed in Alexandria. In early May, there were over 20,000 soldiers protecting Washington. By June, that number would swell to 30,000. On the other side of the Potomac, there were over 20,000 Confederate soldiers. Both sides would spend the next months preparing for war. Lincoln had requested a special session of Congress on July 4, 1861 to delineate his proposed recommendations for funding and militia requests to put down the rebellion of the Southern states. His request for $400,000,000 and 400,000 militia, was not only wholeheartedly accepted, but increased by Congress to $500,000,000 and 500,000 militia.[8]

The highest-ranking officer in the Union army was General Winfield Scott, a physically and historically giant of a man, hero of both the Mexican War and the War of 1812. But by 1861, at the age of 74, his time had passed, and now he was so obese that he could not perform acts of physical stamina, such as riding a horse or even standing for any long period of time. What he did have was the wisdom of experience and a mind like a steel trap. Scott predicted a protracted war with the South, and that it would take time and training to mold the volunteer militias into an effective fighting force.[9]

In time, Lincoln would come to appreciate Scott's military advice, but at this point in his presidency and the war, he ignored Scott's recommendation for the field commander of the Union army, Joseph Mansfield, and instead went with the advice of his cabinet members, thus promoting Major General Irvin McDowell to brigadier general. The selection of McDowell was the recommendation of Secretary of War Simon Cameron and Secretary of the Treasury Salmon Chase, but it would turn out to be an unfortunate choice. Although McDowell was a West Point graduate and career army officer, he had no experience leading men in battle. After two months of organizing the volunteer troops into five divisions and thirteen brigades, with their requisite command structures, McDowell led the Union army into action on July 16, 1861.[10]

Bull Run (Manassas)

The mass of Union forces marched from Washington to Centerville, Virginia, the first reaching the town by 9 a.m. McDowell arrived by the afternoon and spent the next two days with his commanders planning their attack on the Confederate forces behind Bull Run, a tributary of the Potomac River about midway between Centerville and Manassas, Virginia. Scouting parties had determined that the enemy had about 20,000 men behind Bull Run, many stationed at different crossing points downstream of Stone Bridge. McDowell met his subordinate commanders on the evening of July 20, to discuss the plan for the attack which was to start the next morning.

The plan was for two divisions to cross the river upstream of Stone Bridge, while a third division engaged the Confederates at Stone Bridge and downstream, until the three divisions could converge and overwhelm them south of Bull Run. McDowell then asked his generals if there were any questions or comments regarding the plan. General Daniel Tyler responded with a concern regarding the number of Confederate forces at Bull Run, and whether or not they would be reinforced by other enemy forces in Virginia. It turned out to be a prescient question.[11]

The first battle of the American Civil War was not like anyone was expecting. From the Northern perspective, leading papers and local pundits (including Washington Congressmen) were expecting a quick and complete victory. General McDowell commanded an army of 30,000 Union soldiers, who were expected to overwhelm the smaller force of 20,000 Confederates led by General Beauregard (of Ft. Sumter fame). Men (some Congressional leaders included), women, and families took picnic baskets and rode out to the hills overlooking the first major confrontation of the Civil War expecting entertainment. What they were treated to was the harsh reality and horror of war.

All through the early hours of the conflict, it seemed as though the North had the upper hand, but then toward the evening, about 10,000 Southern troops from the Shenandoah Valley reinforced the Confederate side. With a rebel yell and fierce determination, these additional soldiers led by General Joseph Johnston provided a hail of musket fire that unnerved the Federal troops – the Union ranks broke and ran in retreat. In the confusion and chaos that followed, civilians, soldiers, horses, and others caused multiple scenes of anguish as people were trampled in the mad rush to get to safety.[12]

The great confused jumble of people, horses, wagons, carriages, foot soldiers, and citizens arrived *en masse* in Washington, having bypassed Centerville and not stopping until the capital was reached. There they took refuge, as the Federal City took in all they could of the retreating hordes. When the next day dawned, the Confederate Army would gather and discuss a possible invasion and attack of Washington, but it was an opportunity that engendered too much risk, and instead they enjoyed the spoils of victory.

Monday, July 22, was a rainy day that would serve as a watershed moment in the history and the prosecution of the war. It would make the Southerners believe in the invincibility of their army and their cause, and it would force the Northerners to buckle down on their optimism for a quick end to the war and ramp up their dedication and resolve for an ultimate victory.[13]

Army of the Potomac

With General Winfield Scott disabled by his weight and medical condition (an extreme affliction of gout), and with General McDowell having failed so spectacularly at the Battle of Bull Run, Lincoln set about trying to find his next field commander. General McClellan had the look and attitude of a leader, but he would earn his nickname "Little Napoleon" for his huge ego and personality – unfortunately, not for his ability to command troops in battle. He was an excellent administrator, but not a very good general. He consistently overestimated his opponent's strength and firepower, and undervalued his own troop numbers. He also consistently overestimated his ability, and he discredited and badmouthed his superiors and undermined their authority. These character flaws were not discovered by Lincoln until well into McClellan's reign as Commander of the Army of the Potomac. The day after the disaster of Bull Run, Lincoln would hand over Army of the Potomac to McClellan.[14]

General Scott was McClellan's superior officer, and unfortunately McClellan despised him. He wanted General Scott's position and devised ways to make Scott look bad. It added to McClellan's enmity that even though Scott got fed up with the contemptuous nature of their relationship and tried to resign several times, Lincoln refused to allow it. McClellan spent the next several months training his troops, amassing more men and material, and planning his next move. This was as vexing to Lincoln as it was to Scott. Scott publicly questioned McClellan's lack of action, and the anti-slavery Senators in Congress added their voices to this reproach. They took their complaints directly to the President, but Lincoln told them that he would not interfere. In November 1861, General Scott again requested to be relieved of command. This time, Lincoln obliged, and gave Scott's position as Commander of all Union forces to McClellan, in addition to command of the Army of the Potomac. McClellan finally had what he desired – total control –

but he also no longer had someone else to blame if things went wrong. And things would go very, very wrong.[15]

McClellan spent the next several months training and preparing his army. The Army of the Potomac would grow from 50,000 in July 1861 to over 80,000 in November 1861.[16] By December 1861, with no movement of McClellan's troops and no hint of any movement plans, a Congressional committee descended on Lincoln at the White House to complain of McClellan's lack of action. They also demanded that he remove McClellan from command. Lincoln responded with the question, if I relieve him then who would replace him? Toward the end of December, Lincoln forwarded to McClellan a list of suggestions for and questions about forward movement and future plans. McClellan provided a handwritten response ten days later that countered and dismissed each suggestion. Privately, McClellan disrespected Lincoln, and referred to him as an "idiot" and a "well meaning baboon" in letters to his wife. Finally, Lincoln issued Presidential Order No. 1, which required that McClellan move his troops by February 22, 1862.[17]

McClellan finally put a plan, called the Peninsula Plan, in motion in early March. McClellan's scheme called for 85,000 troops to sail down the Potomac River into the Chesapeake Bay and on to Fort Monroe in Virginia, a Union occupied fort on a peninsula between the James and York Rivers. The Union troops would then march 60 miles to Richmond and capture the Confederate capital. The first phase of this plan called for 33,000 troops under General McDowell to march out of Washington to Alexandria, past Centerville then through Manassas Junction down to Fredericksburg. McDowell's troops were intended to be a diversion to preoccupy the enemy north of Richmond while the main force attacked from east of Richmond. When McDowell's troops moved out, so did the Confederates, and Union soldiers found that the cannons facing them from the fortifications at Centerville were merely logs painted black. Many Congressmen were calling for McClellan's head at that point, and Lincoln was forced to do something. On March 11, Lincoln decided to take the Commander in Chief title from McClellan, but still left him in command of the Army of the Potomac.[18]

Monitor and Merrimack

At the beginning of the war, Lincoln had declared a naval blockade of all Southern ports, making Secretary of the Navy Gideon Wells responsible for the blockade's implementation. Some say that the blockade was at least partially responsible for the North winning the war because of the financial impact it struck at the South's ability to wage war. The South's chief export was cotton, which was sent to textile mills in England, France, and New England. In return for this crop, the South received nearly everything it needed to maintain its existence: cash, manufactured goods, produce, spices, and finished products. But with the blockade, the South found its economy strangled and inflation soaring due to the lack of supply of nearly everything. In *Starving the South*, Andrew Smith states, "Over time, the blockade contributed to the South's demoralization and its ultimate defeat. No one can seriously believe that the North could have won the war without the blockade."[19]

The South determined that it must defeat the blockade, and its methodology to do that was with new technology – a metal ship. The Confederate design was simple and straightforward – take an old wooden boat and cover it with heavy iron plates. Its first of this type originated with the hull of a Union vessel called the *Merrimack* that had been set ablaze in the Gosport (Norfolk) Naval Shipyard when Virginia seceded from the United States; once covered with the iron plates the rebuilt ship was named the CSS *Virginia*. In some places the metal was four inches thick, and in its first battle, cannon balls from Union vessels bounced right off. The *Virginia* also had a metal-encased ramming rod that it used to attack the first of two Union ships it encountered, which was on March 8, 1862. What happened next is something that is considered one of the most important battles in naval history – not because of the two participants, but because it was the first ever battle between ironclad vessels – the *Monitor* and the *Merrimack*, or rather more technically correct the *Monitor* and the *Virginia*.[20]

A Swedish engineer and designer, John Ericsson, designed the *Monitor*. He was an inventor who emigrated in 1829, and within a few years had designed ships, optical instruments, and gun carriages. He even won medals for his thermodynamic inventions. His design of the *Monitor* was initially ridiculed, but eventually the government gave him a contract by which he would have to pay back the money if the warship did not meet their expectations. Ericsson provided several innovations with the *Monitor* – one of which was a turret with two guns that could move 360 degrees and fire from any angle, so that it didn't matter which direction the ship was moving. This was a unique innovation – before this invention, ships had to move parallel to their intended target to bear the full power of their weapons upon it. And to this day, revolving turrets are the preferred mechanism used to house weapons on ships at sea.[21]

Only hours after the *Virginia* had disabled two other Union vessels, the *Monitor* made it to the scene. However, the light of day was dim and *Virginia* had already receded to Confederate shores. The *Virginia* had 10 guns, four on each side and one each in the bow and stern (front and back). The *Monitor* had only two guns in its single turret. On March 9, after four hours of fighting through the morning, the battle would be an even draw, as neither crew's cannons could pierce the other ship's armor. At one point, the *Virginia* tried to ram the *Monitor*, but the *Monitor's* able helmsmen maneuvered their ship so that the *Virginia's* impact was just a glancing blow that left no damage. At the end of the battle, the *Virginia* withdrew and sailed back to Norfolk, while the *Monitor* crew rejoiced. After that day, all wooden fighting ships would be a thing of the past

– and the world noticed. Ericsson would get a contract to build more monitors, and Secretary of the Navy Gideon Wells would continue his blockade of the South.[22]

Shiloh

Everything west of the Allegheny Mountains was called the Western Theatre, and in the West a new star was shining, that of Ulysses S. Grant. Grant had earned some hard-fought victories, among them the victories at Ft. Henry and Ft. Donelson in Tennessee. After capturing these Confederate forts, Grant took his army down the Tennessee River to a place called Pittsburg Landing, not far from the Tennessee/Mississippi border. His plan was to build up his army for a siege of the Confederate installations at Corinth, Mississippi, an east-west and north-south rail junction.[23]

The Union camp stretched from the river about two miles out to a church called Shiloh (hence the name of the battlefield). As the Union commanders were training their new volunteer troops at the camp near Shiloh and waiting for reinforcements of 40,000 veterans under General Buell from Nashville, the Confederate cavalry had spotted Grant's army and scouted his positions. The cavalry then communicated the information to General Albert Sidney Johnston, the highest-ranking officer in the Confederate Army. Johnston decided upon a surprise attack that would cut off Grant from his reinforcements and his escape route. What would happen next was the bloodiest battle in American history to that time, claiming more casualties than all of America's previous wars combined.[24] How ironic it was then, that the word Shiloh was a Hebrew term meaning "Place of Peace."[25]

The Confederates surrounded the Union forces, and then attacked at dawn on Sunday morning, April 6. It was a complete surprise – Grant had expected his Pittsburg Landing position not to be a defensive one but the launching place for an offensive operation (and, in fact, it had been Johnston who had left heavy entrenchments and strong defenses in Corinth for the defenseless positions of an open battlefield). The Union troops quickly moved into battle formation, with General Prentiss, General McClernand, and General Sherman divisions in front and General Smith and General Hurlbut divisions in the rear. The Confederate troops attacked head on, with the McClernand and Sherman troops taking most of the initial fire. Sherman himself was shot in the hand and in the shoulder, and he had several horses shot out from under him.[26]

Prentiss and his regiment then took on the fury of the Confederate attack, as Sherman and McClernand fell back. Prentiss found a lane through the brush and used it like an entrenchment, bringing about a furious fire that the Confederates called the "Hornet's Nest." But because Prentiss did not fall back in line with the other commanders, his flank was exposed and he was eventually captured, along with 2,200 of his men and officers, as evening was approaching. Because the defensive line of the Union was not broken, the Confederates were unable to push through to the embankment of the river. Johnston saw what was happening and personally took charge, rallied his troops and led them down the hill toward the Union lines. This was a fatal mistake by Johnston, as several Union bullets ripped through his uniform, one of which pierced an artery in his leg, and he bled out while riding his horse and leading his troops.[27]

With the death of Johnston, the Confederate leadership fell to General P. G. T. Beauregard, who decided, in light of the number of casualties and fatigue of his troops, to reorganize and regroup his army and complete the assault on the Union regiments in the morning. But the inability of the Confederate troops to cut off Grant's hold on the Pittsburg Landing passage across the river allowed Union reinforcements to cross the river and begin the Yankee counterattack. The next day started another surprise attack, this time by the Union army. With large numbers of fresh troops, the force of the Yankee attack shocked Beauregard's troops and the fighting on both sides became as furious as before. By the afternoon of this second day of the battle, the tide had turned, and Grant's forces chased the Confederates back the way they had come, winning a costly victory.[28]

Seven Days Battles

After several months of delays and requests for more troops, McClellan's "Peninsula Plan" was finally put into action. The Peninsula Plan was intended to be an attack on the Confederate capital of Richmond, Virginia, via an oversea transport down the Potomac River, and had started with a siege of Yorktown, Virginia in early April. McClellan badly overestimated the Rebel army holding the town made famous by the Revolutionary War. Instead of an immediate attack that would have overwhelmed the Confederates, he pulled up his heavy guns from the rear and started a slow and deliberate siege of the town. But what worked for Washington didn't work for McClellan. It took weeks to shoulder the guns and mortars into position, and by April 22 Confederate forces led by General Joseph E. Johnston had reinforced the troops at Yorktown.[29]

McClellan still had not attacked Yorktown by the beginning of May, but over the previous six weeks had perfected his siege preparations with 13-inch, 10-inch, and 8-inch mortars, with stockpiles of ammunition and tens of thousands of soldiers ready to storm the walls once they had been breached. Johnston well understood his opponents' advantage and led his 55,000 troops in a retreat back towards Richmond. While McClellan called the capture of Yorktown with minimal bloodshed a success, Lincoln and history had deemed it a failure to seize an easy objective, in sum, a lost opportunity.[30]

McClellan and the Army of the Potomac resumed their march on toward Richmond. When the Army reached the Chickahominy River, engineers had to build makeshift bridges to cross. With only a small portion of the Union army across, rain began to swell the river and make the passage more difficult. The Confederates under Joe Johnston took this opportunity to attack. In what is known as the Battle of Seven Pines, several thousand casualties on both sides were inflicted, but the most significant result of this battle was that Johnston was injured with a bullet to the shoulder and a shell fragment to the chest.[31]

Thus, on June 1, General Robert E. Lee replaced Johnston as commander of the Army of Northern Virginia. This was the same General Lee that McClellan had beaten in one of the early battles of the war in western Virginia. In correspondence with Lincoln, McClellan was pleased with the assignment of his new adversary, and he expected an easy victory. However, his opinion was an incorrect assessment of Lee's capabilities, as history would soon show.[32]

Lee's strategic decisions and troop movements would exhibit an uncanny ability to predict the North's next move. He seemed to be able to get into the head of whatever Union general he was facing, and completely outwit his opponent. This could be because Lee, like McClellan, was a graduate of West Point, and thoroughly knew the Union Army's strategies and tactics . . . and how to defeat them. "Lee concluded that McClellan's attack would be a matter of regular approaches and siege guns, as at Yorktown, and confessed that the Confederates could not play that sort of game."[33]

McClellan waited for the weather to turn in his favor to implement his plan to take Richmond, while Lee prepared his troops for attack. The Seven Days Battles lasted from June 25 to July 1 and occurred on both sides of the Chickahominy River. While the Union forces were split approximately one third on the north side of the river and two thirds to the south, the Confederate forces were situated in the opposite ratio, such that Lee attacked the Union where his own numbers vastly outnumbered those of the enemy, and only feinted an attack on the other side. McClellan was convinced that his whole army was surrounded by overwhelming numbers and ordered a retreat to the James River. In actuality, the Union forces were numerically superior, and could have marched on Richmond and ended the war, but McClellan's hesitation and lack of nerve ended the operation. The Peninsula Plan was a complete failure.[34]

Antietam

McClellan's failures to take the fight to the enemy made Lincoln look for another general to lead the Army. Lincoln removed McClellan from command of the Army of the Potomac and put him in charge of the troops in Alexandria defending Washington. The President found an energetic, but boastful leader in General John Pope. Pope was given command of the Second, Third and Fifth Corps of the Army, renamed the Army of Virginia, and was immediately tested in battle. As Pope tangled with Lee in the Second Battle of Bull Run, McClellan resisted General-in-Chief Henry Halleck's requests to send reinforcements to Pope, stating that they were needed for the defense of the capital. Pope's forces were outmaneuvered and soundly defeated by the Confederates, suffering almost 14,000 casualties. With another disastrous Union defeat, Lincoln was again forced to make changes to the Army leadership. Left with choices between the devil he knew and the devil he didn't know, Lincoln went with the former and on September 2 presented McClellan with command of both Pope's Army of Virginia and the Army of the Potomac, reunited again under a single general.[35]

Antietam was the final battle McClellan oversaw as Commander of the Army of the Potomac. This battle is actually the summation of several clashes near the town of Sharpsburg, Maryland, as Union forces crossed several bridges over Antietam Creek to attack the Confederate positions. The day of the battle, September 17, 1862, was the bloodiest one-day battle in American history, with over 25,000 soldiers killed, injured, or missing as a result of the fighting. The battles were unnecessarily gruesome and bloody due to the ineptitude of the Union generals in the field. General Hooker had his men charge across a field of tall plants where the Confederates could tell exactly where they were, and opened fire as soon as they were in view. General Sumner attempted to fill a gap between the First and Twelfth Corps with Major General Sedgwick's Second Corps, instead of waiting until troops could be gathered for a coordinated assault, and almost half of his 5,000 troops were killed in minutes. General Burnside, who had enormous pork-chop sized sideburns (and became the namesake for the word), futilely sent his men across a bridge that was a clear shot for Confederate sharpshooters defensively positioned above the bridge behind an embankment; Burnside's men ended up being target practice.[36]

Military historians call the battle a draw, but two days after the fighting, McClellan telegraphed Halleck with news of a "Great Victory" by saying he had driven General Lee and the Confederates out of Maryland and back into Virginia. As it was, Lee withdrew to Virginia to escape from the overwhelming numbers of the Union army, and McClellan lost a valuable opportunity to demolish Lee's forces and bring an end to the war. Halleck informed Lincoln of McClellan's telegram and its contents. Lincoln was personally confounded, despondent, and upset by McClellan's lack of action and initiative. However, Lincoln found that with this victory, he was now able to announce his Emancipation Proclamation, which would take effect about 100 days later on January 1, 1863.[37]

The Emancipation Proclamation stated that every slave in every state that was in rebellion against the Union would be immediately and forever free. Politically, this allowed the Border States time to resolve the slavery question by themselves, and kept them strategically aligned with the North while at the same time striking a blow economically at the South, which was dependent upon slave labor for their cotton industry. In addition, the dual effect of the Southern loss of the battle and Lincoln's Emancipation Proclamation kept England from recognizing the Confederacy and joining the Southern cause.[38]

Fredericksburg

Another outcome of the battle of Antietam was the replacement of McClellan as Commander of the Army of the Potomac. Lincoln was completely frustrated by McClellan's inability to be an aggressive commander, and in November 1862, he replaced that impetuous general with General Burnside at the recommendation of Secretary of War Edwin Stanton and General Halleck. Burnside was presented with the orders by a special courier, General Buckingham, directly from Washington. Initially, Burnside refused the assignment, because he was a friend of General McClellan, but was then told that if he didn't accept the offer it would be given to General Hooker instead. Burnside, no friend of the ambitious Hooker, said he would accept. He then accompanied Buckingham to Army Headquarters and witnessed McClellan receive General Order 182, dated November 5, which removed him from command.[39]

Fredericksburg is the midpoint on a line the between Richmond, Virginia (the Confederate capital) and Washington, D.C. (the Union capital), so Burnside recommended it as the next target on the road to capturing the Confederate capital and ending the war. Fredericksburg is situated on high ground overlooking the Rappahannock River, with wood-covered hills behind it. The natural geography of the area made it an easily defendable city if attacked from the north. Burnside counted on the element of surprise, which was lost when his army had to wait 10 days for the promised pontoon bridges from Union Headquarters.

As the men of the Army of the Potomac waited, every night they could see more and more enemy campfires, clear evidence of a buildup of Confederate forces on the other side of the Rappahannock. On December 12 the pontoons arrived, and by the time the Union forces crossed the river they found themselves in a full-blown trap. The Confederate commanders thought that the Union assault was some sort of feint, and that another attack would come from a flank, but there was no ruse. Burnside sent wave after wave of soldiers into an open field in full view of the enemy on higher ground needlessly to their deaths; the Union lines swarmed an impregnable hill and wall behind which there were rows upon rows of Confederate soldiers raining lead upon them. After suffering 13,000 casualties to the South's 5,000 dead, wounded or missing, Burnside finally called off the battle at the end of the day, and under the cover of fog and darkness slipped back across the Rappahannock to the safety of the northern side of the river.[40]

After the defeat at Fredericksburg, Burnside took the Army of the Potomac up the Rappahannock looking for opportunities to attack Lee and the Army of Northern Virginia from the flank and rear. Meanwhile, Lincoln looked for his replacement. Burnside found difficulty in trying to mount a battle in the dead of winter. He attempted a flanking maneuver but the skies above opened with a downpour of water, turning the grounds into intractable mud – he had to call off his planned attack. Burnside knew his days were numbered so he offered Lincoln a choice: clean house within the Army ranks or accept his resignation. Lincoln chose the latter. Lincoln found Burnside's replacement in General "Fighting Joe" Hooker, one of Burnside's most vocal critics. Hooker charged Burnside with incompetence but also and said that the Lincoln Administration was idiotic. Additionally, Hooker stated that what was needed was a dictator to make things go better. Upon his promotion to Commander of the Army of the Potomac, Lincoln provided Hooker with a letter that noted he was aware of Hooker's statements and that he was being promoted not because of what he said, but in spite of it.[41]

Chancellorsville

Hooker devised a plan of attack that certainly had merit. He would use his numerical superiority to overwhelm the Confederate forces still in their winter quarters in the hills around Fredericksburg. At 120,000 soldiers, the Union Army was at least twice the size of the Confederate forces. In late April, Hooker left a third of his army near Fredericksburg and marched the other two thirds up the Rappahannock, taking the same route that Burnside had attempted three months earlier. This time the ground was solid and the weather was cooperating. Hooker's intent was to pin Lee's forces in a pincer, then squeeze the pincer together to destroy the Confederate Army and end the war. Upstream from Lee's army, Hooker took one third of his forces across the Rappahannock to Chancellorsville, and left one third on the other side of the river in reserve that could flow to either side of the pincer, as needed.[42]

By this time, General Robert E. Lee's scouts had determined the Union forces positions, and with General "Stonewall" Jackson's concurrence, decided to try to outflank Hooker's attempt to outflank them. With Hooker dug in at Chancellorsville to the north and Lee's forces positioned to the south, Jackson took over half of Lee's Army and marched them thirteen miles around to the west and attacked the Union forces at this weak flank. This unexpected attack completely surprised and confused the Union forces in the vicinity, forcing them into an immediate retreat towards Chancellorsville and Hooker's camp. Confederate artillery commanded by General Jeb Stuart started bombarding the Chancellorsville mansion, which was Hooker's headquarters, and Hooker was struck in the head by flying debris. With Hooker dazed and confused, there was not enough direction to provide a coordinated counterattack, and the Union forces fell back. Then, in what is probably one of the most significant and tragic cases of "friendly fire" in history, Stonewall Jackson was shot by Confederate troops who thought he and his aides were Union cavalry. Hooker's Army eventually withdrew back across the Rappahannock, thus another lost battle for the Union.[43]

As General Lee contemplated his victories at Chancellorsville and Fredericksburg, he surmised that — with so many casualties and loss of able leaders — too many more such "victories" and the Confederate cause would be lost. He could not afford a war of attrition. He would have to take his fight North to the Union and try to win the war by breaking the will of the Unionists. As he read the Northern papers, he saw the possibility of winning the war by winning enough battles and so demoralizing the North that the general populace would rise up to revolt against Lincoln's policies; thereby, allowing for a freed Confederacy. Lee was also counting on the bountiful Northern countryside to feed and supply his troops, as the Northern Virginia area had been completely decimated by the war.[44]

Lee left a portion of his army at Fredericksburg to both protect the Confederate capital and make it appear as if he was awaiting the next Union attack. Then, he led the majority of the Army of Northern Virginia on a northward trek through the Shenandoah Valley and across the Potomac River into Maryland. His target was Harrisburg, Pennsylvania, and from there he would be able to ravage the Northern countryside, either moving east toward Philadelphia or south to Washington. At least that was the plan. However, as usual with military plans, things did not go to form. The Confederate cavalry, which was supposed to scout the Union forces to keep Lee appraised of their whereabouts, had run into a skirmish with Union cavalry in the Battle of Brandy Station. This battle was a draw, but it had the effect of providing proof that Lee's army was on the move. Now that Lee's forces were out of the way, General Hooker wanted to drive south to attack and capture Richmond, but he was directed by Washington to move the Army of the Potomac northward to stay between the Confederate Army and Washington.[45]

Gettysburg

With Lee's forces on the move and a possible new front opening in the Northern states, Lincoln could little afford to gamble with naming another new general in command of the Army of the Potomac. But that is precisely what he did. He also could not afford the kind of bungled operation that occurred at Chancellorsville, and he no longer trusted Hooker's handling of the position. On June 27, Hooker was replaced by General George Meade. Within a few days, the new commander would lead his army through one of the greatest battles in American history.[46]

As the Union and Rebel forces converged on Gettysburg, the much-anticipated battle to end the war would continue for the first three days of July 1863, and incur over 51,000 casualties. The difference between this battle and prior battles of the war was that this one was located on Union ground, familiar to the Union soldiers. In addition, the Union soldiers held the high ground in a situation similar to that of Fredericksburg, but in reverse. This time the Army of the Potomac was in a defensive stronghold, and this time they were ready. In the first day of fighting, the Rebels attacked the northern flank of the Union line, which was closest to the town. The Union forces that had reached the town first, a First Division cavalry unit under Brigadier General John Buford, and Major General John Reynolds' First Corps, spent the early hours of the battle in a delaying action to provide time for the rest of Meade's army to arrive. Not long afterwards, the Union side was augmented with Major General Oliver Howard's Eleventh Corps. They held on as long as they could through a number of volleys and then fell back through the town and ran to the higher ground immediately south, an area called Cemetery Hill.[47]

The second day of the battle saw the Confederates attack the southern portion of the Union lines, around Big Round Top and Little Round Top, two of the highest vantage points in the hills around Gettysburg. Union General Dan Sickles had his men out of position about a mile ahead of the rest of the defensive forces, and that is where the Confederates attacked. Confederate General Hood could see that Little Round Top and Big Round Top were not occupied and tried to advance on those hills to cutoff Sickles' men from the Union lines. At the same time, Union General Warren directed men from General Sykes 5th Infantry to take the hill. Sykes courier met Colonel Strong Vincent and provided orders to "occupy that hill" (pointing at Little Round Top). Vincent ordered the 20th Maine Regiment under Colonel Joshua Chamberlain to secure the hill and hold it "at all costs." Just when it seemed that all was lost, Chamberlain ordered his men to affix their bayonets and charge the attacking Confederates. This charge swept the enemy off the hill and saved the day.[48]

Later during the second day of battle, the Confederates attacked the northern (Union right flank) portion of the Federal line around Culp's hill. Union commander General George Scott Green (descendent of Nathaniel Green of the Revolutionary War) had fortified their position with a log wall of breastworks that protected his forces from the attack. As night fell, the Confederate forces under General Dick Ewell continued the fight, and ended up with friendly fire in the darkness. The battle continued in the morning on the third day, which became the most momentous of the Civil War to date. General Lee had saved his best for last, with his plan being an all-out effort to break the middle of the Union's line of defense, thus splitting the Union army in two. It started out with an artillery barrage by 163 Rebel guns to soften up the Union defenses, then turned into a precise military operation of thousands of Confederate troops marching into the heart of the Union defensive line.[49]

What's known as "Pickett's Charge" started out like more of a military parade, as the soldiers were flying full colors and marching several men deep and over a mile wide down the hill and into the valley. It was like something out of the European theatre in Napoleonic times. As the Confederates funneled into a narrow gap in the valley, the soldiers would step in unison and maneuver to and through the gap. It was truly a sight to behold, until the Union cannons started bombarding the rows upon rows of troops. Lee had assumed his cannonade would eliminate and silence the Union artillery, but the Confederates had overshot their marks. The 119 Union cannons directed by Brigadier General Henry Hunt unleashed a torrential rain of solid lead balls and grapeshot into and through the Confederate lines. This completely demolished entire rows of soldiers and was as devastating a massacre as the Union's debacle at Fredericksburg. But Pickett's soldiers kept coming, and as they came into musket range each volley of Union guns would tear through the Confederate lines. Few of those thousands of Confederate soldiers actually reached the Union defenders, and when they did, they were either killed or captured. Lee watched in horror as his plans went down in ruin. This day was a terrible loss for the Confederate army and was as a complete and total Union victory as could have been hoped for by Meade. Afterwards, all the Rebels could do was nothing more than retreat back across the Potomac, back into familiar southern territory, to live and fight another day.[50]

Vicksburg

While Lee and Meade were squared off in one of the most consequential battles of the war, another battle was being waged in the West. This battle was for control of the waterways through the heart of the South, and it was at a key town situated on the mighty Mississippi River – Vicksburg, Mississippi. This town was of strategic importance, because it was the last remaining impediment to the Union's complete control of the Mississippi River. However, the city was a fortress almost impregnable from the river; it stood on a bluff overlooking a sharp bend in the river's course. Any ship passing by would have to slow down to navigate the bend and be vulnerable to the cannons pointing from the city's defenses over the river's breadth (the term sitting duck comes to mind). Also, it was just as intimidating to attack the city from the land around it, there being no dry land around from which to mount an attack owing to winter rains.[51]

Grant crossed the Mississippi River at Bruinsburg, 10 miles south of Grand Gulf and about 40 miles south of Vicksburg on April 30. Over the next three weeks he attacked Confederate forces in the area, starting with those stationed at Port Gibson. From there, his army moved on Raymond, and then attacked the Mississippi state capital in Jackson. The Confederate forces in Jackson under General Joe Johnston were overwhelmed by a Union force twice as large, and Johnston wired to President Jefferson Davis that he was too late to save Vicksburg. While in Jackson, the Union army destroyed anything in the town that would support Rebel war efforts. In a move foreshadowing his future war strategy, General Sherman would return to Jackson in July 1863, to send a message to the antebellum South by setting it ablaze.[52] The Union soldiers then marched on to battles at Champion's Hill and Big Black (a tributary of the Mississippi River), defeating enemy forces of 25,000 and 4,000 men, respectively. Finally, it was on to Vicksburg. Grant realized that a frontal assault on Vicksburg would not produce the desired result, so he decided to lay siege to the city.[53]

Although Grant's army had no siege guns, he received large caliber naval guns from Admiral Porter, delivered via the Mississippi River. Grant had the army engineers design parapets on a line 600 yards from the enemy that included sand bags and timber to protect the soldiers while off duty and walking or standing in the batteries. Grant also sent a division under General Blair to flush out any enemy forces within 45 miles of Vicksburg and to destroy all bridges capable of carrying enemy troops or weaponry into the Vicksburg area. During the course of the months-long siege, Grant's headquarters were visited by local Northern politicians, such as the Governor of Illinois, and several assemblymen from the Illinois legislature.[54]

After a month of the siege and with no supplies and no hope of reinforcement by Johnston, the Confederates surrendered the city. The Confederate commander, General Pemberton requested parole (allowed to return home in return for a promise to never take up arms again) for his soldiers, and Grant agreed. On July 4, 1863, one day after the end of the battle at Gettysburg, the Union had captured Vicksburg. Within two days of each other, the Union had two of the most significant victories of the war against the Confederates, and in another good sign they happened on Independence Day.[55]

Chickamauga

Another major front in the Western region was in the eastern half of Tennessee. Union General William Rosecrans had orders from Washington to push the Confederates out of Tennessee, with the objective of taking Chattanooga, a vital transportation center. As Rosecrans' forces moved southeast from Nashville, they encountered the Confederate Army of Tennessee, led by General Braxton Bragg, at the Battle of Murfreesboro. This battle ended in early January, 1863 and was essentially a draw. Convinced he needed more reinforcements, Rosecrans waited until June to make his next move. Lincoln and Secretary of War Stanton prevailed upon Rosecrans to take action toward the capture of Chattanooga, and on June 23, Rosecrans finally led the Army of the Cumberland to push Bragg and the Confederates all the way past the Tennessee River to Chattanooga. There Rosecrans planned his next move.[56]

In July, both Stanton and General Halleck in Washington urged Rosecrans to press the attack, but to no avail. In August, Rosecrans wrote a letter directly to Lincoln stating his rationale for waiting to engage the enemy, which sounded like excuses. Finally, on August 16, the Army of the Cumberland attacked the Confederate forces in Chattanooga. On September 9, Bragg and the Confederate Army of Tennessee evacuated the city and took to the hills and fields of northwest Georgia. Rosecrans followed the retreating Confederates into Georgia and was drawn into a trap at the Battle of Chickamauga Creek on September 19 and 20, 1863.[57]

General James Longstreet and 12,000 soldiers from the Army of Northern Virginia reinforced General Bragg's troops at Chickamauga. Longstreet's men punched through the center of Rosecrans' line, and the Union soldiers retreated. Rosecrans led the retreat back to Chattanooga, but the northern end of the line had held. General George Thomas, who would later be named "the Rock of Chickamauga," held his ground around Snodgrass Hill. No matter how many times Longstreet's men attacked the hill, Thomas' troops repulsed them. The fighting went on into the evening, but as darkness fell, Thomas realized that he could not defend that ground alone. So during the night, General Thomas led his troops in a retreat back to Chattanooga to join the rest of Rosecrans' army.[58]

Lincoln, frustrated with Rosecrans' defeat, and concerned about losing the valuable and strategic town of Chattanooga, decided to reinforce Rosecrans as soon as possible with troops from the Army of the Potomac. Members of his cabinet convinced Lincoln to send troops west by rail, and over 20,000 soldiers, and horses, cannons, and supplies were transported to Chattanooga in 11 days. Lincoln was also concerned about making a change to the command structure, because both Rosecrans and his chief of staff were popular Ohio military officers, and the Ohio elections were coming up. But after the October elections, he promoted General Grant, fresh from his victory at Vicksburg, to the position of Commander of the Western Forces overseeing the Army of Ohio, the Army of the Cumberland, and the Army of Tennessee. Lincoln gave Grant the option to keep or replace Rosecrans, and Grant named

General Thomas as commander of the Army of the Cumberland, removing Rosecrans from command.[59]

Missionary Ridge

The Confederate forces under General Bragg held all the high ground around Chattanooga, which the Federal army occupied, but failed to cut the supply lines keeping the Union forces alive. When Grant arrived in Chattanooga, he found the enemy in possession of Lookout Mountain, overlooking the Tennessee River and the city from the south, Tunnel Hill, overlooking the Tennessee River and the city from the east, and Missionary Ridge, the hills connecting those two end points with a view of the city directly below. Because Missionary Ridge was the easiest to defend and the toughest to attack, Grant decided to start at each endpoint. In the first stage of the battle, Grant assigned General Hooker's men to attack Lookout Mountain. Hooker was the infamous General from the Chancellorsville debacle, but on this day, fortune would be with him. The Confederates were insufficient in number to hold the position, and Hooker's forces (three times as many as the opponent had) swept the enemy off the hill. At the end of the fighting, the Union flag were raised on the hill, and the next morning, old glory was there for all to see.[60]

On November 25, the next day of the battle, General Sherman's men attacked Tunnel Hill. Sherman's men had a much tougher time than Hooker's, and Grant was concerned about troop movement by the enemy. So, Grant directed General Thomas, the Rock of Chickamauga, to attack Missionary Ridge, in order to keep the Confederates from reinforcing Tunnel Hill (although Grant thought he was seeing troop movement from the Ridge to Tunnel Hill, none was actually occurring). Thomas' men were ordered to engage the enemy who were dug in at the foot of Missionary Ridge. In a scene reminiscent of Pickett's Charge (but opposite from the perspective of the combatants), the Union forces came out with flags flying and lines dressed in a two-mile wide stretch of humanity.[61]

As they battled and overtook the men in the trenches at the bottom of the ridge, they found that there was still lead raining down upon their heads from higher up the hills. Slowly at first, and then in a wave, the Union soldiers rushed up the hill to silence the guns above. As more and more boys in blue flew up the hill, it looked from the Confederate perspective as a great wave rushing toward them, so they started to run from their perch at the top of the ridge down the other side and away from the battle. It was over before anyone knew it, and it was a complete and total Union domination. The Yankees celebrated with captured Confederate battle flags and jumping up and down on Confederate cannons, inebriated with the joy of victory. The North would be in total control of Chattanooga, and the path to Georgia and the Deep South was now wide open. But before the final phase of the war started, it was time to convene to winter quarters and resupply and reenergize a depleted army.[62]

Wilderness and Spotsylvania

Ulysses S. Grant was promoted to Lieutenant General in March 1864. Up to that date only one other General in U. S. history had held that rank, and his name was none other than George Washington. While the newspapers and many politicians called for Grant to become the next President of the United States, he wanted nothing to do with it. General Grant felt he already had enough responsibility with just being in command of all of the Union's armed forces. Personally, Lincoln was much relieved to find that Grant did not covet his position, and that put him in that much higher esteem in Lincoln's eyes, and allowed him to trust Grant that much more. He finally felt comfortable handing over all responsibility for ending the war in Grant's capable hands.[63]

In Grant, Lincoln finally found a general who had a vision similar to his own for ending the war. He wasn't just focused on capturing the Confederate capital of Richmond. Grant realized that even if the capital surrendered, he would still have to deal with the Confederate Army. He intended to bring all of the Union forces to bear on eliminating the Confederate Army from the field. His strategy to accomplish that goal was to have Sherman chase Johnston's forces through the South, and he would chase Lee's army in the East. Grant knew that with his numerical superiority and vast resources in supplies and material it was "just a matter of time" before the Union forces would win.[64]

Unfortunately for Grant, he would not win his first battles in his new position as commander of the Army. Grant would face Lee in his first battle in the Wilderness, that area near Chancellorsville where Stonewall Jackson had shocked Hooker's troops in May 1863 and overrun the Union position. About a year later, on May 5 and 6, 1864, Grant would return to these hallowed grounds, and try to get the Army of the Potomac to redeem itself for its prior failures. In these two days of brutal fighting, more leaders from both sides would be cut down or wounded. A Union hero from Gettysburg, General James Wadsworth, would take a bullet to the head while trying to rally his troops. The Confederate General Longstreet repeated Jackson's success, and in an eerily similar situation, was then also shot by "friendly fire" — this time, though, Longstreet survived, but it took him eight months to return to action. Grant was only going be as successful as the strength of his leadership team, and with the flawed leadership of his generals (Burnside and Meade), it wouldn't be very long for him to figure out that changes would need to be made.[65]

After the defeat at the Wilderness, Grant tried to move his troops south to get between Lee's troops and Richmond. Grant thought that would bring Lee out to fight, but Lee anticipated his move and beat him to the punch. At the next battle in

Spotsylvania, the Confederates rushed to gain the higher ground and get there first. Lee's forces were able to set up defensive works and prepare for the inevitable attack by Grant's men. Spotsylvania Court House was only eight miles southeast of Chancellorsville and was not much more than a crossroads. However, it was the scene of another deadly and bloody battlefield, as the armies of the Union and the Confederates repeatedly dealt blow after blow upon each other like two heavyweight prizefighters. Although Grant would continue to push the battle upon the enemy, Lee was successful in countering his moves and effectively negating Grant's superiority in numbers by engaging in defensive "trench warfare" – which would become a standard battlefield method in the years ahead.[66]

Atlanta and Sherman's March

While Grant was fighting Lee in Virginia, Sherman battled General Joe Johnston in Georgia. Johnston fought in a defensive posture, being outnumbered two to one, and slowly retreated towards Atlanta one move at a time. Each time the two armies came in contact, Johnston's troops seemed to be entrenched in a good defensive position. And every time that Sherman tried to hold a front and swing a smaller force around Johnston's flank Johnston would anticipate the move and withdraw to the next defensive position. At one point, Sherman stated that the whole state of Georgia must be laced with Johnston's trenches.[67]

This defensive maneuvering was working quite well, causing frustration and many casualties to the Union side, when inexplicably Confederate President Jefferson Davis replaced Johnston with General Hood on July 17. Hood was a fighter, but took risky chances, and was a rash and unpredictable foe. Sherman was only too happy with the change in Confederate leadership, as he knew he would have the advantage. In less than two days' time, Hood took the fight to Sherman. With his superior numbers and firepower, Sherman predictably was able to fend off Hood's attack and severely weakened Hood's army. In about a week, Hood lost over one third of his forces (about 20,000 men), and it was only a matter of time before Atlanta would fall. One month later, on September 2, the Union army marched into Atlanta.[68]

Atlanta was a major railway hub and communication center for the rest of the South. It was also the main manufacturing center for war supplies for the Confederates. When Hood destroyed an ammunition train in the city to keep it from falling into enemy hands, the explosions were heard 50 miles away. What Hood didn't blow up or burn before he evacuated, Sherman dismantled or destroyed to keep the Confederates from being able to wage war against the North. All the railroads in and around Atlanta were wrecked, with the rails heated up and twisted to be unusable, some wrapped around nearby trees. All machinery and production equipment were smashed, boilers were aerated, furnaces broken, smokestacks torn down, all to ensure they were never used again against the North. In the process, some buildings caught fire. This seems to have been enhanced by arsonists, for whose arrest General Slocum offered a reward of $500 to any soldier. In the end, over 1,800 Atlanta buildings burned. By the time the Union army marched out of the city, there was not much of it left.[69]

Sherman then continued this strategy throughout the rest of Georgia, destroying all the war-making capability of the Confederates, and eviscerating the South's will to fight. His army marched the length of Georgia from Atlanta to Savannah, burning and destroying everything in its path and stripping the land of all food and valuables. The Union army would create "Sherman hairpins" out of the Confederate railroad tracks by twisting the rails into large bows. Just before Christmas, 1864, Sherman made a Christmas present to Lincoln of the city of Savannah. His letter to the President stated, "I beg to present you as a Christmas gift, the city of Savannah, with one hundred and fifty guns and plenty of ammunition, also about twenty-five thousand bales of cotton."[70]

Petersburg and Appomattox

Back in Virginia, Grant and Lee had fought battles across the northeast part of the state, from The Wilderness and Spotsylvania to North Anna and Cold Harbor. Grant kept trying to outflank Lee, to rush past the Confederate forces and push through to Richmond. However, Lee kept anticipating Grant's moves, would get to important points first, then dig in. For the most part, Lee "outgeneraled" Grant in these battles, and the Union lost more troops at each battle than the Confederates. But the Union had more troops to lose, and if it were a war of attrition, then Grant and the Union would eventually win that war. Both armies wound up at Petersburg in June 1864 and dug in for the final time. There they stayed for the next nine months. Each side would occasionally attack the other, but with each side having stout defenses, there was no clear advantage. It was a classic stalemate and would stay that way for a long time.[71]

General Sherman, after making a present of Savannah to Lincoln, marched north toward Columbia, South Carolina. To get there, Sherman's army had to build its own roads through the swamps and lowlands of South Carolina. But the Union army took the capital, their next aim looking upon Charleston. Confederate troops had left Columbia before Sherman's troops arrival, setting cotton stores on fire so they wouldn't fall into Union hands. The Union troops arrived on February 17, 1865 and freed the remaining slaves and prisoners. Wind was blowing the flaming cotton everywhere like tinder, and General Oliver commanded a fire brigade to avert total disaster, but not before more than a third of Columbia burned. The Union army then moved on to Charleston. Sherman's troops showed Charleston no mercy, and the city was burned, because the Federals saw the place as the origination of the insurrection. Union soldiers took pride in capturing the town that had fired the first shots of the war. Sherman's army then fought its way on through North Carolina, with a battle at Bentonville against General Joe Johnston on March 21. After that final battle with Johnston's troops in the Carolinas, the Union army took the town of Goldsboro, North Carolina, with its Confederate supplies and reinforcements. This marked the end of Sherman's March as a military operation.[72]

At Petersburg, the Confederate army had been losing soldiers through desertion at a rate of hundreds per day. Over the course of the nine-month siege, Lee's Army of Northern Virginia's troop strength was drastically reduced by desertions, and during the period of June 1864 to March 1865, fighting had cost the combined armies almost 75,000 casualties. The remaining Confederate soldiers had to be stretched out over a longer and longer perimeter, and Grant continually tried to outflank Lee's defenses. Finally, on April 1, Grant attacked the middle of Lee's defenses, which had been stretched like a rubber band along the almost 35 miles of trenches around Petersburg, and he broke through. Petersburg was taken the next day and Lee sent word to Jefferson Davis to evacuate the capital at Richmond.[73]

Davis' reply to Lee that he needed more time to evacuate the capital was responded to by Lee with an even more urgent message. Lee's response reached Davis while he was attending Sunday services in Richmond at St. Paul's Episcopal Church: Lee's telegram stated that the capital evacuation should occur by nightfall.[74] The Confederate government frantically gathered their valuables and boarded the last trains of the Richmond & Danville line and headed south. As was customary, the evacuating defending troops destroyed anything of value to the invading army and set fires to rations, warehouses, and bridges. On April 3, Union troops marched into Richmond and immediately formed fire brigades to keep the city from burning to the ground. In a turnaround from the destruction of other Southern capitals, Union forces became protectors of the city, putting down a riot and eliminating the looting and arson. On April 4, 1865, President Lincoln toured the vanquished Confederate capital, while crowds of enthusiastic African Americans followed and tried to meet their emancipator.[75]

Lee's army and the Confederate government was on the run. Over the next few days, Lee tried to evade the pursuing and encircling Union army. On April 6, the Federals caught up to him at Saylor's Creek and about 25 percent of Lee's men were killed, wounded or captured. Lee attempted to escape again to Appomattox Station, where a train with railcars packed with supplies awaited, but Grant's army got there first. Surrounded and with no chance to win against a totally superior force, Lee surrendered to Grant at the McLean House in Appomattox, Virginia on April 9, 1965. In an offer of respect to General Lee and his troops, Grant generously offered parole to the vanquished, and even allowed the Confederate Officers to keep their pistols and horses. The next morning throughout the North there were booming celebrations of cannon fire, bells tolling from spires, and flags flying from every flagpole. The Union was now forever bound and forever free.[76]

CHAPTER 7

The Great Emancipator

Abraham Lincoln was not born a crusader. He did not come into the world with a mission to free the blacks. He was not an abolitionist. He was a politician and a realist. It took him a long time to become the man whose name would be so clearly associated with ending slavery in the United States. He would eventually become known as the Great Emancipator, and he would thoroughly deserve that title. But it was a long and drawn-out process of change, because Lincoln grew, learned and matured throughout his years as a farm hand, clerk, businessman, lawyer, politician, Congressman, and President and Commander-in-Chief.

One of Lincoln's first experiences with slavery was during his 1828 trip down the Mississippi River to New Orleans at age 19. He was commissioned by James Gentry to help him and his son Allen navigate over three months a flatboat of goods from farms of mid-Illinois down a thousand miles of the wide Mississippi to the port city near the river's confluence with the Gulf of Mexico. This was a new experience for a young farm hand; the three voyagers witnessed chained slaves heading to the cotton plantations of the South and listened to the babel of languages and dialects from different races and nationalities in a cacophony of sound. Two years later, another entrepreneur named Denton Offutt commissioned Lincoln, his stepbrother John Johnston, and their friend John Hanks to make a similar flatboat run down to New Orleans. Hanks later recounted that on this second trip to New Orleans, Lincoln was very upset by a slave auction he witnessed.[1]

Lincoln was enthralled by the words of the Declaration of Independence, that all men are created equal, and by the ideal and promise of that statement. But as a politician and a realist, he understood that the institution of slavery was embedded in this country and was a part of the customs and culture of the South for hundreds of years. He continually struggled with what seemed like an insurmountable objective and impossible dream, to rid the country of the "peculiar institution" as it was sometimes called that had so intertwined the social, political and cultural fabric of America. As Lincoln moved along his path of increasing responsibility and significance in his political career, he proposed different methods and strategies to slowly eliminate slavery in the United States, from emancipation in Washington, D.C., to colonization in the Caribbean or Africa, to using the financial capacity of the federal government to pay slaveowners for the liberation of each slave. But even then, he had his doubts that the institution would be eliminated in his lifetime.[2]

The forces that forged a legend from an ordinary and humble beginning were constant challenges and disappointments combined with extensive self-analysis and reflection. As one looks at the timeline of Lincoln's progression in self-realization and self-mastery, you can see that the Lincoln from each era or experience is different from the one before. With respect to his stance on slavery, the three most critical and influential periods were his experience in Congress (as an Illinois Representative), his failed bid for a Senatorial seat (the Douglas debates), and his experience as President and Commander-in-Chief (during the Civil War).

As Congressman

When Lincoln was a member of Congress and the Illinois state Representative for the Seventh District, he was a devout

Whig party member and towed the party line. When it came to the subject of slavery, the Whig party line was to keep slavery out of the new territories, and to maintain the Compromise of 1820. The spirit of compromise and reconciliation with the Southern slave states was also maintained in the Missouri Compromise of 1850, which was negotiated and passed through Congress by the politician who Lincoln most looked up to – Henry Clay. Clay was a Whig leader and Senator whose goal was to keep the country together. When Clay died in 1852, Lincoln was one of the people who eulogized Clay in services held in Illinois. Near the end of Lincoln's only term as a Congressman, he attempted to enter legislation to end slavery in the District of Columbia; however, that legislation never received the backing it needed to be submitted, and it went nowhere. Slavery would eventually become outlawed in the District of Columbia during his first term as President (in April 1862).[3]

At the conclusion of the 1858 Illinois Republican State Convention where Lincoln was nominated as the party's Senatorial candidate for Congress, Lincoln delivered an acceptance speech that became known as the "house divided" speech. This speech did a lot to make the abolitionist element of the national Republican Party satisfied with his candidacy and his position on slavery. It also made a believer of Frederick Douglass, a free black who was a famous and outspoken anti-slavery critic of the government. In this speech Lincoln makes the visceral statement, "A house divided against itself cannot stand," – using the words of Jesus in Mark 3:25. He goes on to explain the statement to mean that the country cannot remain perpetually half free and half slave, but that it will eventually become either all free states or all slave states. Lincoln spends the rest of the speech explaining how recent events came to forge the situation of that moment and clarifying and crystallizing the argument for the Republican cause as contrasted to that of the Democratic candidate for U. S. Senator, Stephen A. Douglas.[4]

The Great Debates

The debates between Lincoln and Douglas were more than a race for a political office. They represented a collective discourse on the positions of the pro-slavery forces and the anti-slavery forces. Although Douglas was taking the position of allowing the states to choose if they wanted to be free states or to be slave states (the self-direction philosophy), he still held beliefs of the majority of white racists, and in his speeches, he was promoting the views of the pro-slavery movement.

The seven debates in Illinois during that summer and fall of 1858 were attended by thousands of citizens and written about in newspapers across the country. Douglas kept to the same speech that he repeated with slight variation throughout the seven debates. Lincoln felt he had no need to repeat himself, because as a voracious reader and consumer of newspaper content he realized that he could count on people attending the debates would have read about the previous debates in their local newspapers. He also viewed the newspapers' documentation of the debates as a continuous dialogue on the subject. Lincoln modified his speeches to provide responses to the discussions and issues raised in the previous speeches. Just as today's politicians do, Douglas kept trying to play on people's fears. But Lincoln, trying to bring people from darkness into the light, kept speaking truth to power.[5]

Ottawa

The first debate was held on August 21 in Ottawa, Illinois, a small town with a population of about 7,000 in the upper middle part of the state. It was located on the Illinois River near the Illinois-and-Michigan Canal that linked North/South waterways to the Mississippi River and the Gulf of Mexico, and to East/West waterways through the Great Lakes out the St. Lawrence River to the Atlantic Ocean. Back in those days, politics was one of the main sources of entertainment, there not being much competition from other sources. People poured into the area from miles around, and the attendance was estimated to be 12,000-15,000. All the hotels were filled and people were sleeping on any accommodation they could find. Lincoln arrived by train and was brought to the debate stage by a carriage with the local politicians in it. Douglas arrived by a carriage drawn by several magnificent white horses, and he would maintain that level of showmanship throughout the debates.[6]

Per the agreements made before the beginning of the debates, Douglas had the first hour to speak, then Lincoln would speak for an hour and a half, and then Douglas would finish for the last 30 minutes. Douglas started out by describing his recent congressional record and detailing his involvement with the Kansas-Nebraska Act. He then described Lincoln's record in Congress. He ridiculed Lincoln for his opposition to the Mexican War during his single term as Congressman, which was a popular war at that time. Douglas also denounced Lincoln for his opposition to the Dred Scott decision, and stated that Lincoln supported equality between the races, which would lead to citizenship for Negroes.[7]

Lincoln's appearance on the stage, when compared to his opponent Douglas, could not have been more of a contrast. Lincoln was 6 foot 4 inches tall and ungainly, all arms and elbows, legs and knees. Douglas was short and squat; about 5 foot 3 inches tall, weighing in at 170 pounds. When Lincoln finally had his opportunity to talk, he did so in his folksy way, combining facts and data with humor and wit. He was not bombastic like his fiery foe, but was calm and collected, and spoke in softer tones. He sometimes made fun of himself to make a point, but mostly used humor to offset Douglas' barbs. Douglas, however, did get in the last word. His response to Lincoln's speech was a continued attack on Lincoln's stand on the issues of the day, and on his record while in office. However, that did not affect the crowd's response to Lincoln in this anti-slavery portion of the state. Lincoln's supporters enjoyed his performance so much that when the debate was over, they carried him off on their shoulders.[8]

Freeport

About a week after the first debate, the second debate occurred in Freeport, Illinois, north of Ottawa almost at the Wisconsin-Illinois state line. Freeport was another small Illinois town of about 7,000, and again the crowd for the debate numbered about 15,000. This time, Lincoln would speak first and then have the last word after Douglas' hour and a half speech. Lincoln's supporters were concerned that he hadn't come out strong enough in the first debate, and they urged him to strike the first blow then continue attacking. They came up with some questions for Lincoln to ask Douglas, which would hopefully put Douglas on the defensive.[9]

The four questions were an attempt by Lincoln and his advisers to go on the offensive. The first question was intended to put Douglas on the spot by making him state whether or not he would support a pro-slavery Kansas state constitution, which would lose him votes from the Republican fence sitters. The second question was intended to trip up Douglas on a legalistic interpretation of territory versus state versus federal powers and put Douglas in a box about "popular sovereignty" in light of the Dred Scott decision. The third question was a hypothetical regarding the finality of Supreme Court decisions versus the will of the people via voting rights. The fourth question turned Douglas's question to Lincoln back on him from the perspective of the expansion of slavery – was Douglas in favor of expanding slavery into any and/or all new territories that the United States might own?[10]

Lincoln came out strong with answers to the seven questions Douglas had asked Lincoln at the first debate in Ottawa.

Lincoln's answers to the first five of the seven questions were explicit denials of Douglas' accusations that Lincoln was an unabashed and unapologetic abolitionist. His response kept the door open to compromise and negotiation on the issues of the fugitive slave law, the admission of slave states, the abolition of slavery in the District of Columbia, and the prohibition of the slave trade between states. However, on Question Six Lincoln was adamant that he was pledged to the prohibition of slavery in all U.S. Territories. Finally, to Question Seven, he responded that he would not oppose acquisition of a U.S. territory before the question of slavery therein was resolved. He also went further into clarifying his previous responses by saying that he answered the questions in the manner that they were asked, and provided some follow-up descriptions of his thoughts on those issues. Then, he went after Douglas by asking the four questions he was given from his support team.[11]

Douglas responded to the four questions, chastising Lincoln for making him say in his response the same things he has been saying all along on the campaign trail. He reminded Lincoln of the role he played in the Senate in requiring a minimum population for a state to constitute itself as a free or slave state. The author of "self-determinism" when it came to state's rights on the slavery question, Stephen Douglas reminded Lincoln again that his preference for new territories would be that if any new lands were acquired by Unites States expansion, they should also be able to determine their own path. Then he again went on the attack. He called Lincoln a "Black Republican" for his anti-slavery stance, as if it were a degrading insult. He accused Lincoln of being a friend and confidant of Frederick Douglass, the former slave and well-known black abolitionist. He said that Lincoln was responsible for "Abolitionizing" the Whig party and turning it into a party of Black Republicans. Douglas quoted the platform of the Republican party as it was defined in their organization in 1854, and he accused Lincoln of denying or backing away from those principles in his responses to the seven Ottawa questions. Douglas then derided Lincoln for his "house divided" speech and asked Lincoln how he could say the country must be all free or all slave to survive, a condition clearly against the doctrine of the United States as the founding fathers devised it, with both free and slave states?[12]

Jonesboro

The third debate was about three weeks later in Jonesboro, Illinois, a small town located at the southernmost tip of the state. This area was called "little Egypt" because it was shaped like an inverted pyramid between Kentucky and Missouri (both were slave states). The area was more like the South than the North, and blacks were hated there. Douglas was completely at home in this pro-slavery portion of the state. He started out this speech almost exactly as he did in the first speech, explaining the history of the Whig and Democratic parties and the recent national politics prior to 1854. He also went on to accuse Lincoln of making a deal with Senator Trumbull to get Trumbull elected in 1856. Finally, he repeated the crucial portion of Lincoln's "house divided" speech. He then accused Lincoln of inviting a war between the North and the South for whichever policy and institutions would rule – those of the slave states or those of the free states.[13]

Lincoln, whose father ultimately left Kentucky because he didn't like slavery in that state, was born in Kentucky not far from the area in which he and Douglas now stood in debate and felt he was familiar with the people and their customs. However, the area was overwhelmingly Democratic, and he knew he had little chance of changing the minds or hearts of the people there. Lincoln was also aware that every speech was documented in the papers, and he was very measured and careful with his words. His language was very specific, and he clearly laid out his opposition to Douglas's Kansas-Nebraska Act. Lincoln also explained the history of that Act and why it was actually the cause of the slavery "agitation" in the country. Lincoln's position was that slavery was and had been on the road to eventual extinction because of the limitation by the Missouri Compromise to keep it out of the new territories north of the southern border of Missouri.[14] However, as Lincoln explained, the Kansas-Nebraska Act essentially *repealed* the Missouri Compromise by making *every* new territory potentially a new slave state.[15]

The next part of Lincoln's speech dealt with the party platform that Douglas accused Lincoln of supporting in the Freeport debate. Lincoln's reply sharply contrasted with Douglas's speech at Freeport implying Lincoln was an abolitionist and stated that the platform Douglas referred to in his speech did not reflect the platform he signed up to when he agreed to become the Republican candidate for Senator. In fact, Douglas was wrongly applying a nearly abolitionist platform to a Republican candidate. It was Lincoln's way of casting doubt on Douglas's words in a manner similar to a legal argument in a court of law – to get the jury on your side and convince them of the truth and righteousness of your position.[16]

The majority of the remainder of Lincoln's speech dealt with Douglas's so-called "Freeport Doctrine" – Douglas's position on slavery – the name having been given it by the newspapers after the Freeport debate. In Freeport, what Douglas said in response to Lincoln's question on popular sovereignty in light of the Dred Scott decision by the Supreme Court was that it didn't matter what the Supreme Court says – what matters is what the local police enforces and regulates in each state.[17] Here Lincoln was challenging that response by saying that the Supreme Court's decision was that "any congressional prohibition of slavery in the territories was unconstitutional"[18] because the Constitution recognizes slaves as property, and the Constitution doesn't allow property being taken away without due process.

Charleston

The fourth debate was held on September 18 in Charleston, Illinois, a town with which Lincoln was very familiar on account of having lived there after his father moved the family from Indiana. The town was in the middle of the eastern half of the state and was a critical area for both candidates. At this debate, the crowds again swelled to between 12,000 and 15,000. Once again it was Lincoln's turn to go first and then get in the last word. Lincoln, having been constantly berated by Douglas with racial slurs about his equality leanings and now having been labeled a "Black Republican" and referred to by Douglas as an "abolitionist," fought back by making his own statements about equality. He may have made these comments for political expediency, or he may have been trying to be consistent with the current state law. Whatever the reason, the start of the fourth debate was an unexpected moment of blunt statements from the candidate for Senator. These are some of the most controversial comments by Lincoln that have ever been documented – not at that time, because what he said then reflected the views and sentiments of a majority of whites in the country, but from the perspective of history and his legacy. He said, "I am not, nor ever have been in favor of bringing about in any way the social and political equality of the white and black races, … I am not nor ever have been in favor of making voters or jurors of Negroes, nor of qualifying them to hold office, nor to intermarry with white people; and I will say in addition to this that there is a physical difference between the white and black races which I believe will forever forbid the two races living together on terms of social and political equality."[19]

Lincoln then went into the main thrust of his speech, which dealt with the question regarding Douglas's involvement in attempting to get Kansas entered into the Union as a slave state. Senator Lyman Trumbull had made accusations about Douglas, and Lincoln spent much of his speech quoting Trumbull's points and Douglas's responses to them. He consumed the majority of his hour speech on this one topic, which also questioned Douglas's true feelings towards popular sovereignty, and was surprised when the moderator said he only had three minutes left to wrap up.[20]

Lincoln's final words before Douglas's turn were an accusation that Douglas had changed the wording of the Kansas-Nebraska Act to strike out the provision requiring the Constitution of the State of Kansas be ratified by the people prior to the acceptance of Kansas into the Union. In effect, Lincoln was siding with Trumbull, in Trumbull's charge against Douglas that he was deliberately trying to make Kansas a slave state.[21]

Douglas's reply answered Lincoln's charge of the Trumbull accusation concerning the Kansas-Nebraska Act; Douglas denied it thoroughly. He asked the audience to consider that if the charges were true then why weren't they brought up during the debate of the Kansas-Nebraska Act in Congress? He accused Lincoln of trying to ride into Congress on the back of Trumbull and his lies. Douglas then quoted the *Congressional Globe* multiple times where language specific to the Nebraska Act was entered into the record, and used those quotes to discredit Trumbull's charges while at the same time implying that Lincoln was also guilty of falsehoods by repeating Trumbull's words. Douglas then countered Lincoln's charge with a conspiracy charge against Trumbull of falsifying records regarding the removal of the requirement of the ratification of the State Constitution statement in the Nebraska Act. He further went on to state that the only reason why Trumbull was bringing up these charges against him was to distract from Lincoln's Black Republicanism. Here again he accused Lincoln of attempting to "abolitionize" the Republican Party. Finally, he took the audacious track of claiming that the Republican State Convention during which Lincoln was unanimously nominated as the candidate for Senator was a sham. He claimed that Lincoln was selected as a payback for giving Trumbull the votes he needed to win the nomination for Senator two years previously. He then reiterated that Lincoln and Trumbull were turning the old Whigs and Democrats into abolitionists.[22]

Lincoln's response to Douglas was spirited and humorous. He first clarified his earlier response to Douglas that indeed he was not in favor of Negro citizenship, and he goes on to say that he thinks the states should choose their position on this, not the Supreme Court (Illinois already had a statute that forbad Negro citizenship). Next, he pointed out that Douglas was complaining about Lincoln bringing up the Trumbull charges that were two years old, but Douglas was telling audiences about positions he took when he was in Congress 10 years earlier! He then poked fun at Douglas for his reading of the *Congressional Globe,* where he was quoted as removing the requirement for ratification of the State Constitution in the Kansas-Nebraska Act, and said that this did not mean he didn't put that requirement into the bill in the first place (which was what Trumbull was saying). Lincoln compared that to him telling someone in the audience that he was not wearing a hat — did it make Lincoln a liar if the person in the audience put his hat back on?[23]

The biggest revelation from the Charleston debate, besides Lincoln's position on the "Negro equality" question, was the surprising strength of Lincoln's arguments against Douglas' experienced debate talents and tactics. After the fourth of the seven debates were completed, being more than halfway through the experiment, Lincoln was not only holding his own, but in some people's opinions he was actually winning! It was truly an epic tale of David versus Goliath (not physically, but metaphorically), and David was coming out on top. After the debate, two polls were conducted on separate trains (the only convenient method to poll at that time), and one was 55% Lincoln versus 45% Douglas, while the other was 59% Lincoln versus 41% Douglas.[24]

Galesburg

The fifth debate was held on October 7, in Galesburg, Illinois, in front of the largest crowd to date (some estimated it to be as many as 20,000 people). Galesburg was appropriately named, because before the debate started the wind was blowing so hard across the open town square where the debate was planned that they had to move the debate platform next to a building at Knox College. The three-story classroom building blocked the winds, but made it difficult to get onto the stage, so one of the windows in the building was used as an entrance to the platform. Lincoln entered the building and upon exiting the window onto the platform said, "Well, at last I have gone through college."[25]

Once again, Douglas spoke first and would have final comments after Lincoln's response. However, this time Douglas was showing signs of wear and tear of the tour and the pressure to perform. This was his worst performance; his voice was hoarse and his energy was low. He was fighting bronchitis with the bottle and losing the battle. He stood on the platform with a box of throat lozenges and pushed through to present his arguments. Douglas began with his defense of the Kansas-Nebraska bill, and again proclaimed the legitimacy of the "self-determinism" doctrine for states' rights. Popular Sovereignty was his mantra and he repeated it again and again. He stated that states should be free to choose if they want to be free or slave states, and he would serve to protect that right. If one state allowed slaves and the neighboring state did not, then he would expect the state's laws to prevail and a slave owner should not take his property across the state line, in the same manner that someone who sells liquor should not transport it into a state that has prohibition laws.[26]

Lincoln, for all his disadvantages of not having his own railroad car (versus Douglas), traveling in those conditions without the support of his wife and family (versus Douglas), and fighting an uphill battle against an established and well-known

Senator, came to Galesburg feeling good and hitting his stride. He started his speech by saying that he was not going to respond to everything Douglas said. The reason for this was that all of his previous speeches were in print for people in the community to read them, and understand and acquaint themselves with his opinions. What he wanted to say in this speech was that, from the perspective of the Declaration of Independence, the right to pursue life, liberty, and the pursuit of happiness was equal for all races.[27]

Lincoln followed this train of thought to point out that the decision to allow a new territory or a new state to become a slave state or a free state is actually a moral question. He continued this argument by saying that he is only talking about the new states that are considering that question, not the states where slavery already existed. He said, " . . . in legislating for new countries, where it does not exist, there is no just rule other than that of moral and abstract right!"[28] Lincoln shone the light on the difference between himself and Douglas – and the difference between the Republicans and the Democrats – by pointing that in every speech Douglas made and every statement he uttered, Douglas denies that there is anything wrong with slavery. Lincoln pointed out that if you read Douglas's views on the subject of slavery, you would see that Douglas does not care how it is voted on in a territory or state, which is all right if you believe it is not wrong. But if you do believe that slavery is wrong, then how can you say that someone has a right to do wrong?[29]

Lincoln went on to say, "Now, I confess myself as belonging to that class in the country who contemplate slavery as a moral, social and political evil, having due regard for its actual existence amongst us and the difficulties of getting rid of it in any satisfactory way, and to all the constitutional obligations which have been thrown about it; but, nevertheless, desire a policy that looks to the prevention of it as a wrong, and looks hopefully to the time when as a wrong it may come to an end."[30]

Douglas's response to Lincoln was a repeat of his earlier claims that Lincoln says one thing in one part of the state and a different thing in another part of the state. He was implying that Lincoln pandered to whatever crowd he was speaking to, in order to get their votes, while Douglas was saying his consistency meant he could be counted on. Douglas's platform, and the platform of the Democratic Party, was based on the policy of Popular Sovereignty and states' rights. Douglas put forth that Lincoln's platform, and the platform of the Republican Party, could not be ascertained. Douglas said he stood for the Constitution as it already exists and by the decisions of the Supreme Court, and anyone who didn't "must resort to mob law and violence to overturn the government of laws."[31]

Quincy

The sixth debate was held six days later in Quincy, Illinois, a small town on the western border of the state along the Mississippi River. Quincy was named after the sixth President of the United States, John Quincy Adams, who was in office at the time the city was incorporated. At this debate, the crowd was estimated to be between 10,000 and 15,000 persons. The Quincy region, midway north-to-south of Illinois, was a key battleground for both Democrats and Republicans. The debate was supposed to start at 1:30 p.m. at Washington Square; however, part of the railing around the platform gave way and several attendees sprawled onto the ground. About an hour later the debate started, after the injured were attended to and the platform was repaired.[32]

Once again, it was Lincoln's turn to start the debate, and he would have a chance to respond to Douglas's speech. Lincoln rose to begin, and immediately took to the offense, responding to Douglas's comments from prior debates. From the first debate in Ottawa, and again at the third debate in Jonesboro, Lincoln related that Douglas charged Lincoln with conspiring with the "Black" Republicans to adopt an abolitionist party platform and attempting to "abolitionize" the Republican Party. Lincoln was again pointing out that Douglas had obtained erroneous information about a Republican platform that was specific to some northern counties in Illinois but was not reflective of the state platform or the adopted resolutions for the national Republican Party. However, Lincoln said, Douglas was still fomenting these false notions and had not corrected himself in subsequent speeches. Furthermore, how could Lincoln be held responsible for resolutions made and adopted at conventions he did not attend, some of which were held before he was even a member of that party?[33]

Lincoln also took Douglas to task for saying Lincoln held certain principles and positions in one part of the state and took different positions when he spoke at another part of the state. At Galesburg, Douglas accused Lincoln of trying to dupe the public by telling them what they wanted to hear and changing his story based on the location. Lincoln replied to that accusation during his portion of the debate, but he wanted to emphasize again here in Quincy that he has been and still was consistent with his viewpoints. He said his speeches throughout the state and anywhere else he was publicly quoted were self-consistent, no matter how much Douglas had tried to manipulate his words to "...prove a horse-chestnut to be a chestnut horse."[34]

Lincoln distilled the difference between himself and Douglas, and the difference between the Republican and Democratic parties, down to a single element – that being the belief that slavery a wrong versus those who believe it is not wrong. He went on to explain his belief that it is wrong not to limit slavery to the states where it already exists, and that the ultimate goal would be an eventual end to the practice altogether. Lincoln stated that, due to constitutional considerations, the federal government had no right to change it where it already existed, except for the District of Columbia. He went on to propose that, because the District of Columbia was under Congressional control, slavery could be eliminated there by making emancipation of the slaves gradual and financially compensating the owners (this was something Lincoln had proposed many years earlier when he was a member of Congress).[35]

Douglas came to the podium looking like the grind of the campaign trail was wearing on him. His face was puffy and he spoke slowly, giving some in the audience the impression that he had been drinking. One reporter noted that he spoke as though "bad whiskey and the wear and tear of conscience have had their effect." In fact, Douglas would be dead within three years, owing to alcoholism and other health issues, but not before he would provide a great service to President Lincoln and the country in 1861.[36]

Douglas first complained about what he considered a personal attack regarding Lincoln's accusations of deception by Douglas concerning the Republican Party platform adopted in Aurora in 1854 and the Springfield resolutions. He said he corrected his error about the "spot" upon which the party platform resolutions were adopted in later speeches as soon as he was aware of the mistake, and he wished Lincoln would also be as forthcoming about his own errors. Douglas then accused Lincoln of slander regarding the Dred Scott case. Douglas said that after he had proved the charge of conspiracy against Chief Justice Taney and the Supreme Court was false, Lincoln then charged President Buchanan of being involved in that conspiracy. Douglas said that instead of admitting to his mistake, Lincoln compounded it and didn't correct himself.[37]

Douglas went on to say that under the Constitution, each state had the right to determine its own policy on slavery, and that no other state had any reason or right to object to that policy. He also stated that the Constitution created the Supreme Court to answer all questions in dispute, so that decisions like the Dred Scott case become the law of the land requiring all good citizens to abide by them. By disagreeing with the Dred Scott decision, Lincoln was proposing mob rule and political disruption, and he warned that it could lead to violence, strife and rebellion. Douglas said he believed that by recognizing states' rights and allowing each state to determine its own position on the slavery question the country could forever exist divided into free states and slave states.[38]

Lincoln opened his reply with a joke, "Since Judge Douglas has said to you in his conclusion that he had not time in an hour and a half to answer all I had said in an hour, it follows of course that I will not be able to answer in half an hour all that he said in an hour and a half."[39] He continued by thanking Douglas for finally stating his true intention regarding slavery in his speech that it will last *forever*. Lincoln took issue with Douglas's statement that our forefathers created this country with free and slave states, but instead they found in some states that slavery already existed, and put in place institutions that would put slavery on the eventual course of extinction. He reminded the audience that the founding fathers abolished the slave trade (in 1808 by act of Congress, prohibiting importing of slaves) and had set up a system of restricting slavery from becoming prevalent in new Territories. He continued this line of thought that when the government was established, nobody thought the institution of slavery would last this long. In what could be the most insightful comment of the debate, Lincoln declared that the invention of the cotton gin had made slavery a necessity of the country.[40]

Alton

The seventh and final debate was held in Alton, Illinois on October 15. Alton was a good-sized town, also on the Mississippi River, but about 120 miles south of Quincy. Alton was not only a river town, but also a bustling railway center, as two main east-west railway lines terminated there. Alton was not a friendly place for anti-slavery advocates, by evidence of the publisher of an abolitionist newspaper having been murdered there 21 years earlier, and local attitudes not having changed much since. In an interesting coincidence, Alton is also near the location of Lincoln's infamous duel with James Shields. Or rather, the duel that didn't occur, because at the last moment cooler heads prevailed and the issue was resolved with diplomacy.[41]

Once again, and for the last time, Douglas started the debate with an hour-long speech, then Lincoln would have an hour and a half to respond, and the final half hour would belong to Douglas. As was the case a few days earlier in Quincy, Douglas was still showing the ill effects of the long campaign, with a bloated face, haggard looks, and a hoarse voice.[42] However, regardless of his condition, he did well in his final performance, and summarized the speeches of the previous seven debates like a lawyer performing his closing arguments before a jury.[43]

Douglas started with a historical perspective of the debates. He provided a retrospective of events that had occurred since the Republican State Convention (RSC) and Lincoln's acceptance speech, to the current time, reflecting on the positions they had each taken over the past seven weeks. Douglas said there were three main questions upon which the candidates disagreed: 1) can the United States remain united with slavery is some states but not in others, 2) are Negros denied rights provided by the Constitution due to the Dred Scott decision, and 3) are Negros included in the Declaration of Independence statement of "all men are created equal?[44]

Douglas's position on Lincoln's "house divided" speech at the RSC was that it was politically divisive and could potentially lead to war with the Southern states. He vehemently disagreed with Lincoln that the states could not exist together half slave and half free. In Douglas's view, the United States could maintain the half slave/half free status quo *forever*. He also considered Lincoln's contrary view both an insult and a slander against the founding fathers, who designed the Constitution to provide each state the right to choose its own path with respect to slavery.[45]

Douglas's position on the Dred Scott decision was that it did not keep individual states from choosing how to implement the decision and create "friendly" or "unfriendly" statues and laws to create the environment in which slavery or anti-slavery forces would thrive, depending on how the electorate felt about the issue. He spent a lot of time in this speech talking about states' rights and the people's right to choose their state's destiny. Douglas said each state has the right to choose slavery or anti-slavery only for their own state, not any other state, as the Constitution allows. Finally, Douglas finished with a discussion of the Declaration of Independence. He declared that the signers of the Declaration made no reference to Negroes when it stated "all men are created equal." He said the phrase referred only to white men – men of European birth and European descent. Douglas said that our government was created by white men for white men, and to their benefit in perpetuity.[46]

In contrast to previous debates, Lincoln did not make notes regarding Douglas's speech, or seem particularly interested in what he was saying. For most of the speech, he sat head down with his chair leaned up against the wall, in what seemed to be a trance-like state. When the time came to speak, Lincoln rose up to his full height, walked toward the podium, and began his response.[47] First, he thanked Douglas for giving the current Democratic administration of President Buchanan such a hard time. Then he said he hoped that the Administration would give Douglas just as much of a hard time, and " . . . prosecute the war against one another in the most vigorous manner."[48]

After that bit of humor was over, Lincoln became more serious and defined the difference between himself and Douglas, and the difference between the Republicans and the Democrats, on the question of morality. The moral question was, is slavery a wrong? Lincoln said, "The sentiment that contemplates the institution of slavery in this country as a wrong is the sentiment of the Republican party."[49] Because it is a wrong, Lincoln went on to say, then every effort should be made to make sure that it grows no larger, and ultimately there should be a policy toward a peaceful end to the practice at some time in the future.[50]

Lincoln summarized the past seven weeks of arguments and speeches between the two positions. He said, "It is the eternal struggle between these two principles – right and wrong – throughout the world. They are the two principles that have stood face to face from the beginning of time; and will ever continue to struggle. The one is the common right of humanity and the other the divine right of kings." Lincoln continued, "No matter in what shape it comes, whether from the mouth of a king who seeks to bestride the people of his own nation and live by the fruit of their labor, or from one race of men as an apology for enslaving another race, it is the same tyrannical principle."[51]

For the preceding hour and a half, he had been carefully laying the foundation for his summary arguments, which he knew would be in print for all to see, now and forevermore. Lincoln had chosen the last debate for his best speech to date. He was fresher and stronger than his opponent, and he had the conviction of his principles to guide him – the principle of right versus wrong, freedom versus slavery. He had mapped out his strategy early on, and had planned to use the seven speeches to weave a story from the beginning to the end, and to let the people read the book in seven chapters, as each debate was documented in the papers. From the first debate, when he spent the majority of his time defending himself against Douglas's criticisms, to the last debate, when Lincoln was clearly self-confident and in-control, he refined his message. Lincoln eventually defined the argument of Republican anti-slavery versus Democratic pro-slavery "self-determinism" as the battle of right versus wrong, good versus evil. This was his national political coming out party, and he ended it with a bang. Although he would eventually lose the election for the Senate seat to Douglas, his visibility and viability as a candidate for the Presidency was significantly enhanced. In the end, Lincoln won the debates, and went on to win the 1860 election for President of the United States.

Lincoln's Election

No sooner than Lincoln was elected as President, the great North-South schism opened, and war was inevitable. It started with the succession of South Carolina, and seven more states soon followed. The crisis grew larger and larger each passing day as Lincoln's inauguration day came ever near. A myriad of different proposals to keep the Union together were discussed in Congress. The Southern states would not concede their right to succeed unless certain assurances were obtained from the North. Lincoln made it known to his trusted friends in Congress that he could consider comprise on minor issues, but not the major one, "Let there be no compromise on the question of extending slavery."[52]

The period between his election the previous November and his inauguration on March 4, 1861, was filled with public anxiety and a litany of opinions in the press. Lincoln refrained from making public remarks on his position, saying that his opinion was already a matter of public record. Although he made speeches at every stop on his train ride to the capital for his inauguration, he revealed nothing in those speeches that would arouse suspicion or cause concern for the inhabitants of the Southern states. But in his inauguration speech, he expressed his thoughts on the subject of succession from a legalistic interpretation of the Constitution. He said, "I hold, that in contemplation of universal law, and of the Constitution, the Union of these states is perpetual. . . . [N]o state, upon its own mere motion, can lawfully get out of the Union . . . . I therefore consider that, in view of the Constitution and the laws, the Union is unbroken . . . ."[53]

Lincoln stated that he had no intention of changing the existing laws in the states that currently allow slavery, because he had no legal right or even the inclination to do it. Despite going out of his way in his inauguration speech to recognize the rights of the Southern states to retrieve their slave property as defined in the Constitution, Southerners took his speech as a declaration of federal supremacy over states' rights. The Confederacy interpreted his inauguration speech as a challenge to their legitimacy and a step towards an eventual showdown over the slavery question. Only two days later, the Confederate Congress put themselves on a war footing by authorizing 100,000 troops.[54]

Not long after Lincoln's inauguration, Confederates fired the first shots with their bombardment of Ft. Sumter. Lincoln called for 75,000 troops and received immediate promises of support from the Union states. Four more states succeeded from the Union, and the war was on. Lincoln would famously search in vain for the general he needed to lead the great Union army to victory. One of those early generals that failed him was General Fremont, who was commander of all Union forces in Missouri. Fremont declared martial law in that state, and then on August 30, 1861, he emancipated all of the slaves owned by Rebel forces within Missouri. Lincoln did not want the military making dictatorial proclamations and requested that Fremont modify his decrees to align with his interpretation of the Constitution and legal precedent. When Fremont refused, Lincoln replaced him with Major General Henry Halleck.[55]

Delaware Emancipation

As early as November 1861, Lincoln proposed a voluntary gradual emancipation of the slaves in the Border States by offering to have the government reimburse the slave owners for their property. He proposed that Delaware, the state with the fewest number of slaves, be the test case for his program. Lincoln drafted two bills for Delaware Congressman George Fisher; one was a five-year phased plan for gradual abolition; the other was an immediate emancipation of all slaves over 35 years old, with eventual emancipation of the remaining slaves over a 30-year period. However, he could not elicit enough interest in the program to attempt it, so it was never introduced as a proposal. What he did receive from that experience was a commitment from Senator Crittenden that if there was a Northern battle victory that the people could savor, then it would be a good time to introduce some emancipation legislation.[56]

As it was, the Republicans in Congress were moving steadily against slavery and toward emancipation. In March 1862, Lincoln signed a bill that disallowed the military from returning fugitive slaves to their masters or face a court martial. This law effectively overturned the Fugitive Slave Act, which had been a point of controversy since before the war started. In April 1862, Lincoln signed the law emancipating all slaves in the District of Columbia. The new law allowed for compensation of slave owners loyal to the Union to receive up to $300 per slave. In June 1862, a law that abolished slavery in all of the territories was signed. Although this specific piece of legislation affected only a few (less than 50) slaves, it was an important and symbolic measure that spoke to the root cause of the conflict – arresting the spread of slavery in the United States. Not long after that measure, Congress enacted the Second Confiscation Act (in July 1862). It emancipated all slaves who came over to Union lines or were within Confederate territory that was occupied by Union forces.[57]

Emancipation Proclamation

In July 1862, over the course of two days, Lincoln discussed with his cabinet several important potential resolutions regarding slavery and the course of the war. On July 21, Lincoln proposed four ideas: 1) allow the military to live off the land in enemy territory, 2) allow use of blacks in the military as laborers, 3) require documentation of all confiscated property, and 4) propose the colonization of freed Negroes to "some tropical territory." The next day Lincoln wrote the preliminary emancipation proclamation and showed it to his cabinet. It was another proposal, this time consisting of three points: 1) warn the Confederacy that they had 60 days to cease and desist or the Second Confiscation Act would be implemented, 2) recommit to a policy of gradual, compensated emancipation, and 3) declare that as of January 1, 1863, all slaves in the Confederate states would be declared emancipated and "forever free."[58]

The cabinet was stunned and silent after the reading of Lincoln's proclamation. Only Secretary of State William Seward and Secretary of the Navy Gideon Welles had any inkling of this potential announcement (Lincoln, Seward, and Welles had discussed it privately during a carriage ride on July 13). The cabinet was split regarding the implementation of such a bold initiative, but the most insightful comments came from Seward. He said he was in favor of it but was concerned about its timing. Because of the number of battlefield failures and losses to the Confederate Army in 1862, including the disastrous "Peninsula Campaign" by General McClellan that ended the previous month, Seward stated that announcing the emancipation proclamation at this time would seem like the last act of a desperate nation. He suggested that the President hold off on making the announcement until the fortunes of war turned in the Union's favor.[59]

On September 17, Lincoln finally got his victory at the Battle of Antietam. General McClellan, in his last action as Commander of the Army of the Potomac, called it a complete victory. He said, "I feel some little pride in having with a beaten and demoralized army defeated Lee so utterly, & saved the North so completely."[60]

After Antietam, Lincoln held a cabinet meeting and announced his decision to issue the Emancipation Proclamation, which freed the slaves in the Confederate States as of January 1, 1863. On September 23, 1862, the proclamation was issued to the public. The next day, large cheering crowds descended on the White House to express their support of the announcement, and Lincoln obliged them with a statement from a second-floor window. The President said, "It is now for the country and the world to pass judgment on it." He subsequently focused on the soldiers who were making the ultimate sacrifice in service to their country.[61]

The 13th Amendment

While the Emancipation Proclamation freed the slaves in the Confederate states, there was no guarantee that once the Civil War was over, the slaves would remain free. Many members of Congress, and generally the whole of the Democratic Party, believed that after the war was over, it would be up to the states themselves to determine if slavery would remain the law of the land. A radical Republican and abolitionist by the name of James Ashley, a Congressman from Ohio, wanted to change all that. He was a virulent opponent of the Fugitive Slave laws, and proudly boasted of helping runaway slaves.[62]

In December 1863, Ashley proposed an anti-slavery amendment to the Constitution. James Wilson, a Congressman from Iowa, proposed a similar amendment a few days later. Several weeks after, two Senators also proposed an emancipation amendment, the first being offered by a Senator from Missouri, John Henderson. The second proposal was from Charles Sumner, the well-known abolitionist Senator from Massachusetts. Sumner's proposed amendment went even further than abolition and pushed for social equality. From there, the proposals went to committee for hashing out the final wording and intent. The Senate Judiciary Committee's final version was the following: "Neither slavery nor involuntary servitude, except as punishment for crime whereof the party shall have been duly convicted, shall exist within the United States, or any place subject to their jurisdiction."[63]

The Senate passed the Thirteenth Amendment to the Constitution of the United States on April 8, 1864, one year and a day before General Lee's surrender at Appomattox. However, in June 1864, when the bill came before the House of Representatives, it fell short of the two-thirds majority required for its passage as an amendment to the Constitution. During the course of the remaining year, several slave states (Border States and states occupied by the Union) also modified their state constitutions to abolish slavery. "By the end of January 1865, Arkansas, Louisiana, Maryland, and Missouri had abolished slavery. Tennessee and Kentucky were moving unmistakably toward similar action."[64]

After Lincoln won re-election in 1864, he made emancipation a topic of his state of the union address that December and rallied support for its passage in Congress. He used every bit of his political skill and persuasive talent to ensure there would be enough votes to pass the second time it came up in the House. The House of Representatives voted on the amendment on January 31, 1865. The House was packed to standing room only because in addition to the regular members, Senators, activists, and citizens all wanted to witness history. All of the Republicans were expected to and provided "yea" votes; with each Democrat's "yea" a loud cheer would erupt. As the final vote was tallied, there were 119 yeas, 56 nays, and eight absent members. The two-thirds requirement was met by the slimmest of margins – three votes. Thus, the abolition amendment to the Constitution passed and minutes later the booming of cannons was heard throughout the city in a 100-gun salute of artillery. The next day, throngs of people descended on the White House cheering the passage of the bill and congratulating Lincoln on his accomplishment. Before the day's end, Lincoln's home state of Illinois was the first state to ratify the amendment.[65]

The 13th Amendment was certified on December 6, 1865, when the 27th of the 36 state legislatures (the required three fourths) ratified the amendment to the Constitution.

CHAPTER 8

Lincoln's Legacy

Abraham Lincoln is considered by many historians and political experts to be our greatest president. He consistently is ranked first overall in presidential historical rankings. It is also interesting to note that the two presidents who immediately preceded and succeeded him (Presidents Buchanan and Johnson) are consistently ranked at the bottom of presidential historical rankings. The crisis over slavery that started the Civil War molded and forged this self-made man from an ordinary country lawyer and politician to an instrument of God that saved our country and saved democracy for the world.

Lincoln's unique ability to speak eloquently, but in simple terms and with humility and wit, was one of his most endearing and enduring traits. As described by White in *A. Lincoln*, the classic example of this is his Gettysburg Address. In a few minutes (a speech of 271 words), he was able to paint a picture of simple beauty, taking us from the past, reminding us of the present, and talking about our future beyond the current circumstances. When he said, "Four score and seven years ago" he was reminding us of our commitment to liberty from the Declaration of Independence and that "all men are created equal." When he said, "Now we are engaged in a great civil war, testing whether that nation . . . can long endure" he was explaining that the war was a test of our democratic institutions. When he said, "that government of the people, by the people, for the people, shall not perish from the earth" he was showing us the path to our future, provided that we could overcome the current troubles the country was in.[1]

Lincoln was admired for being such a consummate speaker and speechwriter. According to American historian Merrill D. Peterson, his second inaugural address had English historians comparing his wordsmith ability to that of Shakespeare, noting that, "[w]ith many of his compatriots, [biographer Godfrey Rathbone Benson, Lord] Charnwood ranked Lincoln with Shakespeare in mastery of the English language."[2]

As related by Pulitzer Prize winner Doris Kearns Goodwin in her biography of Lincoln, *Team of Rivals*, Lincoln's legacy is worldwide. Leo Tolstoy, the Russian writer of *War and Peace* fame, once told a story of meeting in the early 1900s in the remote North Caucasus Mountains the chief of a tribe who wanted to hear about Lincoln. Even this tribe had heard about the greatness of Lincoln, who "spoke with a voice of thunder, he laughed like the sunrise, and his deeds were strong as the rock."[3] Tolstoy told them all he knew about the story of Lincoln's life and times. The chief and his family and friends listened with reverence, and afterwards were so appreciative that they gave Tolstoy the gift of a beautiful Arabian horse. Tolstoy's story of the interest in Lincoln in such a remote part of the world shows how great Lincoln's legacy truly is, and he went on to say, "Lincoln was a humanitarian as broad as the world."[4]

As great as Lincoln was, he was continually underestimated by his contemporaries, enemies and peers. This may be one of the reasons why he was able to accomplish so much, in such a short lifetime. His greatness was underappreciated while he was alive, but in death, as Secretary of War Edwin Stanton said, "Now, he belongs to the ages."[5]

The American Dream

Abraham Lincoln is the epitome of the American Dream, for he was born into poverty and rose to become the President of the United States. Lincoln believed that America was a land of opportunity, and that everyone should have those same opportunities to make the most of themselves. In fact, Lincoln was a prime example. He rose from meager beginnings – being raised in a log cabin with a dirt floor – to the highest office in the land. He did that by constantly improving himself and reading any books he could get his hands on. With only a single year of formal schooling in his entire life, he became a lawyer, one of the best lawyers in the state of Illinois. He did this with mental focus and self-discipline. What he did for himself, he believed that others could do also. The opportunities in America were the same for most Americans, except for the black man. The first step in removing those barriers was to take off slaves' shackles and provide them the freedom to make the most of themselves.

Lincoln's prominence on the national political scene seemingly came out of nowhere. From the relative obscurity of a state assemblyman, to a single term as a Representative from Illinois in Congress, to a leader in the brand-new Republican party, his rise to power was an incredible feat of politics and timing by taking advantage of the opportunities that presented themselves to him. Lincoln was not a favored candidate for the Republican nomination in the 1860 election, because more experienced candidates vying for the position made his potential success seem remote. What he did have was enough support as a second choice that, when state delegates found out their favorite sons lacked enough backing for the nomination, they swung their delegates to Lincoln. With the second round of voting, it became a two-man race between Seward and Lincoln, and Lincoln received the Republican nomination on the third round.

Throughout his political career, and especially during his presidency, Lincoln supported and promoted the types of legislation and political change that would promote progress for the American people. He was a progressive before that term was ever applied to political operatives who tried to push the country towards a better future. Lincoln was forward looking and a deep thinker. He endlessly pondered the significant questions of the day, and he tried to anticipate their implications and determine their solutions. Whatever the issue was, Lincoln would saturate his mind with the myriad details and facts surrounding the topic and turn that problem over in his mind until he could see the resolution. In one Washington newspaper of that era Lincoln was called "the most truly progressive man of the age."[6]

Lincoln was a firm believer that the people in America only needed an opportunity to make the most of themselves. He was a proponent of education; he worked to provide homesteading opportunities to individuals and families on federal lands and to use the power of the federal government to create favorable economic conditions throughout the country so ordinary citizens could survive and thrive. For him an analogy was farming: He believed that if the right conditions were available and provided in the environment (opportunity), then that would enable and sustain the growth of the country and its citizens (achievement of the American Dream). In an Address before the Wisconsin State Agricultural Society at Milwaukee, Wisconsin on September 30, 1859, he said, "Let us hope, rather, that by the best cultivation of the physical world, beneath and around us; and the intellectual and moral world within us, we shall secure an individual, social, and political prosperity and happiness, whose course shall be onward and upward, and which, while the earth endures, shall not pass away."[7]

Federalist and Whig Politics

Lincoln was in some ways a reincarnation of George Washington, in that he took an almost Federalist approach to his governing of the country as president. His view was that there were some philosophies that were basic to all states, and therefore could not be interpreted or implemented at the state level – that they must by their very nature be implemented at the federal level. One of these philosophies was that "all men are created equal," and therefore slavery must not be allowed to continue in the United States. Lincoln was enthralled with the words from the Declaration of Independence (a Jeffersonian end) and attempted to use Hamiltonian means to achieve that objective – financing the purchase of "border state" slaves' freedom with federal bonds. Richard Streiner, professor of history at Washington College in Maryland states, "He was the greatest moral strategist our nation has produced."[8]

Lincoln also took a Federalist approach to managing the succession crisis in the Executive branch of the government in that he took action to ensure a strong national direction and response to that crisis. His positions on national matters were a reflection of his Whig politics: anti-Jacksonian positions with respect to support for a national bank; using the power of the federal government for domestic investments in infrastructure; protecting domestic manufacturing with high tariffs on imports; and the sale of public (federal) lands to fund these initiatives.[9] He deftly maneuvered political opinions and national attitudes to garner support for his position before he took action, thereby ensuring the success of his approach before moving in that direction. One of Lincoln's greatest assets was an ability to get a feel for the heartbeat of the nation by reading every newspaper he could get his hands on, in addition to talking to as many people as he could to get their opinions. He may be one of the most empathetic presidents we have ever had, and used that empathy, and the information he assimilated through reading, talking, and thinking, to support his profound leadership decisions while president.

Lincoln considered his principles at least as important as his own personal priorities and goals. When he was elected as a Whig to the Illinois state legislature in 1854, he found out that a position for U.S. Senate would be voted on by the Illinois leg-islature (as was the normal custom, prior to the 17th Amend-ment). In addition, he discovered that the legislature could not elect one of their own, so he decided to decline his elected po-sition in the state legislature. This would give him the oppor-tunity to challenge the incumbent Democrat, James Shields, who was in favor of the Kansas-Nebraska Act that allowed ter-ritories to decide if they wanted to allow slavery. Lincoln cam-paigned vigorously for the Senate seat, with which he would be able to challenge the Senate's pro-slavery Douglas Demo-crats. On February 8, 1855, the election was held in Spring-field. It would take 51 votes to win, and on the first ballot Lincoln received 45 votes. However, with each successive bal-lot, he received fewer votes. After the ninth ballot, Lincoln told his supporters to vote for Lyman Trumbull, an anti-Nebraska Democrat. Lincoln deemed it more important for an anti-slavery man to take that seat in the Senate than to hold out for his own personal vanity or ambition.[10]

The Republican Party

Lincoln was a devout Whig politician, and with the demise of the Whig party, he became a dedicated Republican. Eventu-ally, Lincoln became the face of the Republican Party. He vig-orously supported Whig principles, even when they were unpopular. As a Whig legislator from Illinois in 1848 (his first and only term as a Representative in the U. S. Congress), Lin-coln felt President Polk's declared war with Mexico was unjus-tified. He consistently voted with the Whig minority to oppose Polk's policies of belligerence against the Mexican govern-ment, even though it was a popular war with the American people. It was a young Mr. Lincoln that stuck to his principles, even though his opposition to the war probably caused his dis-trict to vote for the Democrat candidate in the next election. Lincoln's idealism and party loyalty could be blamed for his party's inability to retain his seat in Congress (his seat was still being rotated through the Logan/Hardin/Lincoln Whig candidates, with Logan losing to Democrat Thomas Harris).[11]

In late 1854, after winning a race for the Illinois state legislature representing Sangamon County (comprising Springfield, the state capital) as a Whig, he declined that seat – as noted above – in order to attempt to represent the state as a Senator in Congress. That strategy failed, but it was a learning experience. After his failed bid to become a Senator from Illinois in Congress, Lincoln returned to his law practice, but he followed political events closely. Throughout 1855 he represented several important clients and was involved in many significant cases, all the while agonizing over the direction of the country and the impending demise of the Whig party. He would find himself a target of conscription efforts by different elements of other political movements, but he kept his distance and his options open. In February 1856, he was visited by "free state" supporters for Kansas, who asked him to speak at a meeting. He spoke at the meeting and made a donation to the Kansas supporters, but declined further involvement.[12]

Later that month, he met some newspaper editors in Decatur who were supporting an end to the extension of slavery in the Territories and proposing that he run for governor. They also were organizing an anti-Nebraska convention in Bloomington on May 28. Lincoln made no commitments, but when his partner William Herndon put him on the list of delegates, he agreed to attend. As the final speaker at the meeting that day, Lincoln made what Herndon called the greatest speech of his career. It was so good that reporters at the meeting were in a trance and failed to transcribe the speech, which is now known as the "Lost Speech." Lincoln left that meeting a leader of the Republican Party in the state of Illinois.[13]

As a Republican, Lincoln steadfastly defended his party's platform, and he routinely campaigned on behalf of the Republican Party because his beliefs were aligned with that of the party. For example, in the Douglas debates, Lincoln defended his party and his beliefs in every challenge from Douglas regarding the expansion of slavery into the Territories by Douglas's principle of "popular sovereignty." Regardless of the taunts and insults by Douglas, and no matter how many times he was called a "Black" Republican due to his beliefs that slavery should not be allowed into the Territories, Lincoln stayed true to the party platform – and once he had become the 16th President of the United States, the Republican Party became associated and identified as "the Party of Lincoln" for generations afterwards. From a humble beginning, the Republican Party's establishment and subsequent success is truly a legacy of Abraham Lincoln.

Cabinet Selection

Lincoln had as diverse and powerful a group of personalities in his cabinet as any president before or since: William Seward as Secretary of State, Salmon Chase as Secretary of the Treasury, Edward Bates as Attorney General, Simon Cameron as Secretary of War, Gideon Wells as Secretary of the Navy, Caleb Smith as Secretary of the Interior, and Montgomery Blair as Postmaster General. Seward, Chase, and Bates had been Lincoln's rivals for the presidential nomination at the Republican National Convention in 1860, but Lincoln included them in his cabinet to strengthen his team, while Cameron and Smith had committed their state delegates to Lincoln in order to gain positions in the cabinet.[14]

As Doris Kearns Goodwin noted in *Team of Rivals*, Lincoln was a master at understanding men's motivations and true intentions, and was able to outmaneuver his Treasury Secretary, Salmon P. Chase, and maintain control of the cabinet. When Chase complained to his political allies in the Senate that Lincoln's control of the cabinet was being affected by Secretary of State William H. Seward, they demanded cabinet changes. But if the legislative branch of the government could control and make changes to the President's cabinet against his wishes, this would change the balance of power between the executive and legislative branches in favor of the Legislature.[15]

The radical Republicans in the Senate drafted a resolution that Seward must be removed from the cabinet because they lacked confidence in his abilities. They later modified the resolution to demand a "partial reconstruction" of the cabinet, and they designated a Committee of Nine to present the resolution to the President. On December 18, 1862, Lincoln met the Senators to hear their complaints in a three-hour meeting, listened to their grievances, and promised to review in detail the resolution document they provided.[16]

The next evening, Lincoln met with the Committee of Nine and his cabinet (excluding Seward), and effectively showed that Chase was exaggerating Seward's influence to make Lincoln look bad. Lincoln read aloud the proposed resolution, and they discussed its content for hours. The Senators demanded that all members of the cabinet must be involved in the debate on issues of national interest. Throughout the discussion, each of the cabinet members confirmed that their positions were heard, and that Seward did not control the decisions. Even Chase admitted that there was general agreement on most issues, and there was universal agreement upon measures once the decision was made. In the events leading up to the meeting, Chase's interest was really to make Lincoln look weak and to make Seward look subversive, but the strategy backfired. When the Senators found out about Chase's duplicity, he lost their support and respect.[17]

The result of the affair was that Lincoln was successfully able to thwart the Senate's attempts to control the composition of the President's cabinet. This now and forevermore strengthened the position of the Executive branch of the government. All subsequent presidents are indebted to Lincoln for having the political savvy and skill to delicately handle the challenge by those Senators and retain control of the composition and character of a president's main circle of advisors. This critical ability to name their own trusted intimates, as opposed to having potential adversaries named to those positions by the Legislative branch, effectively restored power to presidents and maintained balance in the government.[18]

Adherence to the Constitution

Lincoln proved once and for all that a democratic country can self-govern, for at no time during the conflict of the Civil War were the democratic institutions curtailed or stopped – all normal elections were held, all regular self-governance was continued, and with rare exceptions, all laws and rights were upheld (except the writ of habeas corpus during the war, and even in this instance the Constitution was followed explicitly for that exception). And with respect to that exception, Lincoln's familiarity with the Constitution due to his experience as a lawyer, provided him the knowledge that the Constitution allowed the suspension of habeas corpus "when in Cases of Rebellion or Invasion the public Safety may require it."[19] Certainly, the Civil War was a situation of public Safety that necessitated this action – rebels in Maryland were destroying railroad tracks and telegraph wires that allowed communication and transportation between the capital and the rest of the Union.

Adherence to the Constitution was also a concept that drove Lincoln to save the Union, as he was sworn to uphold when he took the oath of office. The oath required him to defend the country against all enemies, foreign and domestic. In essence, the successionists were fomenting an uprising against the state and against the Constitution, making their efforts an act of civil disobedience on the level of treason. Lincoln was not the only one who felt that way. There was a general feeling on the part of Union soldiers that spoke of the Confederates in terms of the word "treason" and of their own desire to protect the Union and the Constitution, fulfilling their duty to defend the flag of the United States.[20]

Lincoln stated in his first Annual Message to Congress that the insurrection was "a war upon the first principle of popular government – the rights of the people."[21] Andrew Johnson, before he had become Lincoln's Vice President, had stated that once succession started, there would be no end to it, and the United States would become another European continent, with multiple independent governments endlessly bickering and warring with each other to the point of anarchy. If succession was allowed, then the idea and the ideal of a Constitutional government could not stand. If the minority, represented by the Southern states and personified by their leader Jefferson Davis, was able to rule the majority, represented by the Northern states and personified by President Lincoln as voted in the 1860 election, then the democratic experiment of a representative government had failed.[22]

Ultimately, Lincoln forever ensured that the United States stayed united. By not allowing the Confederate states to separate into another country or group of independent states, he showed the states and the world that our country was a true nation and not a collection of disparate entities. By doing so, Lincoln proved that a democracy based on majority rule could function and govern as an entity.[23]

Commander-in-Chief

Lincoln, more than any other president since George Washington, interpreted the Constitution and defined the presidency in terms of how we understand them to be today. Beyond just the literal meaning of the words, he acted within what he saw were the legalistic bounds and interpretations of what the founding fathers intended the presidency to be. He also demonstrated for future generations that the president would act as "Commander in Chief of all the Army and Naval forces" on account of his making suggestions on troop movement and location during the Civil War and his hiring and firing generals until he finally found one who would do what needed to be done. The eight previous presidents had been titular holders of the leadership position, but they were in reality just puppets for Congress.[24]

Initially, Lincoln brooded with self-doubt when it came to his command of the Army and Navy forces. As a civilian commander with only a few months of militia experience under his belt from the Black Hawk War, his initial directives came with caveats that allowed the officers in charge to take their own advice with respect to the conduct of the war and their own actions. An example of this was his strategy in Ohio and Tennessee to attack the Confederates at multiple points along the battlefront, searching for weak points and overwhelming the enemy with superiority in numbers. However, he included a note in his January 1, 1862 directive that allowed General Halleck flexibility on to how to implement the strategy.[25]

His record as Commander in Chief is still debated, as some of his decisions may have seemed political. For example, he took some 35,000 troops from McClellan to protect Washington when McClellan attempted his infamous Peninsula Plan to capture Richmond – but that was an appropriate defensive maneuver to keep the Confederates from capturing the Union capital. European opinion on his firing of McClellan after Antietam was mixed. Some thought it unwise to dismiss the Union's best general, but ultimately Lincoln was able to bring in a more aggressive and action-oriented persona in General Grant, who brought the war to a successful conclusion. Many years afterward the debate still raged. In the late 1800s, Lincoln was seen as an example of politics getting in the way of military strategy and tactics. However, as time passed, later generations (from World War I and on) saw his involvement as a necessary and important factor in the execution and conduct of the war.[26]

On March 11, 1862, Lincoln took over direct command of the Union armies (via the Secretary of War), because he was displeased with the poor performance and incompetence of the Union generals in command up to that point. Frustrated by General McClellan's litany of excuses for the lack of progress in the war effort against the Confederates, the President issued Special War Order Number 3, which removed McClellan as general in chief of the army. Instead, he had all of the commanders report directly to Edwin Stanton, the Secretary of War. Over the course of the first three years of the Civil War, General McDowell was replaced by General McClellan, who was replaced by General Pope, who was replaced by General McClellan, who was replaced by General Burnside, who was replaced by General Hooker, who was replaced by General Meade, who was superseded by General Grant. It wasn't until after General Grant showed the President that he could be trusted with command of the Union forces, that Lincoln finally gave up the reins and allowed the professionals to take over that work.[27]

Banking and Greenbacks

Lincoln supported a National Bank in his days as a Whig in the Legislature and despised the demise of the Second National Bank during President Jackson's administration. The National Bank Acts, a uniform currency, and the first federal income tax are all examples of legislation that Lincoln's presidency implemented and that are all examples of Federalist type of activities in support of a strong national government. The National Bank Acts of 1863, 1864, and 1865-1866 created a banking system that was a precursor to the federal banking system that exists today. They also helped establish a uniform currency (the Civil War "Greenbacks") by taxing the paper money created and circulated by individual state-chartered banks, and which led to the end of other paper money in circulation. The Greenbacks were a result of the Legal Tender Act of 1862, the Second Tender Act, and the Third Tender Act. These laws helped the federal government pay for the war effort.[28]

The Legal Tender Act was approved on February 25, 1862 and authorized the Secretary of the Treasury to issue $150,000,000 worth of non-interest bearing notes (paper money) payable at the Treasury of the United States. These notes would be redeemable for all taxes, debts, and demands due the U. S. government, and would be "legal tender in payment of all debts, public and private, within the United States"[29] If you look at any paper money in your wallet you will see the following quote, evidence of the lasting legacy of this act: "This note is legal tender for all debts, public and private."

Exactly one year after the Legal Tender Act was approved, the President signed into law the National Currency Act (subsequently known as the National Bank Act of 1863). This act established an office under the direction of the Secretary of the Treasury, called the Comptroller of the Currency. The chief officer of the Office of the Comptroller of the Currency (OCC) would be nominated by the Secretary of the Treasury, appointed by the President, and confirmed by the Senate to a term of five years, unless earlier removed by the President. The act provided for the issuance of $300,000,000 worth of additional notes, at the direction of the OCC, in denominations of five dollars, ten dollars, 20 dollars, 50 dollars, 100 dollars, 500 dollars, and 1,000 dollars.[30]

President Lincoln was extremely proud of the National Currency Act, the result of which was to provide for additional national currency notes for circulation in the economy and to create a total of 584 nationally chartered banks, some converted from state banks. He stated in his Fourth Annual Message to Congress on December 6, 1864, "The national system will create a reliable and permanent influence in support of the national credit and protect the people against losses in the use of paper money."[31] The implementation of the legal tender and currency (banking) acts provided an environment of risk-free use of paper money, in the sense that the notes were backed by the credit of the U. S. government and redeemable for hard money from the issuing bank or any of the reserve banks around the country. For the next 50 years, this system, and the legislative modifications to it, would provide fiat currency to the nation, until the Federal Reserve Act of 1913 established the Federal Reserve notes in use today. Since then, the OCC (which still exists) has been chartered to oversee the financial viability and stability of the nation's banks.[32]

The Homestead Act

Lincoln was a proponent of using the power of government investment for public good. Several measures implemented during the early part of Lincoln's first term were an expanse of federal power, in part fueled by the large majority Republicans held in Congress. Two bills that were vetoed by President Buchanan before Lincoln's election were the Homestead Act and the Morrill Act. The Homestead Act provided 160 acres of federal land free to "homesteaders" – provided that they lived there for five years, farmed the land, and made improvements. This bill passed Congress in 1862 and was signed by President Lincoln on May 20.[33]

The passing and implementation of the Homestead Act was also a plank of the Republican Party's platform of the 1860 election, and a promise to the party's electorate. The act represented an opportunity for the poor to own their own property and farm their own land. At a cost of only $1.25 per acre, any American citizen (or person intending to become a citizen via the naturalization laws of the United States) who was the head of a household or at least 21 years old, could purchase and receive title to up to 160 acres of the public lands they would homestead. This proved a popular program, because by the end of the Civil War over 15,000 homestead claims were filed, and by the year 1900, that number had risen to over 600,000 claims representing over 80 million acres of public lands distributed.[34]

The Homestead Act supported two objectives of Lincoln's strategy for fighting and winning the Civil War: 1) It provided an opportunity for economic incentives and investment in the Western territories that would create an engine of growth in these western lands; and 2) It would create an influx of Northerners to these territories that would be pro-Union and anti-slavery, as an insurance policy for the future in case things didn't go well for the North (and in 1862, the war efforts were not going well at all). In an interesting analogy to another president who dealt with an existential crisis in the country, Lincoln's economic and social policies implemented in the laws passed in 1862 were a precursor to Franklin Roosevelt's use of federal power to implement laws to address a crisis.[35]

Homesteaders did not have an easy life. Separated from their extended families and even from any neighbors close by, they endured hardships on the open plain not unlike the earliest settlers in the Northwest Territories. The appeal of homesteading was the opportunity to own your own piece of the American dream, and the prospects for building a better life for you, your family, and your descendants. It didn't always turn out that way. Seventy years later, interviews of Nebraska homesteaders by members of the Works Progress Administration (WPA) during President Franklin Roosevelt's administration, revealed the stark loneliness and isolation of these pioneers.[36] The "first homesteader" was Daniel Freeman, who settled in Beatrice, Nebraska in 1863. In March 1936, President Roosevelt signed into law the Homestead National Monument Act that created a National Park on the site of the Freeman homestead to recognize the sacrifice and hardships these pioneers went through to settle and cultivate the West.[37]

Land Grant Colleges

In a biography of Abraham Lincoln that his secretary John Nicolay helped write – and was used by his approved campaign biographers such as William D. Howells and John L. Scripps for his 1860 presidential campaign – there is the remark: "He regrets his want of education, and does what he can to supply the want."[38] Lincoln did what he could to remedy that situation by reading whatever he could get his hands on. During his one term in Congress, he was known as a "bookworm," and spent endless hours in the Library of Congress or taking books home to his boardinghouse in the capital. During his Congressional term he was one of the Library's most frequent users.[39]

Lincoln was a proponent of education and did what he could as President to advocate the use of federal power to provide support for the democratization of higher education. In the Morrill Act, he found such a vehicle. The Morrill Act implemented Land Grant colleges in each state that was not in rebellion against the Union, by providing federal lands in each state (or an equivalent endowment if federal land was not available in the state) to start a public institution for agriculture or engineering. The amount of federal lands provided to each state was allocated based on the number of senators and representatives for that state as apportioned per the 1860 census and was equal to 30,000 acres times that number. From the sale of those lands, each state had to provide within five years at least one college, or the grant would cease and the state would have to pay back the federal government any money it had received for those lands. This Act passed Congress in 1862 and was signed by President Lincoln on July 2.[40]

Fifty-nine colleges were established by the 1862 Act, and after the Civil War ended, the Morrill Act was expanded to include the states that had composed the Confederacy. Today, every state has at least one land grant college, and there are now over a hundred Land Grant colleges and universities in the United States and its territories. The Massachusetts Institute of Technology (MIT) is one of the original Land Grant colleges (their land grant was split between MIT and Massachusetts Agricultural College, now known as the University of Massachusetts, Amherst),[41] and so is Cornell, the Ivy League school in

Ithaca, New York. In addition, ten of the Big 10 conference schools are Land Grant colleges, as well as a majority of the schools in the South East Conference, and a number of the universities in the Pacific 12 Conference. These colleges and universities have provided agricultural research, engineering, science and technology advancement for over 150 years, and form the backbone of our public institutions of higher learning in the United States.[42]

Back in the mid-1800s, America was an agrarian society. Fully 50 percent of the population and 60 percent of the labor force were involved in the production of dairy, grain, and meat for delivery to local markets and for nationwide distribution.[43] Lincoln's "New Deal"-like approach to using the power of the federal government to support economic development and growth opportunities also established the United States Department of Agriculture (USDA) in May 1862, and the National Academy of Science in March 1863. The USDA act did as much to support the development of modern farming and the promotion of best practices in the agriculture industry as the Morrill Act.[44]

Manifest Destiny

The westward expansion of the United States was a tradition rooted in both President Washington's treaties with the Indians in the Midwest (considered the "West" at the time) and President Jefferson's purchase of the Louisiana territories. These expansionary policies continued with President Jackson, who pushed the Indians out of Florida and Georgia. Manifest Destiny is described as the fulfillment of this expansionist policy to its logical conclusion, that is, the contiguous east to west expansion of the United States across the North American continent from the Atlantic Ocean to the Pacific Ocean.

In 1840, the Whigs won the presidential contest with candidate William Henry Harrison, a veteran of the War of 1812. On March 4, 1841, Harrison delivered the longest inauguration speech ever on a cold and windy day, without wearing a coat or hat. Unfortunately, one month after his inauguration, he died of pneumonia. Upon Harrison's untimely death, Vice President John Tyler became President, setting a precedent for the transfer of power upon a president's death in office. Tyler asserted his independent views by vetoing Whig-sponsored bills for a national bank and an increase in tariffs. Tyler also challenged Whig anti-expansionist policies by proposing a simple majority vote to annex the Republic of Texas, which passed Congress and was signed by President Tyler days before the inauguration of the next president, James Polk.[45]

After Texas was annexed into the United States, an editorial by John L. O'Sullivan published in the July/August edition of *The Democratic Review* stated that it was our "manifest destiny" to distribute liberty and democracy throughout North America. Texas later ratified annexation on July 4, 1845 and was admitted as a state on December 29, 1845. This concept of manifest destiny was embraced by President Polk when he directed General Zachary Taylor to station his troops in the disputed territory of Texas between the Nueces River and the Rio Grande. The sudden appearance of U. S. forces in this "neutral" area provoked an attack by Mexico on April, 25, 1846, which Polk used as justification for an "existence of a war" with Mexico and for requesting 50,000 volunteers plus an appropriation of $10,000,000 for waging the war effort. It was a popular and quick war, lasting from the spring of 1846 to the fall of 1847, in which battle after battle were soundly won by the Americans. The war was successfully concluded with the Treaty of Guadalupe Hidalgo on February 2, 1848.[46]

As a Whig representative from the state of Illinois in Congress from 1847 to 1849, Lincoln was manifestly against the expansionist policies of President Polk. When he became President, Lincoln did not overtly support expansionist policies, but Congressional actions and laws signed by the President did. Due to the policies implemented by Lincoln's administration, such as the Railroad Act of 1862 and the Homestead Act, westward expansion was further enabled to make Manifest Destiny become a reality. The transcontinental railroad was one of the infrastructure investments that Lincoln, who also saw military and political benefits in the plan, advanced as part of his economic program to promote prosperity in the country. Completing a railroad to California was actually a plank of the Republican party from the 1860 national convention, as was the Homestead Act. The Railroad Act of 1862 provided federal support of a project that had been an ongoing goal of expansionists and capitalists since the 1840s. On May 10, 1869, when East met West with the nailing of the golden spikes on the transcontinental railroad at Promontory, Utah, it drove home the final nail in the implementation of Manifest Destiny for the United States.[47]

Lincoln made the "manifest destiny" of a contiguous continental United States from the Atlantic to the Pacific a reality. The expansion of America "from sea to shining sea" was never an objective of Lincoln as a Republican and was actually rejected by Lincoln as a Whig. But by keeping the United States united, by keeping every state in the Union and not allowing the successionists to succeed, the manifest destiny proclaimed by O'Sullivan is a legacy of President Lincoln.

Religion and Politics

Abraham Lincoln was not a devoutly religious man, but his speeches and writings used phrasing and cadence from the Bible, and he used them to great effect. He also referenced a higher power when speaking about the Civil War, and how God graced us with victories or was teaching us lessons when things were not going well. These messages graced his inauguration speeches, his proclamations, and other speeches and writings. For example, from his Gettysburg Address, the first line "Four score and seven years ago" is an allusion to Psalm 90: "The days of our years are threescore years and ten."[48]

Lincoln lived in a time when religion was a big part of everyday American life. Going to church on Sunday was a ritualistic event, yet he was not a regular churchgoer. Even though he was surrounded by an overwhelming majority of Christian churchgoers, he did not usually participate. The early 1800s experienced a large swath of Midwest communities settled by "revivalist" ministers, and one of those cities was Quincy, Illinois (the site of sixth Lincoln-Douglas debate). Also known as the Second Great Awakening, this movement expanded the Protestant religions (especially Baptist and Methodist) throughout the frontier states of Ohio, Kentucky, and Tennessee, and subsequently to other states. This explosion of conversion of frontiersmen, who heretofore had more of a "Doctrine of Necessity" attitude toward religion, to more civilized God-fearing folk is the background and perspective for Lincoln's attitude towards religion. When he was running for Congress in 1846, his opponent started a rumor of Lincoln's religious infidelity, because Lincoln did not belong to any church. Lincoln responded with publishing a handbill that rebuked the rumor by stating that, although he did not belong to a church, he is not an enemy of religion.[49]

In his second inauguration address, Lincoln quoted the Bible twice, said God's name six times and referred to Him six other times, all in less than 700 words. He quoted the book of Matthew, "Woe unto the world because of offenses," and Psalm 19, "The judgments of the Lord are true and righteous altogether." The closing paragraph of that address is one of Lincoln's most eloquent lines, "With malice towards none, with charity for all; with firmness in the right, as God gives us to see the right . . ." Lincoln's use of language and biblical references show his belief in a higher power.[50]

At his second inauguration, Lincoln was the first president to accept the pledge in the shadow of the new Capitol dome, topped by Lady Liberty. On that cloudy day, as he started his speech the clouds opened up and shone a ray of light on Lincoln, almost like a halo. Some took it as an omen. The end of the war occurred on April 9, 1865, which was Palm Sunday. Lincoln was shot on Good Friday, April 14, and died the next morning. Some have noted those dates as indicative that he did the Lord's work, and like Jesus, God took him to his bosom when his work on earth was done.[51] Even people of Jewish faith saw similarities in Lincoln's life with Moses, and spoke in their synagogues how Lincoln had brought freedom to his people, but was not allowed to reach the Promised Land.[52]

Equality and Civil Rights

Lincoln freed the slaves and made the words and promise of the Declaration of Independence ring true "that all men are created equal." Lincoln was not the only person who had trouble mouthing the words of the Declaration of Independence, in view of how blacks were treated in this country. How could we say that sentence when the reality of our condition was so different? Even the founding fathers had to take issue with those words. John Adams, Samuel Adams, Benjamin Franklin, Benjamin Rush, Alexander Hamilton, and Thomas Paine are just some of the founding fathers who were against slavery. Also, Lincoln discussed in his Cooper Union speech that the founding fathers – or at least those who had signed the Constitution – were in favor of the gradual elimination of slavery by limiting its expansion and not allowing it into new territories. Stephen Douglas and other pro-slavery advocates justified their views by implying that the founding fathers meant "all <u>white</u> men are created equal," and that the missing word was unnecessary. In the first debate with Lincoln in Ottawa, Illinois, Douglas said, "I believe this Government was made on the white basis. I believe it was made by white men for the benefit of white men and their posterity forever, and I am in favor of confining citizenship to white men, men of European birth and descent, instead of conferring it upon negroes, Indians, and other inferior races."[53]

Lincoln's personal views on race and the rights of blacks in society matured over time. He was a creature of his experience and upbringing, and he was slow to come around to the view that the Civil War must not only be about reuniting the country, but it must also be about ending slavery in the United States. He was born in a slave state (Kentucky) and moved to a state that had laws against blacks living there (Illinois). But his father – Thomas – left Kentucky with his family when Lincoln was young because Thomas didn't like slavery, so Abraham did grow up with an aversion to slavery. That negative view of slavery was reinforced during Abraham's trips down the Mississippi River to New Orleans, when he saw firsthand how slaves were treated in the South.

Lincoln's personal experiences and encounters with blacks were rare, so he had a typically biased and uneducated viewpoint. This perspective was greatly modified during his time as President, when he had face-to-face discussions with people like Frederick Douglass. Frederick Douglass commented that Abraham Lincoln was the first important man in America he had met who did not make him feel different or remind him of their differences in color. As Lincoln evolved and became more aware of his own attitudes and biases, he did become more sympathetic and aligned with the abolitionist cause. Lincoln lived in a time when attitudes and beliefs were much more racist than they are today, but even that is a more recent turn of events. Without the prevalence of cell phones with video cameras capturing the reality of race relations in America today, we could still be living in a *laissez faire* attitude toward race. In any case, no president before Lincoln did as much as he did for race relations in the United States.[54]

The End of Slavery
Lincoln is known around the world as the man who ended slavery in the United States. Although he cannot take sole credit for this feat, he was like a catalyst that turned the op-

posing forces into a volatile mix as the nation exploded into a war not originally fought to end slavery but rather to prove that a country "so dedicated" to the democratic process could legitimately manage itself – that is, not devolve into anarchy – and which then became a war to end that "peculiar institution" of human bondage. Although Lincoln did not originally see the War between the States as a battle on the principle of slavery, he eventually came to that conclusion, which was realized in the issuance of the Emancipation Proclamation.

The Emancipation Proclamation is an example of Lincoln's vision, determination, and strategic thinking. In one bold stroke, he took the premise of the war from a question of Union or dis-Union to the crusade of a just cause – the end of slavery in the United States. The national and international reaction was overwhelming and swift. Immediately after the Proclamation was made public, anti-slavery proponents (abolitionists) descended upon the White House to congratulate the President. And at a time when the Confederacy was secretly trying to get European powers, particularly England, to recognize its independence, this action struck a blow to those chances, England having outlawed slavery in 1833. Slavery was abolished in the colonies of France with an emancipation proclamation in 1848, and Lincoln's proclamation eliminated any chance that the European powers would recognize Confederate independence.

Lincoln went on to win the war for the North by continuing to replace general after general in the army, until he finally found a man of action capable of defeating the Confederates. Ulysses S. Grant had succeeded in taking the fight to the South by repeatedly and aggressively winning battles against previously successful Southern generals in the "western" regions (that is, west of the Appalachia Mountains). General Grant, and his second in command, General Sherman, became the two weapons Lincoln most needed to prosecute the war to a successful conclusion. This eliminated the need to pacify his opponents – notably in Congress clamoring to end the financial and human costs of the war – by ending the war without ending slavery. In the end, using the talents of "Unconditional Surrender" Grant and "Uncle Billy" (aka "Crazy Billy) Sherman as his instruments to finally gain control of the conduct of the war to a predictable and certain path, Lincoln was not only able to bind the two sides, North and South, back into the whole – the Union – he was also able to ensure the end of slavery in the United States forevermore.[55]

Lincoln's second inaugural address in March 1865 laid out the reasons for the war in simple and understandable terms. The South, he said, made war on the North, and the North accepted war rather than allow a dissolution of the Union, and although almost 15 percent of the nation's population was in bondage, that part of the population was concentrated in the South. Therefore, slavery was the cause of the war. It had been an interest and a scourge on the nation for 250 years, and that although we pray the war to end, it may be God's will for it to continue "until every drop of blood drawn by the lash, shall be paid by another drawn by the sword."[56]

The end of slavery in the United States was a just and righteous cause, for which the administration would continue the war until that objective was successfully achieved. On April 9, that objective was achieved with Robert E. Lee's surrender at Appomattox, and the South accepted unconditional forfeit of their arms and their cause.

Our Third Great President

Our third Great President was Franklin Roosevelt. He was also a great communicator and used the new radio medium to distinct advantage. His "fireside chats" calmed the frayed nerves of many Americans during the dark days of the Great Depression. President Franklin Roosevelt was first elected during one of the worst crises of our country. He is credited with initiating some of the most sweeping reforms to ever be enacted by Congress. Some of the hallmarks of his administration – the 1934 Securities Act, Social Security, and many of the other New Deal acts – are still with us today.

Franklin Delano Roosevelt followed the same path to the presidency as his older and favorite cousin, Theodore Roosevelt. Theodore Roosevelt started his political career in the in the New York Assembly. From there he became the Assistant Secretary of the Navy. Then Theodore became the New York State governor. In the 1900 Presidential election, he was McKinley's running mate. And after President McKinley was assassinated in 1901, Theodore became President. Franklin Roosevelt followed the same path as his idol. He was a New York State Senator. He became Assistant Secretary of the Navy under President Woodrow Wilson. He was a Vice Presidential candidate for the Democratic ticket in 1920. He also served as governor of New York.

The younger Roosevelt (Franklin) had a love of the sea, and often sailed his father's 50-foot sloop from New York to Massachusetts. He was also enthralled by stories of heroic sea battles, and devoured Theodore Roosevelt's classic book, *The War of 1812*, which dissected the strategy and tactics of the naval battles between the British fleet and U.S. warships. Roosevelt used his knowledge of the sea and Navy history to strengthen U.S. Naval forces during his tenure as Assistant Secretary of the Navy, which occurred just prior to and during World War I. These experiences also prepared him well for the next world war, which happened during his tenure as president.

President Roosevelt guided our country through the most challenging period in world history, the Second World War. Whereas the First World War was mostly a European and Atlantic Ocean conflict, the Second World War engulfed Europe, Asia, and Africa, and threatened Australia and North America. At least 30 countries were involved, making it the most widespread war in human history. Millions of people died, hundreds of millions of lives were affected, and it was the deadliest war in human history.

Franklin Roosevelt is the only president to serve three full terms and the only president to be re-elected three times (his fourth term was cut short by his untimely death in 1945). He broke the unwritten rule about not serving as president longer than George Washington; however, his rationale for breaking that rule was a good one, as the world was already engulfed in the flames of World War II, and it was only a matter of time before the United States would be involved. On that he was quite prescient, and he led the country and the world through the worst crisis it had ever seen. For this and all the other positive and enduring things he did while he was President, he well deserves the title "Greatest President of the 20th Century."

CHAPTER 9

A Beaten Path

Franklin Delano Roosevelt followed the same path to the presidency as his older and favorite cousin, Theodore Roosevelt. They shared more than a name, they shared a zest for life and were both high energy individuals. While neither had to have a job owing to their inheritance and position in society, they both chose the path of making the most of their opportunities for education and realization of their potential. Both went to Harvard, and both went to law school afterwards (though neither finished, Franklin eventually getting into a law firm after passing the New York State bar examination). Theodore was Franklin's senior by over 20 years, and was actually President of the United States when Franklin was in college at Harvard. Ultimately, Franklin would follow his footprints like a path through the forest.

Each decided at a relatively early age he would become a politician. In the late 1800s, politics in the United States was rife with corruption and was regarded by the members of upper society (of which the Roosevelts certainly were) as something best left to the "professionals," like any other distasteful, dirty job. Theodore's father, Theodore Roosevelt, Senior, also felt this way, particularly after being appointed by President Rutherford Hayes to the position of Collector of Customs to the Port of New York. The Senate confirmation process for his nomination was so politicized and drawn out, that Theodore

Sr. was completely embarrassed and distressed by the process.[1]

Given his father's experience with politics, it is ironic that his son would one day become President of the United States. While originally his plan was to specialize in natural history and zoology, he eventually decided on a career in government. Theodore told a friend, even before he graduated from college, that he had a premonition he would be president someday. He also told his family, who were questioning his career choices, that he belonged to "the governing class."[2]

Similarly, Franklin told friends at the New York city law firm – where he had his first job – that he planned a political career that would take him from Governor of New York to President of the United States. He was greatly impressed by the success of his famous cousin and was enthralled that Theodore was to give Franklin's bride away at their wedding. Franklin and Eleanor, his bride to be, were invited to Theodore's 1904 Presidential inauguration, and attended the inauguration at the Capitol building, lunch afterward in the White House, and the inauguration ball that night.[3]

Franklin's experiences along each step of his career path, brought him closer and closer to realization of his ultimate dream: to become President of the United States. The fact that his older cousin had already realized that goal provided him the blueprint of his path forward, and as he checked off each signpost and milestone along the way, he could always look to Theodore's *curriculum vitae* as a reference check for progress. Even the signature difference between their paths to power – the fact that Theodore was a Republican and Franklin was a Democrat – did not deter Franklin's approach, because they both were progressives and ultimately had the common man's interests at heart when making policy and political decisions. In order to understand how both men came to have so much in common despite having started from different perspectives, it is necessary to go back to the beginning.

Worldly View

Both Theodore and Franklin travelled extensively as children. They were afforded this luxury because their parents were extremely well off, and it was something that the people of their class were expected to do. Theodore's first trip abroad was a family vacation throughout Europe, including stops in London, and was an extensive affair. Theodore Roosevelt's Grand Tour of Europe in 1869 was over a year in length (377 days), with visits to England, the Netherlands, Germany, Switzerland, Italy, Austria, and France. At the time, young Theodore was only 10 years old and had terrible attacks of asthma, which his father tried various methods to cure, from Russian baths to chest massages to smoking cigars.[4]

Between Theodore's first and second international vacations, he started private lessons in French, German, and Latin, while his father planned their next cultural experience. Then, in October 1872, the Roosevelt's second European tour started, this one adding on Egypt and the Holy Lands. Theodore Roosevelt, Senior had been appointed as a commissioner to the Vienna Exposition, and wanted to give his family another worldly experience, while the younger Theodore looked forward to an expedition to North Africa. Their family travels would take them from England and Belgium through the European continent to Egypt, then on to Palestine, Syria, Turkey, and Greece before returning to Austria. While their father attended to his business in Vienna, the Roosevelt children spent the summer in Germany, housed and educated by their German hosts (English was not allowed to be spoken in the house).[5]

Franklin Roosevelt's family also travelled extensively while he was young, which gave him worldly experience and a global perspective. James Roosevelt, Franklin's father, was a rich man when he married Sara Delano, Franklin's mother. Their honeymoon in Europe lasted 10 months in the most luxurious places in Italy, Switzerland, Germany, Holland, France, Spain, England, and Scotland, and before the honeymoon was over, Sara was pregnant with Franklin. They would return to Europe as a family eight more times before Franklin was aged 15, and each trip was several months long with visits to aristocracy and persons of affluence in every instance.[6]

On one such trip when Franklin was seven years old, his family stayed at the Palace of Versailles in France, then went on to spending the winter in Pau in southern France close to the border with Spain. While in Pau, they visited with the Princess Christian of Holstein, the Duke and Duchess of Rutland, Lord Clanwilliam – the Admiral of the British Fleet – and Sir Cameron Gull, Member of the British Parliament. It was during this trip that Sir Cameron taught young Franklin how to swim – by tying a rope around his waist and throwing him in the water. If it looked like Franklin was struggling, he would pull him out with the rope, only to throw him back in again.[7]

One day, when Franklin was 14 years old and touring Europe with his tutor, he was in London and wanted to see the bird collection in the South Kensington Museum. As it turned out, that day the Prince of Wales was dedicating a new wing of the museum and entrance required a special invitation. The resourceful Franklin pulled out his gold embossed lifetime membership card to the New York Natural History Museum (a gift from his grandfather, Warren Delano), and he and his tutor were admitted as scientists. Later that same trip, Franklin was also able to use his command of the German language to enable him and his tutor to avoid issues with the Teutonic authorities. The story is that Franklin and the tutor were on a bicycle tour of western Germany, and they were arrested for running over and killing a goose – Franklin was able to convince the police to let them go after simply paying a fine.[8]

Harvard

Both Theodore and Franklin attended Harvard. Both were in the upper echelon of this bastion of New England high society. Neither Theodore nor Franklin was popular at school, because they both associated with strictly the "gentleman sort" of their peers. Theodore was invited to join the oldest club at Harvard, the famous Porcellian. Franklin also hoped to join the Porcellian, but they did not choose him. This would constitute an experience of rejection that he had never felt before, and would serve him as a touchstone for empathy of others who were victims of societal injustice. Instead, he was elected to Alpha Delta Phi (the Fly), ranked as the third highest social club at Harvard.[9]

Another common thread in their college careers was that they were both librarians for their social clubs. Theodore became librarian for the Porcellian, while Franklin became the librarian for Alpha Delta Phi, in addition to being elected to the library committee for the Harvard Union and librarian for the Hasty Pudding club. Both Theodore and Franklin were avid readers and aspiring writers. Theodore published his first book in the summer before his sophomore year, *The Summer Birds of the Adirondacks*.[10] Theodore would go on to publish another 37 books on subjects from naval strategy to hunting and fishing. Both Theodore and Franklin were bird watchers and potential future ornithologists, as Franklin had also written a treatise titled "Birds of the Hudson River Valley" which impressed his grandfather Warren Delano so much that the old gentleman – as previously noted – gave Franklin a lifetime membership to the New York Natural History Museum.[11]

During this time at Harvard, Theodore began to write one of the most significant works on naval strategy ever composed, *The Naval War of 1812*. He started on this project before he graduated from Harvard *magna cum laude* in June 1880 and finished the manuscript by November 1881 during his Columbia Law School years. He used his access to the Astor Library, across the street from Columbia, to research every aspect of his 500-page volume. *The Naval War of 1812* was published in 1882 and became an instant classic. It went through multiple editions by 1884, was used as a textbook for several colleges, and in 1886 became required library material on every ship in the U. S. Navy. For the next 100 years, it remained a reference text for its subject.[12]

Franklin would never become the writer that Theodore was, but he did work diligently on the school's student newspaper, the *Crimson*. He progressed to secretary of the paper, then editor, and eventually to the position of president of the *Crimson*, who was editor-in-chief of the paper and responsible for writing all the newspaper's editorials as well as making news policy decisions. On account of his librarian and editorship positions at the school, he was invited to join the Signet, the school's literary society that included as members most of Harvard's English professors. Franklin's association with the librarian positions and the school newspaper also put him in contact with a book dealer who specialized in old and rare editions. Through purchasing books for the libraries of his clubs, Franklin also started purchasing books for his own personal library, and soon became a collector of rare naval history books, manuscripts, and prints. His collection would eventually become one of the finest in the country.[13]

Father's Death

Theodore loved and adored his father, whom he called "the best man I ever knew."[14] When his father passed away at the age of 46 during his sophomore year at Harvard, it hit Theodore particularly hard. Theodore was away at school in February 1878, studying for the mid-year exams, when he received an urgent telegram to come home immediately. He caught the first train home that afternoon and arrived the next morning, but it was too late – his father had passed around midnight on February 9. Young Theodore returned to school on February

23, and for the next several months, his private diary was filled with his expressions of grief and despair. By sheer force of will, young Theodore managed to complete the remainder of his sophomore year at Harvard without a significant impact to his studies.[15]

Theodore's melancholy continued through the summer and fall, and he expressed his longing to see his father in vivid dreams and daytime visions, as if he were alive. Theodore was wrapped in the guilt of a child whose parent dies when the child is not around, and in his diary expressed his remorse of not being there when his father needed him most. He spent that summer trying to fill every available moment with activity, from swimming to rowing, to riding horses. He also spent time with his brother hiking, hunting and wrestling. Then, during the last few weeks of the summer break, before he had to go back to Harvard for his junior year, he travelled to the back-woods of northern Maine at the suggestion of a friend. There he was introduced to a local guide and hunter by the name of Bill Sewall. Bill was as big as a bear and as tough as a Viking, and stated that his ancestors might have been. Theodore may have found in this giant of a man the father figure he needed and longed for.[16]

Franklin's father died during his freshman year at Harvard. As opposed to Theodore's experience of surprise and shock, Franklin's experience was not far removed from expectations. His father had been sick for many years and had grown older and weaker in front of Franklin's eyes. James had married Sara, his second wife, at the age of 52, exactly twice her age when they tied the knot in June 1880, so James was already 72 years old when Franklin started college. James' health had been failing for many years, and during the first semester Franklin was at Harvard, James had spent time under a doctor's care and took a trip to South Carolina for rest. Franklin had sent many letters to his mother urging her to tell his father to rest and listen to the doctor. Then in late November, he spent time at home in Hyde Park, New York with his parents, stepbrother and stepmother, to all be together. By early December, it was clear that the end was near for James, and Franklin was brought back from school to be at his father's bedside for the man's final hours. On Friday, December 7, 1900, Franklin and his stepbrother Rosy were at home to say their final goodbyes to their father. James Roosevelt passed at 2:20 a.m. the next morning. Franklin was so concerned about how well his mother would hold up after the funeral, that he spent the remainder of the month with her at home in Hyde Park. He returned to college on January 1, 1901.[17]

Marriage

Both Theodore and Franklin would look out into the crowd during commencement at Harvard and see their fiancée, having fallen in love and proposed during their college years. Theodore would wed his "little Queen" within four months of graduation and start law school right after that; his honeymoon in Europe with Alice would have to wait until the summer.[18] Franklin would have a longer engagement, and married his sweetheart in March 1905, over a year after graduating from college and during his first year at law school. Franklin and Eleanor would also have to wait until the following summer for their honeymoon in Europe.[19]

Theodore got engaged on Valentine's Day 1880, and proclaimed his love for Alice in letters to his friends and relatives, and profusely in his diary. He would state that he was lucky to have her, and was so happy it almost made him fearful. Lucky for him, Alice was as in love as he was, as she stated in a letter to her new family. Theodore's family was also supportive and welcomed Alice among them. They knew she came from a good family, and were appreciative of her charm, beauty and grace. Theodore and Alice would have an eight-month long engagement, and would spend endless hours together reading, playing tennis, and riding around campus in a horse drawn

THE NEXT GREAT PRESIDENT

buggy. Theodore's studies were impacted, but this was his senior year, so he felt he could be somewhat "idle." That feeling proved correct when he graduated 21st out of 177 in his class.[20]

The summer flew by as wedding preparations progressed, and Theodore took pains to stay busy and not let the upcoming event overwhelm him. He decided to spend part of the summer hunting in the West with his brother Elliott and tried to overcome his homesickness and longing for his future bride with letters home describing in detail his adventures on the frontier. Then they finally made it back to New York, and it was only six weeks until the wedding. When Theodore was married at noon on his birthday in October 1880, he was 22 years old.[21]

Franklin's experience with his engagement and marriage to Eleanor Roosevelt was somewhat of a different affair. In November 1903, Franklin announced to his mother Sara that he had proposed to Eleanor, and she had accepted. Although Eleanor was a distant cousin and the niece of President Theodore Roosevelt, Sara felt she wasn't "good enough" for her son. Sara went so far as to recommend they keep the engagement private because they were both so young, and to have time to assure they wanted to go through with it. In the meantime, Sara would do what she could to try to make sure they wouldn't go through with it. Sara gave Franklin a cruise to the Caribbean in January 1904, after he had completed his BA studies at Harvard.[22]

As they said their goodbyes to Eleanor in New York, Sara hoped that Franklin, being distracted with the sights and scenery on the six-week cruise, would change his mind about his fiancée. It didn't work. The separation actually caused more longing in Franklin, for when he and Eleanor were reunited after the cruise, he spent nearly every moment he could with her. Their engagement was officially announced in late November 1904, and because Eleanor's father Elliott had died when she was only nine years old, it was decided that her uncle Theodore – the President of the United States – would give the bride away. Theodore was thrilled about the news of the engagement and in his congratulatory letter told Franklin how much he liked and believed in him. When Franklin married Eleanor on St. Patrick's Day in 1905, he was 22 years old, and already working on the next phase of his life – law school.[23]

Law School

Both Theodore and Franklin attended Columbia Law School. Theodore started classes at Columbia a few weeks after marrying Alice and getting situated in New York. From the first day of school on November 17, Theodore charged into class with seriousness and boundless energy. He took the same approach to his studies at Columbia as he did at Harvard, that is to ask questions and challenge answers, with a determination that earned the admiration of his law school classmates. While his classmates appreciated the earnestness and fairness of the man, they understood long before he did that the law was not Theodore's true calling.[24]

Theodore also started dabbling in two other interests that would dominate his life in later years: politics and writing. He got his start in politics by hanging out at the local Republican Association headquarters, Morton Hall. Here he would converse with the people who ran his political district, and he would keep coming back until he was eventually admitted for membership. The other major activity that Theodore undertook during that first year of law school, was his book, *The Naval War of 1812*. He spent countless hours in the Astor Library, researching every aspect of the book. He even sent requests to Washington, D. C., for official documents from the war.[25]

Theodore also took his manuscript and research papers with him on his five-month honeymoon to Europe with Alice. This European tour started in Ireland, and went on to England, France, Italy, Austria, and Germany. On the way back to England via Switzerland, Theodore climbed the Matterhorn. On the last month of his trip, he focused on writing, and while he was in Liverpool, he visited his uncle Irvine, who reviewed his manuscript with the eye of an old sea captain. Then, Theodore and his bride boarded a ship westward bound, and arrived in New York on October 2. He was back at school in November, and by the end of that month had completed his manuscript and sent it off to the publisher. He attended classes at Columbia, but by the next year he proved his classmates' earlier premonitions correct and pursued his other two interests – politics and writing.[26]

Franklin started at Columbia Law School in the fall of 1904, but he was less preoccupied with studying than spending time with Eleanor. In fact, he failed two of his classes that first year, and had to take make-up examinations the next year to continue pace with his classmates. Franklin was more interested in the political events occurring at the time, because his cousin Theodore had been elected President that November, and both he and Eleanor had been invited to the inauguration ceremonies for the following March. Just a few weeks after the inauguration, Eleanor and Franklin were married, and the President was to play a significant role in that event too; he was the man who gave away the bride.[27]

At the end of Franklin's first year of studies at Columbia, he and Eleanor took their official honeymoon. Following in Theodore's footsteps, the trip was also a multi-country tour of Europe. They started in England, then went to France, Italy and Scotland. While in Italy, Franklin climbed the Dolomites. Franklin also spent time studying; he had brought along his school books so he could catch up on the two classes he had failed earlier that year. Upon his return to school that next semester, he passed the two make-up exams and was back on track to graduate with his classmates. However, he didn't graduate and take his law degree. Instead, he took the New York State bar examination in 1907, and, having passed the bar, dropped out of school. With admittance to practicing law in the state of

New York, Franklin took a position in a Wall Street law firm, and waited for an opportunity to get into politics.[28]

New York Legislature

Both Theodore and Franklin served in the New York Legislature as their first political position in their careers, Theodore in the state Assembly and Franklin in the state Senate. They both fought the political "Boss" machine, an engine for political corruption – Theodore as a Republican, and Franklin as a Democrat. Theodore got his start as a candidate for the 21st District of New York Assembly. The day after his birthday in October 1881, he was nominated at the Assembly Convention in Morton Hall and selected as candidate on the first ballot. In the first professional political election of his career, he was elected that November by a 64% to 36% margin.[29]

Theodore started his political career in Albany, New York in January 1882. His first days in the new state capitol building were among the first days of the building itself, construction on the grand white granite structure having not yet been completed. Theodore burst on the scene as a member of the minority Republican party at a time when the New York legislature was staunchly Democratic. At this time in New York, state politics were grossly corrupt, no matter which party was in control. Yet Theodore was determined to do what he could to be a voice for progressive policies and to fight political corruption. Theodore's first year in office, if he were to figuratively look back through his pince-nez glasses in thought, would be considered a learning process.[30]

His second year in office would see those lessons applied in abundance, and the energy with which he threw himself into projects made the impression of a cyclone of political storm. Theodore became a party leader and reformer, leading the effort for civil service reform to reduce the number of political appointees versus government employees who could keep their jobs regardless of which political party was in office. He also introduced the Roosevelt Bill, which would change the New York City political landscape. Instead of the New York mayor having to defer decisions to political appointees called Aldermen, the Roosevelt Bill put that power in the hands of the mayor, who could be voted out of office by the citizens. But on the eve of the pinnacle of his success in the New York State Assembly, that is, passage of the Roosevelt Bill, Theodore was hit by the greatest personal setback of his life – the dual loss of both his wife and his mother on Valentine's Day 1884.[31]

Franklin started his political career in the same way as his cousin Theodore – in the New York state legislature. However, Franklin chose to run as a Democrat for a state senate seat, in a district that was largely a Republican stronghold in the Hudson Valley. He campaigned in an open car, a novelty in 1910, and crisscrossed the three-county district in search of votes. Franklin pledged his independence and railed against the political boss system and special interests. He also self-funded the campaign through the deep pockets of his mother, who was more than happy to support the pursuits of her only child. As often occurs during mid-term elections, the political tide ran against the Republican administration in power, and Democrats won seats in state elections across the country. Franklin upset the Republican incumbent candidate 52% to 48%, a narrow margin of victory but totally unexpected in the heavily Republican countryside.[32]

When Franklin joined his legislative cohorts in Albany that following January, he became embroiled in a political controversy. Before the implementation of the 17th Amendment of the Constitution, the process of nominating and selecting Congressional Senators was by vote of the elected members of the state legislature. Because the Democrats held the majority of both the state senate and the state assembly, it was almost a foregone conclusion that the elected Senator would be a Democrat; however, many of the progressive minded and newly elected members of the legislature (called the "Instigators") were opposed to the party boss politics that required them to choose the Tammany Hall machine candidate, William Sheehan. Although Franklin did not start the movement, and wasn't the Instigators' leader, he became their spokesman. For over two months (January 17 to March 25), the legislators took 58 separate votes, and still could not come up with a two-thirds majority candidate. Finally, the machine politicians came up with a compromise candidate, James O'Gorman, and he was elected on March 31.[33]

Owing to machine politics, Franklin was one of only three Instigators who was re-elected for the next term. He returned to Albany for the 135th New York State Legislature with national publicity and a reputation as a political reformer, much like his older cousin Theodore. Franklin became the public image of a reform politician, a tall and thin Roosevelt wearing pince-nez glasses, fighting "bossism" and Tammany Hall cronyism. This drew the attention of another reformer, the Democratic Governor of New Jersey, Woodrow Wilson. Wilson would become a key political contact in Franklin's next step on his path to the U. S. presidency.[34]

Assistant Secretary of the Navy

Both Theodore and Franklin served as Assistant Secretary of the Navy in Washington, D. C. They both received the appointment after having ingratiated themselves with their presidential candidate and campaign team, and tirelessly campaigning for the candidate – Theodore for William McKinley in 1896, and Franklin for Woodrow Wilson in 1912. Theodore's potential appointment stimulated many people, both for and against, to try to convince McKinley that he was either a hothead and belligerent who could not be trusted with military power (McKinley wanted to avoid a war), or that he was the most qualified candidate for the position due to his knowledge of the subject (Theodore's *The Naval War of 1812* being his calling card).[35]

McKinley named John Long his Secretary of the Navy, and Theodore Roosevelt the Assistant Secretary of the Navy. Long was as old and sedate as Theodore was young and active. Long was also as disinterested in the details and innerworkings of the Navy as Theodore was obsessively absorbing every aspect and intimate nuance of this government bureaucracy. They were a perfect pair. Soon, Long would take his summer vacation, and leave the reins in the hands of his subordinate. Theodore would waste no time in exerting his influence in this temporary capacity to approve fleet maneuvers in the North Atlantic, propose modern artillery for current ships, propose names of famous Navy personnel for future ships, and reduce paperwork. He did what he could to modernize the Navy and prepare for war, as his first public speech as Assistant Secretary of the Navy at the Naval War College emphasized preparedness via a military buildup.[36]

Theodore was so far-sighted that he helped Commodore George Dewey get assigned to command of the Asiatic Squadron, overseeing China and the Philippines, when Rear-Admiral McNair retired. He also made sure that war plans were in place, in case of trouble in Cuba or Hawaii. Theodore provided a memo to Secretary Long that identified several critical actions that should be implemented, such as gathering fleet forces together, fueling and prepping the fleets for deployment, and dispatching them to critical locations. Long ordered the North Atlantic Squadron to refuel at Key West, recalled South Atlantic ships to the equator, and sent a squadron to Portugal to monitor Spain's fleet movements. Theodore's preparations paid off, because when the *Maine* sank in Havana harbor one month later, the Navy was ready to respond.[37]

As a result of Franklin's efforts and contributions to Woodrow Wilson's effective presidential campaign, the second-term New York Senator was invited to the inauguration, and two days before the event was offered the positions of Assistant Secretary of the Treasury or Collector of the Port of New York.

Franklin did not accept either position, because the object of his deepest desire was to be the next Assistant Secretary of the Navy. At a chance meeting in the Willard Hotel on the day before the inauguration, incoming Secretary of the Navy Joseph Daniels offered him the Assistant position. Franklin replied that it was "the one place, above all others" that he wanted to have.[38]

St. Patrick's Day 1913 was not only Franklin's eighth wedding anniversary, it was also the day he was sworn in as Assistant Secretary of the Navy, and at age 31 he was the youngest in history. He now worked for a man who was a newspaper editor in North Carolina, and who had no knowledge or interest in the Navy or the sea. Similar to Theodore's experience as Assistant Secretary, this provided Franklin an opportunity to put his skills and knowledge of the Navy and the sea to its best use. However, he felt indebted to Daniels for the position. He also respected Daniels and they remained friends long after they were both out of office when President Wilson's second term expired.[39]

In 1914, when Germany declared war on Russia and invaded France through Belgium, Franklin immediately understood the implication and historical significance of the start of the Great War. Even though President Wilson declared American neutrality, Franklin focused his attention on preparing the U. S. Navy for the potential of being drawn into the war. He reported to Congress to respond to questions from the House Naval Affairs Committee and was widely praised for his testimony. Franklin's personal and professional growth in the eight years during President Woodrow Wilson's administration prepared him well for understanding the corridors of power in Washington. His experience as the Assistant Secretary of the Navy before and through World War I also served him well as President during World War II.[40]

War

Both Theodore and Franklin played significant roles in the global conflicts the United States became involved in during their tenures as Assistant Secretary of the Navy. Upon declaration of war by the United States against Spain, Theodore resigned his position in the government because he wanted to join the Army and fight in the war. He took his case to the Secretary of War, Russell Alger, and was offered the position of Colonel for the First U. S. Volunteer Cavalry, but due to his inexperience in the military he requested a Lieutenant Colonel position if his friend Leonard Wood, a Medal of Honor recipient from the Apache Wars, could take command. Theodore's request was accepted, and as this news was made public, Wood and Roosevelt received tens of thousands of requests from across the country to join Roosevelt's "Rough Riders."[41]

After training for two weeks at Camp Wood, near San Antonio, Roosevelt's 900 Rough Riders would travel by train to Tampa, where they would await assembly and departure directions. Upon arrival in Tampa, Theodore was informed that only two thirds of his volunteer troops would be needed, and in addition none of the horses (except for those of the officers) would be sent with them – they would become, for all intents and purposes, an infantry division and called the "dismounted" cavalry. Another two weeks would pass, before all the troops, supplies and equipment would be loaded onto ships for their passage to Cuba. In all, over 16,000 troops would make the five-day voyage, in an armada 25 miles long, from Florida across the Gulf of Mexico to that great Spanish island in the Caribbean.[42]

On July 1, 1898, the famous battles of Kettle Hill and San Juan Hill would cement Theodore Roosevelt's name in history and make him a national hero. The First Volunteer Dismounted Cavalry were ordered to move out towards San Juan Heights along Camino Real, the road to Santiago de Cuba, beyond the Heights. As they came upon San Juan Creek, they were met with a murderous volley of artillery and a hail of bullets from the Spanish atop the Heights. As General Kent's Infantry Division attacked San Juan Hill on the left, Theodore noticed a rise to the right from which another source of Spanish bullets was coming. Riding his horse, Little Texas, he led the charge up Kettle Hill, and upon meeting a barbed wire fence 100 feet from the crest, he jumped off and ran up the remainder of the hill killing Spaniards with his revolver. At the crest of the hill, he could plainly see the on-going battle on San Juan Heights, so he led his troops down Kettle Hill and up San Juan Heights. With the Rough Riders and the famous Buffalo Soldiers (the black 10th Cavalry), led by John "Black Jack" Pershing, General Kent was able to defeat the Spanish on San Juan Heights, and eventually take the town of Santiago. In 2001, Theodore would be posthumously awarded the Medal of Honor for his heroic acts on the battlefields in Cuba.[43]

When President Wilson finally asked Congress to declare war on Germany in April 1917, almost three full years after the start of World War I, Franklin had the same feelings as Theodore and wanted to join the military. In fact, Franklin was strongly encouraged by his cousin Theodore to quit working from behind a desk and get to the action. Both President Wilson and Secretary Daniels said they needed him where he was, because that was the best use of his abilities of organization, decision making, and administration. Even General Leonard Wood, Theodore Roosevelt's friend from the Spanish-American War, told Franklin that the country needed him to stay at the Navy Department. The country is lucky he did. At the beginning of the war, the U. S. Navy was a minor player on the world stage. By the end of the war, the number of Navy ships had more than tripled, and the U. S. Navy had more personnel than the British Royal Navy. Franklin was so good in his administrative talents, that he was called into the Oval office in President Wilson's and General Hugh Scott's audience, and directed to share supplies with the Army.[44]

Franklin used more than just his administrative skills in helping the Navy quickly get on a wartime footing; he also used his relationships and salesmanship. He encouraged and finally convinced the Navy to procure 110-foot small ships called "submarine chasers," which would be small enough and cheap enough to be procured and built on a massive scale, and could be effective in patrolling and protecting the East Coast's many harbors from U-boats. He also started a program called "Eyes for the Navy," which requested public donations of binoculars for the duration of the war. This campaign received 50,000 sets of magnifying glasses for Navy lookouts, and the original owners would receive their binoculars back with a signed certificate from the Assistant Secretary of the Navy, Franklin D. Roosevelt, at the conclusion of hostilities.[45]

Perhaps Franklin's most significant contribution to the war effort, was to convince the British Royal Navy of the strategic potential of bottling up German U-boats in their ports by laying mines in the North Sea. At a cost of $80,000,000, a mining force spent four months laying down 70,000 mines between the northern tip of Scotland and the western tip of Norway, a distance of about 240 miles. This mine barrier was credited with having destroyed as many as 23 German U-boats, and, perhaps along with that the German Navy's morale. Franklin's celebrity and reputation for his service as Assistant Secretary of the Navy during the war directly led to his nomination as the Democratic vice-presidential candidate for the 1920 election.[46]

Vice Presidential Candidate

Both Theodore and Franklin were their party's vice-presidential candidates. Theodore became the Republican vice-presidential candidate, and then the vice president when McKinley was elected. He was subsequently sworn in as president when McKinley was assassinated, but before that he had ridden his popularity as a war hero to the governorship of New

York, and then on to his vice-presidential candidacy. Republican National Committee (RNC) members from Wisconsin had visited Governor Roosevelt in Albany to let him know that a McKinley-Roosevelt ticket would be very strong, and they wanted him to be McKinley's running mate. RNC members weren't the only ones interested in getting Theodore on the McKinley ticket. In his first year as Governor of New York, he had managed to upset the bosses and machine politicians in the Legislature, including his biggest opponent, Senator Thomas Platt.[47]

Senator Platt was a corporate executive who was extremely pro-business, and when Theodore managed to get a franchise tax bill approved through the New York Legislature during his first session, the gloves were off. Senator Platt planned his revenge thoughtfully and thoroughly, intending to make sure Theodore would not sniff a second term as governor, and hoping that he could publicly embarrass him as much as possible in the process. Ultimately, it became more of an expedient process to promote Theodore's candidacy for nomination as vice president with the aim of getting him out of New York state politics. When McKinley's then vice president Garret Hobart died in November 1899, it almost seemed a matter of destiny that Theodore Roosevelt would become the vice-presidential candidate on the McKinley ticket for 1900, and the next Vice President of the United States.[48]

After Franklin's eight-year tenure as Assistant Secretary of the Navy, he was nominated to the Democratic ticket in 1920 as the vice-presidential candidate. He also rode his popularity and national prominence as the effective director of the Navy, both before and during the war, and its growth to one of the most powerful naval forces in the world under his direction. Franklin and Eleanor had embarked on a tour of Europe after the end of the Great War, and during their trip had been informed of Theodore's death on January 6, 1919. On the *George Washington* for their trip back to the United States,

Franklin encountered President Woodrow Wilson, who wanted to discuss his League of Nations draft covenant. The League of Nations, an idea ahead of its time, would be doomed to failure both by Wilson's high-handed approach to implementation and by health issues after his stroke in October 1919.[49]

After the war, veterans came back to an economy that was in shambles, because the war engine that had been producing so many ships, planes, bullets, and supplies, was now trying to revert to peace time production. As a result, unemployment was high, labor was in revolt, anarchists were trying to bring down the government, and people were fearful of a Bolshevik type of communist revolution. In this environment, Franklin considered his political future, and his political friends were considering him for the vice presidency. The Democrats were not looking like a good bet for 1920, but there were those in the party who considered a Herbert Hoover-Franklin Roosevelt ticket as an alluring prospect. Since Hoover was from California and Roosevelt was from New York, the east and west coasts could provide enough electoral votes for a win in November. Hoover was being dated by both political parties, but he finally came out as a Republican in March 1920. However, by then Franklin had the bug, and was still interested in continuing his candidacy.[50]

At the Democratic convention that summer, Franklin took every opportunity to look the part. With a speech that was short but effective, he seconded the nomination of New York Senator Al Smith for president. Eventually, Governor James Cox of Ohio was nominated for president on the forty-fourth ballot. Cox chose Roosevelt as his running mate, and Franklin was unanimously selected as the vice-presidential candidate at the next day's proceedings. His boss, Joseph Daniels, provided a convention-concluding speech that spoke to his organization's feelings for the Assistant Secretary as a patriot and clearly competent leader. Although the convention concluded in high spirits, and the candidates did all they could to campaign across the country and promote the ticket, they could not turn the tide of nationwide unrest and discontent. In November, Republican Warren G. Harding won the day with a "return to normalcy" refrain. And in 1921, a return to normalcy would become Roosevelt's greatest objective.[51]

Personal Tragedy

Both Theodore and Franklin endured personal tragedy that would impact their present, shape their future, and affect them for the rest of their lives. At the height of Theodore's political career as a New York state assemblyman, his fortunes changed, and over the course of 48 hours his life would alter forever. He was frantically working in Albany to ensure the passage of the Roosevelt Bill, right up to the due date of his first child. His "sweet dear" Alice and his mother Mittie were back at the family home in New York City, awaiting the arrival of the baby. On the morning of February 13, 1884, Theodore received a telegram announcing the birth of a daughter, and he made arrangements to catch a train ride home. Before he left Albany, he received a second telegram that changed his composure and caused him to accelerate his departure.[52]

Theodore arrived home and ran upstairs to take his beloved Alice into his arms, but she was so ill with an undiagnosed kidney ailment, that she could barely identify him. Meanwhile, his mother Mittie was downstairs dying of typhoid fever. He was informed that he needed to say goodbye to his mother before it was too late. It was early Valentine's Day morning, when he went downstairs and watched his mother take her last breath. Then he trudged back upstairs to spend the last moments with Alice. In the early afternoon of Valentine's Day, four years to the day from when they were engaged, Theodore said goodbye to Alice.[53]

Theodore would finish out the spring session of his legislative term, and in June would travel west to the Badlands of South Dakota. He would spend the next two years in the wilderness, hunting, fishing, ranching, and catching criminals to bring them to justice. It was all in an effort to bury the past, or at least live a life so close to the edge that if it didn't kill him, it would at least kill the pain in his heart. The pain was so great that Theodore would never again mention Alice's name. Although his daughter Alice Lee was named after her mother and would be cared for by his older sister for the first three years of her life, Theodore called her "Baby Lee." He liked living the life of a cowboy, because at the end of the day he was so exhausted he couldn't think, so at least he would be able to sleep at night.[54]

In August 1921, while vacationing with his family in Campobello, New Brunswick, Franklin Roosevelt came down with a mysterious illness that had him bedridden for two weeks. He was mis-diagnosed by two different doctors, and his friend Louis Howe recommended a third diagnosis. Eventually they sought the advice and consultation of Dr. Robert Lovett, a Harvard professor and a national authority on poliomyelitis. During Dr. Lovett's visit to Campobello on 25 August, he confirmed that Franklin had polio. Dr. Lovett provided the hope that recovery was possible, but only time would tell.[55]

After weeks of waiting and hoping, reality started to set in. Franklin was transported by private railroad car to a hospital in New York for specialized care. The secrecy surrounding Roosevelt's condition was vaporized by a front-page headline in the *New York Times*. Doctors implied that he had a mild case of polio that would not result in permanent paralysis, but the truth was he was not getting any better, he was getting worse. By the end of September, he had completely lost the use of his legs, and his back and arms were also affected. In October, he gradually began to get the feeling back in his arms and his back, and by the end of the month he was able to lift and turn his body with his arms and shoulders. Franklin was discharged on October 28 and taken by ambulance to his home in New York City.[56]

Like Theodore, for the next few years Franklin spent time in his own wilderness, a political wilderness that kept him from even thinking about a future in politics. Franklin also spent those years attempting to find a cure. He eventually established the National Foundation for Infantile Paralysis (NFIP), nicknamed by entertainer Eddie Cantor as the "March of Dimes" and which was a non-profit agency dedicated to the eradication of polio in children. Ten years after Franklin's death, the Salk vaccine for polio immunization was announced by the chairman of NFIP. Franklin's experience with polio had the double effect of fulfilling his understanding and sympathy for the less advantaged while making him a more sympathetic person to others. In these years he dealt with his condition in the most positive way and put a good face on.[57]

In April 1924, he was asked to chair a committee for the Democratic candidate for president, Albert E. Smith, Governor of New York. At the Democratic National Convention, held that summer in New York's Madison Square Garden, Franklin was the chairman for the New York delegation. He was asked to give the nominating speech for Al Smith and accepted. When he walked on crutches out on the stage, the crowd held their breath until he reached the podium, then exploded in wild applause as he smiled and clutched the sides of the lectern. At the end of his 34-minute speech, the Garden crowd "went crazy" with a demonstrative parade through the aisles and cheering that lasted over an hour. Franklin had returned from the political wilderness on the biggest stage and in the most convincing way. His future seemed brighter, and he allowed himself to start thinking about his political future again.[58]

Governor of New York

Theodore Roosevelt became Governor of New York, after his successful experience in the Spanish-American War, most notably his famous charge up San Juan Hill. Colonel Roosevelt was now the most famous man in America and would eventually leverage that popularity and fame all the way to the White House. In the meantime, the next appropriate step in his political career was to seek the Republican nomination for Governor of the State of New York in the 1898 election. Theodore knew full well from his previous experiences fighting corruption that he was persona non grata from the perspective of the political bosses in the Republican party, especially the "Easy Boss" – U. S. Senator from New York Thomas C. Platt.[59]

To ensure that he would get the nomination, Theodore played to the Independent Party interest in a progressive candidate with popularity, against the Republican Party interest in a famous candidate who could be placated, and possibly controlled, by his obvious ambition. Theodore would disappoint the Independents by accepting the Republican nomination, and then campaigned throughout the state on the issue of corruption of the judiciary by the machine politicians of Tammany Hall. He would win the election by a narrow margin and would take over the New York governorship in January 1899. As Theodore arrived in Albany, he decided he would try to work with Senator Platt and the machine in order to accomplish as much as possible during his tenure. He became a man of compromise and middle ground, with the notion of accomplishing the greatest good. In addition, he would operate with a level of openness and frankness to the press that was unprecedented in the 1800s, so the public would know what was going on. By the end of his term in 1900, he would become known as a friend of labor, a progressive on civil service reform, and a force against an alliance that combined politics with nameless, faceless corporate interests.[60]

Franklin also became the Governor of New York after his tour of duty as Assistant Secretary. However, for Franklin, there was a several year gap between serving as Assistant Secretary and Governor. The first few years of his polio illness were a period of adjustment and acclimation. His next few years were a period of transition and triumph. He started visiting Warm Springs, Georgia after the Democratic convention in 1924, and discovered the springs' therapeutic effects. The natural buoyancy of the warm waters helped him swim and exercise longer, to the point of being able to feel his toes for the first time in years. Franklin later purchased the land and hotel around the springs and created a foundation there that was dedicated to treating polio patients and performing research for finding a cure. He would split his time between New York and Warm Springs for the next two years, becoming an "adopted son" to the people of Georgia. This time of his life taught him a lot about rural America, and how people really lived in the country, often without basic necessities such as electricity, running water, education, shoes and proper clothing. Franklin became an advocate for these people and would carry that advocacy with him into the presidency.[61]

Franklin's nomination speech at the Democratic convention in 1924 started his road back into politics, and in 1926, he was asked to provide the keynote address at the state Democratic convention in New York. Al Smith was re-elected Governor of New York, and in 1928, he became the front runner for the Democratic presidential nomination. At the 1928 Democratic National Convention, Franklin again gave the nomination speech for Al Smith, and again he was cheered wildly. This time, he had learned to walk without crutches, by leaning on his son's arm and swinging his legs with his upper body while supporting his weight with a cane as he traversed across the stage. This time, his popularity and apparent good health, along with his speechmaking ability, made him an obvious candidate for higher office. The leaders of the Democratic party recognized that they needed him and his famous name to help them win the governorship of a key state like New York. Although Franklin wasn't sure the timing was right, he accepted being drafted as the Democratic candidate for Governor of New York. During the campaign, and straight through election night, the race was too close to call. But by the end of the evening, even though the 1928 Presidential election was a Republican landslide, Franklin won the race for governor with 50.3% of the vote. As he took this step on the path that was previously travelled by cousin Theodore, he knew the next step, the presidency, was now within reach.[62]

President

Both Theodore and Franklin took the road of governor of New York to the presidency. Theodore took a pit-stop as vice president, before his ascendency to the presidential office, but they both deservedly achieved their ultimate political goals by staying true to themselves and standing up for the rights of the common man. And Theodore's pit-stop as vice president did not last long. Six months after the inauguration, President William McKinley was shot by an anarchist at the Pan-American Exposition in Buffalo, New York. A week later, McKinley was dead, and Theodore Roosevelt, Jr. took the oath of the President of the United States.[63]

As the youngest leader of the youngest world power, Theodore would put his energy and enthusiasm into ensuring that the second century of the United States, and the 20th century of the modern world, would be America's century. He used an African proverb in a speech about foreign policy: "Speak softly and carry a big stick, and you will go far." But he was quoted as saying only the first phrase of the proverb. Theodore created an addition to the Monroe doctrine about the Americas in the Western hemisphere, and stated in his address to Congress that the United States has the right to police these countries. He created a commission for the building of the Panama Canal and considered a canal of critical importance for worldwide commerce and U.S. security. Theodore also proposed the construction of a great fleet of battleships and sent them around the world on a goodwill tour of six continents and a dozen countries over 14 months. The tour of the Great White Fleet was not only a successful attempt at "sabre rattling" diplomacy aimed at the Japanese (which convinced Japan to sign the "Gentleman's Agreement" on immigration), but was also an education for the U.S. Navy in circumnavigation and the ineffectiveness in the construction of their battleships. These are but a fraction of Theodore's actions and impact in shaping America's future destiny.[64]

Franklin ran for president after serving as the Governor of New York. Franklin's was not the exact same path as that of his cousin, but nearly identical, and being of the same last name, it was almost expected of him. It is, however, a sad note to realize that because Theodore died in 1919 at the age of 60 years old, the older Roosevelt never saw his admirer and cousin rise to that same level of prominence and distinction. Franklin became president long after Theodore had passed away, but he used Theodore's blueprint and his political legacy as a path to his ultimate political goal. Franklin not only followed Theodore's beaten path, but he also improved on the result, and became one of the greatest presidents in the history of the United States.

Franklin's years as Governor of New York were an important stepping stone and training ground for his years as president. He took the governor's office in January 1929, less than ten months before the Great Crash of the stock market and the beginning of the Great Depression. His initial focus as governor was to help farmers and rural New Yorkers with proposals on agricultural tax relief, on using a dam system to supply rural electricity, and on providing subsidies for farming research. After the stock market crash, Franklin would become a proponent for unemployment insurance, and he created the first state employment commission in the United States. He was re-elected governor in 1930, and from that moment on was favored to become the next Democratic nominee for president. In his second term as governor, Franklin would try out different assistance programs to help the people of New York endure the economic hardships of the Depression. He also attracted national attention by his condemnation of the Hoover administration with his "Forgotten Man" speech, a criticism of Hoover for not addressing the core issues of the Depression.[65]

Franklin would attend the Democratic National Convention in Chicago and receive its nomination as the presidential candidate. As time progressed to the national elections in 1932, Franklin continued to attack Hoover and the Republicans for their lack of empathy for the American people and their *laisse faire* approach to economic recovery. Franklin was elected during a landslide for Democratic candidates across the board, from the states to a plurality in both houses of Congress. Franklin Roosevelt was the right person in the right place at the right time to lead the country out of the Depression and into better days.[66]

CHAPTER 10

The Great Depression

Before the Great Depression began, unemployment was running at about 3%. By the time it was in full swing, unemployment peaked at about 25%.[1] This means that 15 million Americans were jobless. In part, the increase in unemployment was driven by a reduction in production, which itself was driven by a reduction in consumption. During the Great Depression, more than 32,000 businesses went bankrupt and more than 5,000 banks failed. Wages dropped by 42%, prices fell by 10% per year, and GDP nearly halved (from $103 billion to $55 billion).[2] Farm prices dropped so low that most of the independent farmers went bankrupt or lost their farms to the bank. In addition, weather patterns in that decade provided record droughts, and the Midwest became a "dust bowl" – unable to sustain any crops whatsoever. As a result, many American farmers moved west, to California, in search of work. The great book by John Steinbeck, *The Grapes of Wrath*, fictionalized the stories of some of these people.[3]

The depression hit the banking system especially hard. The life blood of the banking system was the loans that were provided to businesses and other banks. In this period of severe contraction, less and less loans were being made. In addition, the Federal Reserve was trying to save the biggest, most financially stable banks, while the majority of the smaller banks, and especially the state-chartered banks (which were not overseen by the Fed) were left to flounder. To make matters worse,

Americans were losing their jobs, and because of not being able to pay the mortgage, losing their houses at an alarming rate. It was an ever increasing and self-sustaining effect. These were some of the most difficult days for Americans in our history, and these difficulties were not helped, but were actually made worse by President Hoover.[4]

The Great Depression began after the stock market crash in 1929, lasted throughout the 1930s, and ended at the start of World War II.[5] The severity of the downturn was actually made worse by the action (or inaction) of President Hoover and Congress. The Smoot-Hawley Act imposed severe tariffs on products shipped to the United States. The thinking was that this "protectionist" act would save U. S. jobs, when actually the opposite occurred. By increasing tariffs and limiting imports, the United States incited reactionary tariffs from other countries, thereby reducing sales of U. S. products overseas by over 40 percent.[6] This led to a further slowdown in production and subsequent layoffs at exporting companies.[7]

Another action taken by President Hoover that worsened conditions leading to the Great Depression was a tax cut he proposed at the end of 1929. In and of itself, the tax cut would not have caused much damage. However, President Hoover was also a champion of a balanced budget. He even urged the incoming president, Franklin Roosevelt, to maintain a balanced budget. By reducing revenues via the tax cut, he was also required to reduce spending at a time when additional federal spending was warranted. The fear of going off the gold standard and risking inflation also made things worse. The country had experienced significant inflation over the previous decade, and all the financial advisors and economic policy experts were "looking in the rearview mirror," that is, concerned about additional inflationary effects, when in fact the opposite was the case – the country was experiencing the worst deflation since the post-Civil War period.[8]

Hoover's Failure

Hoover's inaction to take appropriate steps were as impactful to the deepening and worsening of the Depression as the steps he did take. The Smoot-Hawley Act called for the highest tariffs in U. S. history, and was passed by Congress, but Hoover had the opportunity to veto the bill. He would receive requests and encouragement to veto the tariffs, domestically and from around the world. Thomas Lamont, a J. P. Morgan executive, later said he had almost begged Hoover to veto the bill. General Motors offices in over a dozen different countries sent him telegrams that also complained, and their European director said it would result in "economic isolation" for the United States. Over one thousand economists signed a letter to President Hoover recommending a veto of the tariff bill, which was later published in the *New York Times*, and also predicted retaliatory tariffs which would reduce exports and increase unemployment.[9]

Bank runs occurred as a result of Hoover's failure to take action to ease the public's sense of panic and mass hysteria. Also, those fears were augmented by rich society's anticipation of what the new president would do to face the growing problem (nationalize the banking system, declare capitalism dead, become a dictator, embrace communism, socialism, or fascism, etc.), and their withdraws of cash from the banking system. State by state bank closures, starting in Detroit, Michigan started a new wave of panic in 1932, and President Hoover still refused to take action to stem the tide. He insisted on a joint announcement with the incoming administration of Franklin Roosevelt on how to approach the problem. This was interpreted by Roosevelt as a trap by the current administration to support their failed policies and accept some responsibility for Hoover's failures. Roosevelt side-stepped Hoover's advances for a combined approach to the crisis, in order to avoid committing to any specific program, and to give himself and his new administration the flexibility to respond to the crisis as it evolved. Ultimately, Franklin Roosevelt's landslide election gave him and his new administration the public approval and a calling to take unprecedented action or whatever else was required to address the economic, social, and political issues facing the nation.[10]

Franklin's acceptance speech at the Democratic National Convention in July 1932 promised "a New Deal for the American people," and these were the words the American people wanted to hear. All of President's Hoover's fear mongering and claims of the Democratic Party representing mob rule, ended up being self-inflicted wounds. Hoover had dealt with thousands of unemployed veterans' requests for early payment of their WWI bonus pay by sending a military response led by General McArthur to disperse or arrest the veterans' large assembly near the Capitol at Anacostia Flats. Hoover's actions and his message were not well received by the American public.[11]

Roosevelt's Election

From the convention in June, to election day in November, the result was a foregone conclusion. Roosevelt and the Democratic Party won an unprecedented majority across the country. Unfortunately for the nation, and for President Roosevelt's chances to make an immediate positive impact, there would be a four-month delay between his election and being able to take over the reins. This was because the 20th Amendment of the Constitution, which moved the Presidential inauguration from March 4 to January 20, was not ratified until January 1933. The Lame Duck amendment, as it is also known, attempted to limit or eliminate actions of the President or legislators who have been voted out of office. In the case of the transition from Hoover to Roosevelt, the transfer of power could not come soon enough, because of the economic state of the nation and its impact on the majority of Americans across the country. Farm income had been cut in half from before the Depression, commodities prices were so low that it cost more to harvest the crops than what they were worth, hundreds of thousands of children were malnourished, and states were closing thousands of schools.[12]

As the season deepened into winter, the Depression deepened also. By February 1933, almost 400 banks had closed since the beginning of the year, and the entire nationwide banking system was on the verge of failure. In Michigan, one of the largest banks in Detroit, Union Guardian Trust, was perilously close to collapse. Their largest depositor was Henry Ford, who was asked to promise not to withdraw the $7.5 million he held there. Ford not only refused to make that promise, but also threatened that if Union did not remain open, then he would pull all $25 million in deposits that Ford Motor Company held at First National Bank.[13] This caused the Governor of Michigan, William Comstock, to close all of the state's over 500 banks for the next eight days or longer, in order to provide time to resolve the situation. The crisis spread like an epidemic, as banking depositors across the country stood in long lines to withdraw their funds and stash it under their mattress. The next state Governor to close its banks was Maryland's Governor Ritchie, and Kentucky and Tennessee soon followed.[14]

On February 15, Roosevelt was scheduled to address the American Legion annual convention at Bay Front Park in Miami. He made his speech from the back seat of a convertible, and at its conclusion slid back down into his seat. To his left was the Mayor of Miami, seated in the car. To his right, standing next to the car was the Mayor of Chicago, Anton Cermak, who was making arrangements for a meeting in Roosevelt's railway car at Miami station. At that moment five shots rang out, one of which mortally wounded Mayor Cermak. All five shots missed their mark, as Roosevelt was not hit, but the car sped away with the wounded Mayor, and rushed him to the hospital. Afterwards, it was discovered that four others were wounded, but only Cermak would perish. The unrepentant assassin would later die in the electric chair as a result. A side effect of the assassination attempt, would be to further Roosevelt's image as a chosen leader for the American people, and the nation rallied to his support.[15]

Like a perfect metaphor for the country, the incoming President had overcome his condition of paralysis with work and physical effort, so too must the paralysis of the nation be overcome with effort and energy. Roosevelt's inauguration address was short, but as he asserted that "the only thing we have to fear, is fear itself" he gave people hope and courage. Inauguration day was rainy and gloomy, a reflection of the mood of the country. However, as Roosevelt's speech ended and he waved his hand to the adoring crowd, the clouds parted and sunlight illuminated the new President, as if anointed by God.[16]

A Bank Holiday

During the transition period between Roosevelt's election and his inauguration, panic and fear caused by the worsening Depression had people across the nation scrambling to get their savings out of the nation's banks. Depositors had removed more than $1.3 billion of gold and gold certificates from the banking system, and either held onto it or transferred it to foreign accounts. The resulting bank runs had caused multiple bank failures, and several governors closed banks throughout their states. By the day before the inauguration for President-elect Roosevelt, 32 of the 48 states had closed their banks, and more closures were looming. President Hoover was advised by both the Treasury Department and the Federal Reserve to take action to stem the mounting crisis by using the 1917 Trading with the Enemy Act as the authority to close all of the nation's banks. However, Hoover decided not to take action, but instead continued to make demands of Roosevelt to declare a joint approach to the resolution of the banking crisis.[17]

Finally, after the inauguration on March 4, and with the power of the government firmly in his hands, President Roosevelt had the authority to take action. Already his aides had been working with the prior administrations' men in both the Treasury and the Fed. They had put together a plan for closing the remaining open banks throughout the country for four days, then slowly reopening them until the financial system was back on its feet. They had devised three classes of banks that would provide a structure for dealing with the situation. Class A banks were deemed the healthiest and would be reopened as quickly as possible. Class B banks would be opened as time went on, determined by their ability to receive additional funding to support their reopening. Class C banks were considered unredeemable and would have to stay closed indefinitely.[18]

On Sunday night, the day after his inauguration, Roosevelt issued two presidential proclamations: the first was a call for an emergency special session of Congress to start on Thursday, March 9, and the second was a declaration of a bank holiday, closing all the nation's banks until Monday, March 13. These acts were met with immediate acclamation by the pubic, for at last there was a commitment to take action. On the Monday after the proclamations, at a planned meeting of the governors of all 48 states, Roosevelt spoke for ten minutes to explain the banking closures. After his speech he was given a standing ovation.[19]

The First Fireside Chat

A week after Roosevelt had been in office, he held the first of many radio broadcasts to the nation. These were the first of their kind, as radio was a new technology that had only recently become accepted *en masse* by the public. In ten years, the number of radio sets had gone from a few thousand to almost 20 million in the country, which represented about half of the households in the United States. When Roosevelt spoke to the

American people that Sunday night in March 1933, he was reaching out to 60 million people in their homes throughout the country, as if speaking to them from a chair next to the fireplace in their own living room. In a new approach to reach listeners, Roosevelt spoke in a conversational tone, as if talking to a friend. This was different from most speakers who were new to the radio medium – their speeches typically were almost shouted out as if to reach the people in the back of the room, but with a good radio microphone that was no longer necessary.[20]

The context of the speech was to talk about his first week in office and explain the banking situation. He walked through the banking crisis and what the administration was doing about it. He explained that some banks would open the next day, and that these would be the strongest and safest banks to use. Roosevelt stressed that it would be safer for persons to put their money in these banks than to keep it at home. He said that it would be a patriotic act to put their money back into these banks, and he chastised those who were considering withdrawing their money, that it was "unfashionable" to do that now. He ended the chat by putting the responsibility on the public to help make it work, and lastly said, "Together we cannot fail."[21]

The public response to Roosevelt's speech was overwhelming. Monday, March 13, saw thousands of people standing in long lines at banks across the country to redeposit their funds. By the end of his second week as President, 75% of the banks that had closed were reopened. In addition, the stock market rallied and had its best one-day showing in 50 years. Roosevelt had saved banking and the financial institutions it was based on, and he may have saved capitalism itself. His success in these first few weeks of his presidency exceeded everyone's expectations, and even their hopes and dreams. But he was just getting started on the ambitious programs that would collectively be called "the New Deal" – programs which would have a lasting impact on Americans individually and collectively, and on American society and culture as a whole.[22]

The New Deal

Just as Roosevelt promised during his acceptance speech at the Democratic National Convention, he was intent on providing a New Deal for the American people. He did not know what that deal would be composed of yet, but he would take action and keep taking action until he improved the lives of the American people and got them through the worst of the Depression. Like a general on a battlefield during a war, he took responsibility, gave orders, and directed his staff with such confidence and optimism that they became confident and optimistic themselves.[23]

The banking crisis resolution was the first success of what would become multiple successes in his first three months in office. From the passing of the Emergency Banking Act on the first day of the special session of Congress opening on March 9, to the passing of the National Industrial Recovery Act on the last day of the special session exactly 100 days later on June 16, the New Deal delivered 15 major pieces of legislation, more than any other session in the history of the United States. To put this into perspective, President Roosevelt worked with Congress to pass one major piece of legislation, on average, every single week of the first 15 weeks of his presidency. All subsequent presidents have been held to this standard of their first 100 days in office, and none have come close to this level of achievement.[24]

The New Deal was actually a collection of legislation that would attack the Great Depression with three different types of programs: 1) Relief Programs, 2) Recovery Programs, and 3) Reform Programs. The relief programs included the Civilian Conservation Corps, the Federal Emergency Relief Act, and the Emergency Farm Mortgage Act. The recovery programs included the Tennessee Valley Authority Act, the Agricultural Adjustment Act, and the National Industrial Recovery Act. The reform programs included the Emergency Banking Act, the Glass-Steagall Banking Act, and the Truth in Securities Act. These programs composed the bulk of the New Deal legislation passed in the first 100 days of Roosevelt's presidency. Each of these programs required Roosevelt's unique abilities to respond to events as they occurred, taking a hardline when he could, being flexible when required, and negotiating the process with the nimble fluidity of a political ninja (figuratively, of course). Roosevelt's success in pushing his legislative agenda through Congress was astounding, and a victory for the American people.[25]

Relief Programs

The relief programs of the New Deal were intended to provide immediate financial aid for people in need from the overwhelming crush of the weight of the Depression. With unemployment running at over 20%, these programs were critical to priming the economic pump by putting spendable income in consumers' pockets and providing an injection of confidence. The first of these programs was the Civilian Conservation Corps (CCC), and it was Roosevelt's brainchild. Like his cousin Theodore, Franklin was a dedicated conservationist, and at his own estate had planted tens of thousands of trees every year. As Governor of New York, he had implemented a similar program in 1932, which had employed thousands of men in the state. Incredibly, organized labor was opposed to the concept, but Roosevelt was able to get Congress to act quickly on the measure, and it passed both houses by March 30. He named Robert Fletcher, Vice President of the American Federation of Labor (AFL), as its top administrator.[26]

The CCC was the first of its kind and the model for all National service programs that followed (Job Corps, Peace Corps, VISTA, etc.). It put three million men to work, while positively impacting the economic scene in the local areas where the construction and forestry conservation occurred and the camps were located. In addition, these young unmarried men (18-25 years old) who were employed by the CCC were required to send the majority of their salary back home to their families. After its initial rebuff from labor unions, it became one of the most popular programs of the New Deal. The CCC was phased out in 1942, another casualty of WWII.[27]

Other relief programs of the New Deal were intended to provide immediate financial aid to the states, which could then fund programs at the local level. President Roosevelt had implemented a similar program in 1931 when he was Governor of New York, called Temporary Emergency Relief Administration (TERA). The Federal Emergency Relief Act provided $500 million in federal grants (instead of loans) to the states and established the Federal Emergency Relief Agency (FERA) to provide the oversight and administration of those funds. Immediately, FERA provided millions of dollars to a multitude of states. Harry Hopkins, Roosevelt's administrator for TERA in New York, was named the top administrator for FERA. Within one year, FERA provided assistance to 17 million Americans, and by the end of the program in 1935, it had disbursed over $3 billion in funds.[28]

FERA provided two mechanisms for disbursing funds: direct payments (called the "dole" by recipients), and state and local government employment positions for out-of-work unskilled laborers. The latter was both psychologically and emotionally preferable to those in the program because at least they were working or doing something to deserve payment. In the critical early years of the New Deal, especially during the winter of 1933, there were significant concerns for the public welfare of the unemployed, so a new employment administration was set up. This new program was called the Civil Works Administration (CWA) and was funded with $400 million from the Public Works Administration (PWA) to immediately get people to work. The CWA employed over four million people at its peak, and provided construction projects (public building remodeling, park and greenbelt cleanup, sewers, roads and schools) for local areas. However, conservatives attacked the agency as being too wasteful, and by 1935 the CWA was replaced with the Works Progress Administration (WPA).[29]

The Home Owners' Loan Act (HOLA) created the Homeowners Loan Corporation (HOLC), which provided relief to middle class homeowners by guaranteeing low interest mortgage loans for financial institutions. HOLA mirrored EFMA (see below), in that it allowed for refinancing of mortgages at lower rates for longer terms, and also allowed financing for taxes and repairs.[30] This program made everyone happy, because homeowners were granted lower payments for their mortgages, allowing them to afford their homes, and banks and other financial institutions received guaranteed payment if the mortgagor (homeowner) defaulted on the loan. Eventually, almost 20% of all urban housing would receive these mortgage guarantees and lower interest rates and payments. Some recipients went so far as to say the HOLC saved their life, because if they lost their home they would have lost their will to live.[31]

Recovery Programs

Recovery programs were a key element of Roosevelt's economic recovery plan. These programs funded significant economic projects that the states could not fund themselves, the source being the overwhelming power and financial backing of the federal government. One of these programs was the Tennessee Valley Authority Act. Roosevelt's personal experience and close friendships with people of the rural south in Warm Springs, Georgia, made him particularly sensitive to the conditions on the nation's small non-electrified farms. He was aware of an unused dam on the Tennessee River in Muscle Shoals, Alabama, and had visited the site in January, 1933. The dam had originally been built to provide power to a nearby weapons munition facility during World War I. Now it was abandoned and the nearby area was depressed, but Roosevelt intended to use it as a model for development of government-run power systems nationwide. He sent to Congress a request for legislation that would harness the power of the Tennessee River to make people's lives better. The resulting legislation was signed by Roosevelt on May 18. The TVAA would electrify thousands of households throughout Tennessee and the South, and in addition provided employment for tens of thousands of people throughout Tennessee, Alabama, Mississippi, Kentucky, Georgia, North Carolina, and Virginia.[32]

The Tennessee Valley Authority (TVA) eventually provided low cost electricity through 16 hydroelectric plants throughout the valley, in addition to flood control, conservation, irrigation, and other positive impacts to the region. It has been called the most successful of all the New Deal programs, for it improved the lives and welfare of hundreds of thousands of people in impoverished rural areas through jobs, education, and economic opportunity. President Roosevelt's vision was to use the TVA as a model for improving communities throughout the country, but private utility companies successfully lobbied Congress to put an end to that dream. Wendell Willkie, legal counsel and later president of one of those companies – Commonwealth and Southern Corporation – successfully defeated future efforts to build other similar public utility agencies.[33]

Two more recovery programs were the Agricultural Adjustment Act (AAA) and the Emergency Farm Mortgage Act (EFMA). The intent of these programs was to support the recovery of the farming and agriculture industry. These programs provided support to farmers by: 1) paying farmers to *not* harvest crops or livestock, and 2) providing farmers with low interest loans to reduce their payments and save their farms. President Roosevelt was personally invested and interested in saving and preserving the small family farms in America because he saw them as an important cultural heritage and an economic growth engine. As a senator in the New York legislature at the beginning of his career, he had presided over the Agriculture Committee, and as a candidate canvassing for votes in his district in upstate New York, he had become intimately familiar with the people and the problems of the farming communities.[34]

The AAA was one of the less successful and more controversial programs of the New Deal. The economic condition of the farmers was such that owing to the existing market conditions it cost more to produce cotton, wheat, and livestock than they would receive when harvested. The prevailing conventional wisdom was that farm prices were too low because there was too much available supply of product. If production were lowered, wouldn't prices necessarily rise? That theory was put to the test via AAA's scarcity program, which would plow under excess cotton and feedstock, and slaughter and dispose of excess livestock. However, when theory met publicity, the public shock and outrage about the gross waste of hundreds of millions of pounds of pork being destroyed in meat grinders and processed into fertilizer or thrown away was quite a reaction. Millions of starving and destitute people were going hungry, yet the government was paying farmers to throw away or destroy perfectly good product. Anti-New Dealers fanned these flames of discontent, and newspapers fed on the story. From that reaction came a proposal by Jerome Frank, AAA general council, and Rex Tugwell, AAA director, to create a non-profit organization called the Federal Surplus Relief Corporation, that would distribute the excess farm production to relief recipients. In October 1933, the Surplus Relief Corporation was incorporated in Delaware and started operations, and for the next two years distributed pork, dairy, flour, cornmeal and other products from AAA to the needy.[35]

The National Industrial Recovery Act (NIRA) was the last major piece of legislation crafted during the first 100 days. It provided jobs and protected workers; it also protected the workers' right to unionize as well as collectively negotiate contracts with businesses. Title II of the Act was Roosevelt's jobs program, which included legislation for the creation of the Federal Emergency Administration of Public Works that would administer construction projects throughout the country. It allocated $3.3 billion in spending for public works in its first two years of operation and $6 billion overall, putting 1.2 million people to work. However, there were major flaws in its origination and implementation. The act put too much power in big business to police themselves, and that power was abused. Businesses were allowed to create codes and practices defining how businesses would be regulated, and ultimately these codes were written to be favorable to their own businesses and reduced competition.[36]

The NIRA was challenged in the Supreme Court in 1935 and lost, with the ruling that the Act usurped too much power from the legislative branch by allowing businesses to regulate themselves. In 1935, the Federal Emergency Administration of Public Works was renamed the Public Works Administration (PWA); it continued its operations through 1939. The PWA succeeded in providing the economic "force multiplier" that was intended, because for every person employed through the program, two addition workers were indirectly employed. There were over 34,000 PWA projects, including airports, dams, ships, bridges, schools, courthouses, and hospitals. Some of the notable projects were the Lincoln Tunnel, the overseas highway through the Florida Keys, the Triborough Bridge in New York City, the Hoover Dam, the Fort Peck Dam, and the Grand Coulee Dam.[37]

Reform Programs

The reform programs included the Emergency Banking Act, the Glass-Steagall Banking Act, and the Truth in Securities Act. As discussed previously, the Emergency Banking Act allowed the President to close all of the banks, then reopen the ones that were solvent; provided authority to regulate gold and foreign exchange; and authorized printing more money to increase the nation's currency supply (needed because of cash hoarding). The Glass-Steagall Banking Act separated investment banks from consumer banks, and provided to the Federal Reserve interest rate control by means of the interest rate the Fed could charge private banks. The Glass-Steagall Banking Act also included one of the most successful ideas in the entire New Deal – deposit insurance through the Federal Deposit Insurance Corporation (FDIC). Consumers deposits would be federally protected up to $2,500, or about $50,000 today, which represented all but the top 5% of individual accounts in the country (circa 1933).[38]

Carter Glass was a Senator from Virginia and a former Secretary of the Treasury under President Wilson, who founded the Federal Reserve. He chaired the Senate Appropriations Committee, and was a powerful proponent of the Act, which was intended to keep banks and financial institutions from using their depositor's funds to speculate in risky investments in the stock market. Henry Steagall was a U. S. Representative from Alabama, who was chairman of the Committee on Banking and Currency. He insisted on including federal deposit insurance in the Act, and also reduced the time allowed for consumer banks to eliminate their associations with investment banks from five years to one year. Those two additions are credited with helping the Act pass through both houses of Congress.[39]

The Securities Act of 1933, also known as the Truth in Securities Act, was enacted by Congress in May 1933. The intent of this legislation was to rein in the fraud and corrupt practices of securities dealers that had led to the collapse of the stock market in 1929. It was the first federal law that regulated the sale of stocks. This act required disclosure of all the facts involved in the sale of a security, including financial records of the company, a prospectus, information about the security, and other business information. It also made the company and the security's underwriter fiscally responsible for the accuracy of all of the information in the documentation provided. This law would be administered by the Federal Trade Commission (FTC), which had the power to revoke security registrations that contained inaccurate information, making the sale of those stocks illegal. Roosevelt felt that if the security seller bore the burden of truth, then investors would have more confidence in the information and in the overall market.[40]

The Securities Act of 1933 was followed with the Securities Exchange Act of 1934, which created the Securities and Exchange Commission (SEC). Both of these Acts were the result of President Roosevelt's desire for regulation of the stock market, and the fact that Roosevelt asked multiple people to draft such legislation. The 1933 Act came about by his asking Secretary of Commerce Daniel Roper to provide a securities regulation draft bill. The 1934 Act was the result of the efforts of the former legal counsel for the House Committee on Banking and Currency, Samuel Untermyer, to perform the same task. The two bills were completely different and approached the problem from different perspectives, so instead of trying to weave them together into a single law, they both became enacted. The 1934 Act provided reforms that everyone, including the business community, thought were necessary on account of the excesses of the 1920s: 1) It provided federal control over the sources of funding and credit for the exchange; 2) It curtailed insider trading and stock price manipulation; and 3) It put teeth into the requirements for providing detailed information regarding each company that was represented on the exchange. The 1934 Act also changed the regulatory agency of the stock market from the FTC to the newly created SEC. The most controversial aspect of the SEC's creation was the person who Roosevelt selected to lead the agency, Joseph P. Kennedy, patriarch of the Kennedy family and father of a future president. To those who complained about Kennedy's selection owing to his enrichment by the stock market crash, Roosevelt replied, "Set a thief to catch a thief." These actions in 1934 were followed by the mid-term elections as an early referendum on the New Deal thus far.[41]

The Second New Deal

The Democratic Party's success in the 1934 mid-term elections was unprecedented. For the first time in American political history, the party in power won more seats (increasing their majority) in *both* houses of Congress. The Democratic Party also increased their number of governorships across the country. President Roosevelt took this as a validation of his presidency and his policies, and he intended to strike while the iron was hot. Roosevelt had several initiatives in mind and went about immediately to put those thoughts into action. In addition, a majority of the newly elected legislators were "New Dealers" who were eager to implement the President's programs.[42]

In keeping with the approach of the original New Deal, the Second New Deal (as it would later be called) implemented a relief program, a recovery program, and a reform program. The relief program was the result of the Emergency Relief Appropriations Act of 1935, a bill that authorized $4.8 billion in funding for work relief activities and was up to that time the largest appropriations bill in the history of the United States. The bill was authorized on April 8, and on May 6, President Roosevelt created the Works Progress Administration (WPA) by executive order. He wanted to replace relief aid with relief work, and his rationale was that, although it cost less and was more efficient to provide direct aid to the needy, those who received the aid were much more interested in working for it than being paid for nothing. In a speech later that year, he said ". . . most Americans want to give something for what they get. That something, which in this case is honest work, is the saving barrier between them and moral degradation."[43]

President Roosevelt named Harry Hopkins, former director of the Federal Emergency Relief Administration and the Civil Works Administration, the top administrator of the WPA. The WPA was a controversial program in that its detractors on the right called it a "patronage boondoggle" for the Democratic Party, and its detractors on the left called it an opportunity to work for "depressed wages." It was called a patronage boondoggle because it replaced the local influence on patronage for similar work – under the new arrangement city and state jobs usually associated with whoever was elected would now be provided by the federal government. It was called an opportunity to work for depressed wages, because federal jobs had consistent pay across the country – these positions would compete for opportunities to work from sunup to sundown on a farm for half as much money. Notwithstanding these complaints, the program put over 8.5 million people to work over the next eight years, performing construction, employing people in the arts (including music, theatre, and artwork), and providing funding for teachers whose salaries were not being paid by bankrupt municipalities. The WPA worked hand in hand with the PWA by providing the labor that implemented the designs and used the raw materials funded by Ickes' PWA programs. Examples of this are the Bonneville Dam and the Boulder Dam. The Boulder Dam was started by Hoover but completed by Ickes and the PWA and WPA programs, then subsequently renamed the Hoover Dam by a Republican administration.[44]

The recovery program that Roosevelt pushed for in 1935 was the Rural Electrification Administration. This was a concept that was as close to Roosevelt's heart as any other and was his vision for America since his concept for the Tennessee Valley Authority was implemented in the First New Deal in 1933. Utility companies had successfully blocked his plans to use the blueprint of the TVA for replicating that success across the country. So, he created the REA by executive order in May 1935 using the authority and funding of the Emergency Relief Act of 1935. Low interest federal loans provided financing for rural community cooperatives to build up their power infrastructure and bring electricity to the homes and farms of their region. The success of this program is reflected in the fact that at the time it stared, only 10% of the country's non-metropolitan areas were electrified. By the beginning of World War II (for the United States) in 1941, nearly half of the rural areas were electrified. During the war, a halt was put on the construction of new power infrastructure, but after 1945 and through that decade, construction continued and accelerated, so by the end of the 1940s, nearly 100% of the country had electricity.[45]

The most significant program implemented in the Second New Deal was a reform program. It was the biggest goal that Roosevelt had set for his administration after the mid-term elections in 1934. It was almost a personal project for the President, as he had envisioned a social security program and announced in June 1934 his intention to enact a one. It would be drafted by committees in Congress in January 1935 and would eventually become the Social Security Act of 1935. Roosevelt's vision was that the program would fund itself, as opposed to being funded by a tax. His reasoning was that this would force the program to work on a financially sound basis, as it would pay for itself through payroll deductions. The second benefit of this approach was that it would be viewed as property by the beneficiaries – because they had contributed to it all of their working lives, they would own the benefit when they retired. Once the program was funded by Americans' payroll deductions, no politician would dare attempt to use those funds in the Treasury for some other political purpose. Social Security was approved by the House in April and by the Senate in June. FDR signed the measure into law in August 1935, a guarantee for all Americans that their golden years would not end in poverty.[46]

A second successful reform program of the Second New Deal was the implementation of the National Labor Relations Act (NLRA). New York Senator Robert Wagner started pushing the NLRA through Congress in 1934, but momentum stalled, and he would have to wait another session to see the fruits of his labors. By 1935, the momentum swung in Wagner's favor as he negotiated the NLRA through the halls of Congress. With the signing of the NRLA (also known as the Wagner Act), and the implementation of the rest of the legislation of the Second New Deal, Roosevelt aligned himself politically and ideologically with the "forgotten man" – the poor, downtrodden workers, and the rising labor movement that would become a major political force supporting the Democratic party through the 1960s. With the success of all these new programs and legislation implemented in 1935, the election of 1936 would become a foregone conclusion.[47]

Roosevelt's Reelection

The Roosevelt administration started their reelection campaign in January 1936 and never looked back. Franklin correctly predicted and told his cabinet that the election would be about a single issue, that of his presidency. Either it would be a vindication of his approach to the economic crisis of the Depression and his course of action to address it, or it would be a conviction by the American people that he had taken the wrong path. Roosevelt and his advisors were convinced that the lives of ordinary Americans had been improved by the myriad of New Deal programs implemented in that first term, and they would want the progress to continue. At his State of the Union address in January 1936, Roosevelt addressed Congress in a special evening session (the first president to ever do so) and to a live radio audience, and blasted the rich and powerful for their greed and lust for power.[48]

The economy was gaining strength all through 1936, and Roosevelt emphasized the need to keep it going strong. He directed his aides to make sure there would be no let-up of the WPA work relief programs, and he wanted to do whatever could be done to keep crop prices high. By all accounts and statistics, the economy was on a roll. By all reasonable measures, progress since 1932 was incredible. Farm income had almost doubled, unemployment was down by 35%, corporate profits were higher, and industrial production and the stock market were almost double since the start of Roosevelt's first term.[49]

In stark contrast to the strength of the economy was the weakness of the opposition's candidate. Alf Landon was the Governor of Kansas, a Republican progressive, and a New Deal sympathizer. But he was not a great speaker. One of Roosevelt's staff joked that the campaign should pay for Landon to make more speeches, because it would turn more voters into Democrats. The selection of Landon was almost by default, due to the lack of legitimate candidates elsewhere. He was one of only seven Republican governors in the country, and the Republican Party could ill afford to lose a Senator or Representative giving up their seat to run for president.[50]

There was still, however, Herbert Hoover, who had only served one term as president, and could legitimately seek a second term. Former President Hoover was touring the country, trying to set the record straight about his four years in office, and promoting the same policies that failed to get him reelected in 1932: maintaining the gold standard, a balanced budget, and conservatism. However, the American people had tuned out that message in 1932 and were not listening now. In fact, most people still blamed Hoover for the Depression. Even Republican candidates were distancing themselves from Hoover, fearful that a Hoover scent would run afoul of voters in November.[51]

Initially, the Republicans ran a crusade against the New Deal, attacking it as a step on the path toward communism. Al Smith, former Democrat and associate of Roosevelt, the same Al Smith who had run as the Democratic Presidential Candidate opposing Hoover in 1928, spoke to a convention of 2,000 members of the American Liberty League at the Mayflower Hotel in Washington. The Liberty League was a collection of some of the wealthiest people in the United States, and their association with the Republican party did not help Landon's cause. The more the rich expressed their hatred of Roosevelt and denounced the New Deal, the more likely ordinary Americans were to vote Democratic, and Smith was at his vitriolic best when he said "There can be only one atmosphere of government, the pure fresh air of free America, or the foul breath of communistic Russia."[52]

Most Americans saw the contrast between the Democrats and the Republicans as the party of the common man (or the forgotten man) versus the party of the rich man (or the wealthy). Roosevelt took the Liberty League and Chamber of Commerce's hate as a badge of honor, and proudly declared in speeches and radio addresses that he would rather represent the interest of "ordinary" people than big business. He made the most of a class divide between the haves and the have nots, and his speeches took on more of an us-versus-them tone. In the end, he declared that to the wealthy, he was the most hated man in America, and that he was proud of that fact. During his last speech on the campaign trail at Madison Square Garden, he declared, "They are unanimous in their *hate* for *me – and I welcome their hatred.*"[53]

The results of the election were a landslide of epic proportions, even greater than the 1932 election. In 1932, Hoover received 58 electoral votes to Roosevelt's 472, while in 1936, Landon only received 8 electoral votes to Roosevelt's 523. The popular vote was just as impressive; Roosevelt took in 27.8 million votes to Landon's 16.7 million, an incredible 60.8 percent of the vote (the Union, Socialist, and Communist parties taking in another 1.1 million votes combined).[54] In addition, Democrats cleaned up in the other elections across the country, and their majority increased in both houses of Congress. They gained 11 more seats in the House of Representatives, and seven more seats in the Senate. It was an unprecedented victory beyond Roosevelt's wildest dreams. In January 1933 (Roosevelt was the first president inaugurated after ratification of the 20th Amendment), his inauguration speech reflected his intent to continue progress towards a complete recovery of the nation from the effects of the Depression, and "make every American citizen the subject of his country's interest and concern."[55]

The Supreme Court

In stark contrast to the composition of the executive and legislative branches of the government, which had both turned more liberal and progressive during Roosevelt's first term, the judicial branch had not changed at all. It still represented the most conservative establishment in the federal government. For the first time since President Monroe, a president's first term expired without an opportunity to name a single judge to the Supreme Court. As a result of 12 years of Republican rule (Harding, Coolidge, and Hoover from 1921 through 1933), the Court was staunchly conservative, with seven of the nine judges appointed by Republican presidents (in addition to the above Republican presidents, President Taft had appointed Justice Willis Van Devanter in 1910). In addition, since the Supreme Court building had not yet been completed, the judges worked in separate offices spread throughout the D.C. area. As New Deal legislation was challenged in the lower courts, appeals would take those issues all the way to the highest court in the land. When New Deal liberalism met the Supreme Court conservatism, conservatism won out. Between 1935 and 1936, the Supreme Court declared the National Industrial Recovery

Act, the Farm Mortgage Act, the Railroad Retirement Act, the Agricultural Adjustment Act, and the Bituminous Coal Act unconstitutional. Roosevelt would go on the offensive to fight for the New Deal, as the rejection of these programs by the court could mean a dismantling of nearly everything he had accomplished in his first term.[56]

During a press conference in May 1935, Roosevelt complained about the Supreme Court's decision regarding the NIRA by saying, "We have been relegated to the horse-and-buggy definition of interstate commerce." That comment set off a firestorm of debate in the press and complaints from conservatives. Senators were expecting a wave of anti-New Deal rhetoric, but the opposite occurred. They started hearing from their constituents who agreed with Roosevelt, and voiced their concerns about a lack of federal control of interstate commerce, with all 48 states having different rules and regulations (the NIRA was based on the Constitutional statement regarding federal control of interstate commerce).[57]

There was another Constitutional amendment that some had in mind, which would change the Supreme Court's decision-making process. Their approach would require a two thirds majority to overturn legislation from Congress, as opposed to a simple majority.[58] This approach did not go far enough in Roosevelt's eyes, and he had an entirely different plan in mind. After his reelection and the inauguration to start his second term in office, Roosevelt and his aides (primarily his Attorney General, Homer Cummings) put together what became known as the "court packing plan" to add up to six additional justices to the Supreme Court bench. The purported purpose of this plan was to provide more personnel to spread out the case load, so that the court could hear more of the cases brought, as average caseloads had increased 150% since 1913. In reality, everyone saw through that thin veil and understood that if Roosevelt was allowed to name six more Supreme Court justices, then he would be able to swing the decision-making process decidedly more favorable to his New Deal programs.[59]

In 1937, over the span of 168 days, from the day Roosevelt's plan was announced on February 5, to the day the associated bill was defeated in the Senate on July 22, the court packing plan roiled Congress and the public, and was the biggest political mistake of Roosevelt's presidency and possibly of his career. It was mostly a failure of his approach – in previous policy change implementations Roosevelt worked his magic with a personal touch and convinced the public and his political cohorts of what needed to be done before trying to do it.

The court packing scheme was an example of Roosevelt attempting to implement change with brute force as opposed to his usual style of finesse. Whether it was due to his riding a wave of popularity with the 1936 election landslide and thinking nothing could stop him, or that he had lost the guiding influence of the two people he was most able to confide in (owing to the death of his advisor and chief-of-staff Louis Howe in April 1936 and his bodyguard Gus Gennerich in December 1936), the court packing scheme of 1937 earned him a lot of contempt and would permanently split the Democratic Party.[60]

In August 1937, Roosevelt appointed his first justice to the Supreme Court, Hugo Black. By the end of his second term in office, he would name four additional justices to the court (Reed, Frankfurter, Douglas, and Murphy). He would soon have his own majority rule to preside over litigation regarding the New Deal and the rest of his programs. Until then, whether it was due to the public outcry from the court packing debate, or a shift in attitude by the two "swing" voters (Roberts and Hughes), the Wagner Act, the Social Security Act, and the Fair Labor Standards Act decisions went in favor of the New Deal. In the end, Roosevelt achieved what he had set out to do – change the makeup of the Supreme Court to make it more aligned and responsive to the economic and social realities of the country. As time moved on, Roosevelt would run for and win an unprecedented third term in office. In his third term as President, Roosevelt would go on to elevate Justice Stone to Chief Justice (replacing Charles Hughes) and nominate three more justices, so that ultimately all nine judges on the Supreme Court were his appointees.[61]

Breaking Precedent

Franklin Roosevelt is the only president in U. S. history to serve more than two elected terms. The precedent set by George Washington to step down after two terms as president, was one no prior president had dared to break. It was an effective term limit for all subsequent presidents to follow, for who could possibly entertain the thought of serving more terms in office than the first and greatest president of our country? However, there existed no rule, no Constitutional limit or Amendment that would prohibit any president from seeking a third term. How then would events conspire to cause such an occurrence?

Two short months before President Roosevelt was inaugurated as the 32nd President of the United States, Adolf Hitler was appointed Chancellor of Germany. A few weeks after Roosevelt became President, the German Reichstag (equivalent to the U. S. Congress) pronounced Hitler dictator of Germany. While Roosevelt was dealing with the joblessness, hunger and fear of millions of Americans at home in an unprecedented domestic crisis surpassed in our national history only by the Civil War, world events progressed toward an eventual collision course between militaristic fascism and capitalistic democracy in a fight for the very survival of the democratic form of government.

In 1935, while Roosevelt was implementing the Second New Deal, Hitler armed Germany, Italy invaded Abyssinia (modern day Ethiopia), and Japan attacked Shanghai. In 1936, while Roosevelt was busy running for a second term, Hitler absorbed the Rhineland back into Germany (it had been vacated by Germany and declared a demilitarized zone as a part of the Treaty of Versailles after World War I) and the Spanish Civil War began. In 1937, when Roosevelt was reeling from the Supreme Court debate, Japan expanded its attacks on China (including an unprovoked attack on an American ship that resulted in an apology from Japan and reparations)[62] and Italy joined Japan and Germany in the Axis pact. In 1938, Roosevelt was dealing with an unexpected recession and also attempting to influence mid-term elections to more liberal and New Deal friendly Democrats (which was unsuccessful), while Germany annexed Austria and then swallowed up the Sudetenland, a part of Czechoslovakia. In 1939, Germany occupied the remainder of Czechoslovakia, Italy invaded Albania, and Germany signed a non-aggression pact with Russia. Then, in September 1939, Germany invaded Poland and started the greatest worldwide conflict in history, the Second World War.[63]

With the backdrop of these history-making events, Roosevelt was convinced that he was the only person who could lead the country from the brink of war to the successful conclusion thereof. He had been the Assistant Secretary of the Navy in the First World War and felt like it had been a dress rehearsal for what he was about to do as President. His knowledge of Europe from his many travels there as a child through adulthood, his understanding of European languages and cultures, and his intimate relationships with the aristocracy, royalty, and personalities there combined to provide him a clear advantage over any other candidate to run in 1940. There were, however, obstacles to achieving his vision of leading the country through those difficult and trying times in American's lives.

Isolationism and Election

One of the biggest obstacles Roosevelt had to deal with was American's feelings towards participation in another European war. Public sentiment and even some of his own administration (including Secretary of War Henry Woodring) were against involvement on any kind in Europe's troubles, mostly due to the feeling that America's involvement in the First World War had been a mistake.[64] Isolationists, like Senators Hiram Johnson, William Borah, and Robert La Follette, led the Congressional opposition to modification or abrogation of the Neutrality Act, which prohibited the export of arms, ammunition, or implements of war to foreign nations at war. Even famous public figures, like Charles Lindberg, came out in opposition of participation in European troubles, saying it was just a continuation of the prior war's issues.[65]

The other significant hurtle for Roosevelt to overcome was the expectation that he would not seek a third term as President. At times, it seemed as if he had not made up his own mind. He received a contract from *Collier's* magazine to provide bi-weekly articles for three years, starting in 1941 after his second term expired. His Presidential Library was nearing completion in Hyde Park, the first ever housing of presidential papers and memorabilia in what has become an established expectation of all subsequent Presidents. He was preparing himself for the eventual end of that part of his career, and even looked forward to the organization and management of his personal papers for the National Archives at his Hyde Park library. His longing to retire was counterbalanced by world events, as the months-long "Phony War" (October 1939 to March 1940, during which no significant battles occurred) continued, while Hitler consolidated his resources after the successful Blitzkrieg of Poland. If things got worse in Europe, he would have to reconsider his thoughts regarding a third term candidacy.[66]

Things would get much worse. In April 1940, the German army swept into Denmark and the German navy attacked Norway. Both countries capitulated in a few weeks. In May, German forces overran Holland and Belgium, and by June they occupied France. After Germany's invasion of France, Italy declared war and also invaded France, which prompted Roosevelt to say in a commencement speech at the University of Virginia that "the hand that held the dagger has struck it into the back of its neighbor."[67] On June 22, France surrendered, and only Britain remained as the sole surviving democratic nation in Europe opposing the forces of fascism.

Back in the United States, the Democratic primaries marched on, and state after state went to Roosevelt. Roosevelt did not actively campaign, but he also did not dissuade any of the activities being performed on his behalf. At the Democratic National Convention in Chicago, President Roosevelt had a message read to the delegates that he was not a candidate and that they were all free to vote their conscience. Then pandemonium ensued as the chant arose "We want Roosevelt" from the loudspeakers and then was joined by the delegates. Roosevelt received almost 950 votes and all the remaining candidates received a total of less than 150 votes combined. Eleanor Roosevelt spoke at the convention in place of Franklin, giving her "no ordinary time" speech. Her appearance and speech provided a salve for the discontent and bruised egos at the convention, and engendered party unity.[68]

Roosevelt's Republican opponent for the election of 1940 was none other than Wendell Willkie, the former litigator-Democrat and current political outsider-Republican, who had opposed Roosevelt's Tennessee Valley Authority Act on behalf of private utility companies. Willkie campaigned extensively over 18,000 miles, through more than 30 states, and made almost 600 speeches, but it seemed the more he campaigned, the farther he fell behind Roosevelt. The problem for Willkie was that his message was quite similar to Roosevelt's: Both men were in favor of the draft and war preparations while supporting Britain to keep Germany at bay. When Willkie came out against the war and became more isolationist, the polling numbers started to reverse their trend.[69]

Up to that point, Roosevelt had stayed in the White House tending to the business of the presidency and not campaigning. After polling started trending in Willkie's favor, Roosevelt announced that he would respond to the challenge and campaign the last two weeks before the election. He started on October 23, in Philadelphia, then spoke at Madison Square Garden on the 28th. In Boston on October 30, he said he would not send Americans into foreign wars. Two days later in Cleveland, he wrapped up the campaign with a speech that laid out his vision for America, and some say it was his best speech ever. Voters must have agreed, for they elected Roosevelt for a third time, with a five million vote plurality (55% of the popular vote), and 449 electoral college votes to Willkie's 82. The stage was set for Roosevelt's next act as America's Commander-in-Chief during the greatest conflict the world has ever known.[70]

CHAPTER 11

The Second World War

President Roosevelt walked a political tightwire during the crisis in Europe. Most Americans were focused on domestic issues such as the economy and labor unrest while at the same time isolationists were adamant about not getting involved in another war. But the experience Roosevelt had had as Assistant Secretary of the Navy during World War I gave him insight on just how unprepared the United States was for handling another similar conflict. So, he instituted vigorous programs to get the country prepared with the manpower and equipment required to act when the time came, the benefit of which was to put millions of Americans to work. In May 1940 at a joint session of Congress, he asked for an additional $1.2 billion for defense spending to modernize the Army and Navy. By the end of that month and as the situation deteriorated in Europe, he asked for another $1.9 billion.[1]

In May, the German forces conquered Holland and Belgium with ease, and were pouring into northern France. With the French army in disarray and the French government preparing for evacuating Paris, coordination between the French defense forces and the British Expeditionary Force (BEF) was impaired. By the end of May, the BEF and what was left of the French northern army were surrounded at Dunkirk. Much has been written, and a recent movie released, about "Operation Dynamo" and the deliverance from Dunkirk of 338,000 Allied troops, including 26,000 French troops, the importance of which cannot be overstated.[2]

After the British evacuation from Dunkirk, where they were forced to abandon thousands of tons of ammunition and over 100,000 military vehicles, British Prime Minister Winston Churchill requested U. S. assistance in the form of military equipment and ammunition to resupply the British defense forces. Roosevelt relayed the request to General George C. Marshall and arraigned for thousands of weapons and millions of rounds of ammunition left over from World War I to be shipped to the British. Everything that the British requested was provided within six weeks, with the exception of tanks (there were too few available).[3]

After the fall of France, Churchill also put to Roosevelt a desperate plea for a minimum of 50 destroyers for the defense of the British Islands against an expected imminent invasion by the Germans. In August, after coordination with the British government, the Roosevelt administration used the President's authority as commander-in-chief to trade 50 U. S. WWI destroyers for 99-year leases to use British military facilities on six islands in the Caribbean (the Bahamas, Jamaica, Antigua, Saint Lucia, Trinidad, and British Guiana).[4]

These transactions were not nearly enough to supply England with the amount of material and arms necessary to compete with the Nazi offensive and Hitler's intent to rule Europe as well as possibly the rest of the world. What came next was Roosevelt's solution to England's predicament. He told the White House press corps that it was like letting your neighbor borrow your garden hose if his house was on fire – would you ask him to pay for the hose before he used it, or would you just expect it back after he was finished? This became known as the Lend-Lease agreement, and it was the subject of Roosevelt's next fireside chat. The United States would lend England all the weapons and war material it needed to defend itself against Germany's war machine and England would just give them back to the United States when it was finished. Roosevelt said, "We must be the great arsenal of democracy." That way, "we and our children will be saved the agony and suffering of war."[5]

Pearl Harbor

As long as the fighting was far away on foreign shores, we were saved the agony and suffering of war, but the Japanese had conquest and imperial visions in mind. Those visions brought war to our doorstep, on an idyllic and peaceful island in the middle of the Pacific Ocean. Pearl Harbor was thought to be an "impregnable" fortress, on the island of Oahu in the middle of the Hawaiian Islands chain, with a harbor that was thought to be too shallow for airplane-dropped torpedoes. It was also protected by two airfields, one on Ford Island in the middle of the harbor, and another on Hickam airfield located at the mouth of the harbor (close to the present-day Inouye International Airport). How then, did this seemingly safe and protected location become the target of the most infamous and dastardly surprise attack in American history?

President Roosevelt had sympathy for the Chinese people and their plight in 1937 during the Japanese invasion of Manchuria. However, in 1937 his hands were full with domestic issues, so no significant steps were taken in response. By 1940, Japan was heavily invested in Manchuria, which they had renamed Manchukuo and in which they had settled over three million Japanese. When the Japanese military moved southward and took over airfields in Indochina (present day Vietnam), President Roosevelt used a trade embargo to deny aviation fuel and all types of iron and steel to the Japanese in hopes of curbing their southward expansion. But the embargo only stoked the fires of Japanese imperialists who sought further rationale for their expansionist plans. Roosevelt attempted to use economic measures to put Japan in a box while nonetheless trying to avoid all-out war. He decided to put a freeze on Japanese assets in the United States, the purpose being to force approval of the use of those funds for trade, though allowing trade for oil and gasoline. Unfortunately, the freeze was implemented without the oil and gasoline caveat, and Japan took the embargo as a threat to their existence (Japan imports nearly 100% of their oil). These events put Japan and the United States on a collision course for war.[6]

Japan's Admiral Yamamoto conceived the war plans for the attack on Pearl Harbor from the perspective of a Harvard graduate student who had travelled extensively across the United States and knew its immense industrial capacity. He understood explicitly that the only way for Japan to win the war would be to wipe out the U. S. Pacific Fleet and then consolidate power throughout the Pacific Rim. The Japanese authorities approved Yamamoto's plan, and he and his staff set about implementing it. The Japanese Navy performed a dress rehearsal of the attack in early November 1941. By the end of that month, Yamamoto's plans were put into action. All that stood in the way was the final formal approval by the Japanese Emperor. On December 2, that approval was given, and the message "climb Mount Niitaka" was transmitted to the ships in transit – the attack was on.[7]

At 6:10 a.m. on December 7, the Japanese fleet was 200 miles north of Oahu and turning into the wind. The first half of a wave of 350 airplanes was launched and on its way toward the American bases, and within an hour the second half of that wave was off as well. The first planes reached their targets by about 8 a.m., and by 10 a.m. the attack was over . . . but the effect never was. "Remember Pearl Harbor" became a rallying cry for Americans throughout the war, and a visit to the USS *Arizona* memorial at Pearl Harbor is proof that it will never be forgotten. The toll was 2,403 dead and 1,178 wounded, with 18 ships and 162 aircraft destroyed. But the attack forged a bond and united a country like no other event ever had – until September 11, 2001.[8]

Doolittle Raid

After the attack on Pearl Harbor and America's declaration of war response, the news got consistently worse for the cause of democracy. The Japanese attacked Malaya, Hong Kong, Guam, the Philippines, Wake Island, and Singapore. In addition to American losses, the British had significant naval and army reverses, the Dutch and French colonies were attacked, and Australia was imperiled. Two weeks after Pearl Harbor, Roosevelt knew that something had to be done to boost the public's morale. He asked the Joint Chiefs of Staff what could be done, and stated his desire was to take the fight to the enemy, by attacking the heart of Japan as quickly as possible. This request flowed down from the armed services chiefs to their staffs, and with an idea of Captain Francis Low on Admiral King's staff, they came up with a plan to fly Army bombers (with their longer range than Navy carrier planes) off a Navy carrier to bomb Japan.[9]

The mission was led by Colonel James Doolittle, who was a famous American test pilot and a member of General Henry "Hap" Arnold's staff. The crews were selected from the 34th, 37th, and 95th squadrons of the 17th Bomber group out of Pendleton, Oregon. They flew on specially modified B-25 aircraft that had every spare ounce of equipment removed so they could carry extra fuel (almost double) and extend their range. The crews had to be specially trained at Eglin Field in Florida to take off from a short runway and fly on a low-level bombing mission for hundreds of miles that might include bad weather and nighttime flying. Two dozen planes were prepared for the mission, but only 16 were loaded on the USS *Hornet* in Alameda, California at the end of March.[10]

The USS *Hornet* and its carrier group of two cruisers, four destroyers and an oiler left San Francisco Bay on April 2, 1942. They rendezvoused with the USS *Enterprise* (to provide air cover and protection) and its carrier group of two cruisers, four destroyers and an oiler on April 13, in the middle of the Pacific. On April 16, the oilers refueled the ships in the carrier group, and then they and the destroyers were left behind (due to heavy seas). The carrier group that included the USS *Hornet* and its 16 B-25 bombers were sighted by a Japanese picket ship about 650 nautical miles from Japan. This was much further out than planned and affected the planes' ability to reach safe airfields in China, but Colonel Doolittle and *Hornet* Captain Mitscher decided to launch the aircraft immediately, to keep the precious aircraft carriers and the rest of the ships in the carrier group out of harm's way. All 16 aircraft were successfully launched, and flew to their assigned military targets in Tokyo, Yokohama, Yokosuka, Nagoya, and Kobe.[11]

The first aircraft (Doolittle's) arrived over its target in Tokyo at 12:30 p.m. local time. None of the 16 aircraft were shot down by enemy fighters, and only one was slightly damaged by anti-aircraft fire. One of the airplanes was extremely low on fuel and flew to Russia, which was significantly closer than China. The crew of that aircraft was imprisoned and held captive on account of a neutrality agreement signed in 1941 between Russia and Japan. The remaining 15 aircraft, low on fuel, ditched in the water off the China coast or bailed out over the China mainland. Of the 80 men who flew the mission, 77 survived, one died bailing out of his aircraft and two drowned in the China Sea. Eight of the men were held as Japanese prisoners of war, of whom three were executed, one died in captivity, and four were repatriated after the war. The remaining 69 crewmembers of those aircraft were eventually returned to the United States from China (and Russia). All of the members of the mission received the Distinguished Flying Cross and were promoted. Doolittle was promoted from lieutenant colonel to general (skipping the rank of colonel), and he received the Medal of Honor from President Roosevelt upon his return to the United States in June 1942.[12]

Battle of the Coral Sea

With the announcement of the successful raid on Tokyo, Americans felt pride and some sense of revenge that the United States could carry out an attack on the enemy's homeland. Events then proceeded to the next significant battle in the Pacific, the Battle of the Coral Sea. The Battle of the Coral Sea was historic in that it was the first time in naval history that two combatants fought each other using air power only and never fired a single cannon or gun salvo against the other foe. It was also the first major battle between the Imperial Japanese Navy and the U. S. Navy, and the first time in the war that the U. S. forces battled on par with the Japanese forces. The battle's strategic importance was to challenge the Japanese superiority in the area, and to slow their southward advance. Its success was in stopping the Japanese planned attack on Port Moresby and takeover of its airfield, which would have put northeastern Australia at risk.[13]

On May 5, the aircraft carrier *Lexington*, assigned to Task Force 11 under Rear Admiral Aubry Fitch, and the carrier *Yorktown*, assigned to Task Force 17 under Rear Admiral Frank Fletcher, rendezvoused about 325 nautical miles south of Guadalcanal in the Solomon Islands chain. At 10:30 the next morning, a Japanese reconnaissance plane sighted them and radioed the U. S. position to Japanese headquarters. Admiral Hara, the commander of a Japanese carrier group located 300 miles to the north, gave chase to the U.S. ships traveling south and out of range, intending to catch up and attack by the next morning. At dawn on May 7, both carrier groups launched search aircraft to locate the enemy's position, and by 8:15 a.m., both navies had sighted the other's ships. The Japanese found their targets first, but only sighted the support and cover ships of the battle group, a destroyer (*Sims*) and a refueling oiler (*Neosho*). The *Sims* was hit by three bombs and sank immediately; the *Neosho* was hit by seven bombs and was slowly sinking, buoyed by her half empty oil tanks. The U. S. Navy pilots found their opponents next, the light carrier *Shoho*, which was hit with two bombs and five torpedoes from the *Lexington's* aircraft. Then it was hit with 11 more bombs from the *Yorktown's* aircraft. The *Shoho* sank shortly thereafter.[14]

At 9:15 a.m. on May 8, the Japanese fleet carriers launched a combined force of 69 aircraft, including fighters, bombers, and torpedo bombers. At the same time, the *Yorktown* launched 39 aircraft and the *Lexington* launched 36 aircraft immediately afterwards. At 10:55 a.m., the Japanese aircraft sighted both U. S. carriers and attacked both ships. Four torpedoes missed the *Yorktown*, but two torpedoes hit the *Lexington*. Two bombs hit the *Lexington* and one hit the Yorktown. The *Lexington* was staggering like a heavyweight boxer that has taken too many punches, but was still moving forward, while the *Yorktown* was severely damaged though also capable of moving. Meanwhile, aircraft from the *Yorktown* and *Lexington* were arriving above the Japanese carriers at about the same time the Japanese aircraft had attacked the U.S. carriers. The *Yorktown* aircraft attacked at 11:05, with the dive bombers scoring two hits on the *Shokaku*, but all the torpedo bombers missed their targets. The *Lexington* aircraft arrived about 30 minutes later, with the dive-bombers attacking the *Shokaku* and scoring one hit, and the torpedo-bombers attacking the *Shokaku*, with all torpedoes missing their target.[15]

One of the bombs that hit *Lexington* damaged the aviation fuel storage room, and fuel fumes spread throughout the deck. Sparks from electrical wires ignited the gasoline vapors in a series of three explosions that rocked the vessel. At 5:07 p.m., the order was given to abandon ship. After the survivors were rescued, torpedoes from the destroyer *Phelps* scuttled the *Lexington*. The *Yorktown* was sent to Pearl Harbor for repair. The Japanese carriers *Shokaku* and *Zuikaku* were eliminated from operations so the *Shokaku* could be repaired and both carriers could receive additional aircraft and trained pilots. The stage was now set for the most significant battle of the Pacific Theater, and one that changed the fortunes of war in favor of the Americans, the Battle of Midway.[16]

Battle of Midway

The Battle of Midway was the decisive battle that the Japanese naval command was seeking; however, the outcome was the complete opposite of what the Japanese expected. U. S. intelligence had cracked the Japanese secret codes and was able to intercept and understand their naval strategy and plans even before they were put into action. Admiral Yamamoto had taken pains to convince his superiors that a final strike on the U. S. Navy in the Pacific would kill their will to fight and their ability to wage war. In addition, if Midway was taken, then the Japanese homeland would be safe from attacks like the Doolittle raid months earlier. Yamamoto was so convinced of the correctness of his plan, that he pulled nearly the whole of the combined Imperial Navy into the conflict: four large carriers (the *Akagi*, *Kaga*, *Hiryu*, and *Soryu*, all participants in the Pearl Harbor attack), 11 battleships, 16 cruisers, and 53 destroyers. Yamamoto's flagship was the battleship *Yamato*, and at 67,000 tons, it was one of the largest battleships in the war.[17]

To counter the expected attack on Midway, Admiral Nimitz used the two carriers from Task Force 16, the *Enterprise* and the *Hornet*, and would supplant that with the remaining carrier from Task Force 17, the *Yorktown*, which was undergoing repairs in Pearl Harbor from damage incurred at the Battle of the Coral Sea. Rear Admiral Spruance would take command of Task Force 16, while Rear Admiral Fletcher would command Task Force 17. Nimitz directed Task Force 17 to join Task Force 16 and rendezvous at a location about 325 miles north of Midway to lie in wait for the expected Japanese attack.[18]

At 4:30 a.m. on June 4, the battle started when over 100 aircraft from the Japanese carriers were launched to attack Midway atoll. At 5:30 a.m., a U. S. search plane from Midway spotted two Japanese carriers headed toward the atoll. Radar installations at Midway identified the Japanese aircraft approaching, and fighters were scrambled to intercept the incoming threat. At 6:20 a.m., the Japanese aircraft struck Midway, and heavily damaged the Army base. The island-based aircraft suffered heavy losses (15 aircraft destroyed and the remainder damaged); however, the airfield at Midway weathered the attack, and the Japanese pilots reported that a second wave would be required to soften up the American defenses for the amphibious landing planned for phase two.[19]

At 7:00 a.m., both the *Enterprise* and *Hornet* began flight operations and launched their aircraft to hunt and destroy the Japanese carriers, with the *Yorktown* starting at about 8:00 a.m. (having held their aircraft in reserve). The American carriers launched their aircraft at maximum range from the enemy fleet, and by doing so, lost the protective support of their fighter escorts, which ran short on fuel and had to turn back. By 9:20 a.m., the first torpedo bombers from the *Enterprise* reached the Japanese carriers, and, without fighter escort, all 15 aircraft were shot down, while nine of the 14 from the *Hornet* were shot down. Next, the *Yorktown's* torpedo bombers reached the target, and 10 of 12 of them were shot down, with none of the torpedoes launched from any group of U. S. aircraft having any effect whatsoever. Fortunately for the Americans, the Japanese fighter cover was drawn down to lower altitudes to attack the U. S. torpedo bombers and did not notice the U. S. dive bombers circling for attack. At 10:22 a.m., the *Enterprise's* aircraft split up to attack the *Kaga* and the *Akagi*. The *Kaga* suffered four direct hits, while the *Akagi* was hit with only one bomb, but it pierced the middle deck elevator and exploded in the middle of the armed and fueled Japanese aircraft being readied for the next wave of attacks on Midway. Simultaneously, the dive-bombers from the *Yorktown* attacked the *Soryu*, and scored three direct hits.[20]

The remaining unscathed Japanese carrier, *Hiryu,* wasted no time launching a counterattack. Its 24 aircraft attacked the first enemy carrier it came in contact with, the *Yorktown.* The *Yorktown* was hit with three bombs, and Admiral Fletcher moved his command to the cruiser *Astoria.* Damage control groups were able to put out the fires and patch up the flight deck, and she was put back into operation. But about an hour later, a second wave of 16 aircraft from the *Hiryu* arrived above the *Yorktown,* and hit her with two torpedoes – and the damage control operations previously performed had been so effective, the Japanese thought they were sinking a second carrier. The Americans then counterattacked; 24 dive-bombers from the *Enterprise* successfully found the *Hiryu* and struck with four direct hits. By nightfall the *Soryu* sank and later that evening the *Kaga* sank. By early the next morning the *Akagi* sank, and later that morning the *Hiryu* sank. With the loss of four of their six fleet aircraft carriers, the Battle of Midway marked the beginning of the end of the war for the Japanese.[21]

Guadalcanal

With the advance of the Japanese across the Pacific stopped by the victory at Midway, the tide turned, and it was time for the Americans to take to the offensive. In August 1942, 12,000 U. S. Marines landed on Guadalcanal, Tulagi (which was a Japanese seaplane base), and Florida Islands (Tulagi and Florida were due north a short distance from Guadalcanal) in the Solomon Islands chain. The Japanese defenders, who were surprised by the attack, were outnumbered and overrun. The Marines took over Tulagi and Florida, and the airfield on Guadalcanal, which were the objectives. The Japanese immediately responded and over the course of August to November 1942 attempted to retake the airfield multiple times.[22]

On August 19, about 1,000 troops from Rabaul under Colonel Kiyonao Ichiki, were delivered by Japanese destroyers to Guadalcanal; they then attacked the U. S. encampments around Tenaru, near Henderson Airfield. The Japanese had woefully underestimated the size of the American build-up on the island, and their forces were almost completely wiped out. Only 30 of the attacking Japanese remained to join the 10% reserve that did not participate in the raid, returning to the landing point to notify their superiors and await further instructions. After the Tenaru battle, Admiral Yamamoto established a naval force of three carriers (the fleet carriers *Shokaku* and *Zuikaku*, and the light carrier *Ryujo*) and 30 other ships to counterattack the U. S. invasion of the Solomon Islands. On 24 August, these forces were met by Admiral Fletcher's carrier task force, which included the fleet carriers *Saratoga* and *Enterprise*. Japanese Rear Admiral Tanaka sent out the light carrier *Ryujo* in front of the fleet to draw the Americans into battle, and the bait worked. The *Ryujo* was struck with several bombs and a torpedo, and it quickly sank, but the *Shokaku* and *Zuikaku* were not attacked. Meanwhile, Japanese dive bombers hit the *Enterprise* with three bombs, and almost put her out of commission; valiant effort by the damage control teams saved her. The *Saratoga* escaped attack on this day, but one week later a Japanese submarine (the *I-26*) torpedoed her, and the *Saratoga* was sent to dry dock for three months.[23]

On September 14, a U. S. naval convoy delivering over 4,000 men, with food, fuel, ammunition, and equipment headed toward Guadalcanal. This task force included the fleet carriers *Wasp* and *Hornet*. The next day while providing air cover for the operation to resupply the island, the carrier *Wasp* was hit by three torpedoes from a Japanese submarine (the *I-19*) and seriously damaged (it was later scuttled). Another torpedo from that submarine hit and damaged the battleship *North Carolina*. With both the *Enterprise* and the *Saratoga* having been damaged in action the month prior, this left the *Hornet* as the only U. S. fleet carrier in the Pacific, at least until the *Enterprise* and *Saratoga* repairs could be completed.[24]

The Japanese high command, after reconsidering their strategy and tactics with respect to Guadalcanal and Henderson Field, decided they were not committing enough resources to achieve their objectives. Thus, they also upped the ante and decided to reinforce Guadalcanal with another 17,500 men. On October 14, two battleships (the *Kongo* and the *Haruna*), one cruiser and nine destroyers all under Admiral Takeo Kurita started shelling Henderson Field from about 10 miles away. They poured over 900 fragmenting shells onto the airfield in less than 90 minutes, damaging both runways, and destroyed all of the aviation fuel and half of the parked aircraft.[25]

Regardless of the damage, Seabees and maintenance personnel got one of the runways back in working order within hours, and aircraft and fuel supplies were flown in immediately. The Japanese had planned the naval bombardment to soften up the U.S. defenses and destroy the airfield in preparation for a land attack. On October 23, the Japanese 4th Infantry Regiment and the 1st Independent Tank Company attacked U. S. Marine defenses and were nearly wiped out at very low cost to the Americans. Then the main Japanese force attacked over the next two days but suffered complete carnage. By the morning of October 26, the Japanese commander called off the attacks and ordered a retreat.[26]

Santa Cruz Islands

At the same time as the land battles on Guadalcanal, the Imperial Japanese Navy under the command of Admiral Yamamoto engaged U. S. carrier forces under Admiral Halsey, facing off northeast of Guadalcanal near the Santa Cruz Islands of the Solomon Islands chain. The Japanese were again hoping for a decisive carrier battle in their favor, and they also wanted to eliminate the U. S. naval forces in the area, thus allowing them unrestricted maritime access to supply their ground forces at Guadalcanal. The Japanese fleet had two fleet carriers (the *Shokaku* and *Zuikaku*), two light carriers (the *Junyo*, and *Zuiho*), four battleships, ten cruisers and 25 destroyers. The U. S. fleet had two fleet carriers (the *Hornet* and *Enterprise*), one battleship, six cruisers, and 14 destroyers. Assuming that Henderson Field had already been destroyed and believing that their overwhelming numbers were successful in their land attacks, the Japanese warships sailed toward Guadalcanal intent on supporting the ground troops with air cover.[27]

On October 26, the two combatants' search planes spotted each other, and raced to launch their attack aircraft. The Americans were first to strike, with two bombs hitting the *Zuiho* and heavily damaging it. The *Shokaku* was also hit with at least three bombs, making the flight deck completely unusable. Also, the heavy cruiser *Chikuma* was hit with two bombs and was heavily damaged. Shortly afterwards, Japanese aircraft found the U. S. carrier forces and attacked the *Hornet*, hitting her with three bombs, and one aircraft intentionally dived into its smokestack. At the about same time, multiple Japanese torpedo bombers attacked the *Hornet* from both sides of the ship, hitting her with two torpedoes and leaving her dead in the water. Meanwhile, the *Enterprise*, which had been hidden by the clouds of an ocean storm, emerged from the squall and was immediately attacked and hit by two bombs, causing heavy damage. With one carrier out of action and another carrier damaged, the U. S. commander decided to withdraw, and the task force retreated to New Caledonia. The battle, though a technical victory for the Japanese due to the number of ships damaged or sunk, was too costly for them in terms of aircraft and aircrews, which were irreplaceable. The U. S. would deliver many more warships to support the Pacific battles, and Japan would engage in battles of resistance and retreat for the rest of the war.[28]

On November 1, U. S. ground forces on Guadalcanal took to the offensive and several land battles took place across the island. The result of these operations provided information to U. S. commanders about the strength and capacity of the Japanese. By mid-November a stalemate evolved from which no side could gain the advantage, and the status quo remained for the next six weeks. The Japanese then attempted one last effort to rid the island of its American inhabitants, and to take over Henderson Field.

Admiral Yamamoto sent a fleet of two battleships, one cruiser and eleven destroyers to shell Henderson, along with a troop convoy of additional men to reinforce Japanese ground forces already on Guadalcanal. Admiral Halsey sent two battleships and four destroyers to interdict the Japanese naval force, and airplanes from the *Enterprise* and Henderson Field to intercept. In this final naval battle for Guadalcanal, three U. S. destroyers were sunk and one destroyer and the two U. S. battleships were damaged, while one Japanese battleship was severely damaged. However, the Japanese withdrew without attempting the bombardment of Henderson field. At the end of December, in light of the continuing drain on resources of ships, supplies and personnel, the Japanese high command determined that Guadalcanal was impossible to retake from the established U. S. forces there. In January, they started evacuating men and supplies back to Rabaul, and by February 1943, Guadalcanal was secure; it became the foundation of the U. S. offensive to win the war in the Pacific.[29]

North Africa

Although the Pacific front was seeing progress and victories on the American side, things were still going badly in the Atlantic for the Allies. Roosevelt had committed to Churchill that the emphasis and priority in the war would be a "Hitler first" approach, but there were some conflicts in the perceived order of battle. Roosevelt was in favor of attacking the continent of Europe through a build-up of forces on the British Islands, and Stalin was continuously demanding a "second front" be engaged against the Germans to draw their forces away from the siege of Moscow and Stalingrad.[30] Churchill was convinced that an attack through the soft underbelly of Europe (e.g., Italy) was the way to go, but that could not be accomplished until the Mediterranean Sea was controlled from the straights of Gibraltar to the Suez Canal. This meant North Africa would have to be recaptured from the Italian and German forces that had taken over in 1940-1941, taken over despite that fact that British forces had been fighting them there since January 1942, with significant battles at Tobruk and El Alamein. Operation Torch, the Allied invasion of North Africa, began in early November and went more smoothly than expected – Churchill would call it "the end of the beginning."[31]

In January 1943, Churchill met Roosevelt in North Africa for the Casablanca conference. Interestingly, at the end of December 1942, Roosevelt had held a New Year's Eve dinner, and after the dinner there was a movie presentation at the White House theater which, when released nationwide a few days later, would become a blockbuster hit and instant classic. The name of the movie was *Casablanca*. The Casablanca conference was set in a hotel five miles south of the city and about a mile from the Atlantic Ocean.[32] It was also surrounded by beautiful villas, which would house the principal delegations represented: the English, the French, and the Americans (the Russians had declined to participate). At the conference, it was decided that the next Allied target, after victory in North Africa, would be the Italian island of Sicily. At a news conference on the lawn of the hotel after their meetings, Roosevelt called for the "unconditional surrender" of the Axis powers, which caught Churchill by surprise. The comment would become a headline in the United States and provide an additional boost of confidence to Americans back home.[33]

By the end of January 1943, Hitler had committed an additional 243,000 men and 870,000 tons of supplies and equipment to the North African theater, thus a "second front" was empirically constituted. The Allies countered Hitler's military buildup in Tunisia with their own in Algeria. This took the combined Allied forces from 130,000 personnel to over 500,000 troops, 1,800 tanks, and thousands of aircraft. The fighting in Algeria, Tunisia, and Libya initially resulted in heavy Allied losses, and the American forces were demoralized, which caused much consternation and reflection. The resulting "lessons learned" were applied to the command structure in North Africa, with General George S. Patton replacing the II U. S. Corps Commander General Frendendall, who was sent back to the States to become a training, rather than combat, general.[34]

The final phase of the North Africa campaign started on May 1, with the U. S. II Corps holding the left/northwest flank, the British First Army in the center/southwest area, and the British Eighth Army holding the right/southern flank. The II Corps then advanced through the western mountains of Tunisia towards Tunis and fought several battles through to the western regions surrounding Tunis. While the British First and Eighth Armies attacked from the south, the U. S. II Corps attacked from the west via Bizerte. The Allied forces overwhelmed the German and Italian forces at Tunis and Bizerte. With no retreat or escape via the port of Tunis due to the total command of the seas around the port by the British Navy, the Axis forces laid down their arms, and 240,000 Germans and Italians surrendered on May 13.[35]

Sicily

As the Allies were on their way to victory in North Africa, Churchill was on his way to visit Roosevelt in the United States. He travelled by ship, the *Queen Mary,* because it was considered fast enough to outrun German U-boats in the Atlantic. Churchill wanted to ensure that the victory in North Africa was not wasted, and that the next step in the Allies' strategy was agreed-to and deliberate. This was called the Trident conference, and it occurred in mid-May 1943. At this conference, British and American military planners coordinated the future invasions of France (called Overlord) planned for May 1944, and Sicily (called Husky) planned for July 1943. The other significant discussion was regarding plans after Sicily was taken. The Americans said that Sardinia and Corsica should be the next targets, while the British insisted on Italy. Roosevelt was not convinced, and so it was decided to wait until after Sicily was conquered for the next target to be determined.[36]

The Sicilian battle began on July 3 with an intense air bombardment of the airfields on both Sicily and Sardinia. The intended target of the overall attack was kept in suspense, as Allied naval and military movements appeared to indicate an attack on Greece. On July 10, the amphibious landings on Sicily began, assisted by bad weather that scattered the Allies' transports but provided cover from discovery and the expectation that nobody would attempt amphibious landings in that weather. As such, the surprise landings were successful, and the British forces, landing at the southern tip of Sicily near Pachino as well as further north near Avola, were met with scant resistance. The American forces, landing on the southwest beaches near Licata, Gela, and Vittoria, were also able to quickly establish supremacy and consolidate their forces. The battle plans for Sicily called for the British Eighth Army under command of General Montgomery to attack the strategic objective of Messina, a city on the northeastern tip of Sicily across from the boot of Italy (due north of his landing sites), while the American Seventh Army under command of General Patton was to cover Montgomery's left flank.[37]

While Patton's Seventh Army achieved all of its objectives to the "yellow line" – an arc from the middle of the southwestern coast of Sicily (near Palma de Montechiaro) to Caltigrione in the middle of the bottom third of Sicily, Montgomery's Eight Army was held down by German forces outside of Catania along the middle of the eastern edge of the island. Patton then divided his forces, sending the 3rd Division northwest towards Agrigento, and the 2nd Armored Division north towards the town of Palermo on the northern coast. By

July 17, the 3rd Division entered Agrigento and Patton ordered them to clear out the rest of the western part of the island of combatants. By July 22, the 2nd Armored Division took Palermo, and the next day the remainder of western Sicily was cleared of enemy troops. Now the race was on for Messina.[38]

By August 5, Montgomery's troops finally captured Catania and began moving north toward Messina. On August 9, German and Italian forces began to withdraw towards Messina, and for the next three days it appeared they were in full-scale evacuation mode. By the time Patton's troops reached Messina on August 17, the remaining German forces in Sicily had transferred off the island to the Italian mainland. Montgomery's Eight Army was not far behind and arrived in Messina shortly after the Americans. It was after his triumphant capture of Messina that Patton's famous "slapping" incident occurred. He was visiting a base hospital to talk to his wounded warriors and happened upon a soldier who was hospitalized for battle fatigue. Patton became incensed and verbally berated the soldier. When he came upon a second soldier who was also hospitalized for battle neurosis, Patton flew into a rage and struck the soldier's helmet with his hand and had to be restrained by the attending doctors and nurses. Patton later personally apologized to both soldiers, the hospital personnel and his troops on Sicily.[39]

Italy

Roosevelt and Churchill met in Quebec City, Canada for the Quadrant conference on August 17. Once again, Churchill crossed the Atlantic in the *Queen Mary*, but this time he arrived a week early and spent personal time with Roosevelt at his Hyde Park, New York home. Churchill left early for the conference, which allowed Roosevelt a day to go back to Washington before boarding a train for Quebec. The purpose of this conference was to make firm plans for Overlord, the cross-Channel attack of Europe. When Churchill agreed to a May

1944 date for the invasion, the main objective of the conference was attained. The two leaders also agreed that an American would be the overall commander of the operation. While
at the conference, the two leaders received the good news
about the Allies' success in Sicily, and when General Eisenhower recommended the next target to be the mainland of Italy,
they both concurred.[40]

In Lisbon, negotiations with the Italians were going well. On
August 20, the Allies' demands for an unconditional surrender
were met. Italy's General Cantellano was given ten days to
communicate the agreements to his government, and the negotiations concluded. After ten days, the Italian government
had still not agreed to the Lisbon offer. The next day, General
Cantellano was called to the Allies' encampments in Sicily for a
final answer. Once again, he was sent back to the Italian government with an ultimatum. This time, the Italian government
capitulated, and two days later, they sent a telegram to Allied
Headquarters accepting the peace arrangements. On September 8, General Eisenhower announced the surrender of Italy,
and the Italian Navy left their harbors in Genoa and Spezia and
made their way to the British port at Malta. The next day, Allied troops landed on beaches near Salerno (Operation Ava-
lanche), and British troops seized the port of Taranto
(Operation Slapstick).[41]

On September 10, the German army surrounded Rome, and
occupied the city after brief resistance from Italian troops. On
September 12, Mussolini was freed by the Germans by means
of a daring raid on a remote ski resort hotel in Gran Sasso, near
Assergi, Italy (about 100 miles from Rome), where he had been
held captive. Two days later, Mussolini met with Hitler in Mu-
nich in an emotional reunion. The strategic result of the Allied
attack on Italy and the coup of Mussolini was a disastrous decision by Hitler to move significant resources of men, material,
and supplies to the Italian front to defend that territory and
prop up a fallen dictator. That decision drained defenses from

other areas and provided the "second front" in Europe that Stalin was demanding. Hitler sent 20 divisions to Italy and directed his armies to defend the line from the mouth of the Garigliano River on the Tyrrhenian Sea (western side) to the mouth of the Sangro River on the Adriatic Sea (eastern side). This was called the Gustav Line (also known as the "Winter Line"), and it became a major front for the next eight months of the war.[42]

The overall commander of the Allied armies in Italy was British General Sir Harold Alexander. The strategic plan was for the British Eighth Army led by General Sir Bernard Montgomery to take the eastern route up the boot of the Italian peninsula parallel to the Adriatic Sea, and for the American Fifth Army led by Lieutenant General Mark Clark to take the western route of the Italian peninsula parallel to the Tyrrhenian Sea – with the Apennine Mountains ("Spine of Italy") separating the two forces. Both armies' progress was halted at the Gustav Line, the Eighth Army at the city of Ortuna, and the Fifth Army at the city of Cassino, and the major battles of Monte Cassino and Anzio were fought there. Above Cassino, there was an historic hilltop abbey founded by Benedict of Nursia in the year 529 AD, called Monte Cassino. From this hilltop, the Germans could observe the Allies' movements and direct artillery assaults on the troops below.[43]

Cassino and Anzio

The Battle of Monte Cassino started on January 17 and lasted through four attacks, until the final surrender of German forces there on May 18. The first attack started with a seaside assault across the Garigliano River by the British X Corps, causing the Germans to reinforce that portion of the line with troops from Rome. Then the main thrust of the Allies came through the Liri valley across the Rapido River on January 20. This advance was effectively repulsed by the German forces with heavy Allied casualties.[44]

The Battle of Anzio started as an amphibious landing (Operation Shingle) behind the Gustav Line to support the attack at Monte Cassino on January 22. The commander of the operation was Major General John Lucas, a subordinate of General Clark. The initial landing was a complete surprise, and it would have been an overwhelming success if General Lucas had taken initiative and gained the high ground in the mountainous territory immediately surrounding the beachhead. Instead, while Lucas was consolidating his forces on the beach, his German counterpart, Field Marshal Kesselring, moved all available German forces to a mountainous ring around the beach and started shelling everything that moved. With the opportunity lost to break through the German defenses, Anzio became a controversial example of bold strategy with lackluster implementation.[45]

The second attack on Monte Cassino began with an Allied bombing of the Monte Cassino abbey and the surrounding area. On February 17, the Allies tried to take Monastery Hill, but with little success. On March 15, after a heavy bombardment by Allied airpower, the third battle for Monte Cassino began. The 4th Indian Division and the 2nd New Zealand Division were called upon to do the fighting. The New Zealanders' advanced on Monastery Hill with an artillery barrage of hundreds of cannons. By March 26, after severe losses by both divisions of the New Zealand and Indian Corps, the remaining personnel from the attack were extracted from the battleground.[46]

The fourth and final battle for Cassino was called Operation Diadiem. The Allies brought together 13 divisions to fight Field Marshal Kesselring's six divisions, and the strategy would be to move troops, armor, and supplies only at night over the next six to eight weeks to keep Kesselring from pulling reserves from Rome. The strategy worked, and when the battle started on May 11 with a massive artillery bombardment of 1,060 guns from the Eighth Army and 600 guns from the Fifth Army, Kesselring thought he was only facing six divisions. Within two days, the German right flank gave way to the Fifth Army, and the French Expeditionary Force under the command of General Juin captured Monte Maio. All that was left, was for the Fifth Army to join the Eight Army to encircle Monte Cassino. The Polish II Corps launched multiple attacks on Monte Cassino, and after the second attack on May 17, the Germans defending those positions retreated and regrouped to the north (called the Hitler Line). The next day, the Poles raised a Polish flag over the ruins of Monte Cassino.[47]

On May 23, a new offensive at Anzio began, the aim being to push to Rome or break through the German defenses and destroy their Tenth Army. Owing to Field Marshal Kesselring's decision to pull every available resource to counter the Allies' May offensive at Monte Cassino, the Anzio offensive was violent but effective, and General Truscott's troops were able to breakout of the Anzio beachhead. On May 25, General Truscott received orders from General Clark to strike toward Rome. Five days later, General Clark added the U. S. II Corps to the fray, which joined Truscott's forces to push north along the road to Rome. On June 2, German defenses collapsed, and the U. S. Fifth Army rushed north, entering Rome two days later. Hitler, desiring to avoid another Stalingrad, directed Kesselring not to defend Rome. Later that morning of June 4, General Clark held a victory press conference on Capitoline Hill, one of the seven hills of Rome. Two days later started the greatest Allied offensive in the history of the war, the long-anticipated cross-Channel amphibious landing on the shores of northern Europe: D-Day.[48]

D-Day

In November 1943, President Roosevelt and his staff began their journey to the first meeting of the "Big Three" (Churchill, Roosevelt, and Stalin) in Tehran, Iran. The most significant agreement from the conference was the U. S. and British commitment to establish a western front in northern Europe (operation Overlord) to battle fascist Germany, with a corresponding commitment from Russia to engage the Germans on their eastern front to keep Germany's military resources divided. The conference ended with the commitment by Roosevelt to name the commander for Operation Overlord within a week. Roosevelt had only two people in mind: General Marshall, current Chief-of-Staff of the Armed Forces, and General Eisenhower, current commander of U. S. forces in Europe. On December 5, after discussing it with Marshall (who gave him no preference either way), Roosevelt decided: it would be Eisenhower.[49]

For the next six months, General Eisenhower was the center hub of a wheel of activity for planning the seaborne invasion of northern France. On January 15, Eisenhower arrived in London to take over as "Supreme Commander" of Allied forces in Europe. One of his first actions was to move headquarters from the center of London to a seaside town. Another action Eisenhower took was to transfer General Patton from the Mediterranean theater to his headquarters. Although he almost regretted it initially, owing to some public statements by Patton that received extremely negative press, eventually Patton would go on to show his worth in leading the U. S. Third Army through France, Belgium, and Germany. Eisenhower also took care to maintain morale of the troops, and he did this by constantly visiting them to show that he cared for them. Between February 1 and June 1, Eisenhower visited "twenty-six divisions, twenty-four airfields, five ships of war, and numerous depots, shops, hospitals, and other important installations."[50]

On D-Day, June 6, 1944, the U. S. landings at Utah Beach and Omaha Beach, and the British and Canadian landings at Gold, Juno, and Sword, were supported by the greatest naval armada in the history of the world. There were 150,000 soldiers, 12,000 aircraft, thousands of tanks, troop carriers, specialized vehicles, jeeps, and equipment of every kind delivered by 7,000 ships.[51] Every soldier participating in the landings that day carried a special message from General Eisenhower that said (in part):

> "You are about to embark upon the Great Crusade, toward which we have striven these many months. The eyes of the world are upon you. The hopes and prayers of liberty-loving people everywhere march with you. In company with our brave Allies and brothers-in-arms on other Fronts, you will bring about the destruction of the German war machine, the elimination of Nazi tyranny over the oppressed peoples of Europe, and security for ourselves in a free world."[52]

All of the attacks that morning were challenged by the Germans in their prepared defensive positions, but the fiercest fighting was at Omaha Beach, where the Germans had been engaging in defensive exercises. The "Battle of the Beachhead" lasted longer than the military planners expected, and at the end of June, progress was slow; indeed, some observers were concerned about a repeat of the World War I experience of trench warfare. However, the supplies of troops, armor, and equipment kept coming. Even a hurricane on June 19 did not stop the machinery of constant movement of materiel from reaching the Normandy shores. By the beginning of July, over 170,000 vehicles, half a million tons of supplies, and a million men had landed at the beach, supported by constant Allied aircraft overhead. The overwhelming numbers for the Allies had a cumulative effect, and a "breakout" occurred on July 25, with the U. S. First Army breaking through Saint Lo. This was the beginning of an all-out offensive through northern France, and assuaged fears of a trench warfare stalemate on the minds of the soldiers in the field and their loved ones back home.[53]

Philippines Invasion

The last day of the Democratic National Convention in Chicago was July 21; Roosevelt was again nominated President, and Harry Truman was nominated Vice President. As Truman accepted the nomination in Chicago, Roosevelt was boarding the USS *Baltimore*, a cruiser headed to Pearl Harbor, for a meeting with General MacArthur and Admiral Nimitz. Five days later, he arrived for the meeting with those two military leaders, who were in disagreement over the next military target in the Pacific. MacArthur wanted to return to and liberate the Philippines, and Nimitz and the other joint chiefs wanted to bypass the Philippines and attack Formosa, the better to attack the Japanese mainland sooner. MacArthur made the convincing argument that the Philippines was a more strategic target and would provide better air base coverage for attacking Japan and at the same time controlling the South China Sea. Admiral Nimitz grudgingly agreed, and so Roosevelt approved the operation – the Philippines would be the next Allied target in the Pacific.[54]

On October 20, General MacArthur made his triumphant return to the Philippines, setting foot on Leyte Island shortly after the start of amphibious landings there. MacArthur brought with him the President of the Philippines, Sergio Osmena, and addressed the Filipino people on a small radio transmitter to remind them of his promise kept ("I have returned"). He asked them to support the liberation of the island from their Japanese captors. By the end of the day, U. S. forces had overwhelmed the Japanese defenders and were solidly established on the island with minimal losses.[55]

The Japanese had been expecting an assault on the Philippine Islands, and their plan was to carry out a trap, dividing their naval forces into a decoy group of four aircraft carriers, three light cruisers plus eight destroyers, and a main attack group of seven battleships, 11 heavy cruisers, five light cruisers and 28 destroyers. The decoy group of carriers would be the bait to draw off the U. S. Navy's protective battleships and cruisers so the attack group could then demolish the U. S. invasion force landing in the Philippines. Another aspect of the Japanese plan was that the attack group be split in two – half of the ships planned to approach Leyte Gulf from the south, taking the Surigao Straight between Dinagat and Leyte, and the second half of the attack group led by Vice Admiral Kurita planned to approach Leyte Gulf from the north, taking the San Bernadino Straight between Luzon and Samar. The final aspect of this plan, which was complex with multiple time dependencies as Japanese strategies typically were, required the first half of the attack group to be a combination of ships commanded by two vice-admirals. Ships led by Vice Admiral Shima were to come from Japan, skirting the China coast down past Taiwan, then heading south toward the Philippines to meet up with Vice Admiral Nishimura's ships coming from Borneo, a large island southwest of the Philippines.[56]

The Japanese Fifth Fleet, led by Admiral Kurita, was spotted by American submarines *Darter* and *Dace* operating in the area; these two submarines attacked on October 23, sinking the Japanese cruisers *Atago* and *Maya* and damaging the cruiser *Takao*. Kurita's flagship was the *Atago*, and he was among over 600 crewmen plucked from the sea by a destroyer; he transferred to the battleship *Yamato*. Kurita's force was thus reduced by three cruisers and two destroyers, because Kurita directed the *Takao* to head back to Brunei, Borneo with two destroyers as protection. The next day, aircraft from the U. S. carriers *Intrepid* and *Cabot* attacked the super-battleship *Musashi*, hitting her with a bomb and five torpedoes. The heavy cruiser *Myoko* was also damaged in this first wave. A second attack of U. S. planes hit the *Musashi* with ten more torpedoes and bombs. They also damaged the battleships *Yamato*, *Nagato*, and *Haruna*, plus an additional destroyer. After a third attack, a combined total of 19 torpedoes and 19 bombs hit the *Musashi* rendering her dead in the water. Kurita ordered the fleet to turn west, taking them away and out of range of the onslaught from the American planes. He radioed the Japanese high command to inform them of the losses and requested direction. The reply was to attack.[57]

Battle of Leyte Gulf

On October 24, aircraft from the carriers *Essex* and *Franklin* spotted the Japanese southern group under Admiral Nishimura and damaged the battleship *Fuso*. By midnight, Nishimura approached Surigao Straight where the U. S. Seventh Fleet was guarding the American forces on Leyte. On both sides of the Straight were 20 destroyers of Rear Admiral Jesse Oldendorf's trap for the Japanese. At the end of the Straight just before it opened fully into Leyte Gulf steamed Oldendorf's battleships and cruisers in a formation that would "cross the T" when the Japanese arrived, that is, form the top of a "T" to the Japanese line that made the vertical stem of the "T," a positioning which would give great advantage to the U. S. warships and their fire power. Oldendorf's battleships were survivors of Pearl Harbor: the *West Virginia, Pennsylvania, Maryland, Mississippi, Tennessee,* and *California*, all repaired, refitted, and refurbished with the latest technology.[58]

At 2 a.m., as Nishimura's ships slowed and lined up to navigate the narrows, five American destroyers fired torpedoes on the ships, sinking one destroyer and damaging the battleships *Fuso* and *Yamashiro*. Then six more destroyers attacked the *Yamashiro*, which received a direct torpedo hit, and two other torpedoes hit the Japanese destroyer *Yamagumo*, which sank immediately. At 3:30 a.m., Nishimura's ships were coming into range of Oldendorf's battleships and cruisers as they sailed in single file up the Surigao Straight. Here was the revenge for Pearl Harbor as the *Tennessee, West Virginia,* and other battleships that were bombed without warning that December 7, had their own surprise attack on the Japanese ships sailing up the Straight. As the Japanese ships emerged, thus forming the vertical stem to the American battleships' "crossing the T," they ran into withering fire from the Americans. The battleship *Fuso* sank, along with a third destroyer, and the battleship *Yamashiro* was blasted and sank. The *Mogami*, a heavy cruiser, was extensively damaged and attempted a retreat. As the Japanese turned to run away, the ships from Admiral Shima's group were entering the Straight. Shima's flagship, the heavy cruiser *Nachi*, unexpectedly rammed the *Mogami*. Both ships then made their way back out of the Straight to escape the carnage. Oldendorf's ships pursued the cruiser *Mogami*, mercilessly pounding the ship until it also finally sank. Shima's ships survived to fight another day, but of Nishimura's ships, only the destroyer *Shigure*, while badly damaged, escaped total destruction.[59]

At almost the same time as Nishimura was being hammered by U. S. battleships, Kurita's center force was exiting the San Bernadino Straight. Kurita's experience was completely the opposite of Nishimura's – there was not an enemy vessel in sight. Then at dawn, his lookouts sighted aircraft carriers and their support ships, and Kurita assumed that this was Halsey's fleet. As the Japanese center force approached Leyte Gulf, with the super-battleship *Yamato*, battleships *Nagato*, *Kongo*, and *Haruna*, and the heavy cruisers *Caokai*, *Chikuma*, *Tone*, *Jumano*, *Suzuya*, and *Haguro*, the only defense Admiral Kinkaid had comprised 16 escort carriers and 21 destroyers. Kinkaid had broken his task force into three groups: Taffy 1, in the southern portion of the Gulf near Mindinao; Taffy 2, in the center of the Gulf; and Taffy 3, consisting of six escort carriers and seven destroyers, at the northern end. At 7:00 a.m., the Japanese battleship *Yamato* opened fire on the ships of Taffy 3, hitting the escort carriers *White Plains* and *St Lo*. The U. S. destroyers *Hoel*, *Heermann*, and *Johnson* launched torpedo attacks against the Japanese ships, hitting the cruiser *Kumano*, but the destroyer *Hoel* was counterattacked and sunk, and *Heermann* was hit and damaged. By 8:00 a.m., aircraft from the escort carriers attacked the Japanese ships and sank the cruisers *Caokai* and *Chikuma*; in addition, the cruiser *Hagurao* was hit with a bomb that disabled a gun turret. The *St Lo*, already damaged by shells from the Japanese cruisers, was struck by a kamikaze pilot and sank. The escort carriers *Santee*,

Suwannee, and *Kalinin Bay* were also hit by kamikaze planes and damaged. By 12:30 p.m., the Japanese ships withdrew to the north, the ships and planes of Taffy 3 having successfully protected the landings at Leyte. Because of the courage of the sailors and airmen of Taffy 3, who defeated an overwhelming enemy wielding the firepower of the largest battleships and cruisers in the Japanese Navy, the Leyte landings were protected and the Philippines invasion forces were saved.[60]

Battle of the Bulge

The success of the landings in the Philippines and the naval battles in Leyte Gulf could not have come at a better time for President Roosevelt, because he was in a bitter battle with his Republican challenger Thomas Dewey in the 1944 presidential election campaign. Roosevelt was the first president since Lincoln to be running for president during a war, and as can be said of General Sherman's victory march into Atlanta in September 1864, the positive impact of winning these battles in the Pacific had a positive impact on the campaign for the incumbent president. In addition, the September and October successes of the Allies' armies in northern France and Belgium pushing the Nazis back to the German border, was also welcome news to the American public. Roosevelt was easily elected to his fourth term, with 432 electoral votes to Dewey's 99 and a popular vote of almost 54 percent. But the good news could not last forever, and that winter the Allies were hit by a surprise counterattack by the Germans in Belgium.[61]

By the middle of October, the Allies were encountering more issues with logistics and supplies than they were with the vaunted German army and armored divisions. French railroads had been extensively damaged, so the alternative plan for providing supplies to the troops was to rebuild the port of Antwerp, which had been under heavy attack by Hitler's V2 rockets from Dutch islands.[62] With the overextension of Allied forces, Hitler saw an opportunity. He would counterattack the weakest portion of the Allies' line from Belgium to Luxembourg, that is, the middle of the line, which was in the region of the Ardennes. He would use overwhelming force to break through and advance to Liege, Belgium. If things went well, the Panzers could race all the way to Antwerp and complete the task that the V2s had started. Hitler's military planners expected a seven-to-one advantage of 30 divisions to four, and since the campaign would occur in the winter months, bad weather would wipe out the Allies' air-superiority advantage. In addition, this strike through the heart of the Ardennes' forest would provide maximum cover from aerial observation the covert movement of troops leading up to the attack.[63]

On December 16, the Germans struck, tearing a whole in the Allies' defenses and pushing them back 20 miles in four days. In addition to the German Panzer tank units blowing up everything in their path, secret units of English-speaking German commandos infiltrated the American lines, dressed in American uniforms and driving captured U. S. vehicles. These units caused confusion and suspicion in the American lines by changing signposts on the roads, destroying communication lines, and blowing up supplies and ammunition. Before long the U. S. troops caught on to the subversion and sabotage; they set up new checkpoints all along the front and interrogated every soldier in every vehicle details about Americana, such as the names of comic strip characters, baseball players, and Hollywood stars. Even General Bradley, commander of the 12th Army, was questioned.[64]

Bastogne

The Germans completely bypassed and surrounded the Belgian town of Bastogne, a critical east/west and north/south crossroads in the heart of the Ardennes. It became the "donut hole" of the German offensive, and the German high command fully intended to lay siege to the town if the Americans did not surrender. The American commander of the 101st Airborne and 82nd Airborne units in Bastogne was General Arnold McAuliffe.

McAuliffe had confidence in his troops and their defensive positions in and around Bastogne. He believed in their ability to hold off the Germans until relief came, and that was his mindset at noon on December 22 when German officers – having signaled with a flag of truce – were led into his camp blindfolded by an American escort. The message from their commander was an entreaty to surrender, to save the Americans and their Belgian hosts from complete annihilation. When Colonel Harry Kinnard read the message's English translation to him, McAuliffe's first response was "Aw, nuts" – because his initial reaction to the white flag had been that the Germans were surrendering, though having heard their message he could then see this was not the case. McAuliffe sat down to write out a response and asked Kinnard what he should say. Kinnard said the General's first response would be best, but McAuliffe didn't remember what he had said. Kinnard recounted McAuliffe's initial reaction to the reading of the message, and they both laughed out loud. McAuliffe agreed that nothing more needed to be said, and simply wrote "Nuts" on the back of the German commander's letter.[65]

Word of McAuliffe's response to the Germans' surrender demand instantly lifted spirits of the Allies across the Western Front, and even across the globe. General George Patton said, "Anyone that eloquent deserves to be saved."[66] Patton was determined to rescue the 101st Airborne and other units at Bastogne. Patton also asked his unit's chaplain to provide a special prayer for good weather so that Allied air power could be used in the effort to sustain and relieve the beleaguered troops at Bastogne. As the surrounding Germans prepared their "hammer and anvil" attack on Bastogne, the Allies were also preparing their operations to send air support, relief supplies, and armor.

On Christmas Day the Germans struck. It started with an artillery barrage at 2:45 a.m., followed by German infantry, which began streaming into the outskirts of town. By 7:00 a.m., a column of Panzer tanks rolled down the streets, but they did not get very far. McAuliffe's troops from the 101st and 82nd Airborne distinguished themselves by magnificently engaging and destroying the tanks and eliminating the troops on sight. By 8:00 a.m., owing to the clearing skies, American P-47 fighter-bombers were winging their way to Bastogne, providing air cover and support for the beleaguered American troops. They blasted away at the tanks, transports, armored vehicles and gun positions surrounding the Americans. Later that day, C-47 cargo planes dropped supplies to the besieged town.[67]

Not far from Bastogne, commanders of the 37th Tank Battalion and 53rd Armored Infantry Battalion discussed battle plans for the relief of Bastogne. Their directions from HQ were to attack the Germans in Sibret, a town southwest of Bastogne. As they were coordinating their next steps, they observed the C-47 planes and unarmed gliders winging their way through anti-aircraft fire to provide the needed medical supplies, food and equipment for the 101st. As they were watching, multiple aircraft were being hit and falling out of the sky to unknown results beyond their view. This inspired a change of plans.

Colonel Abrams of the 37th and Colonel Jacques of the 53rd reasoned that attacking Sibret was taking them away from their objective, which was relief of Bastogne. Instead, they decided that the route through Assenois, only two miles from Bastogne, was a more direct and efficient path. These men of the 4th Armored Division of Patton's Third Army surprised the Germans at Assenois and easily overwhelmed them. The day after Christmas they arrived in Bastogne and surprised the Americans defending the town. They called out and when nobody answered, they said, "Come on out, this is the 4th Armored." Finally, an officer crawled out of a foxhole and introduced himself. It was the beginning of the end of the German counterattack, and from that point forward, the Germans would be fighting a defensive rear guard action, falling back closer and closer into the heart of the third Reich.[68]

Victory in Europe

After the Allies pushed the Germans back through the Ardennes to the German border and beyond, the next objective was the Rhine River. Allied planning targeted February or March for the Rhine crossing, with objectives being securing and holding the bridges and crossing points for entry into the heart of Germany. While the planning and execution of this offensive was ongoing, the next major conference between the leaders of the Allied countries took place at Yalta, Crimea in February 1945. The Yalta conference (also known as Argonaut) started on February 4, the Americans, British, and Soviets meeting eight times in eight days for three to four hours a day. For the most part, all three leaders achieved their goals; however, Yalta has been seen in hindsight as a major setback for U. S. and British interests.[69]

Roosevelt returned to the United States somewhat rejuvenated from the conference and the journey, feeling that it had accomplished its major goals. On March 1, he spoke to a special dual session of Congress to give a speech about the Yalta Conference and his plans for bringing a speedy conclusion to the war. For this public appearance, he made his speech while seated in a chair, instead of standing at the lectern, for the first time. He made a quick reference to his seated position, explaining that his leg braces made it difficult to stand after having "just completed a fourteen-thousand-mile trip." The real reason for this change in appearance was his failing health.[70]

At the end of March, Roosevelt travelled with his cousins Laura Delano and Margaret (Daisy) Suckley to Warm Springs, Georgia, in another attempt to convalesce. He was also accompanied by his personal secretary Grace Tully, and his personal doctor, cardiologist Dr. Howard Bruenn. By the end of the first week in Warm Springs, it appeared that the President was recovering, with the color coming back to his face and regaining his appetite and spirits.

On April 9, Lucy Rutherford arrived at Warm Springs with her friend Elisabeth Shoumanoff, who was a painter. Roosevelt had dinner on April 11 with his Secretary of the Treasury, Henry Morgenthau, and Henry was profoundly and sadly surprised at the President's memory and physical appearance. The next day, after Shoumanoff had painted the President's portrait and the butler was preparing lunch, Roosevelt suffered a brain hemorrhage. Dr. Bruenn was immediately summoned, and an emergency call was placed to a doctor in Atlanta, Dr. James Paullin, who had examined the President at Bethesda the previous year. Dr. Paullin would not arrive in time. Dr. Bruenn made Roosevelt as comfortable as possible, while the President's labored breathing indicated the inevitable conclusion. Around 3:30 p.m., Roosevelt took his last breath.[71]

As the world mourned and the war continued, Vice President Harry Truman took up the reins of leadership as President of the United States. Two other world leaders died that April, both of them leaders of the Axis powers. Benito Mussolini had established his headquarters at Lake Garda in the Italian Alps. As the Allies pushed farther north towards the Alps, more Italian partisans were emboldened to resist and revolt. Eventually Mussolini was captured, along with his mistress and a dozen other leaders of the shadow Italian government of the Republican-Fascist party. They were executed on April 28 by members of the Italian communist party. On the last day of April 1945, Adolf Hitler committed suicide in the Chancellery Bunker in Berlin with his wife of one day, Eva Braun. On May 8, Germany finally succumbed to the Allies' unconditional surrender terms, and the world celebrated Victory in Europe (VE) day.[72]

Victory in Japan

With victory in Europe assured, the Allies were able to focus their energies on bringing the war in the Pacific Theater to closure. Just as the war across the Atlantic had progressed steadily since January 1945, so had the war in the Pacific. On February 19, U. S. Marines landed on Iwo Jima, and fought a bloody contest for several days until the Marines were able to raise the U. S. flag on Mount Suribachi on February 29. However, that was not the end of the battle, because the Japanese had created a labyrinth of caves and tunnels deep in the hillsides of the island. Japanese General Tadamichi Kuribayshi and his men would battle to the death for over a month in an attempt to delay the use of Iwo Jima's airfields for bombing Japan.[73]

After Iwo Jima, the next target of the Allies was Okinawa, an island only 340 miles from Japan's southernmost island of Kyushu. The Allies began the attack (Operation Iceberg) on April 1, and it would take almost three months to complete the takeover of the island and at an alarming cost (75,000 Allied casualties, over 110,000 Japanese casualties, and over 80,000 of the indigenous population of the island killed). The goal was use of the large airfields at Kadena Air Base as the launching point for Operation Downfall, the invasion of the Japanese islands of Kyushu and Honshu. The Okinawa invasion was the largest amphibious operation in the Pacific Theater, with 1,300 ships involved, and it became notorious for the number of Japanese kamikaze attacks.[74]

The Potsdam Conference (codenamed Terminal) was held between July 17 and August 2, 1945. It was held in Potsdam, Germany, and was the last of the conferences of the "Big Three" – this time consisting of Prime Minister Winston Churchill, General Secretary Joseph Stalin, and President Harry Truman. The intent of the conference was to determine what to do with Germany now that it had surrendered. Another result of the Potsdam conference was the Potsdam Declaration,

which provided terms and conditions for the Japanese to surrender (unconditionally); it was basically an ultimatum. The
Potsdam Declaration was met with suspicion and contempt by
the Japanese, because they considered the "unconditional surrender" unacceptable, notably on account of their belief that it
would end their imperial system of government and rule by
their deity, Emperor Hirohito.[75]

Meanwhile, in order to push the Japanese to surrender
without having to suffer the estimated 500,000 to one million
Allied casualties from an invasion, President Truman made the
decision to deploy the atomic bomb. On August 5, the first one
was dropped on the city of Hiroshima, which was a shipbuilding port that also contained other war material factories, and it
was the Japanese Second Army headquarters. Although millions of leaflets had been dropped on the city documenting the
Potsdam Declaration and warning of an impending attack, over
70,000 residents were instantly killed. The next day, President
Truman again asked for Japan's surrender, but no response
came. Three days later, a second atomic bomb was used, this
time on the city of Nagasaki. Millions of leaflets warning of the
impending bombing were dropped on the city before the attack. Another 75,000 residents died in this bombing, and this
time the Emperor took a stand. He spoke to the Supreme
Council and directed them to accept the terms of surrender.[76]

Emperor Hirohito recorded a message to the Japanese people that explained his reasoning for the surrender, owing to
the new and terrible weapon of the enemy, and his desire not
to see the country totally destroyed. At noon on August 15,
the Emperor's recorded message was played on the radio and
over loudspeakers all over Japan. It was the first time most of
the Japanese people had heard the Emperor's voice, and most
accepted their fate. The official surrender ceremony occurred
on the deck of the battleship USS *Missouri* on September 2.
This last act ended the most bloody and devastating war in

world history, and Americans and Allies all over the world celebrated Victory in Japan (VJ) day.[77]

CHAPTER 12

Roosevelt's Legacy

Roosevelt's shadow is long and imposing. He set a record of legislative accomplishment that has not been matched and is the standard against which all subsequent presidential efforts have been measured – his first 100 days in office. In those first 100 days, which equates to about fifteen weeks, he was able to request or create 15 major pieces of legislation, garner support for that legislative effort, and push those legislative acts through Congress onto his desk for signature. In that legislative record are laws still on the books today, and some withstood the test of time so well they were only overcome by newer legislation some 70 years or more later.

He also set a number of other firsts: He was the first president to attend his political party's presidential national convention and to accept the nomination for president in person; he was the first president to repeat the Oath of the President word for word, instead of just saying "I do;" he was the first president to have the First Lady, Eleanor Roosevelt, hold a press conference; he was the first president to connect to the American people through a new medium (radio); he was the first president to have a movie, play, and book created about him during his presidency; he was the first president to hold his inauguration in January (owing to the 20th Amendment); he was the first president to name a woman to a cabinet position (Secretary of Labor Frances Perkins); he was the first president to support a peace-time draft (the first ever) to prepare the country for war; he was the first president to travel by airplane while in office (for the Casablanca Conference); and he was the first president to build a Presidential Library to hold his official documents after leaving the presidency (which is now a tradition, as all subsequent presidents have followed his example).

In addition to his accomplishments as President, Roosevelt also was a significant contributor to the eventual passage of the 17th Amendment to the Constitution, which allows for Senators to be directly elected by citizens. This came about on account of his activism in progressive policies against the Murphy political machine (bosses) in New York state while a state senator. In his fight against polio, the disease that brought his greatest personal tragedy and challenge to his political career, he became much more appreciative of his position and potential to do right for the common man. He created the National Foundation for Infantile Paralysis (NFIP) – nicknamed the "March of Dimes" by comedian Eddie Cantor – and he provided his name and invested his own personal wealth for comforting others with the disease and for attempting to find a cure.[1]

Roosevelt led the United States as a leader on the world stage – under his political and strategic leadership and direction, the United States became the dominant world power after World War II. His legacy of large government programs and a social contract with the American people remain to this day in the form of labor laws; farm support through crop prices and other agriculture regulations; regulation and oversight of the stock markets; use of the media and modern technology to communicate to the masses; and the Social Security programs that form the backbone of the safety net for seniors throughout our country today. Given all of his achievements, it is easy to see why Franklin Roosevelt is considered by many to be the greatest president of the 20th century.[2]

The End of Prohibition

Ending Prohibition and the Volstead Act, including a repeal of the 18th Amendment, was actually a position Roosevelt held as he was campaigning before the 1932 election. At a campaign stop in New Jersey, Roosevelt demanded Republicans reform Prohibition to at least allow modification of the law to allow beer to be produced and sold. He also stated that the revenue gained by the taxation of beer would provide much needed relief to government budgets decimated by the Depression. As President, Roosevelt would quickly make that proposition come true.[3]

As Roosevelt bathed in the glow of his first Fireside Chat, he turned to his most trusted aide and confidant Louis Howe and said, "I think it's time for a beer."[4] With that statement, he started down the path toward his next activity, accelerating the progress toward ending Prohibition. Prohibition was already a patient on deathwatch – the "lame duck" Congress of 1932 had voted for repeal of the 18th Amendment. It was only a matter of time before the mandatory number of states ratified the Blaine Act, which would repeal Prohibition and become the 21st Amendment. Amending the Volstead Act, which was written to implement Prohibition in 1918 and ratified in 1919, was already a plank of the 1932 Democratic platform. Now was the time to make that promise a reality.

Roosevelt, quoting the text of the Democratic platform, sent his request for modification of the Volstead Act to allow the sale of 3-2 beer (that is, 3.2 percent of the beer is alcohol by weight) and light wine to Congress. With a flurry of activity, the House Ways and Means Committee completed a draft of the Beer and Wine Revenue Act (BWRA) in less than a day. The next day, the House of Representatives overwhelmingly (more than 75% voting Yea) passed the measure. Only two days later, the Senate also voted for the Volstead amendment to allow the sale of beer and wine. On March 22, President Roosevelt signed the BWRA into law, and citizens across America were singing Roosevelt's theme song from the Democratic National Convention, "Happy Days are Here Again." By the end of 1933, the requisite number of states passed the Blaine Act, and Prohibition was repealed altogether.[5]

Conservation

Roosevelt was a conservationist at heart. He lived in a farming community in upstate New York and was fully aware of the issues involved with maintaining soil health and farm productivity. In August 1934, he was travelling by train from Portland to Chicago and passed through the northern reaches of the "Dust Bowl" of the Great Plains. His train stopped at Devils Lake in North Dakota whereupon he took an automobile tour of the surrounding countryside. On this tour, he saw a sign addressed to him stating, "You gave us beer, now give us water." After the tour was over, he addressed a large crowd at Devils Lake and provided his personal views on the causes of the current soil conditions. Roosevelt said he believed that action could be taken, despite the natural phenomenon of drought and windstorms, to provide windbreaks of trees or shrubs to maintain soil health and reduce dust storms.[6]

Dust storms caused by soil erosion were a national menace according to a pamphlet written by Hugh Hammond Bennett. Bennett was a soil scientist working for the Department of Agriculture who believed that sheet soil erosion caused by conventional farming methods was the root of the problem and that massive dust storms were the result. In 1933, Harold Ickes set up a Soil Erosion Service within the Department of the Interior, and installed Bennett as its Director. Withing months, Bennett had CCC camps in 31 states working on soil conservation and erosion control projects on four million acres of land. In April 1935, Roosevelt transferred the Soil Erosion Service to the U.S. Department of Agriculture (USDA), where it belonged, and it was renamed the Soil Conservation Service. In Senate hearings that month, Bennett provided expert testimony on the causes of soil erosion and their consequences. As he did so, a dust cloud, having travelled 2,000 miles from the Great Plains, dramatically hit the capital, blocking out the sun and blackening the sky as the Senators stared out the window.[7]

Roosevelt was ahead of his time when it came to views on forestation, soil erosion, and water conservation. He was also ahead of his time when it came to the Civilian Conservation Corps (CCC). The CCC was similar to a program Roosevelt had created as Governor of New York. The government hired unemployed young people to perform conservation activities in national parks across the country; they planted thousands of trees, cut fire breaks, constructed thousands of miles of trails, and provided treatment for diseased trees and soil erosion.[8] In another first, some of those 125,000 miles of trails cleared by the CCC were used for downhill skiing in Stowe, Vermont – one of the first ski resorts in the United States. The numbers are astonishing; during the life of the program, over three billion trees were planted by the CCC, 800 state parks were developed, and 20 million acres were protected from erosion.[9]

Roosevelt's initial goals were much more conservative than the above numbers indicate, but when he initially rolled out his objectives even his own cabinet complained about how audacious his plan was. Roosevelt expected 250,000 men working by the summer, and he had only proposed the CCC on March 21. This example of a leader demanding greatness and helping his team achieve it is evidenced by the fact that by early April the first members of the CCC had enrolled, and by the end of June the quarter-million-man goal had been met. Almost 275,000 CCC workers were enlisted and located in 1,300 military style camps throughout the United States. The camps were run by the Army, which supplied tents and food, as well as direction and discipline. As such, the CCC was a perfect opportunity to employ World War I veterans, since their benefits had seen a 50-percent cut owing to the Economy Act, Roosevelt's attempt to produce a balanced budget. Roosevelt waived the age requirement of the CCC to allow any veteran to seek enlistment in the program – within a few years 250,000 veterans would serve their country a second time as members of the CCC. In the end, the CCC was Roosevelt's most popular and successful New Deal program, and the Soil Conservation Service has remained an agency of the USDA to this day, although it was renamed the Natural Resources Conservation Service by President Clinton in 1994.[10]

Emergency Relief

In 1933, at the peak of the Depression when unemployment hit 25 percent, people were desperate. Staring into the abyss of an unprecedented calamity, Roosevelt had to act fast, especially in light of the coming winter and the potential for huge numbers of Americans being out on the street on account of loss of income and no way to pay the mortgage or rent. The Federal Emergency Relief Act was signed on May 12, 1933; it created the Federal Emergency Relief Agency (FERA), which provided direct grants to states as a means of overseeing and supercharging local relief efforts, down to the county and city levels. Instead of creating a whole new bureaucracy, FERA used the existing structure of the state relief organizations and funded cash payments and state-directed work efforts for the unemployed. In a 30-month span, FERA distributed more than $3.1 billion in funds and provided jobs to over 20 million workers.[11]

Roosevelt installed Harry Hopkins as the administrator for FERA, which was authorized $500 million for grants to states. Hopkins resigned his position as the head of New York's Temporary Emergency Relief Administration (TERA), and took a 37 percent cut in pay to work for FERA, which was a reflection of his belief in this role and its mission.[12] Hopkins immediately brought his team in from New York and got to work. Within two hours on the job, Hopkins spent $5 million of his allocation, and some were projected he would run out of money in a matter of months. Hopkins believed it was necessary to "prime the pump" to get the economy moving, and this was his method of priming. His objective was to serve the most at risk, the 30 million Americans without a regular source of income.[13]

In November 1933, the Civil Works Administration (CWA) was established; it provided jobs for unskilled laborers to work on local construction projects such as schools, sewer lines, and public building improvements. The CWA was created under the National Industrial Recovery Act (NIRA), and Hopkins was named its administrator. The CWA was a means of providing employment – not mere cash ("the dole") – and so helped to give those it helped a boost of confidence and self-esteem. The CWA hired 2.6 million workers by December (two million came over from FERA), and at its peak in January 1934, the CWA employed over 4.2 million people. The CWA accomplished a lot in its short lifespan (the agency was shut down by July 1934): Over 40,000 miles of new roads were paved; thousands of miles of levees were built up; a thousand miles of water mains were laid; and thousands of new schools were built. Years after the CWA program ended, Hopkins proudly stated his belief that these buildings and achievements would stand as monument to the efforts the CWA workers performed in every state of the nation, long after they and the difficult days they endured were dead and buried.[14]

The CWA was such a popular and successful program that a new program was created to take its place and replicate its achievements. In late 1934, Roosevelt decided to create a massive work relief program that would help the unemployed endure the effects of the Depression, without the negative personal and societal impacts of a handout. This would become known as the Works Progress Administration (WPA). The WPA was created by the Emergency Relief Appropriation Act of 1935, which allocated nearly $4.9 billion to multiple programs, the single highest appropriation to that date in U. S. history.[15]

The WPA was not without its detractors. It was derided by liberals and labor organizations claiming the wages paid were too low, and it was chastised by conservatives who said the organization was communist, that the agency was "Sovietizing" Americans. The WPA would quickly become the largest employer in the nation, and over its eight-year lifespan provided employment to over eight million people. The agency also created jobs for out-of-work musicians, actors, writers, and artists. The Federal Music Project employed 15,000 out-of-work musicians, provided free concerts of classical music to cities that had no prior orchestras, and documented and preserved American folk music. The Federal Theater Project (FTP) employed aspiring directors, playwrights, and actors like Orson Wells, Arthur Miller, John Huston, and Burt Lancaster. The FTP also produced such highly acclaimed productions as *Voodoo Macbeth*, *Triple-A Plowed Under*, and *Power*. The Federal Writers Project (FWP) offered jobs to unemployed writers, teachers, and librarians for documenting 1930s' Americana, from state travel guides to recording oral histories of different ethnic groups. The FWP employed future writing luminaries such as Richard Wright (who wrote *Native Son* and *Uncle Tom's Children*), Saul Bellow (Pulitzer Prize, Nobel Prize for Literature, and National Medal of Arts), and John Cheever (Pulitzer Prize, National Book Award, and National Medal for Literature). The Federal Arts Project was one of the most controversial of these programs because it provided murals by local artists in or on public buildings such as post offices. The murals tended to celebrate the oppressed or working class and attracted the attention of the House Committee on Un-American Activities. Regardless, these projects left an American cultural legacy all their own.[16]

Infrastructure Investment

By executive order on June 16, Roosevelt set up the Public Works Administration (PWA) under the National Industrial Recovery Act (NIRA) as a means to infuse a shot of economic stimulus into the moribund economy of 1933. However, the leadership he installed to effect that change, in the form of Harold Ickes, was incapable of executing on Roosevelt's vision. By the end of 1933, Ickes had only spent $110 million of the $3.3 billion allocated the PWA program from the NIRA. This is because Ickes was a micromanager who demanded to be involved with and approve every detail and decision of every project. To counter this constraint, Roosevelt created the Civil Works Administration (CWA) and assigned $400 million of funding from PWA to execute the CWA projects under Harry Hopkins, which were much smaller in size and spread out across every state in the nation. Thus, the CWA provided fiscal stimulus on a local/micro-scale whereas, the PWA needed to and was intended to implement fiscal stimulus on a national/macro-scale. Eventually, this macro-scale process did occur, but it took time to take effect, and by then the NIRA was doomed. Fortunately, Roosevelt separated the PWA from the NIRA before it was declared unconstitutional by the Supreme Court.[17]

The PWA over its ten years of existence (1933-1943) left a legacy of massive construction projects that are still in use today. These notable projects include the Lincoln Tunnel and Triborough Bridge in New York City, the overseas highway/series of bridges that connect the Florida Keys to the mainland, the Fort Peck Dam in Montana, the Grand Coulee Dam in Washington, the Bonneville Dam in Oregon, the Boulder (Hoover) Dam in Nevada (begun under President Hoover), the San Francisco Mint (new building dedicated in 1937 where the mint still resides), and the Washington National (Ronald Reagan) Airport. The PWA also included thousands of smaller projects so that the total number of projects was over 34,000. These smaller projects included funding (grants and loans) for thousands of construction projects for hospitals, libraries, and schools; it also funded electrical power, sewer, water projects and other improvements.[18] In addition to these projects, the PWA funded the construction of naval vessels, army posts, and military airports. These military projects and expenditures helped the United States prepare for and win World War II, including building the aircraft carriers *Yorktown* (commissioned September 30, 1937) and *Enterprise* (commissioned May 12, 1938), which served in major naval battles in the Pacific.[19]

Another source of infrastructure investment was the Works Progress Administration (WPA). Although the WPA was conceived and intended to be a relief program – providing jobs to the unemployed – it also served up construction funding for major projects across the United States. WPA construction projects included schools, roads, and government buildings, but another major contribution was the funding spent on developing, expanding or modernizing hundreds of airports across the country. Some of the significant airports that received funding and construction projects from the WPA are: Berry Field (Nashville International Airport), Chicago Municipal (Midway) Airport, Drew Field (Tampa International Airport), Geiger Field (Spokane International Airport), Mills Field (San Francisco International Airport), Mines Field (Los Angeles International Airport), and New York's LaGuardia Airport.[20]

Farm Subsidies

President Roosevelt was almost Thomas Jefferson-like in his admiration for the American farmer and the agrarian way of life. His experience of living on the Hudson River near a rural farming community in upstate New York gave him an appreciation for the effort and hardships of living off the land. As a state senator in New York early in his political career he represented the interests of farmers in the Hudson Valley and was also the head of the Agriculture Committee. He related to the plight of millions of Americans in farming communities hit so hard by depressed agriculture prices that often the cost of production was higher than the market price of the products.

As a consequence, the farmers in the Midwest and Plains States were starting to take matters into their own hands: Stories abounded about farmers banding together to thwart the bankruptcy process by bidding $1 for their neighbor's farm then selling it back to him for $1 (many farmers were losing their farms to foreclosure) and even attacking bankruptcy judges. In addition, at that time in America's history over 30 million people, or 25 percent of the population of the United States, were living and working on over six million farms in rural communities, so relief or financial assistance to this segment of the population would positively impact a large number of Americans.[21]

Roosevelt believed he understood the problem, that agriculture prices were too low, and to develop a solution he summoned a group of experts to Washington. They came up with the Agricultural Adjustment Act (AAA), which was signed into law on May 12, 1933. The solution to the problem was an application of the supply and demand theory of economics – if the supply was reduced, then prices would rise. To execute this solution, farmers would be paid not to produce, and excess supply would be destroyed, plowed under, or thrown away. The bill offered something for almost everyone, with the exception that the costs for implementation would be borne by the "middlemen;" these were believed to be the profiteers in the farm-to-table production system and they would pay an excise tax for the privilege.[22]

In a 1996 analysis of the history and effects of agriculture legislation, Edward Lotterman stated that although the destruction of crops and pigs in a time of starvation was criticized, the AAA achieved its objective of increasing agricultural prices. After the Supreme Court struck down the taxation aspect of the AAA, legislators revised it in 1938 – and multiple times thereafter – such that the act "remained in force" for 60 years. Because Lotterman's paper was written on the occasion of the passage of the Federal Agricultural Improvement and

Reform (FAIR) Act in April 1996, it is interesting to note that although FAIR was intended to repeal the provisions of the AAA, that aspect of FAIR was dropped in committee conferences. Thus, parts of the AAA, though not implemented, are still on the books today.[23]

In 1933, nearly 50 percent of the National Farm Loan Associations were failing, and foreclosures were occurring across the country. The second action Roosevelt took was to help farmers keep their farms by supplying a source of low-cost loans through the Emergency Farm Mortgage Act (EFMA). The EFMA, also approved on May 12, 1933, allowed two federal agencies to purchase farm mortgages and then facilitate the refinancing of the loans at lower interest rates as well as over longer repayment terms. On March 27, Roosevelt created by executive order the Farm Credit Administration (FCA), combining the Federal Farm Board, the Federal Farm Loan Board, the Crop Production Loan Office, and the Seed Loan Office of the Department of Agriculture into a single unit to be effective within 60 days. On May 27, Henry Morgenthau, Jr., became the FCA's first governor; he named William Myers, his technical advisor, the deputy governor. Myers created the Farm Credit System (FCS), a structure of financial institutions that organized financial cooperatives for farmers to provide short, medium, and long-term loans. In 1934, the FCA facilitated the creation of the federal credit union system and was assigned the responsibility of overseeing all federal credit unions. The success of FEMA, FCA, and FCS is evident in the fact that they have consistently and reliably provided agricultural credit for farmers for over 80 years, and that the FCA and FCS organizations still exist today.[24]

Rural Electrification

Roosevelt spent a considerable amount of time in Warm Springs, Georgia, where he enjoyed the therapeutic effects of the waters and created the National Foundation for Infantile

Paralysis (NFIP). In Warm Springs he became an adopted son of the South, where he first observed and became concerned about the abject poverty of some of its people. If a regional planning organization, with governmental power but without governmental encumbrances, could be set up to serve the inhabitants of the Tennessee River, its tributaries and watershed, then it would be possible to provide economic opportunities and employment to an area of 44,000 square miles encompassing parts of seven states. To this end, the concept of the Tennessee Valley Authority (TVA) was created, and a bill for the TVA was proposed.[25]

When the Tennessee Valley Authority Act (TVAA) was written, Roosevelt and U. S. Senator George Norris of Nebraska made sure it included a provision that allowed the TVA to distribute its power over its own power lines, because whoever owned the power lines could dictate who received the power and at what price. This provision of the TVAA received immediate and vehement opposition by the existing Tennessee Valley power company, Commonwealth & Southern. At congressional testimony on Capitol Hill, Wendell Willkie, representing the interests of Commonwealth & Southern, stated that he was not opposed to the TVA generating power, but said the provision allowing TVA to build its own transmission lines was tantamount to confiscation of Commonwealth & Southern market and property. Willkie also charged that there already existed an overcapacity for power in the area, a supposition ignoring the fact that the community was overbilled and underserved. The TVAA cleared committee review unchanged, then was passed by Congress and signed by Roosevelt on May 18, 1933. The legacy and success of the TVA is evidenced by its continued service to the Tennessee Valley across seven states for over 85 years, and that it currently serves over four million households and 744,000 commercial and industrial consumers.[26]

Roosevelt wanted to replicate the model and success of the TVA across the country to electrify the countryside, but he was thwarted in these efforts by the utility companies. So, on May 11, 1935, Roosevelt used an executive order to create the Rural Electrification Administration (REA), and defined the head of the organization to be an administrator whose objective was: "To initiate, formulate, administer, and supervise a program of approved projects with respect to the generation, transmission, and distribution of electric energy in rural areas."[27]

The administrator whom Roosevelt assigned to carry out this objective was Morris Cooke, a utility trustee he had previously worked with when he was Governor of New York. Cooke originally attempted to work with utility executives to carry out his duties, but they were uninterested in his proposals. Cooke then decided to borrow a page from the TVA playbook and strove to encourage farmers to organize their own non-profit power utility co-ops to build power transmission lines and electrify their own regional rural areas. This was accomplished by obtaining low-cost, long-term loans from the Reconstruction Finance Corporation (RFC).[28]

On May 20, 1936, exactly 74 years after President Abraham Lincoln signed the Homestead Act, the Rural Electrification Act (REA) became effective. While the Homestead Act provided up to 160 acres of free land to cultivate and settle the great prairies of the West, and an opportunity for citizens to own their own land and make their own way in pursuit of the American dream, the remoteness and undeveloped nature of Homestead Act's rural areas made it difficult for beneficiaries to have the same living conditions and opportunities enjoyed by those born and raised in towns and metropolitan areas of the nation. The REA, co-sponsored by Senator Norris of Nebraska and Speaker of the House Sam Rayburn, would facilitate electrification of rural America from less than ten percent in the early 1930s to over 90 percent in the late 1940s. In another corollary to the Homestead Act, the first homestead claim was filed by Daniel Freeman in Gage County, Nebraska, the location of the first Rural Electrification District some 70 years later.[29]

Banking Reform

When Roosevelt entered office, the country was in a severe banking crisis, as thousands of banks were failing across the country. Although there was animosity between outgoing President Hoover and President-elect Roosevelt, the lower level administrations in the Treasury department (incoming and outgoing) worked together to coordinate a plan to close all banks (a banking "holiday"), and then re-open them in stages until all healthy, financially solvent banks were reopened. All banks, including the Federal Reserve Banks, were closed for a week, while the administration worked on proposed legislation to respond to the crisis.

The resulting legislation, called the Emergency Banking Act of 1933, was introduced and passed on March 9. In order to ensure cash flows to the banking system, on March 11 Roosevelt wired New York Fed Governor George Harrison to state that the government would guarantee Federal Reserve Bank loans to their member banks. Roosevelt's first Fireside Chat on March 12 assured the public of the safety and security of the banks that would reopen the coming days, and the public responded by depositing their cash (within a month Americans deposited almost $1.8 billion back into their bank accounts), thereby resolving the bank run crisis.[30]

With the near-term crisis behind them, the administration worked with Congress and banking experts to put in place regulations that would provide long-term solutions and avoid repeating a similar crisis in the future. The Banking Act of 1933, also known as the Glass-Steagall Act of 1933 (for the cosponsors of the bill), was signed by President Roosevelt into law on June 16, 1933. There were two significant aspects of this reform: 1) It required banks to separate their investment operations (selling stocks and bonds, underwriting securities) from their commercial operations (maintaining savings and checking accounts, providing loans and mortgages), and 2) It required federally chartered banks to be stockholders (members) of the Federal Deposit Insurance Corporation (membership was optional for state chartered banks). In addition, Glass-Steagall restricted the rights of bank officers of member banks to borrow money from banks they controlled (specifically with respect to Federal Reserve member banks).[31]

In 1999 the Gramm-Leach-Bliley Act repealed the 1930s Glass-Steagall separation of investment and commercial banking. Some believe that the repeal of Glass-Steagall led to the excesses of the financial services industry in the 2000s, and the financial crisis of 2008 that caused the Great Recession. However, others, like Alan S. Blinder, author of *After The Music Stopped*, stipulate that the blame for the financial crisis shouldn't go to the investment banking activities of these firms, but rather to "the dangerous mix of high leverage with disgraceful lending practices, precisely what has been getting banks into trouble for centuries."[32]

At a time when Roosevelt was being told he should "nationalize" the banks and take them under federal control, he instead restructured the industry and helped provide confidence in the system that was sorely lacking. While it is not evident that corporate titans and the upper class ever gave him credit for it, Roosevelt managed to help save capitalism from itself. What is evident from the banking reforms enacted by Roosevelt, and the outstanding success and legacy of those reforms, is that depositors are guaranteed their money is safe up to an amount that covers most Americans' deposits (currently $250,000) in any member bank of the FDIC. Per the FDIC, "Since the start of FDIC insurance on January 1, 1934, no depositor has lost a single cent of insured funds as a result of a failure."[33]

Securities Reform

Owing to the stock market crash in 1929, which was a major cause of the Great Depression, the public's anger against and distrust of the business and financial systems in the United States were intense and widespread. And no single business or financial enterprise in the country was more representative of the disastrous excesses of capitalism than the securities exchanges. As the Senate hearings by the Pecora Commission (misnamed by the press – it was actually a Senate committee led by Senator Peter Norbeck of South Dakota and Senator Duncan Fletcher of Florida) would soon discover, public distrust in these exchanges was well founded. The Pecora investigations, named for Ferdinand Pecora, a former assistant district attorney for New York County, disclosed through public testimony the chronic and systemic abuses of Wall Street. Because of the high profile industrial and financial titans who were subpoenaed to testify, such as Richard Whitney, president of the New York Stock Exchange (NYSE), and Charles Mitchell, chairman of National City Bank, these investigations received significant press coverage and became front-page news. The testimony provided at the hearings disclosed practices of stock price manipulation, abuse of margin financing, and deliberate stock disinformation distributed by sellers and brokers.[34]

These investigations, which Pecora joined in January 1933 and reported on in June 1934, resulted in two significant acts of Congress that would affect the future of the securities market and protect the interests of individual investors: The Securities Act of 1933 and the Securities Exchange Act of 1934. Although the language of these two acts came from different attempts by Roosevelt to obtain a securities bill that could be passed through Congress and presented to the public as quickly as possible, the Pecora investigations provided public support and Congressional interest in passing long-term securities reform legislation. Stock shenanigans did not go away with the passing of the Securities Act in 1933, as evidenced by a collapse of the market that July, and some operators were said to have profited handsomely by (shorting) that collapse. This episode convinced many of the need for a securities law with more teeth in it. The resulting legislation was the Securities Exchange Act of 1934, which created a Securities & Exchange Commission (SEC) that was empowered to oversee and regulate the securities markets.[35]

A similar reaction by the business community to the Securities Act of 1933 greeted the SEC upon its implementation, that is, a "strike by capital." This was evidenced by a dearth of new stock issues, which was interpreted by the administration as a concerted effort by businesses and financial institutions to force Roosevelt to bend to their will and not enforce the new regulatory measures. This is where Roosevelt's political genius came to the fore – by naming Joseph Kennedy as the SEC's first chairman he put on the board one of the savviest stock operators in the country, a man wishing to redeem himself both to Roosevelt and to the public by making the SEC do its job. Kennedy proved Roosevelt's faith in him correct when in 1935 a new bond issue worth $43 million hit the market. At the end of one year as chairman, after which Kennedy resigned his post, new stock issuances had reached $1 billion, and by the end the calendar year would be double that amount. As the businessmen who initially opposed the restrictions and regulations embodied in the SEC discovered that the SEC was actually beneficial to their business by bringing confidence back to that disgraced industry, the nation further believed Roosevelt to be the right man in the right place to save capitalism from itself.[36]

Home Ownership

In the dark days of the Great Depression, families were losing their homes to foreclosure at a furious rate of over 1,000 per day.[37] On April 13, 1933, Roosevelt asked Congress to provide a bill for saving small urban dwellings from foreclosure similar to the one that had established the Emergency Farm Mortgage Act (EFMA). Exactly two months later, Roosevelt signed the Home Owners Loan Act (HOLA) into law. HOLA created the Home Owner's Loan Corporation (HOLC), which purchased loans that were at risk of foreclosure. HOLC then refinanced those loans back to the original mortgagor over a 15-year amortization at a lower interest rate (this was at a time when most home loans were amortized over three to five years).[38] Within one year, about 20 percent of all home mortgages in the United States were owned by HOLC. In a few more years, HOLC would own 75 percent of the value of all non-farm home mortgages in America.[39]

In June 1934, Roosevelt signed the National Housing Act (NHA), which created the Federal Housing Administration (FHA). The FHA provided mortgage insurance (federal loan guarantees) to the mortgagee (banks or savings and loan institution providing the loan) as long as the loan met specific federal guidelines. These loan guarantees encouraged more financial lending firms to provide capital for construction, home improvements, and refinancing, which directly led to a boom in housing construction and employment in the building trades. In 1938, the Federal National Mortgage Association (Fannie Mae) was created by amendment to the NHA, which helped create a secondary market for home mortgages. Thus, Fannie Mae was able to purchase FHA loans. This sent capital back into financial institutions, capital they could reinvest in more loans to consumers.[40]

In October 1943, Roosevelt was looking forward to a postwar future when he asked Congress for a means to provide education and job training for returning servicemen.[41] This bill, which became an even larger program of benefits including low-cost and low-down-payment home loans, medical coverage, job counseling and unemployment insurance, was called the Servicemen's Readjustment Act of 1944, but became more commonly known as the GI Bill of Rights. The GI Bill of Rights passed on unanimous votes of both houses of Congress in mid-June 1944 and was signed by President Roosevelt on June 22. Although the education and training benefits of the bill were more widely used by veterans, the GI Bill's low-cost mortgage benefit was taken advantage of by almost 2.4 million veterans by 1952.[42]

The legacy and success of the housing programs implemented by Roosevelt during his presidency are evidenced by the incredible changes they effected. In the 1930, U. S. citizens were typically renters – about 60 percent of households rented – and only about 40 percent of Americans owned their own homes. In the 2000s, that number had increased to nearly 70 percent. The FHA, though it was incorporated into the newly created Department of Housing and Urban Development (HUD) in 1965, still guarantees home loans that meet established federal criteria. Fannie Mae still exists as an organization, although it was nearly extinguished by the Financial Crisis of 2008. Finally, the GI Bill is still providing veterans an avenue for home ownership with low cost mortgages.[43]

Social Security

As the initial wave of attempts to lessen the impact of the Great Depression through the First New Deal passed through the economy, not everyone was satisfied with the results. This gave rise to several evangelists for the common man, whose populism worried some and frightened others. Principal among these men were Father Charles Coughlin, Dr. Francis Townsend, and Senator Huey Long. Their movements peaked in the mid-1930s, as Americans who once were firmly set in the middle class saw their status fall with their incomes during the Depression. Father Coughlin, the Radio Priest, had millions of listeners, to whom he told stories of capitalism's demise due to its exploitation of the workers. Toward the end of his popularity, he turned anti-Semite and pro-fascist, praising Mussolini and Hitler.[44]

Dr. Townsend believed he had an economic cure for the Depression called the Townsend Plan. This plan would pay all citizens over 60 years old a $200 monthly stipend that would have to be spent withing 30 days. His theory was that the spending would stimulate the economy, and the Depression would be over – the problem was the program would be paid for by a national sales tax of two percent. Regardless of the impracticality of the program, it was immensely popular, as 89 percent of Americans polled were in favor of it. In addition, Townsend received 20 million signatures on a petition for his program, an astounding 20 percent of the adults in the country.[45]

Senator Huey Long represented Louisiana in Congress but had his own ideas on how the country should be run. He was in favor of a program for redistribution of wealth in the United States, a plan he called Share Our Wealth (SOW). It would provide an estate of $5,000 to every family in America. These funds would come from redistributing the wealth of anyone whose fortune was greater than $10 million, wealth above which Huey Long said was in excess of what the rich families needed or could use. The 27,000 clubs and 8 million members were evidence of the popularity of Long's SOW proposal. History may have taken a different turn if Senator Long had not been assassinated in September 1935.[46]

The popularity of these populist organizations and their radical-to-extreme solutions for the economic crisis put even more pressure on the President and his political party to perform. However, Roosevelt was already working on a plan to provide a national program for unemployment insurance and old-age benefits, a cradle-to-grave system that would cover sickness, disability, unemployment, and retirement. In the middle of 1934, Roosevelt created an advisory committee to investigate solutions to the problems with individuals' financial security. He wanted the committee to consider a program that would include unemployment insurance and be funded by employee contributions at the workplace. Roosevelt also wanted the implementation of the program to occur before the 1936 election in order to counteract the popular SOW and Townsend plans. In January 1935, multiple Social Security bills were debated in Congress. They were eventually merged into a single bill, and on August 14, President Roosevelt signed the Social Security Act.[47]

Social Security is one of the crowning and lasting achievements of the Roosevelt administration. Admittedly, it did not end up being the all-encompassing cradle-to-grave coverage that he desired, but it marked a significant departure from prior American attitudes and expectations, because culturally Americans had always been a people of rugged individualism and independence. To now have a social safety net of coverage for unemployment, disability or sickness, and old age – at least for those who were covered (domestic and farm workers were not covered, which was one of the failures of the act) – was a significant accomplishment. It is possible that without the crushing weight of the Depression fraying the social fabric of American society, Social Security may never have become law. And by making it a contributory (through payroll deduction) social contract between the government and its people, Roosevelt ensured that it would not be considered "charity," nor would it be a "general fund tax" that future politicians could manipulate or eliminate.

Labor Relations

During the depths of the Depression, when up to a quarter of Americans lacked a steady job, many laborers were simply happy to be among the employed, as opposed to the alternative. But as the New Deal programs began to take hold, the economy started a comeback. As the fear of losing the precious commodity of employment eased, the sense that employers were taking advantage of their employees while at the same time seizing an unfair proportion of the recovery's economic prosperity ensued. A law of nature states: to every action, there is an equal and opposite reaction. For a very long time, employers had held all the cards and all the power in the relationship between employers and employees, management and labor. Now the second half of that equation was starting to push back; labor was demanding its fair share.

Two examples of this push back occurred in the summer of 1934: The Minneapolis Teamsters' strike and the San Francisco Longshoremen's strike. The Minneapolis local members of the International Brotherhood of Teamsters went on strike, and it became class warfare. Two of the union members were killed and 67 injured. The resulting funeral provoked unity across Minneapolis, as nearly all of the union members in the city and a majority of its middle-class citizens joined in the funeral procession of almost 100,000 people. A general strike of the city, which encompassed all city services and most of its restaurants and shops, brought the employers to the bargaining table, and the strike settled peacefully. Similar events and results occurred in San Francisco when the International Longshoremen's Association (ILA) went on strike. Nearly all of the ports on the West Coast were affected, with only the Los Angeles port being effective in hiring replacement workers. The ILA gained support of the city's unions and middle class, and successfully shut down the city until both sides were brought to the table and negotiations started. The strike ended successfully for the union when the majority of their demands were met.[48]

During the prosperous 1920s, organized labor, or collective bargaining associations known as unions, had lost about half their membership. The first half of the 1930s were not kind to unions either, but the implementation of the 1935 Wagner Act, which curtailed the ability of companies to discourage employees from organizing, began to turn that around. New York Senator Robert Wagner actually started trying to push his bill through Congress in 1934, but President Roosevelt successfully leaned against it to halt its passage. By 1935, the momentum swung in Wagner's favor as he negotiated it through the halls of Congress. When the Supreme Court declared the National Industrial Recovery Act unconstitutional in May 1935, effectively eliminating the collective bargaining and minimum wage aspects of that law, Roosevelt jumped on board and tagged the Wagner Act as a high priority for his administration. The National Labor Relations Act (NRLA) became law on July 5, and the National Labor Relations Board (NLRB) was implemented soon afterwards. With the implementation of the NLRB, which still exists today, organized labor received legal remedy to cases involving collective bargaining disagreements and unfair labor practices of employers.[49]

The final significant legislation of the New Deal era struggled to come to fruition. It had actually passed the Senate in July 1937 but stalled in the House of Representatives conference committees due to significant opposition. This bill was called the Fair Labor Standards Act (FLSA) and was also known as the wages and hours act. The intent of the bill was to set a minimum wage per hour and also define the number of hours in a work week.

Two powerful organizations opposed the bill: 1) Southern Democrats, who wanted to keep wages low in the South in order to attract business to their communities, and 2) Organized Labor, which was concerned that defined minimum wages would become actual maximum wages, and they also wanted to take credit with their membership for any increase in wages. FLSA was finally approved by the House in May 1938, but then was delayed further by consolidation of the separate bills approved by both houses of Congress. The joint resolution was approved on June 14, and President Roosevelt signed the measure on June 24. The final version of the bill outlawed child labor used for interstate commerce, set a minimum wage of $0.25 per hour, set a maximum workweek of 44 hours, and established time-and-a-half for overtime pay. The bill also included a provision that the minimum wage would increase to $0.40 per hour and the maximum workweek would reduce to 40-hours within two years. Although the minimum wage has increased over the years, the workweek is still defined as 40-hours, another legacy of the Roosevelt presidency.[50]

Commander-in-Chief

Roosevelt considered himself the best person to lead the United States through another World War. This was because of his experiences as Undersecretary for the Navy during World War I, which he felt was a dress rehearsal for World War II. In addition, he had travelled extensively throughout Europe as a child, as a maturing young man, and even on his honeymoon. Just like his older cousin, President Theodore Roosevelt, President Franklin Roosevelt had a near photographic memory, and could easily remember people, places, and things he had seen or read. He remembered all of the people in high places that his late father had introduced to him during their travels, and he was on a first name basis with many of the heads of state in Europe. These experiences and capabilities uniquely qualified Roosevelt to be the Commander-in-Chief of the United States during the greatest global conflict the world has ever known.

Even before America's participation in World War II, Roosevelt was thinking and strategizing about how to support the democratic countries and institutions in Europe and the rest of the world, while placating an isolationist public at home. He went as far as he thought he could to prepare the United States for the eventuality of the coming war, whether that came before or after Hitler conquered all of Europe would only be known with the elapsing of time. Until then, Roosevelt did the following to put America on a war footing: authorized billions of dollars for defense spending; promoted the first peacetime draft; approved trading England 50 World War I destroyers for defense installation leases in the Caribbean; created the Lend Lease program to allow England to receive war materials without paying for them; and met Churchill and his staff to discuss strategy to defeat Hitler.[51]

During the war Roosevelt had numerous conferences with the Allies to ensure a cohesive approach to defeating the Axis powers. He also installed a Map Room in the White House to track the daily activities of the opposing forces and success and failures of U. S. movements and operations throughout the world. The Map Room also contained all of the correspondence between the President and the leaders of the Allies (Churchill, Stalin, Chang Kai-shek, and others), and the correspondence he had with U. S. military leaders. Additionally, the Map Room contained all of the documentation regarding the conferences he held with Churchill and the other leaders of the Allied forces. Roosevelt was intimately involved in strategic decisions throughout the war, and especially with respect to critical personnel decisions (e.g., naming Dwight Eisenhower as Supreme Commander for Overlord – the cross-Channel invasion of Europe).[52]

Roosevelt put America on a path to worldwide supremacy in a post-war world. At the end of 1939 the United States had the 18th largest army in the world, but by the end of the war America could boast the most powerful military in the world. His commitment to becoming the Arsenal of Democracy pushed the manufacturing capability of the United States to dominance, for which none other than Joseph Stalin had commended the President and America. At the Tehran Conference, Stalin offered a toast to Roosevelt, and said, "The United States is a country of machines. Without use of these machines, through Lend Lease, we would lose this war."[53]

Roosevelt also looked to a future for America that would have to prepare and adjust for the millions of returning servicemen. He thus championed the GI Bill of Rights that provided unemployment, training, and disability benefits for all veterans. Roosevelt also envisioned the United Nations, a revamped version of President Wilson's League of Nations, to be a collective organization by which nations could resolve their differences rather than resorting to war. He coined the name at the Arcadia conference in 1942 and discussed its implementation with Stalin and Churchill at the Yalta Conference in 1945. Unfortunately, Roosevelt would not live to see his vision come to fruition; he died in April 1945 not long after his return from Yalta. Senator Robert Taft eulogized Franklin Delano Roosevelt in the following way: "He dies a hero of the war, for he literally worked himself to death in the service of the American people."[54]

Presidential Library

Roosevelt was the first president to have a Presidential Library, and actually designed and oversaw the construction of the building. In another first, he had the library constructed during his presidency, before the end of his second term. Roosevelt had already collected a massive amount of records and personal material from his years as a New York State Senator, Assistant Secretary of the Navy, and Governor of the State of New York. He also added to this body of documentation his personal papers from his first two terms as President. In addition, Roosevelt was an avid collector of naval material, manuscripts, books, and charts dating back to his days as librarian for several clubs during his college years.[55]

On June 19, 1934, President Roosevelt signed into law the National Archives Act. This act provided for the creation of a repository to preserve documents related to America's history. In 1938, Roosevelt stated at a press conference the need for creating a place to house his own presidential papers. Funds were privately raised for the construction of the library, which was built on Roosevelt family property in Hyde Park, New York. In November 1939, at the dedication of the cornerstone for his presidential library, Roosevelt spoke of his appreciation for the letters he received from the public telling him about their issues and opinions, and that they too would be included in the documents preserved in the building. The library was under construction during 1939-1940, and it was dedicated on June 30, 1941.[56]

At the dedication ceremony in Hyde Park, to which Roosevelt invited his friends, family, and neighbors from the surrounding Hudson Valley countryside, he emphasized his belief in the library and how he hoped it would be used in the future as an opportunity to study the past and apply its lessons to the future. Because this dedication occurred after his unprecedented election to a third term, and in light of worldwide events, Roosevelt also stated: "This latest addition to the archives of America is dedicated at a moment when government of the people by themselves is everywhere attacked."[57]

After the dedication, the library was opened to the public, but not all reactions to the opening were positive. Some newspaper articles compared Roosevelt to Julius Caesar, in that he was erecting buildings to celebrate himself. Some articles decried the library as a publicly built and publicly maintained shrine to the President. This may have been backlash to Roosevelt's audacity to seek a third term, or just the normal political party rhetoric of rival views. However, some articles recognized the historical significance of this collection of private papers, books, memorabilia, and correspondence for future generations to access and study.[58]

Interestingly, even though Roosevelt expressed his desire that his collection of papers be provided – by means of his will – to the government through the library, the transfer was challenged in court, and government ownership was not declared for three years. In addition, President Truman objected by saying that the documents should not be made public until they could be reviewed for sensitive or classified information. Ultimately, the FDR Presidential Library must be considered a success, as every succeeding president has also housed his presidential papers in his own library. This tradition was codified in two subsequent Congressional bills, the Presidential Libraries Act of 1955 and the Presidential Records Act of 1978.[59]

Term Limits

Action and reaction: These words not only describe a written law of physics but also an unwritten law of politics. Although presidential term limits were considered and rejected by the writers of the Constitution, and were proposed well over a hundred times between 1788 and Roosevelt's unprecedented third term, term limits were never a concept that could be agreed upon by the parties in Congress. All that changed with the audacity of Roosevelt to run and win not only a third election to the presidency, but a fourth term also. The Republican National Committee added presidential term limits to both its 1940 and 1944 party platforms, but could not make headway toward that end with a Democratic president and a Democrat-controlled Congress – the 79th Congress, elected in November 1944, had 36 Republicans in the Senate and 190 Republicans in the House. But the 80th Congress, elected in November 1946, had 51 Republicans in the Senate and 242 Republicans in the House. With the landslide of the Republicans in the elections of 1946, they were in full control of the legislative agenda for the remainder of Truman's first term as president after Roosevelt's untimely death in April 1945.[60]

No sooner had the Republicans taken control of Congress, than they put a term limit bill on the table. A proposed amendment to the Constitution was introduced in the House by Earl Michener, chairman of the Committee on the Judiciary and representative of Michigan's 2nd District, which limited future presidents to two terms in office. It was approved in February, barely a month into the new legislative session, and the Senate began work on their version. The Senate version would be similar, with the exception that Senator Robert Taft added a clarification regarding how a vice president elevated to the presidency would be handled. The Senate version of the proposed amendment passed on March 12, 1947, and the House accepted the Senate's version on March 21, allowing the proposed amendment to go forward to the states for ratification. It took nearly four years to become ratified, when the 36th state (Minnesota) ratified the amendment on February 27, 1951.[61]

The final wording of the 22nd Amendment to the Constitution is: "No person shall be elected to the office of the President more than twice, and no person who had held the office of President, or acted as President, for more than two years of a term to which some other person was elected shall be elected to the office of the President more than once. But this Article shall not apply to any person holding the office of President, when this Article was proposed by the Congress, and shall not prevent any person who may be holding the office of President, or acting as President, during the term within which this Article becomes operative from holding the office of President or acting as President during the remainder of such term."[62]

Although he broke an unwritten rule and served just over twelve years as President of the United States, Franklin D. Roosevelt was the right man in the right place at the right time to lead our nation through some of the most difficult challenges in its history. For all of his accomplishments, and a legacy of programs and institutions that are still with us today, he certainly deserves recognition as one of the greatest presidents ever to serve the United States of America.

The Next Great President

The next Great President will be elected in 2020, 2024, or 2028. There will be an epic crisis that will challenge this president to prove the country's belief in him or her was well founded. Let's hope that this person in time of crisis will be able to rise to the challenge and prove his or her mettle. In the subsequent chapters the types of challenges the president is likely to face at that time will be discussed. It might not be a war, but if past history provides insight to our future path, then war is possible.

The work of William Strauss and Neil Howe in the book *Generations* points to a coming crisis in the 2020s. What form will this crisis take? Will it be a global pandemic? Will it be a nuclear terrorist attack? Will it be a world war? Or will it be some cataclysmic climatic event? It may be too soon to tell, but one can make some educated guesses. The world continues to be a dangerous place. Multiple hot spots around the globe are sparking like flash points in a California wildfire. A single flash point could end up being the start of an escalating chain of events leading to worldwide conflict, such as the seemingly minor occurrence (assassination of Franz Ferdinand, the Archduke of Austria-Hungary) that ignited the First World War.

Current events are pointing toward another great worldwide crisis in our future. Events unfolding in the Middle East are dynamic and dysfunctional. There is civil war raging in Syria, a bloody sectarian war ongoing in Yemen, threats of nuclear proliferation in Iran, and a host of other regional conflicts. In addition, there are hot spots around the world: Afghanistan and President Ghani are at odds with President Trump and the security forces there; President Trump's decision to pull troops out of Syria could result in a reestablishment of ISIS/ISIL in the area; North Korea's leader Kim Jong Un is testing missiles and threatening the stability of the Korean peninsula (and the world) while building up stockpiles of nuclear weapons; and Ukraine is struggling to maintain control against insurgents while Russia's President Vladimir Putin is challenging their independence with the of annexation of Crimea and the potential for further land grabs.

Climate change is affecting weather patterns around the globe and impacting millions of farmers and ranchers. Serious drought conditions are affecting the Western United States and large parts of Africa. And other areas of the world are getting much higher than normal rainfall. Hurricanes and tornadoes are coming more frequently and wreaking more damage. There are more storms causing more damage than ever before. The number of storms causing more than $1 billion has been increasing exponentially since the 1980s, and all you have to do is say the name of one of these storms (Sandy, Irene, Katrina, etc.) to provoke an emotional response in whomever you are talking to.

Besides climate change and weather damage effects, there are other environmental issues that potentially could be catastrophic. Worldwide air and water pollution are severely affecting our quality of life. Bad air is affecting asthma patients and is a general health concern. Water pollution of our oceans is causing dramatic changes to sea life and our fish food stock. What will all of these issues lead to?

CHAPTER 13

Common and Uncommon Traits

The three greatest presidents to serve the United States had traits common to all of them, while these traits – or the combination of them – are uncommon amongst the general public. Of course, you would expect a leader to be "better" than a common man or he wouldn't have been put in the position to lead. But what does better mean? A lot of people don't know how to be a good leader, or how to even define or explain it, but they would recognize it if they saw it. Some of the typical descriptions would include words like: decisive, courageous, self-confident, intelligent, and other similar positive attributes. The remainder of this chapter is devoted to describing the attributes common to the presidents discussed in the previous pages to see what kind of a picture emerges, the better to evaluate the qualities necessary to describe a great leader or a great president.

Washington and Lincoln shared traits in part because their eras were closer in time than theirs to that of Roosevelt or our own. Washington and Lincoln both spent time as surveyors. And both were farmers, although Washington farmed more as a desire to increase his wealth while Lincoln farmed more of a necessity to support his father and family. Roosevelt, while not a farmer, was a proponent of supporting rural life and farming both as a New York politician and later when he became president. Washington and Lincoln were self-taught, and that lack of formal education and training drove both their ambition to excel and their fear of failure or embarrassment owing to want of knowledge. Washington and Lincoln both credited their successes in the Revolutionary War and the Civil War to divine providence.[1]

Lincoln and Roosevelt were great speakers and gifted at making logical arguments. This may be why both of them decided to become lawyers, both passing the bar examination in their home states: Lincoln became a practicing lawyer and Roosevelt joined a firm that wanted to capitalize on his name as being related to President Theodore Roosevelt. Lincoln and Roosevelt had a variety of interests, including curiosity and a sincere interest in learning and in reading books (the same could be said of Washington). Lincoln would read any book he could get his hands on and was famous among his friends for borrowing and reading their books. He also borrowed books from the Library of Congress during his first and only term as a Congressman. Roosevelt was the librarian for several clubs and organizations while at Harvard. He also collected books, especially those on naval topics, and donated thousands of books to his Presidential Library.

All three presidents were tall, each over six feet, and literally stood head and shoulders above the crowd. They were all great leaders, but each his own way – each grew into the man he would become through constant study and application of his unique gifts. Washington, Lincoln, and Roosevelt each became larger than life figures in American history: each became the right men in the right place at the right time to lead our nation at critical junctures, and each left a significant legacy for posterity. All three presidents were Commander-in-Chief in times of severe crisis and the crucible of fire: during the birth of the nation, the social transformation of the nation, and the defense of the principles of the nation.

Ambition

Ambition is a primary attribute in politics, for what other attribute would possess you to suffer potential ridicule in public for how you look or what you say? Without the driving force of ambition, who would stand in front of a crowd and try to get them to vote for you? At a very young age, each of our three great presidents set goals that put him on the path toward his destiny.

George Washington was only 21 when he was commissioned by the Virginia Colony Lieutenant Governor Robert Dinwiddie to risk his life on a secret mission to determine the intentions of the French trespassers who were inhabiting the western frontier lands of the Ohio country. By the time that adventure was over and Washington had written and published a journal of his travels, he became one of the most famous men in the British colonies of America. The document was titled, *The Journal of Major George Washington*, and it was both praised by the colonial partisans who wanted the French out of the region and derided as a work of fiction by a paid operator in support of a private interest (the Ohio Company).[2] At that time in America, one of the quickest ways to earn your way to fame and fortune was through the military, and Washington's plan was to become a regular in the British Army, then rise through the ranks. Contrary to his plan, the British military took no interest in Washington's desire – how ironic it was then that he would lead the colonies to an unexpected victory over the haughty English.

Abraham Lincoln came from humble beginnings – having been raised in a log cabin in the Kentucky wilderness – and rose to greatness by the application of his ambition for becoming "truly esteemed by my fellow men." In Lincoln's time, politics was the proven field for young men to advance their position in life and to make the most of their ability and ambition. At the tender age of 23, Lincoln ran for a seat in the Illinois state legislature, and although he didn't win that election, he entered the political arena again two years later. In those two years he applied himself in every way to become a well-known, liked and respected member of the community. He was already the clerk of the local general store, where he was known for being kind, considerate and attentive. He became the town's postmaster, widening his circle of acquaintances. Lincoln's next move was to learn geometry and trigonometry from a book (self-taught), and he became deputy surveyor for the county, a role that took him throughout the area to settle boundary disputes between farmers and other property owners. Lincoln did his best to positively impress his future constituency, and when it came time to stump for the next election, he was so well known that he easily won a seat in the Illinois assembly. At age 25, Lincoln was on the road to his political future and never looked back.[3]

Franklin Roosevelt led a privileged and protected life, one that included annual vacations to Europe beginning when he was an infant (he was even conceived during his parent's ten-month European grand tour honeymoon)[4] and continuing through his own honeymoon tour of Europe when he was 23. Two years later, as a clerk for the New York law firm of Carter, Ledyard, and Milburn, he declared to his fellow clerks he would one day become President of the United States. It was all part of his master plan to follow the footsteps of his older cousin Theodore, who became president after a position in the New York legislature and stints as Deputy Secretary of the Navy, governor of the state of New York, and Vice President of the United States.[5]

Adversity

Adversity is the anvil and hammer that forges the steel of your character, and all three great presidents faced significant adversity in their personal and professional lives. Owing to these experiences, all three leaders experienced growth through resilience, and came out the other side of their trials and tribulations more improved versions of themselves.

Not long after Washington's initial visit to the Ohio country, he was again sent by Dinwiddie to that region to confront the French, and if challenged, capture or kill them. Washington, now a Lieutenant Colonel in the colonial Virginia militia, commanded a force of about 150 men in addition to a group of sympathetic Indians of about the same number. A skirmish in the forest led to the unfortunate killing of a French officer who was carrying diplomatic papers. This led to an inevitable escalation by the French, who sent an army of 1,200 to meet Washington's challenge. Washington made a strategic error in his choice of locating his defenses in the middle of a meadow surrounded by trees. Although reinforcements of 100 colonial militia arrived from Virginia, Washington's defenses at Fort Necessity were woefully inadequate, and the British-American garrison was soon surrounded and overwhelmed by the French. Washington surrendered and returned to Virginia to report the bad news to Dinwiddie. Rather than accept a demotion to captain, Washington turned over his commission and retired. One year later he volunteered as an aide to a British general in another campaign against the French and redeemed himself as a soldier.[6]

It was the third year since the start of the depression of 1837, and the Illinois economy still had not yet recovered. Three years previous, Lincoln had campaigned on the promise of economic expansion and fulfillment by saying that if the improvements to canals, roads, railroads, and the like could be agreed to and a bill passed to support those projects, then all of the inhabitants of the state could prosper. By the time this bill made it through the state legislature in December 1836, a something-for-everyone approach was in play, as neglected counties wanted their share. The final version voted on totaled $10,000,000 in improvements, a staggering sum in those days considering the total state annual income was just under

$60,000 and expenses were just over $55,000.[7] This approach to fiscal management was bound to end badly, and it did. With half-finished projects halted across the state, Illinois defaulted on its debt, and Lincoln saddled himself with the blame. Businesses failed, homes were foreclosed, and banks shuttered, on account of which Lincoln felt guilt and personal anguish. He fell into a deep depression from which his friends worried he would never recover. At that time, he also called off his engagement to Mary Todd, which caused him additional melancholy. He quit the legislature at the end of the session and returned to private life. Only by reapplying himself to the legal profession did he rehabilitate his reputation and finances. Once this was accomplished, he restored his personal honor by reacquainting himself with Mary Todd, and eventually marrying her.[8]

"That which doesn't kill you makes you stronger" is a saying that could be applied to Roosevelt in the year 1921. In August, he and his family sailed to Campobello for their annual summer holiday. Roosevelt's first day of vacation he felt a little off, but he pushed through the queasiness for the day's activities of fishing and sailing. The next day he woke not feeling well, but spent all day exercising by sailing, swimming and jogging, and put out a small brush fire on a nearby island. By that evening he felt a chill and went to bed early, without dinner. When Eleanor took a tray of food to him for breakfast the next morning, Roosevelt could barely stand. When his temperature showed 102 degrees, she sent for a doctor. The doctor examined him and, finding nothing obviously wrong, said he had a serious cold then prescribed bed rest. As his symptoms worsened, losing the feeling in his legs and extremities, his family called in another doctor, who recommended massages to his legs to maintain circulation (which was extremely painful to the patient). It wasn't until the third doctor saw him, that a correct diagnosis was provided – poliomyelitis. Polio would have seemed to be a political death sentence, but Roosevelt, and his closest personal friends and advisors kept his political hopes alive. Three years later he would deliver the nomination speech for Governor Al Smith at the Democratic National Convention in Madison Square Garden, and Roosevelt would be commended across the country for his noble and dignified speech.[9]

Communication

Communication is an important leadership quality because leaders need to be able to convince their followers of the logic and veracity of their approach and direction in order to maintain their following. The written word was the key form of communication in the early years of the country, whether that was via newspapers, letters, or memorandums to Congress.

George Washington wasn't known as a great speaker, but the volume and content of his writings were key elements to his success. His official correspondence goes back as far as his reports to Lieutenant Governor Dinwiddie on his travels to the Ohio country. Although his writing style was initially stilted in the convention of the mid-1700s, by the time he was commander of the Continental Army, Washington's writing style was more compact and to the point. In order to keep up with the volume of correspondence from and to Congress and with the other demands on his attention from various sources he employed over 20 aides-de-camp. Washington dictated responses and oversaw and edited the content until he was satisfied. None other than that famous author of the Declaration of Independence, Thomas Jefferson, commended Washington's correspondence.[10]

Speeches were a key aspect of Abraham Lincoln's repertoire of communication; he was very good at gesticulation and imitation, aspects that added depth and humor to his communication. As far back as his childhood, Lincoln was a great storyteller, and other children would gather around him to listen. He would also mimic the preachers who would occasionally pass through the countryside, and retell their sermons complete with gestures and tone. As he got older, he impressed the visitors in the general store where he worked with his stories and jokes, and at that social center he became the focus of attention. When he won the election in 1834 for assemblyman in the Illinois legislature, he became known for both his written and oratory style, which retained his storytelling and gift of humor. He also was known for his excellent penmanship, which was important in those days – because legislative bills were usually written out in longhand – and his writing style was legible and accurate, with very few errors. Over time, Lincoln refined his writing and speaking style to the point of greatness, and in the future, Lord Charnwood would compare his prose to that of Shakespeare.[11]

A relatively new medium, radio, was used by Franklin Roosevelt to communicate his messages directly to the masses. Roosevelt initially used radio communications as Governor of New York in 1929 to provide his perspective on political events in the state and as a means to cut through the chatter and party politics in the Republican-controlled state legislature. He leveraged that experience into the now famous "fireside chats" that would be the first radio communications by a sitting president in our history.

Roosevelt used the opportunity of the completion of his first week in office and the passing of emergency legislation in the form of the Emergency Banking Act of 1933 to explain how the country would rebound from the current crisis in banking and ongoing depression. He had declared a bank "holiday" on his first day in office, and one week later, a day after his first fireside chat, the first banks reopened. Roosevelt and his administration wanted to make sure there was no panic withdraws of funds, so he calmly explained that citizens' money would be safe and they could redeposit their funds. He went so far as to say that depositing their money would be the patriotic thing to do, and that panic withdrawals were now unfashionable. Roosevelt's speech was so successful that billions of dollars of funds were deposited – Americans even waited in long lines to make their deposits – and the banking crisis ended.[12]

Courage

Michael Beschloss, in his treatise on *Presidential Courage*, states: "Since George Washington, courage has been a requirement of the Presidency."[13] Washington's courage under fire literally occurred via French and Indian muskets during the French and Indian War and British muskets during the Revolutionary War.

Washington was a self-taught student of the classics; he had read about the life and beliefs of the Roman statesman and philosopher Seneca the Younger, who preached stoicism and the control of one's emotions and fears to face death with dignity. Perhaps it is this philosophy that enabled Washington to endure a torrent of bullets raining down on him while surrounded by a pile of corpses at Fort Necessity, or two horses shot out from under him and several holes through his hat and coat during the battle at the Monongahela River during the French and Indian War. Certainly, he didn't lose that confidence in battle, that fearlessness, during the Revolutionary War. For example, Washington famously led the Continental Army against the British Redcoats while conspicuously on horseback in front of his troops and leading the charge during the battle of Princeton. In addition, Washington suffered the same conditions as his troops, exposed to the elements and living in camp conditions including the winter of 1777-1778 at Valley Forge. Washington also led his men during a counterattack at the battle of Monmouth Courthouse after General Lee had ordered a retreat and the American troops were in disarray. Washington's courage and quick actions saved the day and turned a morning's decisive defeat into a near victory (or a tie) by sundown.[14]

Lincoln's courage was established early in his life. He never backed down from a fight. When he first arrived in New Salem, Illinois, he was 21 years old and had struck out on his own, leaving his parents and the rest of his family behind in Decatur, Illinois. He started working at the local general store, where the owner bragged about the new boy's physical strength. Word got around about the new kid in town, and soon the leader of the local gang – the Cleary's Grove Boys – challenged Lincoln to a fight. The leader of the gang, Jack Armstrong, was strong and muscular, and known for his wrestling ability. Lincoln had a height and reach edge over Armstrong that he used to his advantage in the wrestling match, and the result was a tie. What Lincoln won was the respect and admiration of Armstrong and his gang. Later, when Lincoln volunteered for the Illinois militia in a unit representing New Salem during the Black Hawk War, Armstrong and his boys voted for Lincoln as captain, and Armstrong served as his sergeant. As captain in the militia, Lincoln learned that discipline in volunteer organizations was difficult to maintain. When an Indian named Jack arrived, bearing papers signed by General Lewis Cass that protected Jack's passage, members of Lincoln's company wanted to kill him. Lincoln protected Jack's life by stepping in front of him. Some of the men in the unit called Lincoln a coward for saving the Indian's life, to which Lincoln challenged, "any man thinks I am a coward let him test it."[15]

Roosevelt's courage was demonstrated when he risked his political future and public humiliation should he fall on the stage at Madison Square Garden while delivering his 1924 presidential nomination speech of governor Al Smith. Only three years earlier, Roosevelt had been diagnosed with polio, and had been paralyzed from the waist down. He fought to recover the use of his legs, but they were too far gone, although the day he was able to wiggle one of his toes was an event worth celebrating. Roosevelt had become dependent on his wife Eleanor to be his eyes, ears, and voice at Democratic

Party events and public meetings around the country. He had also become dependent upon his friend and political consultant Louis Howe for meeting with politicians throughout the country to keep Roosevelt's name and interests alive. But to remain a true political force, Roosevelt had to be seen in public at some point, demonstrating his viability as a future candidate for public office, so he decided to accept Al Smith's offer to give the nomination speech. Risking a fall while walking on stage at the Democratic National Convention was truly a gamble of his political future. When the moment came, he walked on crutches while dragging his legs in steel braces across the stage to the podium. Twelve thousand people held their collective breath until he finally reached the lectern, grabbed it with both hands, threw his head back and smiled, then they erupted into shouts of joy, admiration and applause for Roosevelt's display of bravery. At the end of his speech, they exploded into an hour-long celebration of Roosevelt's triumph.[16]

Empathy

Per Daniel Goleman's classic book on *Emotional Intelligence*, empathy "is the fundamental 'people skill.'"[17] In Goleman's follow-on book *Social Intelligence*, he states empathy in one sense is "*responding compassionately* to another's distress."[18] All three great presidents demonstrated this uncommon quality (not everyone is compassionate or demonstrates empathy).

Washington felt compassion for the Indians whose lands the government and speculators were continually taking, and whose treaties with the whites were continually being broken. As a colonial officer in the French and Indian War he thought the Indians were the savages, but later he understood it was "the white men who stole Indian land as the villains of the forest."[19] The first treaty that Washington negotiated as President was the Treaty of New York. It was between the United States government and the Creek Nation, the tribes of Indians who inhabited the southeastern part of the country. The treaty defined a border between the Creek Country and the United States, which no sooner had the ink dried was being violated by white settlers from Georgia and other areas. While President Washington and Secretary of War Knox felt duty bound to protect the Creeks and their land, and Knox sent federal troops to defend the border, the tidal wave of American citizens was impossible to restrain from Creek Country. Washington was infuriated by the settlers' wanton disregard for the treaty and their "disorderly conduct."[20]

From a very young age, Lincoln felt empathy for other people and their plight. One evening while walking home with his friends, he found a drunken man lying in a ditch by the side of the road. He stopped to pick the man up and carry him to his cousin's house where he could warm up and not die of exposure. He also had compassion for animals. When other children were catching turtles and putting hot coals on their backs to watch them escape from their shells, he chastised them, saying that "an ant's life was to it as sweet as ours to us."[21] He was so distressed about this practice, he wrote an essay about animal cruelty for school. Another time, he was walking with his friends and saw a pig stuck in a bog. They kept walking, but after a while, Abe turned around and went back to save the pig. He couldn't stand the thought of the pig suffering. On another occasion, he was learning how to shoot a rifle and shot a wild turkey. After that experience he never again killed for sport.[22]

Roosevelt felt compassion for his fellow "polios," whose spirits he tried to raise and for whom he created a non-profit organization that purchased the Warm Springs resort and that was dedicated to finding a cure. He had found the buoyancy and warmth of the mineral water of the springs there to be therapeutic and helped him exercise his affected muscles. He even encouraged the other polio victims to exercise with him in the pool and taught some how to swim. They called him Dr.

Roosevelt (though in truth there was no physician at the resort) because he provided charts that showed how the disease affected the muscular-skeletal system and which muscles needed special attention during exercise. Roosevelt felt encouraged by the positive feedback he received from the other polios, and they were uplifted by his positive attitude. The respect, admiration, and love they bestowed on him made him care for them and their plight that much more. He spent two thirds of his net worth to purchase the resort, and then put in tens of thousands of dollars more to upgrade the facilities. Eventually, Roosevelt chartered the Georgia Warm Springs Foundation as a non-profit organization and encouraged donations from some of his more well-off friends. If he accomplished no more in his life, the foundation itself would be enough to represent a lasting legacy, but of course he would go on to do much more.[23]

Growth

All three great presidents achieved significant personal growth through their individual personal or professional adversities to rise above the challenges and become more capable leaders. These challenges are what forced the growth and changed these men from the inside out in a metamorphosis of their character.

Washington changed from the immaturity of his younger years to the wisdom and maturity of his later years. In particular, the arrogance and ego that drove him to ignore the advice of his Indian guides and locate his inadequate defenses of the Virginia militia at Fort Necessity in the middle of a field surrounded by trees (natural defensive positions for an attacker) was naive. Washington also took offense from the leader of the reinforcements sent by Dinwiddie, James Mackay, when Mackay stated that by right of his commission as captain in the British Army, he outranked Washington and would take over command. Mackay was an 18-year officer of the army and veteran of Indian battles in Georgia, but Washington in his defiance said a colonel outranked a captain and would not take orders from Mackay. The resulting conflict between Washington's troops and the reinforcements, each committed to their own leader, eliminated any possibility of working together in their common defense to the point where Mackay's men refused to help dig trenches and build walls to expand the defenses at Fort Necessity. In addition, because Washington wouldn't listen to Indian leader and ally Half-King, the chief rounded up his men and disappeared into the woods. The resulting defeat by the French was an experience and a failure that Washington would never forget, and one that he would leverage in a heroic stand at the battle of the Monongahela one year later.[24]

Lincoln felt remorse for his role in the Illinois improvements bill that passed just before the depression of 1837, the subsequent calamitous impact on the state and local economies, and the dire effects on the finances and livelihoods of many of his friends and acquaintances. He would dedicate the next several years to his legal practice, and as his finances improved, along with the general economy of the state and the nation, his personal growth expanded along with his professional acumen. In addition, he would wed Mary Todd, and they would start to raise a family. Lincoln experienced an ever-expanding period of growth over the next two decades (essentially, the rest of his life), but the period immediately after his one session in Congress – the 30th Congress from March 1847 to March 1849 – was his most significant. He embarked on a period of study and reflection that would take his legal talents to the next level and beyond. Lincoln was on the circuit court in the area and spent four months of the year (two months each spring and fall) traveling through towns and villages with the rest of the court personnel (judges, other lawyers, bailiffs, etc.) to try cases in different counties throughout the state. Almost like a traveling circus, these court workers played their parts in providing entertainment in the trying of cases from assault to wills in dispute. Being on travel provided Lincoln an opportunity to read, study and focus on subjects ranging from astronomy and mathematics to poetry and science. As he broadened his base of knowledge, he became more adept at breaking down each case to its root elements and to provide juries a logical argument they could follow to conclusion. Through this constant evolution and growth Lincoln became so good at his craft that he became one of most sought-after lawyers in central Illinois.[25]

As a result of his physical limitations and his association with his fellow "polios" at Warm Springs, Roosevelt grew in depth of character and likeability because he had finally learned to care for others as much as he cared for himself. He evolved from his previous aloof and self-absorbed (pre-polio) persona into a convivial and genuine progressive who would become the defender of the common man, the *forgotten* man. This transformation would occur over many years, but the first big step was that introduction for Al Smith at the 1924 Democratic National Convention. Then, in 1928, Al Smith asked Roosevelt to campaign for governor of New York, to fill his seat while Smith ran for President of the United States. Smith lost the presidential race in a Republican Party landslide, but Roosevelt won the governor's seat by a slim margin. Roosevelt then chose his staff by selecting the top men (and women) at their positions. He chose three professors from Columbia University to serve as his scientific and economic advisors, and they became known as his "brain trust" – which Roosevelt expanded with additional experts as necessary. Frances Perkins, who would become the first woman selected for a presidential cabinet position as Secretary of Labor in 1933, was also on his New York staff. Roosevelt didn't allow his physical limitations to become an excuse for his intellectual capacity and growth, so he had the experts come to him, and they would discuss subjects in their fields of expertise until Roosevelt became as informed on that subject as he could possibly be.[26]

Intelligence

Intelligence is a critical component of leadership because leaders are constantly required to make decisions, ones that could affect the fate of a village, company, state, people, or nation. Without a foundation of knowledge upon which to make those decisions, and the implications of them for the future, a leader is lost in determining which direction to take, or worse leaves decisions up to his or her advisors. Although two of the three great presidents were self-taught and the third downplayed the quality of the education he received, all three great presidents were intelligent, thoughtful leaders who understood the significance and consequences of the decisions they made.

Washington, who felt personal embarrassment at his lack of formal education, strived constantly to understand the world around him. With the foundation of a grade school education and tutors provided by his father, he created within himself a desire to learn and rise above his station in life. During the throes of the colonial uprising against British rule and in keeping with the Enlightenment period of political dialogue, Washington sought out information regarding the on-going political discourse, which was enhanced by his friend and neighbor George Mason. When the time came for action and Washington was named the Commander of the Continental Army, he immediately procured books on military strategy and tactics. At the time of his death, he had collected a personal library of over 900 books, and when possible personally talked to the authors of the books he owned to reap a better understanding of what he had read. Although Thomas Jefferson belittled Washington's reading as being that only of history and agriculture, and John Adams ridiculed Washington as being unread, unlearned, and illiterate, Washington actually was a sponge for information, and what he didn't know he would seek out that knowledge in books.[27]

Lincoln was another president who did not have a formal education. Although he attended school on and off for many years, he calculated that the entire length of his education did not span more than three years' worth of schooling. Still, what Lincoln saw in himself compared to his classmates and others he met was an above average intelligence and an ability to grasp concepts by applying himself to it. He also had an innate curiosity and an insatiable need to comprehend what he saw or heard. Lincoln's application of his will to force his mind to think through to the essence of a thing brought about a thorough understanding and an ability to explain what he learned. His natural gift as a storyteller was then applied to these explanations, and he entertained his friends and schoolmates with these stories. As he grew older, he was rarely if ever without a book in his hands – he spent every spare moment reading during idle time while working in the fields of his father's farm or in the evening by firelight. Lincoln became a self-taught lawyer by studying the law books of John Stuart, a friend from the Black Hawk War experience. Stuart helped Lincoln by providing him access to the law library at Stuart & Dummer, Stuart's law office. Lincoln applied himself to this opportunity with discipline and effort, which led to his becoming a full-fledged lawyer, and eventually Stuart's partner.[28]

Roosevelt grew up the favored, coddled only son of a wealthy New York family. He led a very structured life as a child, and his mother Sara was intimately involved with his daily activities. Roosevelt also traveled extensively with his family. When he was five, the Roosevelt family spent the winter in Washington, D. C., because his father was a major contributor to President Grover Cleveland's presidential campaign and was looking for support of a trans-oceanic canal through Nicaragua. Franklin and his family visited the President several times in the White House because Grover offered the elder Roosevelt a diplomatic post. Franklin was tutored until he was 14 years old, and was fluent in German and French, languages he used on frequent family vacations to Europe (eight times by that age). At age 14, Roosevelt was sent off to Groton, the most prestigious prep school in the country at the time. He did well there, because the school was as regulated and disciplined as his upbringing. Groton's headmaster was Endicott Peabody, whose approach to shaping the lives of his young students was through an ethos of cold showers, uniforms, exercise, religion, discipline and scholarship. Peabody assessed Roosevelt as having an "above average" intellect but being physically "slight." After Groton, Roosevelt attended Harvard, along with several of his Groton classmates. The Groton curriculum being so advanced, Roosevelt was allowed to skip all of the mandatory classes and went straight to electives. He could have graduated in three years but stayed for his senior year to execute his duties as editor-in-chief of *The Harvard Crimson*, the school's undergraduate newspaper. After graduation, he decided to earn a law degree from Columbia University, but after two years of school he passed the New York bar, and became a practicing lawyer.[29]

Leadership

Although you are born with the physical attributes you exhibit when you mature, according to John H. Zenger and Joseph Folkman's *The Extraordinary Leader*, the characteristic or attribute of leadership is a skill you can develop. "There is no question that some people come into the world endowed with self-confidence and a keen intellect. That is clearly an advantage. But of that group, only a small number move on to remarkable achievements as leaders. The difference appears to be hard work, thoughtful and tenacious effort, zeal for learning, and a willingness to extend beyond one's comfort zone."[30] All three of our greatest presidents exhibited these elements and are considered the greatest leaders in our country's history, so we are indeed fortunate that these three came along at the exact moment they were needed to see this country through some of its darkest days.

Washington, after leading the Continental Army to victory in the War of Independence and presiding over the Constitutional Convention, was unanimously elected President of the United States (twice). Of all of the intense moments of Constitutional clarification and establishment of the foundation of the government of our new nation, the formal treaty that established the permanency of the end of the Revolutionary War with the British and that cemented our international relationship as trading partners was the most critical. The American public was divided in its affections between supporting France or Britain in those two countries' ongoing war with one another, the majority of Americans supporting the French for their support of the United States in our battle against the English during the Revolutionary War, and hating the British for the same reason. Washington declared an unpopular Neutrality Proclamation in 1793 to keep the United States out of any European conflict.

In 1794, Washington sent Supreme Court Chief Justice John Jay to England to negotiate a treaty to retain peace between our respective nations, and in 1795 Jay came back with a treaty draft. Officially named *The Treaty of Amity, Commerce, and Navigation, Between His Britannic Majesty and The United States of America*, and nicknamed Jay's Treaty, it decidedly favored England, but promised to clear the remaining Northwest Territory forts of British soldiers and provide for a ten-year trade agreement between the two countries. In June 1795, a secret session of the Senate debated the merits of the treaty, but a Virginia Senator provided a copy to the anti-Federalist newspaper *Aurora*. Soon a public outcry over the contents of the proposed treaty enveloped the nation. On Independence Day, a crowd burned an effigy of John Jay and soon other cities followed suit. By August, nearly the entire country was aflame with indignation over the contents of the treaty. Although the Senate approved the treaty in late June by the required two-thirds majority, Washington held off signing because of the nationwide controversy. After careful consideration, on August 18, Washington signed the treaty and handed it over to his Secretary of State, Edmund Randolph, to give to the British foreign minister, George Hammond. This act of leadership to do what he thought was right, and in the best interests of the country regardless of his popularity and good name, sets Washington apart and confirms his greatness in the pantheon of American presidents.[31]

Barely a month after Lincoln's inauguration as the 16th President of the United States, the states were no longer united, but instead at war with each other. In a challenge to the principles of republican government, the minority had risen up to defy their elected representatives and declared themselves the Confederate States of America. This was a repudiation of the very essence of the Constitution, and even democracy itself. If the minority could rule the majority, who's to say that the minority couldn't be a member of one, and then what difference would there be between democracy and monarchy, or even a dictatorship? This was the original principle and argument used by Lincoln to organize his thoughts and actions against the insurrection. However, as the war raged on, one battle after another was lost to the Southern armies.

Lincoln contemplated the available options and struggled with the constitutionality of slavery versus his moral abhorrence of it. From a legal perspective, he reasoned that the Constitution provided the president as Commander-in-Chief with the authority to outlaw slavery in the rebellious states on the premise that their forced labor supporting the Confederate cause was a military advantage. Therefore, Lincoln was within his rights as president to eliminate that military threat through emancipation of the slaves in the Confederate states. In July 1862, Lincoln called a meeting of his cabinet to read to them his Emancipation Proclamation and listened to their comments and concerns afterwards. One concern he concurred with was to wait to make the pronouncement until after a Union battlefield victory so as not for it to seem like an act of desperation. In September, the Union battle victory at Antietam provided that just opportunity, and on September 22, Lincoln issued the Emancipation Proclamation, stating that it would become effective on the first day of 1863. On that fateful day, with millions of people waiting in anxious anticipation, Lincoln signed and released the proclamation, freeing 3.5 million slaves in the South.[32]

From his very first day in office, President Franklin Roosevelt was dealing with a crisis of momentous proportions. The inability or refusal of President Hoover to deal with the banking crisis – thousands of banks were failing and shutting down across the country – was threatening the lifeblood of the economy and the circulation of money through the financial system. As this circulation constricted, capitalism itself floundered – businesses failed, homes and farms were foreclosed, and millions of people lost their jobs and joined the ranks of the unemployed. Fear was palpable. Some persons were in a daze and it seemed like a Biblical "End of Days." However, starting with his inaugural address, Roosevelt set an expectation that things would get better, and committed himself and his administration to make it so. "The people of the United States have not failed," he said in the address. "In their need they have registered a mandate that they want direct, vigorous action. They have asked for discipline and direction under leadership. They have made me the present instrument of their wishes. In the spirit of the gift I take it."[33]

Roosevelt promised the American people he would act, and act NOW to actively pursue remedies for their suffering. In the first 100 days of his first administration he did just that. In a presidential record that is still unbroken, he pushed through Congress 15 major pieces of legislation in 15 weeks, from jobs programs to relief programs to reforms and infrastructure investment. These programs proved a commitment between the American people and its government. All subsequent presidential efforts have been compared to this 100-day milestone as a barometer to the success or failure of presidential administrations. In Roosevelt's case, he set the bar for crisis leadership and what the American people can and should expect from their future leaders.

Temperament

Temperament is a quality of your character that represents how you carry yourself. It has to do with a person's nature, and how he or she would be predisposed to respond to a situation. Behavior is another term that could be used to describe temperament, in that it is an external manifestation of one's internal traits. Although these three presidents had different temperaments, they used other aspects of their characters to offset or control the less desirable attributes of their natures. To use the current business management leadership vernacular, they emphasized their strengths and minimized their weaknesses.

The people who observed him in his day described Washington's temperament in a variety of positive ways: composed, dignified, graceful, regal, majestic, superb, and powerful. One would recognize him as being a general or some other important person just by looking at him and how he carried himself. He was also leadership-oriented and was a natural born leader if there ever was one. Some of the less positive words used to describe Washington were: sensitive, irritable, fierce and savage. These descriptive terms were reflective of his temper, which could explode like a volcano if left uncontrolled. Fortunately for Washington, and for America, he was a student of Seneca's writings. Seneca was a Roman philosopher who preached stoicism, and railed against the emotions of anger and grief, calling anger "the most outrageous, brutal, dangerous, and intractable of all passions."[34] Washington's internal battle with this flaw of temper in his character was the main weakness he overcame to achieve greatness. His dominant, results-oriented outlook reflected his ambition and his striving to better himself and his condition. This effort to improve himself and his station was driven by his ambition that itself was mastered by his internal moral compass.[35]

Lincoln was melancholic, a reserved and self-reliant deep thinker, whose ambition seemed out of place with his station in life. This condition, as he thought about it, brought about great sadness in the man. "Lincoln was engulfed by sadness, revealing a pensive, melancholy side to his temperament that became more pronounced as time went by," wrote Doris Kearns Goodwin.[36]

Lincoln's natural proclivity to sadness and depression intensified whenever bad things occurred. After his friend Ann Rutledge died, he wandered around New Salem like a lost soul, and even took his gun into the woods (he wasn't a hunter). During the economic depression occasioned by the 1837 financial panic, all of the infrastructure projects that Lincoln worked so hard to promote in the Illinois legislature were stopped, and the state slid into bankruptcy. This caused Lincoln to fall into despair and a deeper depression, unable to eat, sleep, or carry on his duties as an assemblyman. His Springfield doctors believed that Lincoln was headed for an insane asylum, but his friends pulled him back from the brink.[37]

Other aspects of Lincoln's personality offset the deepest depths of his melancholy, and one of those was the driving need to make something of himself, so he would not be lost to history. Lincoln wanted to be respected and worthy of admiration by his fellow man, an ambition which drove him to make the most of, and in some ways perfect, his natural gifts and abilities. The harder he worked on himself, the better lawyer, speaker, and politician he became, to the surprising point that was named the Republican candidate for the 1860 presidential election. Upon his election that November, Lincoln took over the reins of leadership at the most critical juncture in America's history. All his life experience had led to this moment, and the combination his temperament with the compassion, humility, morality and integrity of his personality led to his success in achieving his life's ambition – to make his mark and be truly esteemed.[38]

Four days after President Franklin Roosevelt's inauguration, the new president visited former Justice of the Supreme Court Oliver Wendell Holmes to pay him respects and wish him a happy 92nd birthday. Roosevelt knew Holmes from his earlier stint in Washington as the Undersecretary of the Navy for Wilson's administration, and had attended many lunches the Justice had hosted for the rising stars in government. Although it is debated if he actually said it, Holmes was reputed to have uttered of Roosevelt after he left, "A second-rate intellect, but a first-rate temperament."[39]

Sanguine is a good word to describe Roosevelt's temperament, because he was naturally positive and optimistic, even in difficult situations. There could have not been a better disposition in our president to deal with the Great Depression. His calm smooth voice that carefully explained the banking situation in his first "fireside chat" radio address allayed the public's fears and allowed them again to trust the financial system they had been worried to death about only days earlier.

Roosevelt was confident and charming, an engaging and convivial persona, who enjoyed activities like sailing, golfing, swimming, and horseback riding (before polio struck, of course). He was also a very social person and was active in many different clubs in his school years as well as during his early political years by virtue of joining the Metropolitan Club, the Army & Navy Club, and the Chevy Chase Club. Roosevelt's social activities included annual fishing trips with a group of wealthy friends in Florida, which continued into his presidential years. These and other gatherings were famous for his "cocktail hour," when he would relax and wind down with his staff and family while serving drinks and entertaining. Roosevelt exuded optimism in a time of fear and dread, and buoyed the spirits of a depressed nation, providing them hope for a brighter future, then leading them to a promised land of unimaginable strength, power, and influence in the post-war world (which, like Moses, he would imagine but never see).[40]

Underestimated

All three of our greatest presidents were underestimated and were believed to be less capable than the people around them. The perception was, to some, that the person in the role of the executive was a puppet for some other person who was pulling the strings. This was because the person in charge surrounded himself with the best available talent and was not afraid to receive input from contrarian or strong opinions in his cabinet or elsewhere. The fact that these leaders chose the best available minds to surround themselves is evidence of their self-confidence and ability, as opposed to leaders who surround themselves with weak minds or yes-men they can easily control. Through the strength of their character and the legacy of their presidencies, they all proved that they themselves were truly the forces behind the successes they achieved.

Washington was a good judge of ability and surrounded himself with superior talent, both as the Commander of the Continental Army and as President. Washington created the first presidential cabinet, and brought in one of the most capable teams in history. Thomas Jefferson, author of the Declaration of Independence and a future president, was Secretary of State, and Alexander Hamilton, main author of the *Federalist Papers* and Washington's aide-de-camp during the Revolutionary War, was Secretary of the Treasury. Hamilton was a brilliant financial wizard who set up the country's treasury and financial systems, including the national debt, the national

Mint, the Coast Guard, and the Customs Service. Jefferson and Hamilton squared off incessantly during Washington's first administration to the point that Washington told them both he was going to quit after the first term. Jefferson, in particular, believed that Washington was under the spell of Hamilton, and was only in favor of the national debt Hamilton proposed because he didn't understand it. Jefferson also believed that Hamilton was attempting to install a monarchy along the lines of the British system and that "Hamilton had hopelessly bewitched the president."[41]

Lincoln rose from meager beginnings, was self-deprecating and known to all as the Illinois prairie lawyer. He was so humble, candid, honest and kind that others took it as a sign of weakness. When Lincoln created his cabinet, he brought in all of his political rivals from the Republican National Convention, men who believed they should have been nominated for president instead of the person who became president. Lincoln deliberately brought in strong personalities who would provide a myriad of opinions, men of outstanding experience and education who were experts in their fields, the purpose being to have the best available team to provide the support he and the country needed.

Lincoln ended up with five of the top seven cabinet names he wanted: William Seward, Salmon Chase, Edward Bates, Montgomery Blair and Gideon Wells. His plan all along was to imbed the cabinet with former Democrats and Whigs, along with his party's Republicans, to ensure political balance in the cabinet. Seward, Chase and Bates had all been nominees for the Republican national ticket, and Chase, Blair and Wells were former Democrats. To those names he added Simon Cameron as Secretary of War, another former Democrat, and Caleb Smith as Secretary of the Interior, a Republican. This balanced the cabinet with four former Democrats and four Republicans (including Lincoln, of course). Seward was selected as Secretary of State, the highest-ranking member of the cabinet after the president, and thought it was up to him to "save freedom" and his country.[42]

On January 12, just under two months before Lincoln's inauguration, as U. S. Senator from New York, Seward provided a two-hour speech to Congress about the evils of succession and a civil war, and offered resolutions in a last-ditch attempt to keep the country together. Then, during the first few weeks of Lincoln's first term, Seward operated as if he was the man in charge behind a weak president. He was wrong. When Lincoln responded to Seward's memo regarding what ought to be done, Lincoln made it clear that the decisions were the President's and the President's alone to make. Seward would come to understand that Lincoln was more than capable of leading the country through the crisis, and would do it his own way, though with much needed and appreciated assistance of his cabinet members. In December 1862, another challenge to Lincoln's leadership, based on an underestimation of his ability and an assumption of his weakness, came when Secretary of the Treasury Chase implied to his friends in the Senate that Seward was running the presidency and Lincoln was a puppet. That episode is discussed in a prior chapter and won't be rehashed here; suffice to say that Chase would discover what Seward already knew – Lincoln was his own man and was completely in command.[43]

Roosevelt was underestimated by nearly everyone before his presidency and called a political lightweight by his rivals. In particular, Al Smith, the New York governor and presidential wannabe, was a force in Roosevelt's life who served as both a measuring stick and an obstacle. The position that Smith held from January 1919 to December 1920 and January 1923 to December 1928 – the governorship of New York – was the position Roosevelt wanted as his stepping-stone to the presidency. Smith was almost ten years older than Roosevelt and looked upon his mentee (of sorts) as a tool to be used, when it was convenient for him. Smith was a graduate of the school of life, taking his first job at age 14 and working his way up. He lived his entire life in New York City and became a savvy political operative and member of the Tammany Hall political machine. When Smith was nominated as the presidential candidate, Roosevelt was urged to run for governor of New York to fill his seat. When Smith lost the presidential election and Roosevelt won the governorship, Smith expected to go back to his old job and run the show by pulling the strings on Roosevelt. When Roosevelt didn't allow that to happen and called his own shots, it proved just how badly Smith had underestimated his understudy, and how the student had become the master. Political rivals were not the only ones who underestimated Roosevelt; that club included intellectuals and reporters as well. The most famous columnist of his day, Walter Lippmann, who was a fellow Harvard grad (a few years after Roosevelt), also considered Roosevelt a political lightweight, and called him "a kind of amiable boy scout."[44]

Lippmann wasn't the only reporter who underestimated Roosevelt – H. L. Mencken, Herbert Bayard Swope, Arthur Krock, and Frank Kent were all doubtful of Roosevelt's qualifications for president. But they all actually did Roosevelt a favor, because by lowering expectations in a time of great crisis, the effects of the President's success were spectacularly magnified. In an era when fascism had become fashionable, and talk of converting to communism had become common, the savior of capitalism and democracy proved to be that underappreciated and underestimated Governor of New York and future 32nd President of the United States, Franklin Delano Roosevelt.[45]

CHAPTER 14

Parallel Lines, Pressures & Problems

The greatest presidents to serve the United States faced similar issues they had to address or were challenged by during their presidencies. They all had to deal with the greatest questions or issues of the day: George Washington was elected president during the birth of our nation, and was deemed the only man who could save the country from infant mortality; Abraham Lincoln was elected president during the social and cultural crisis over slavery and was counted on to save the country from disunion; and Franklin Roosevelt was elected president during an economic crisis of biblical proportions and was hoped could save the country from a dark depression that threatened democracy itself; then, democracy would be threatened again by even darker forces.

Although the specifics of each crisis were different, there were similarities. The purpose of this chapter is to delve into those similarities to determine the commonalities and parallels that the presidents experienced. With those parallels in mind, what conclusions can be drawn and lessons learned from each leader's approach to address and resolve those problems? Such lessons learned could then be applied to problems of the present and the future, thus to avoid the tendency to "reinvent the wheel" when a new leader comes along to address similar circumstances.

In each of these instances, seeds of great conflict grew into the overwhelming crisis that confronted the nation. In the early years of our colonial history, the New World subjects of the British Empire looked upon the motherland with reverence. But as time passed, and American colonialists started feeling the bite of taxation and the seeming indifference of British royalty and Parliament to their plight, the result was a Declaration of Independence and an eight-year long war. The United States Constitution was established on the basis of a compromise, a seemingly temporary expedient between the northern and southern states that would allow a special type of property to die out. This agreement would be embellished and expanded until one day it exploded in civil war. The seeds of conflict in World War II were rooted in the onerous treaty agreements of reparations for World War I, which were exacerbated by the economic conditions of worldwide depression in the 1930s. This combination of debt and depression begat the dictatorial fascist and communist regimes of Europe that led the world into another global conflict.

In addition to these core problems, there were other similarities that were not necessarily issues, but instead were parallelisms among the situations of the three great presidents and could be considered opportunities. Risks, issues and opportunities are three categories of analysis that should be considered when addressing a situation before making decisions about it and determining a path forward. Not all of the topics were necessarily issues to contend with, but commonalities or parallels among the three great presidents. First are the domestic topics, which encompass banking, education, national debt, and politics. Second are the international topics, which deal with alliances, global issues, trade, and war (realizing of course that the Civil War was a domestic issue, but with international implications and consequences).

Banking

Banking was a problem common to all three great presidents. Washington dealt with government financial issues both as Commander of the Continental Army and as President of the United States. As commander, he was constantly frustrated by Congress's inability to provide pay and provisions for the army. As President, he had to deal with the legacy of the Articles of Confederation, which had allowed states to print their own money even though that was expressly prohibited by the Constitution. The U. S. Mint would be established by the Coinage Act of 1792, which was signed in April 1792. But the first coins would not become available until 1793, and due to production issues Congress would allow certain foreign coins to remain in circulation until 1857.

Washington also dealt with the establishment of the first central bank for America, the Bank of the United States, the charter of which Alexander Hamilton based on the Bank of England. The bank bill that would establish this bank passed both houses of Congress by early February, 1791, and Washington was urged by members of his cabinet (Jefferson and Randolph) to veto it. Washington listened to their concerns regarding the legality of the bank, because such a bank was not expressly authorized by the Constitution, but was convinced by Hamilton that the implied powers of the executive to execute the needs of the federal government authorized its existence. He signed the act on February 25, putting America on the course of a richly interpreted and living Constitution.[1]

In the establishment of the federal government, one of the first acts of the Secretary of the Treasury was to establish financing for the national debt. Hamilton's *Report on Public Credit* was well regarded and served as the rationale for the Assumption bill, which established federal assumption of all states' Revolutionary War debts and created a payment system that would be financed by import duties. The Assumption was approved in Congress in July 1790, through a deal that

Hamilton made with Jefferson and Madison to locate the nation's capital to the shores of the Potomac River.[2]

As with most systems, issues don't usually reveal themselves until – at the worst time – the stress associated with running the system at its peak shows the cracks and weaknesses. The federal banking system during the Civil War is an example. With the cost of the crushing debt of the war, Lincoln was challenged to overcome multiple issues in the banking system and devise an effective means of handling them. To that end he had an effective Secretary of the Treasury, Salmon P. Chase, who understood the need and how to finance the war effort. This was accomplished by a multi-level effort. First, it was established that paper money, provided by the federal government and which would be legal tender for all government debts, would replace or be an alternate to payment of debts using silver or gold specie. This freed the federal government from the requirement to maintain silver and gold reserves at the level of hundreds of millions of dollars, a considerable burden because the cost of the war was in excess of $2 million per day.[3]

Second, the Revenue Act of 1862 authorized an Internal Revenue Bureau in the Treasury Department plus a broad number of tax changes to help finance the war, including the first general income tax. The Act defined the taxation and the power to collect it. Third, the National Currency Act (renamed the National Bank Act of 1863) provided a national banking system that required member banks to purchase government bonds and deposit them in the Treasury. These banks would then put an equivalent amount of paper money into circulation that could be redeemable for gold or silver. Because the paper money was redeemable for hard money, confidence in this system of federally backed paper money increased (because it was accepted at face value) and eventually other forms of paper money disappeared (because other forms of money traded at a discount depending on the confidence in the issuer of the money).[4]

President Franklin Roosevelt was inaugurated during one of the worst banking crises in the history of our country. Over 5,000 banks had failed, wiping out the life savings of millions of Americans. By the eve of Roosevelt's first inauguration, 34 out of 48 states had shut down their banks indefinitely, including New York, Pennsylvania, Michigan, and Illinois. The unemployment rate was 25%, with up to 50% of the working population at work less than full time – but several regions were hit even worse, with some cities seeing unemployment as high as 80%. Capitalism was failing and people were losing faith in democracy. With fascism and communism on the rise in other countries, many wondered publicly if these marked a better way. Roosevelt projected self-confidence, which inspired confidence in him and through him to the rest of the system. Roosevelt's first action upon taking over as President was to declare a banking holiday for the next four days (it would end up lasting a week), so the new administration could determine a path forward. Roosevelt had also called Congress back from recess for a special session, to start on March 9 and with no specific end date (it would last for 100 days).[5]

The first legislation Congress addressed was the Emergency Banking Act, which was approved the first day of the session by acclamation. The Act retroactively provided the President approval to close the nation's banks, gave the Comptroller of the Currency the authority to restrict banks' operations, gave the Secretary of the Treasury the power to review bank health and financial conditions, and gave the Federal Reserve the power to print Federal Reserve Bank Notes ($200 million was printed). When banks reopened, there was such a surge of deposits that the Bank Notes were never used and were subsequently retired. Roosevelt also wanted to implement bank reform, to ensure that this type of banking crisis never occurred again. During the next few weeks and months, the

Banking Act of 1933, also known as the Glass-Steagall Act for the two Congressmen responsible for championing it, passed through the houses of Congress. This Act implemented two crucial changes that led to reducing consumer risk: first was separating financial investment (buying and selling stocks and bonds, acting as a broker for individual investors, and underwriting securities) from regular "commercial" banking (savings, checking, loans and mortgages), and second was providing depositors' insurance (via the Federal Deposit Insurance Corporation (FDIC)). This legislation would stand for nearly 70 years (revised by Gramm-Leach-Bliley Act in 1999 to repeal separation of investment and commercial banking), and the FDIC is still with us today – the effectiveness of which is evidenced by the elimination of "bank runs" in the United States since its implementation (notable international examples are the runs on Northern Rock (United Kingdom) in 2007 and the Bank of East Asia (Hong Kong) in 2008).[6]

Based on history, the next crisis in American life may again be reflected or initiated in the banking industry. If history truly rhymes, what tune will the country be singing when the next banking crisis hits (they were singing, "Brother Can You Spare a Dime?" in the early 1930s)? What would potentially be the driving factors in a future financial or banking meltdown? The answers to these questions may be found in the current stock market rise, where values of the Dow, the S&P 500, and NASDAQ are unprecedented and seemingly divorced from fundamentals.

In the historic peaks of spectacular rises in the stock market, there has always been a catalyst for their demise. In John Kenneth Galbraith's *The Great Crash 1929*, he attributes causes of the stock market crash in 1929 to five weaknesses: 1) income distribution, 2) corporate structure, 3) banking structure, 4) foreign account (trade) imbalance, and 5) economic intelligence. Income distribution currently in this country is skewed between the 'haves' and the 'have nots' on a level not seen since the late 1920s. The weakness of corporate structure in the 1920s was attributed to nested and multi-level holding companies. The weakness of corporate structure in the 2020s may be deemed (in hindsight) caused by the interrelatedness of global commerce. The weakness of the banking structure in the 1920s was the lax oversight and the ability of bank officers to use consumer deposits in speculative investments. In the 2020s, current quarterly pressures to meet analysts' and investors' expectations may be driving corporate officers to take speculative risks to meet those expectations. In the 1920s, the United States was a huge current account creditor. Today, the U. S. is a current account debtor, in the number of hundreds of billions of dollars. What would happen if those debts were called due? In the 1920s, government and financial expertise in the area of economics wasn't nearly what it is today. Today's financial analysts and government economists have a wealth of experience and body of data to determine the health and balance of the economy. But is that enough? The velocity of change and the explosion of derivatives may well be beyond the comprehension and experience of even the most intelligent and experienced economists.[7]

Education

While many presidents have attempted to be known as the "Education President," few have actually deserved that moniker. There is a difference between vision and action, between desire and results. From the perspective of primary education, few could argue that President Johnson's "Great Society" vision was not realized with respect to K-12 education in his Elementary and Secondary Education Act of 1965. From the perspective of analysis of the three greatest presidents, all three were visionaries who took action with respect to their visions regarding college education.

Washington, who was self-conscious about his lack of formal education, especially with respect to the other founding fathers, was a continual advocate of a national university. His commitment to this vision is evidenced by references to it in his correspondence to other leaders, in his annual address as President, and in his final will and testament. Washington wrote letters to the commissioners of the District of Columbia, to Thomas Jefferson, and to Alexander Hamilton proposing a national university for the education of American citizens in the republican form of government. He was concerned that, by sending their youths to foreign countries for university education (which was the norm at the time), their young minds were potentially being impressed in favor of other forms of governance and other nations' modes of thought. Washington also believed that a national university, located in the central location (at that time) of the nation's capital would encourage attendance by "the Youth from *all parts* of the United States." In his eighth and final annual address to Congress, he asked it to consider the establishment of a national university that would educate our young "in the science of *government.*" In his last will and testament, Washington bequeathed 50 shares in the Potomac Company as an endowment for a university in the District of Columbia under the federal government (he also bequeathed 20 shares in the Bank of Alexandria to the town of Alexandria toward a free school for orphans and poor children).[8]

Lincoln was a self-educated man whose amount of education in what he called "A, B, C" schools (primary education) did not total more than one full year. Although he would attend these contributory schools on and off for a number of years during his childhood, he spent more time practicing writing or reading at home when not performing his chores or helping his father on their farm. His father, Thomas Lincoln, believed that reading was a waste of time, and occasionally beat his son for reading too much.[9] Regardless of his father's opinion, Abraham Lincoln reveled in reading; he borrowed and read anything he could get his hands on. This self-education, self-reflection, and self-realization put Lincoln on the path to greatness, and fueled his desire to support other's needs in education. In his very first attempt at political office, he described his position on education as: "I view it as the most important subject which we as a people can be engaged in." Later, during a speaking tour leading up to his candidacy for the presidency, Lincoln spoke at a Wisconsin Agricultural Society meeting and stated that he was a proponent of the melding of education and agriculture as a means of profitably applying technology and the latest advances in machinery to chemistry and botany. As president of the country, Lincoln was a proponent of the Morrill Act and the land grant colleges in agriculture and engineering it created.[10]

Roosevelt was a member of the wealthy class. He was educated at the best prep school in the country (Groton), was college-educated at Harvard, and went to Columbia Law School, so he knew the value of a good education. He was a vocal proponent of providing education to the returning veterans of World War II, the better to assimilate them into the national economy as quickly as possible. The unspoken concern was, with 16 million veterans returning home at roughly the same time, up to 75% could end up unemployed (estimates of postwar unemployment was 8-15 million by the National Resources Planning Board and the Department of Labor).

Roosevelt recommended a bill that would cover returning service men and women for education, hospitalization, rehabilitation, disability pensions, business loans, home loans, and unemployment. Competing plans soon made their way to Congress, and the one that took root came from the American Legion. When the GI Bill of Rights hit the floor of the Senate, it was passed without modification. A difference between the House version of the bill led to some debate regarding the unemployment benefit, but that too was accepted – although, it was the least utilized benefit by veterans. The most utilized benefit of the GI Bill was for education. By 1947, almost half of the country's college enrollees were veterans, and by 1956, 7.8 million of the veterans of World War II had used the benefit for education or training.[11] Ultimately, the GI Bill was a gift of thanks to World War II veterans for what they had done for their country. But that investment of an estimated $50 billion in costs of the program was more than made up for by the return in the way of an expanded middle class that included doctors, lawyers, engineers, and teachers who would contribute to the future prosperity of a grateful country – another contribution to America by what Tom Brokaw called its "greatest generation."[12]

That education is a catalyst for future growth is a lesson the three greatest presidents learned and believed and could be a lesson learned for future leaders to take advantage of. If the above examples are not enough evidence to believe in the power of education, the example of California free education is one of the most cited, and its success is hard to argue. Education in California's three-tier system of community colleges, Cal-state colleges, and UC schools, was largely free for a time (through the 1970s and into the early 1980s). While the education was not entirely free – "education fees" and other costs were not covered – it was a popular program for residents and drew an influx of transplants from across the country (education was free for residents only). With a high population of well-educated workers, technology companies in computers and aerospace were drawn to the area, and prosperity ensued.

If California was a country, it would have a Top-5 international GDP, and it is the home of some of the most technologically advanced companies in the world. In an attempt to rekindle that fire, California Governor Gavin Newsome introduced a program in September 2019 that would provide free tuition to any of the state's 115 community colleges for the first two years, provided the students are enrolling for the first time and attend full-time.[13]

National Debt

In times of severe crisis, the solution usually involves a financial burden. This burden has usually resulted in an order of magnitude increase of the national debt. Looking back through history, empires rise and fall based on their ability to maintain their credit, and their ability to finance the ongoing costs of supporting the empire, including border protection, raising armies to defeat invaders or expanding the empire, domestic investment in infrastructure, and paying for the cost of administration. Wars are typically the most costly and significant of expenses of maintaining an empire, and an efficient method of taxation is critical to that end.

As the first president, Washington inherited war debts from the Revolutionary War and the dysfunctional Continental Congress, since rendered obsolete by the new Constitution. The amount of the debts from the war was about $43 million. Added to that were debts owed to France and other nations in excess of $11 million.[14] Although many tried to convince him not to repay the foreign debts, Washington stood fast to honor them, which started the reputation that the United States would always stand by its financial commitments. Because we as a nation have never defaulted, United States Treasury Notes are assumed to have zero risk, and we have enjoyed some of the lowest borrowing costs for debt in the world. In addition to the prior debt of the country, the 1790 Assumption Bill also financed the war debts of the various states, which added another $25 million to the tab. So, at the start of the Washington administration, the national debt went from *zero* to around $80 million (in percentage increase terms, infinity).[15]

Abraham Lincoln inherited a national debt of less than $91 million, and by 1865, the national debt was in excess of $2.6 billion, more than double an order of magnitude increase. What caused this incredible increase in the debt? The extreme costs associated with mobilizing, training, and arming the Union armies started with an initial request for funding by Lincoln of $400 million, which Congress immediately increased to $500 million and authorized. So, within four months of his presidency, Lincoln had already authorized spending half a billion dollars to address the crisis, at a time when up to that time the national debt had never exceeded $130 million. By the end of 1862, the debt was more than $524 million, and in 1863 the debt reached over $1 billion and never looked back (the lowest it came down to since 1864 was $1.5 billion in 1893, and it has been in excess of that number ever since). The costs to finance the Civil War were tremendous, but Lincoln also included domestic investment projects in his budget proposals, thus adding to the national debt. A few of the domestic investment programs that Lincoln recommended to Congress (almost New Deal-like in their concept and implementation) were the Transcontinental Railroad, public Land Grant colleges, and investment in railroad infrastructure throughout the country, especially with respect to regions to and from the battlegrounds that would aid in troop movement across the country.[16]

Franklin Roosevelt oversaw an order of magnitude increase in debt from $22.5 billion in 1933 to nearly $259 billion in 1945.[17] Initially, the national debt grew from less than $20 billion at his inauguration to almost $43 billion at the end of his second term due to fighting the Great Depression with a combination of domestic investment in infrastructure, relief efforts for those on unemployment, and financial assistance for farmers and homeowners. These investments included: the Federal Emergency Relief Act, which initially provided $500 million in federal grants to the states and by the end of the program had disbursed over $3 billion in funds; the National Industrial Recovery Act, which allocated $3.3 billion in spending for public works in 1933 and spent $6 billion overall; and the Emergency Relief Appropriations Act of 1935, which authorized $4.8 billion in funding for work relief activities and was up to that time the largest appropriations bill in the history of the United States.[18]

In May 1940, as a result of the breakout of war in Europe and militarism of the Hitler regime, Roosevelt requested authorization of $3.1 billion in defense spending from Congress. During the war effort from 1941 to 1945, the national debt exploded to over a quarter trillion dollars as the United States funded not only U. S. needs for machinery, ammunition, and supplies, but also Lend-Lease of the same materials to England (initially), China, the Soviet Union, and other allied powers in an all-out effort to win the war. Eventually, 30 different countries would sign Lend-Lease agreements with the United States at a cost to the U. S. of $50 billion.[19] Spending on the war effort increased at an exponential rate for the first three years, then leveled out at around $60 billion per year from 1943 through 1945. The Manhattan Project alone, the program that created the atomic bomb, contributed to $2 billion in military spending.[20]

Will the next national crisis cause another order of magnitude increase in the national debt? If that occurs, the U. S. debt would be greater than $200 trillion, and if that occurs, the debt would be over ten times the annual Gross Domestic Product (GDP) of the country. The U. S. already has more debt than any other country in the world, but it also has the largest economy in the world, and the debt ratio is only 104%, which doesn't even make the list of the top 25 highest debt ratios in the world. Japan and Greece have the two highest debt ratios, on the order of 200% (double their GDP); what would happen if the U. S. debt ratio were five times that amount?[21]

Politics

The word "politics" is sometimes used as an epithet and blamed for negative things that occur. When people don't get the raise or promotion they think they deserve, "office politics" is often blamed, but politics is actually a critical element in working with other members of society or organizations to achieve an objective, any objective. Great leaders are able to use their God given gifts of personality, persuasion, communication, empathy, strategic analysis, and other elements to achieve great things. The term "leadership" also implies followers, so leaders should remember that they're not a leader if they have no followers.

All three of our greatest presidents used their skills to move the country in the direction they thought best for the results they pursued. Washington was a political master. Even before he became president, he honed his skills at achieving his objectives through experience and a thorough understanding of peoples' motivations, both while in the Virginia militia and the Continental Army. As a colonel in the Virginia militia, while working for the governor and lieutenant governor to make his preferences known, Washington played with skill the political game of deference and patronage within the Virginia aristocratic hierarchy. As Commander of the Continental Army, he effectively dealt with challenges to his authority, such as the Conway Cabal. This experience prepared him for the political challenges he faced as the first president of our country.[22]

As President, Washington espoused the altruistic objective of doing what he believed was the right thing, the best thing for the nation, and he set those expectations not only for himself, but also for his cabinet. He would become truly disappointed, then, when his two greatest cabinet members, Secretary of State Thomas Jefferson, and Secretary of the Treasury Alexander Hamilton, would become locked in a long struggle for Washington's ear and implementation of two completely opposite visions for America's future. Hamilton's vision was of a strong central government and executive, with a national bank and international trade, along the lines of the British Empire, and he was known as a Federalist (Hamiltonian). Jefferson's vision was of representative government and a strong legislative branch, with a focus on agrarianism and states' rights (particularly southern states rights with respect to slavery), and he was known as a Democratic-Republican (Jeffersonian). This division and rivalry within Washington's cabinet created the two-party system dynamic in American government and is one of the enduring legacies of Washington's presidency.[23]

Abraham Lincoln was no neophyte when it came to presidential politics, as he had been practicing his political acumen in the Illinois legislature for eight years and was a U. S. Congressman for an additional two years. On top of that, Lincoln was an adept observer of human behavior from many years as one of the best trial lawyers on the Illinois circuit court. That he received the presidential nomination for the newly formed Republican Party (six years old) in 1860 as a political newcomer and relative unknown against some of the most experienced and well-known members of the party (a collection of governors, Senators, and former Congressmen) was a significant accomplishment. He did this by letting the political factions fight it out against each other and remaining friends with everyone, then attempting to be everyone's second choice for the nomination. When Lincoln won the election for president, he took the unprecedented step of elevating the strongest of those political rivals into his cabinet. He did this in a conscious effort to retain the services of the best and brightest in the party to help him govern, and it also allowed him to keep his rivals from throwing rocks at his administration when things didn't go well. When that happened and his Secretary of the Treasury (Chase) was colluding with Senators to remove the Secretary of State (Seward), Lincoln masterfully exposed the issue and resolved the conflict while retaining the services of both Secretaries.[24]

Franklin Roosevelt was a political master and was able to handle multiple issues and their political intricacies with flair. He was well versed in the art of persuasion, and the political ability of saying a lot without really saying anything. To some observers, Roosevelt's most frustrating habit was to nod while listening to people talk to him, which they took as agreement but to Roosevelt only meant he was following along with the conversation. His political skills were honed in the New York state legislature, in Washington as the Assistant Secretary of the Navy, and as Governor of New York before his elections to four consecutive terms as president. There were some misjudgments, in particular with respect to the Supreme Court in 1937, but overall, his political acumen was almost incomparable. For example, leading up to the 1940 election, Roosevelt put two of the Republican opposition's most talented leaders, Henry Stimson and Frank Knox, in his cabinet – Stimson as Secretary of War and Knox as Secretary of the Navy. This was a move almost Lincolnesque in political nuance.[25]

Another example of Roosevelt's political ability leading up to the 1940 election was his handling of Joseph Kennedy, Sr., the U. S. Ambassador to England. Kennedy was appointed to that position by Roosevelt in 1938, but by 1940, it was apparent that the appointment was a bad fit – Kennedy was anti-British, anti-Semitic, and convinced that England was going to fall to Hitler's Germany. Roosevelt knew about Kennedy's beliefs, so he kept Kennedy out of the communications with England about the destroyers-for-bases deal, which infuriated Kennedy. However, as the presidential race tightened, Roosevelt felt he needed the 25 million Catholic votes that Kennedy could supply, so he planned to ask for a political endorsement.[26]

When Kennedy returned from England in late October 1940, Roosevelt asked him to come to the White House immediately upon arrival. Kennedy and his wife met with Roosevelt, Senator James Byrnes, and Missy LeHand in the upstairs Oval room for dinner. Roosevelt charmed Kennedy, and then asked him for his endorsement for President (to be provided by a radio address). Kennedy voiced his displeasure about being left out of the destroyers-for-bases deal and then said he would provide the endorsement, but that he would pay for the radio time himself, and he would say whatever he wanted. When he went on the air, Kennedy endorsed Roosevelt, and said the president was not trying to get the country into the war.[27]

Some people think politics is bad and imply it is the cause of their troubles. The great presidents realized that political discourse and persuasion is required to achieve great accomplishments. In our republican form of government and the democratic experiment it represents, its leadership will succeed or fail based upon its ability to convince the public of the correctness of its intended path. If the epithet of "politician" is used, then that should be a badge of honor, because that word was used to describe Lincoln and Roosevelt, and as I describe above, it could also be aptly applied to Washington.

Alliances

With respect to alliances, Washington set America's path early on with his Neutrality Proclamation. He believed that without its own Navy to protect its interests the United States was in no position to go to war with any of the European powers, and that to do so would be the equivalent of infant suicide of our young republic. The French Revolution went the route of chaos and anarchy as rival revolutionaries contended for the upper hand. In time, the Jacobins would unleash the Reign of Terror, and many would lose their heads to the guillotine, including King Louis XVI.

When France declared war on England, Holland, and Russia, there was internal and external pressure on the Washington administration to join forces with France in the name of liberty and democracy. The internal pressure was from the pro-French Secretary of State Thomas Jefferson in addition to a very large pro-French segment of the civilian population. The external pressure was from France itself, as their ambassador, Citizen Genet, attempted to collaborate with the pro-French movement and American merchant sailors to set up privateers that would battle the British on the high seas. Washington, who saw no benefit in coming to France's aid and was distressed by the wanton acts of violence and murder perpetrated upon French citizens by its government, wanted no part of that European conflict. With no precedents to guide him, Washington was left to steer the nation's course through these troubled waters of alliances and war, with the implication that whatever path he chose would set a precedent that would dictate American's future for decades. Washington called a momentous cabinet meeting to discuss the path forward; the result was a unanimous decision to issue a proclamation. The proclamation would state that the United States would "adopt and pursue a conduct friendly and impartial to the belligerent powers."[28]

President Lincoln was desperate to keep the European powers from recognizing the South or even offer to mediate in the conflict, because mediation itself would be recognition of the Confederate States. Lincoln left communication with those European powers in the capable hands of his Secretary of State, William Seward. Soon after the Confederate attack on Ft. Sumter, Lincoln announced a blockade of Confederate ports, also known as General Winfield Scott's "Anaconda Plan."

In May 1861, the British announced the Proclamation of Belligerency, recognizing the South as a belligerent, which fell short of recognizing them as a separate country. France did not follow Britain's lead, as they were allowing the scene to unfold. Seward provided instructions to America's minister in England to protest any unofficial discussions with Confederate representatives and warn the British of the implications for future relations with the U. S. government. One year later, the British and French had still not recognized the Confederacy as an independent nation, even though the impact to each of their textile industries was severe owing to their reliance on Southern cotton. This position was at risk of changing as the

North was routed in several battles with the South and as Lincoln tried – unsuccessfully – general after general to lead the Union armies to victory.[29]

Then Seward tried a different tact, this time to leverage Russia as a U. S. ally in case England and France considered recognizing the South, which would lead to war. In the 1800s, relations between Russia and the United States were very good owing to the arms and supplies support America provided Russia during the Crimean War against France and England. Lincoln received a letter from the Russian foreign minister that stated Russia's support of the American Union, and Seward provided a response that emphasized the friendly relations between the two nations. Then Seward asked the Russian minister, Baron Stoeckl, permission to publish both letters. In the press, the implication of the letters was that Russia would come to the Union's aid if war broke out between the United States and France or England.[30]

The United States had two distinct phases of alliances during World War II. The first phase was before America's entry into the war as Roosevelt carefully negotiated a path between the military preparedness he knew was right, and the extreme view of American isolationists who wanted nothing to do with another European war. In the first phase, the United States was a neutral party, but engaged in coordinated activities with the British (some public, some secret) that would facilitate a seamless transition if and when the Americans joined the Allies against the Axis powers. On May 10, 1940, Winston Churchill was named British Prime Minister, and over the course of time Roosevelt would develop an intimate friendship with him, which would become a foundation of trust and mutual respect that would enable open and honest communications between the two world powers.

During this first phase, the Roosevelt administration would do everything they could to supply England with the materials and machinery for England to make war against Germany. After the Dunkirk evacuation in early June, Roosevelt had General George Marshall provide thousands of weapons and millions of rounds of ammunition to the British. By late June, Germany had defeated France, and the next target would be England. Churchill asked Roosevelt for 50 destroyers to help defend the country against invasion, and Roosevelt was willing provide, but the difficulty was how? Ultimately it was decided to trade the ships for 99-year leases of military bases in the Caribbean, plus Bermuda and Newfoundland bases. This deal was coordinated in August and finalized in September.[31]

After Roosevelt was reelected in November 1940, he came upon the idea of Lend-Lease. Roosevelt described this concept with the analogy that if your neighbor's house was on fire, and you could lend him your hose to help put the fire out, you wouldn't ask him for money. You would just ask for the hose back after he was finished. Lend-lease was an important program for England, because the British were critically short of money to pay for the material and supplies, but Lend-Lease allowed them to continue to fight the war without having to end up bankrupt for doing so. Churchill called it the most magnanimous act by one country for another in the history of the world. Roosevelt and Churchill would continue to work together, and would meet in the United States in August 1941, the outcome of which would be the Atlantic Charter, a declaration of common purposes and principles.[32]

The second phase of World War II alliances started that infamous day of the Japanese sneak attack upon Pearl Harbor, December 7, 1941, and ended with the unconditional surrender of Japan on September 2, 1945. The first coordinated event between the countries of the Grand Alliance was the Arcadia Conference, also known as the Washington Conference. On New Year's Day, 1942, Roosevelt signed a declaration of alliance of 26 United Nations against the Axis powers. The signers of this declaration included the United States, the United Kingdom, the USSR, China, Australia, and many other countries at war with Germany. The combination of the leaders of the U.S., U.K, and USSR would become known as the Big Three (Roosevelt, Churchill, and Stalin), and they would dominate the overall strategy of the United Nations alliance.[33]

What lessons can we learn from the above examples on how to deal with alliances with other countries? I think the example of Roosevelt is most applicable to the present day, in that alliances formed to deal with a common enemy or a common cause are the most effective means of achieving your goals. For example, in the last 30 years, the United States has had two wars with Iraq. The first one, in 1991 under President George H. W. Bush, was led by a coalition built up through international cooperation with allies across the world. That campaign was very successful, and the objective was achieved in a very short period of time. The second one, in 2003 under President George W. Bush, was led by the United States with a smaller number of international participants, and, though initially a successful campaign, became a nearly decade-long fight that devolved into a bloody civil war. The point here is not to argue the case for or against the second Iraq war, but to illustrate the power of a cooperative, combined international approach to resolving issues.

Global Issues

International issues were a challenge to all three great presidents. The issues took the form of precursors of things to come or augments or stresses on preexisting conditions threatening to make matters worse. Washington faced challenges from European colonialism and European competition for domination of the New World. England, France and Spain held significant claims to territory on the North American continent and were potential and actual constraints on U. S. growth and expansion. In addition, these three nations were constantly at war or threatening war with each other in their attempts to maintain or expand their empires. In winning its independence from England, the United States was in a precarious position, squeezed on three sides by England to the north (Canada), Spain to the south (East Florida and West Florida), and Spain or France to the west (the Colony of Louisiana was French until 1762, then Spanish from 1762 to 1800, and then French from 1800 until sold to the U. S. in 1803).[34]

Late in Washington's second term in office, he achieved peace with the two world powers at America's borders. The Treaty of London (also known as the Jay Treaty or Jay's Treaty) was signed on November 19, 1794, between the United States and Britain; it provided resolution of the occupied forts in the Northwest Territories that the U. S. believed should have been abandoned as part of the Treaty of Paris of 1783. Jay's Treaty decidedly favored the British, but ultimately Washington was convinced it was better than to risk war.[35] The Treaty of San Lorenzo, also known as the Treaty of Madrid (or Pinckney's Treaty), was signed on October 27, 1795, between the United States and Spain, and provided resolution of a long held dispute of lands west of Georgia that the U. S. thought Britain had ceded at the end of the Revolutionary War. This treaty also guaranteed U. S. navigation rights on the Mississippi River (the east/west boundary between the U. S. and Spain).[36]

During the Civil War, Lincoln's administration spent a considerable amount of effort trying to ensure that other countries such as England and France did not recognize the rebel states. While the Union was trying to douse that fire, the Confederacy, and especially its leader Jefferson Davis, was trying to do all he could to win legitimacy of his government through international recognition. In their arrogance, the Confederates thought their cotton exports, or lack thereof, would bring France and England to their knees, or at least cause so much disruption to their textile industries as to require redress. Some international incidents ensued during the political intrigue and economic concerns that occurred over the next few years. The most significant incident was the *Trent* affair, which was the capture of two Confederate representatives bound for England on a British merchant ship, the *Trent*. The ship was fired upon and boarded by the USS *San Jacinto*, whose captain (Charles Wilkes) confiscated the Confederate passengers and brought them back to the United States.[37]

Walter Stahr, in his biography of Lincoln's Secretary of State William Seward, equated this event to a 19th-century version of the Cuban missile crisis. It was an event that had the potential to lead to war between two global powers, the United States and England. As Seward awaited word of England's response to the incident, rumors of British preparations for war were rampant. Some rumors had British ships and supplies sailing for Canada, filled with soldiers and weapons. Other rumors implied a British embargo on gunpowder and gunpowder-ingredient exports. Not only was England offended by the *San Jacinto* confiscation, but there were also rumors of the French taking offense at the flagrant violation of international law, perhaps presaging French support of the British position.[38]

Seward was formally notified of the British response on December 23; it demanded a return of the captured Confederate passengers, an apology for the incident, and formal response within seven days. The British foreign minister Lord Lyons also notified Seward that if a response was not received within seven days, he was instructed to leave America and head back to England. Lincoln called a cabinet meeting for December 25, at which Seward presented the details of England's request and his draft response letter; also presented at the cabinet meeting were letters from envoys in England and France detailing the mood and reaction of their governments and populace (which was indignant anger towards the United States).[39]

Lincoln and other members of the cabinet were not convinced that Seward's draft response was the best course (return of the prisoners and an apology) and held to the course of mediation by a foreign government (like France). At the end of this five-hour cabinet discussion, it was agreed that they would meet again the next day to continue the discourse. At the cabinet meeting on December 26, all agreed that Seward's draft response to the British demands was the appropriate course of action: to release the prisoners with an explanation of the event. This reply was given to the English foreign minister Lord Lyons, the prisoners were released and taken to a British warship for their cross-ocean travel to England, and a war between the United States and the United Kingdom was avoided.[40]

In the late 1930s, the American public was in an isolationist mood, and wanted nothing to do with European wars, but when Germany attacked Poland in September 1939, Roosevelt called a special session of Congress to deal with the crisis. He asked for a repeal of the arms embargo of the Neutrality Act he had signed in 1937. Congress responded with the Neutrality Act of 1939, which allowed cash purchases of military arms if the purchaser picked up the purchases on American shores (and took the risk of sailing the high seas laced with German U-boats). On April 9, 1940, Germany invaded Denmark and Norway. By April 10, Denmark surrendered, and by May 1, Norway was overrun. In May 1940, the German Blitzkrieg struck again, this time through Holland, Belgium, Luxemburg and into France. At the end of May, the British Expeditionary Force (BEF) was forced out of continental Europe – on June 4, the last of the ships of Operation Dynamo departed with British soldiers from the shores of Dunkirk. France fell three weeks later.[41]

Roosevelt did what he could to provide arms and ammunition to beleaguered British forces, including trading ships for leases on British bases in the Caribbean, while U. S. election year activities ensued. Roosevelt was unanimously nominated as the Democratic candidate and won the November contest by five million more votes than his opponent, while dominating the electoral count. In March 1941, he committed the United States to Lend-Lease, a program of giving military equipment to the British in support of their fight against the fascist regimes of Germany and Italy. Roosevelt assigned Secretary of Commerce Harry Hopkins the task of overseeing this critical program for supporting the British, and Hopkins moved into the White House to become one of Roosevelt's special advisors and a member of his inner circle. After Germany invaded the Soviet Union in June 1941, Roosevelt extended Lend-Lease to Russia. In August 1941, President Roosevelt and British Prime Minister Winston Churchill met for the first of many conferences to plan the defeat of Germany and winning World War II.[42]

The lessons of the above instances of global issues and their impact or potential impact on future presidential actions or constraints provide guidance on the implication of international events on presidential decisions. Awareness of ongoing political developments and participation in the international community is key to preparedness and the ability to have options and backup plans as events unfold. Risk mitigation analysis and strategies should be a constant and ongoing activity to track and monitor evolving events. Intelligence is another factor in preparedness, as it will assist in understanding and anticipating the reaction and countermoves that could occur.

Also note that key trusted team members are valuable contributors to the ideation and decision-making processes that leaders need to execute. Washington worked through envoys John Jay and Thomas Pinckney to achieve treaties with America's neighbors that would allow her future growth. Lincoln worked through his preeminent Secretary of State William Seward to avoid a war with European countries that probably would have split the Union. Franklin Roosevelt leaned on his inner circle made up of his wife Eleanor, Harry Hopkins, and Missy LeHand, all of whom provided advice, opinions, and insight into the on-going crises of the day in the dangerous years preceding World War II.

Trade

Trade has been a critical element of international relations since recorded history. International trade between the United States and other countries has been key to the economic health of the nation, and when that trade has been interrupted or compromised, it has significantly impacted growth. Early in our history as a country, the U. S. trade with England was mostly a one-way street, especially with respect to the total value of the goods exchanged. Seventy-five percent of that commerce was for British products, while our exports only constituted about 10 percent of England's imports, and 90 percent of U. S. federal revenues were as a result of tariffs on imports.[43]

George Washington personally experienced the vagaries of international commerce as a Virginia planter and homeowner. He was continually indebted to his London merchants, Carey & Company, due to his appetite for the finer things in life, while the value of his export crop of tobacco was notoriously undependable on account of vacillating Virginia weather of droughts and heavy rains.[44]

Alexander Hamilton, George Washington's (and America's) first Secretary of the Treasury, implemented tariffs on imports as a means of funding the U. S. government. In order to analyze a country's trading stance, it is important to understand its tariff level and policies; however, federal statistics on the average tariff were not kept until 1821. Douglas Irwin, researcher at the National Bureau of Economic Research (NBER), has analyzed available data to determine tariff levels before these records were kept and computed the average tariff to be roughly 15 percent during Washington's tenure as president. Irwin goes on to say in this report on U. S. trade policy that Hamilton designed the tariffs to be low enough so as not to discourage the critical income source for the nation – imports – which were funding the debt.[45]

Abraham Lincoln was an advocate of high tariffs and protectionist duties, which was also a plank of the 1860 Republican National Convention. As the president-elect, Lincoln boarded a train in Springfield on February 11, 1861 (a day before his 52nd birthday), for a trip to the nation's capital and his inauguration. While Lincoln's presidential train traversed the country from Illinois to Washington, D. C., it stopped in several large cities, among them Pittsburgh, Pennsylvania. Because Pennsylvania was a heavy manufacturing state, protective tariffs were an important topic to the electorate there, and Lincoln gave a speech on that topic providing the analogy that a tariff is like a meal for the government.[46]

Lincoln arrived in the capital on February 23, and during his transit to Washington, a protectionist tariff bill that had been languishing in the Senate (it had passed the House in May 1860) was moving toward final approval. When several states seceded from the Union in December 1860 and January 1861, opposition to the bill diminished as Republicans took control of the Senate in February. On February 20, the Morrill Tariff was approved in the Senate, which then required reconciliation with the House version of the bill. The final version of the Morrill Tariff was unanimously approved on March 2, 1861, two days before Lincoln's inauguration, and would become effective on April 1, 1861.[47]

While this first version of the Morrill Tariff significantly increased duties on imports (some 70 percent higher than in 1860) and was denounced in England because of its financial impact to their industries, it was still not high enough to service the debt induced by the costs of the Civil War. A second Morrill Tariff bill was created as part of the Revenue Act of 1861 to increase tariffs another ten to twelve percent. The combination of these acts raised the average tariff from around 25 percent pre-Civil War to around 45 percent from 1861 to the end of the century. It is interesting to note that these high rates were still not enough to pay for the cost of the war, and additional sources of federal revenue were implemented, including the first federal income tax.[48]

Before Franklin Roosevelt's election, the Smoot-Hawley bill increased tariff drastically, leading to reduced U. S. exports – on account of other countries raising their tariffs in reply – at a time when U. S. exports were desperately needed to counterbalance the lack of domestic growth. The Smoot-Hawley tariff, also known as the Tariff Act of 1930, increased duties on imports from around 40 percent to 59 percent, but they instigated reactive tariff increases by other countries. This action-reaction caused an overall decline in international trade of over 60 percent by 1933. Upon his inauguration in March 1933, President Roosevelt worked with Secretary of Commerce Cordell Hull to get Congress to enact tariff reform.[49]

In 1934, Roosevelt signed the Reciprocal Trade Agreement Act, also known as the Trade Act of 1934, which allowed the President to raise or lower existing tariffs up to 50% if other countries would reciprocate the tariff concessions. This act also delegated specific product duties to the Executive branch, thereby minimizing or eliminating Congressmen from pressure by special interests and lobbyists to enact product-specific protective trade barriers. The Trade Act of 1934 established a seismic shift in U. S. trade policy from protectionist to liberal; it ushered in a new era of global trade, trending toward minimal tariffs and eliminating trade barriers. An extension of the Reciprocal Trade Agreement passed Congress in 1945, and President Truman continued Roosevelt's liberal trade policies by signing the General Agreement on Tariffs and Trade (GATT) in 1947. When GATT became effective in 1948, it allowed every nation that signed the agreement to participate in tariff concessions of every other nation. This agreement provided the vehicle for war-torn countries around the globe to participate in post-war prosperity and peace.[50]

In reviewing the history of trade and tariffs of the three great presidents encompassing 230 years of America's history, there are a few pearls of wisdom that can be surmised. The first is that duties on imports can be an important source of revenue for the country, but if they are raised too high, then they become counterproductive and other countries will retaliate with higher tariffs or find different sources. The second is that reduction of tariffs among countries with bi-lateral agreements can "lift all boats" and create prosperity for all countries engaging in those agreements provided the agreements are maintained and no other trade barriers are erected between those countries.

War

War is another common thread through the three great presidents. It presented a challenge and crisis through which their mettle was tested. One president dealt with a great war before serving two terms as president, one president had to deal with war within weeks of becoming president, and one president led the country through a global war after serving two terms as president guiding the country through the worst economic crisis in our history.

Even before he was president, Washington was the Commander of all the American forces in the Revolutionary War. This War of Independence put the United States on the map, and Washington was singularly responsible for the strategy and tactics used in prosecuting the war. When Washington was named Commander in Chief of the Continental Army in 1775, he was a 43-year-old man of courage and action. His tenure over the next eight years would see highs and lows from the vicissitudes of war. From victory in Boston, where Washington chased the British Redcoats out of town, to embarrassment in New York, where the militia fled before the English (and Hessian) invaders without firing a shot, Washington worked with the materials a young country provided and tried to work a miracle. Out-numbered and out gunned, Washington and the Continental Army fled New York on the run but provided a Christmas-Boxing Day surprise for the Hessians in Trenton after secretly crossing the Delaware River. Another victory over the British at Princeton ensued before both armies settled in for the winter of 1776-1777. In the summer and fall of 1777, the English and Americans fought battles at Brandywine and Germantown near Philadelphia, with the British getting the upper hand via a surprise attack at Brandywine, and Washington making a defiant statement with the battle of Germantown that impressed the international community. That winter, the British settled in the American capital of Philadelphia, while Congress fled to Trenton, and Washington's army settled in for a bleak Christmas and battle for survival in their Valley Forge winter quarters 18 miles from Philadelphia.[51]

In the summer of 1778, the British broke camp and left Philadelphia bound for New York. Washington and the Continental Army caught up with the English at Monmouth Court House and Washington turned certain defeat, due to the cowardly retreat by General Lee, into victory by rallying the troops and getting them to attack. After that battle, the British concentrated their efforts on battling in the southern states; Washington kept an eye on the English garrison in New York and sent General Green to the Carolinas to harass the British forces there. In September 1781, Washington was informed of the British taking up defensive positions in Yorktown, Virginia, and raced his army across New Jersey down to Virginia to meet them. This time, the Continental Army was aided by French army and naval forces, which surrounded the English and lay siege on Yorktown in October 1781. The British surrendered, and it was the last major battle of the war. Although it was not officially over until the Treaty of Paris was agreed to in 1783, the war was won with the British defeat at Yorktown in 1781.[52]

Abraham Lincoln was barely a month into his presidency when the Confederate States attacked Fort Sumter in South Carolina. This unprovoked incident initiated a full-scale military buildup in both the North and South and kicked off a bloody four-year war between the Union and the Confederate states. The North expected a quick end to the rebellion and was shocked and disappointed by the result of the first battle at Bull Run. More disappointments followed, as Lincoln's generals proved to be more adept at administration than fighting.

After a military buildup of nearly 100,000 men and the associated weapons and supplies, General McClellan put into motion his Peninsula Plan in March 1862, nearly a year after the start of the war. McClellan's plan failed spectacularly, mostly due to his hesitation and lack of aggressiveness. However, in the West (the West being defined as west of the Appalachia Mountains) a new star rose by the name of General Grant. Grant's victories at Fort Henry, Fort Donaldson, and Shiloh, forced the Confederates out of Kentucky and Tennessee and inspired a grateful President to send him a box filled with 10,000 cigars. The year 1862 brought more difficulties, but after the victory at Antietam, Lincoln announced the Emancipation Proclamation – freedom for all slaves in the states of the rebellion to become effective on New Year's Day 1863. From that day forward, the Civil War became a war of emancipation and the end of slavery. With that purpose, it succeeded.[53]

In the late 1930s, the world was on fire and it seemed only a matter of time before the conflagration would also consume the United States. In May 1936, Italy completed its conquest of Abyssinia (present day Ethiopia), a nearly 500-year-old monarchy, after nearly two years of war in Africa. On July 17, 1936, the Spanish Civil War began, pitting neo-fascist nationalists from Spanish Army units that included General Francisco Franco, against the existing left-leaning Popular Front republican government. In a live-fire type training opportunity for the Hitler and Mussolini war making apparatus, Germany and Italy helped Francisco Franco defeat the government troops, who were supported by Soviet equipment and personnel. The final battles occurred in Madrid and Alicante, and the U. S. formally recognized the government led by dictator Francisco Franco on

April 1, 1939. Six days later, Italy invaded Albania, seeking to expand its Mediterranean possessions in a second coming of the Roman Empire. On September 1, 1939, Germany invaded Poland to start World War II.[54]

Although the world was at war, the United States would not enter until more than two years later, and it would take a Japanese surprise attack on Pearl Harbor to force the issue. Franklin Roosevelt was Commander-in-Chief and dictated strategy for the war. He successfully maneuvered America into a position of preparedness at a time when national sentiment was mainly against participation in another European conflict, owing to the fact that the last one had cost so many American soldiers' lives and the United States bore such a significant financial cost (the national debt skyrocketed from $3.6 billion to $27 billion during Wilson's administration to pay for the war effort).[55] In addition, war reparations and the costs that other countries owed the U. S. were not being repaid.

Roosevelt's position as President Wilson's Undersecretary of the Navy provided invaluable experience and expertise in how things got done in a war economy, and how the levers of politics and power worked in Washington. From his understanding of the regional dynamics in Europe, to his handling of Congress, to working with the Allies across the world, Roosevelt was the most experienced and adept executive in handling the pressures, problems, and issues of the war-torn world during World War II. Although he did not live to see the Promised Land, his guiding hand during the war effort ensured America a successful conclusion and unconditional victory.

What are the commonalities and what conclusions can be drawn from the three great presidents and the three great wars they fought? Although the three presidents fought these wars in different phases of their presidencies – Washington before he became president, Lincoln throughout his presidency, and Roosevelt at the end of his presidency – there are distinct similarities. All three presidents suffered early defeats that shook their confidence, and the public's confidence in them. All three maintained their faith in their objective and persevered through the challenges. Other similarities deal with how the wars were started – some claim that Roosevelt maneuvered the Japanese into attacking Pearl Harbor, and others claim that Lincoln maneuvered the South into attacking Fort Sumter. By analogy, would these critics also claim that Washington had baited the British into the Boston Massacre? These claims are far-fetched and require one to suspend logic to believe. Suffice to say, that these three great leaders rose to the occasion, and executed their duties and responsibilities to the best of their abilities. One hopes that through the next great crisis our next great leader will emerge to lead the country again safely to the Promised Land.

CHAPTER 15

The Next Great Crisis

Consider the comparisons of the last three Great Presidents with the conditions necessary for the next one and think of how the geographic progression has gone. George Washington's experience and geographical involvement in the American Revolution was limited to the east coast of the United States. Abraham Lincoln's experience and geographical involvement of the Civil War was mostly with the eastern half of the United States, basically from the Mississippi to the Atlantic Ocean, though politically it did extend into Texas and as far west as California. Franklin Roosevelt's experience and geographical involvement was from the United States to Europe and North Africa for the eastern limit, and from the United States to Japan and East Asia for the western limit. This portends a trend for the next major conflict to be truly worldwide in geographical involvement.

In the book *Generations* by William Strauss and Neil Howe, Strauss and Howe describe how the different generations of American civilization affect, or reflect, history. They state that, *"Generations come in cycles. Just as history produces generations, so too do generations produce history."*[1] The combination of the four current generations of Boomer, Generation-X (named Thirteenth by Strauss and Howe), Millennial, and Generation-Z (unspecified by Strauss and Howe) cohorts will all participate in the next great secular crisis of our country. They state that this crisis will be as significant as the American Revolution, the Civil War, or World War II, and that "The Crisis of 2020 will be a major turning point in American history and an adrenaline-filled moment of trial."[2]

Theodore Roosevelt, in the introduction to his classic naval history book *The Naval War of 1812* wrote, " . . . it is the old, old lesson, that a miserly economy in preparation may in the end involve a lavish outlay of men and money . . . " which was a comment on the unpreparedness of the country to fight a war against the British that everyone knew was coming. He said his reason for not writing about the land battles of the War of 1812 was that " . . . these operations were hardly worth serious study." In effect, he was saying that all of the land battles were predictable outcomes of the large disparity between the well trained and disciplined British regular Army versus the undisciplined and poorly trained American militia. Here Roosevelt argued that because Presidents Jefferson and Madison had not prepared the country for war, America suffered the consequences.[3]

The parallel here is clear. Owing to the impact of COVID-19 and the virtual shutdown of major segments of the American economy, the second quarter 2020 national Gross Domestic Product (GDP) fell at an astounding 31.7 percent. This is unprecedented in American history. In addition, this drop followed a first quarter GDP of -5 percent, and these two consecutive quarters of negative GDP growth by definition indicate a recession. The potential is that this recession will drive changes in domestic priorities and financial decisions. In these times of financial crisis and economic lethargy, let us hope that cuts to defense spending and military preparedness do not cause a similar crisis in our ability to react to worldwide threats against our interests abroad and the defense of our homeland and way of life.[4]

Climate Change

Climate change is a potential destabilizing force. As changing weather patterns increase the frequency and severity of floods, droughts, and other natural disasters (tornadoes, hurricanes, and the like), they could have a drastic effect on the ability of worldwide agriculture to keep up with feeding the global population. This could carry its own seeds of destruction, as countries and cultures fight over the remaining sources of fish, meat, fruits and vegetables to feed their populations. If it came to that, it wouldn't be the first time that man consumed to extinction the resources of a location and caused their own population demise (Easter Island, Australia, etc.).

Climate change has been affecting America's weather, and we can expect to experience more severe and catastrophic droughts, floods, hurricanes, and tornadoes. These natural disasters affect food production, commerce, and economic activity, and there is also a human cost in deaths, injuries, and personal impacts. These events are occurring with greater frequency and at a greater cost. A paper by Adam B. Smith titled "2010-2019: A Landmark Decade of U. S. Billion-Dollar Weather and Climate Disasters" provides insight into the number and cost of these effects. In the 2010s, there were 119 billion-dollar disasters, twice as many as the previous decade. The human and financial costs were 5,212 lives and over $800 billion. Since the 1980s, there has been a total of 258 billion-dollar disasters at a cost of $1.75 trillion, so in the last 25 percent of that time, almost 50 percent of the number and costs of the billion-dollar disasters have occurred.[5]

In the first six months of 2020, the United States has already had ten billion-dollar weather events, the quickest rise to double digits in history. It also represents the sixth year in a row (2015-2020) that there were ten or more billion-dollar weather events. The only previous years of double-digit billion-dollar weather events were 1998, 2008, 2011, and 2012. This information should shock even the most casual observer to the profound truth of the data, which is that climate change is significant and undeniable – and its impact is getting worse.[6]

According to a report by the Institute for Economics and Peace (IEP), the worldwide picture is even bleaker. Per the Ecological Threat Register (ETR) 2020 report, even though the United States has had a higher number of climatic disasters than any other country since 1990, the United States also has more economic resources to handle the shock and provide recovery assistance. As poorer nations are impacted by climate change, fewer economic resources translate into more human displacement as survivors flee the area in search of better circumstances. Around the world in 2019, almost three times as many people were displaced by climatic/ecological events (24.9 million) than by conflict/war (8.6 million). The ETR also identified specific regions that are "particularly susceptible to collapse," notably the Middle East (Syria, Iraq, Iran, Afghanistan, and Pakistan) and several African nations. These hotspots are among the world's most fragile countries trapped in continual conflict and competition for resources, and when challenged by climatic or ecological stresses are more susceptible to the kinds of forces that lead to social and civil collapse: economic upheaval, societal instability, and political disintegration.[7]

Civil Unrest

Are there any historical perspectives to help in understanding our current situation? In a review of their mammoth multi-volume work, *The Story of Civilization*, historians Will and Ariel Durant wrote a concise and insightful summary entitled *The Lessons of History* describing what they had learned and offering conclusions both hopeful and cautionary. In the chapter on "Government and History," they ended with a comment that seems particularly apt at this time: "If our economy of freedom fails to distribute wealth as ably as it has created it, the road to dictatorship will be open to any man who can persuasively promise security to all; and a martial government, under whatever charming phrases, will engulf the democratic world."[8]

In these strange days of COVID-19 lockdowns and protesters in the streets, it feels like we are on the verge of a seismic shift – when things could significantly change one way or another, for better or worse. There are a myriad of different challenges facing this country, and we are not alone. A recent survey by the Pew Research Center identified consistent trends in data collected across 14 countries, from the United States and Canada to nine European countries, South Korea, Japan and Australia. With respect to the pandemic, there was agreement among the majority of respondents that international cooperation could have mitigated the outbreak (59 percent). Per the respondents, the economic outlook for their country dropped significantly from 2019 to 2020, on the order of 25 percent on average, as significant a drop in confidence as that recorded during the global financial crisis of 2008. Across all 14 countries surveyed, the highest threat cited was that of global climate change (eight of the 14), and either climate change or the spread of infectious diseases (like coronavirus) was number one or number two in all 14 countries.[9]

The social fabric of our country seems to be tearing in front of our very eyes; either via television, social media, or live and in-person, the conflict between left and right, black and white, angry and afraid, seems violent and uncontrollable. The bitter divide within our own political institutions and the fractious voices of internal domestic struggle is another potential source of the coming storm. As the presidential election of 2020 plays out before us, the behavior of both protesters and anti-protesters has been deplorable. The temper and extremism on all sides of the political and national debate is reminiscent of that during the pre-Civil War era. However, at that time the divide and the debates were much more focused and clearer – slavery and the socio-economic system and culture of the

South versus the abolitionist and industrial-manufacturing forces of the North. Today, the debate is being framed as the far right versus the far left, while a wide range of common ground in the middle is being ignored. More emphasis is being placed on what divides us, as opposed to what unites us, and that is a recipe for disunion and revolution. Revolution to some would be a better alternative to what exists today, but evolution is what is needed. Change is needed, but positive change through the existing democratic processes is the best solution – and that will occur over time. The demographics of our country are changing and that may be the wave of the future as the population of swing states like Florida, Arizona, and North Carolina have had significant increases in the proportion of minority voters eligible to vote. In addition, the population of white voters in Texas now barely hold a majority (51 percent) of the electorate.[10]

The situation in the United States is not unique. Worldwide issues of cultural, political, and religious divides are driving social engagement and expression of discontent. A driving factor for social change is social media. It is changing norms and behaviors more quickly and radically than anything since the advent of modern advertising on television. World events in recent history, like that of the Arab Spring in 2011, were facilitated by Facebook and other social media platforms. These platforms have the ability to unite, but they also have the ability to divide, and more and more people across the world use them to promote their causes.

With respect to radical Islam, several examples of trouble spots could become the sources of conflict. Syria, Lebanon, Iraq, Egypt, Libya, Turkey and other Middle East and North African nations are undergoing civil strife and are potential breeding grounds for discontent and radicalization. Taliban and radical Islam clerics could potentially leverage this situation into extreme measures, such as major terrorist activities that impact the Western world. What would be the potential outcome of a bad actor (like Iran) to obtain a nuclear weapon with the intent to use it? If North Korea could use expertise in centrifuge technology and weapons design from Abdul Qadeer Khan of Pakistan to develop a nuclear weapon capability, why couldn't Iran? That potential, as scary as the thought is, exists.[11]

Global Resources

Global resources in basic needs like food, water and arable land are at a premium, as the world population increases and as climate change reduces the amount of arable land due to rising sea levels. These issues can cause major instability in some countries because they could provide an impetus for mass migration or population displacement from one country to another, thereby driving political instability. As many as 1.2 billion people could be displaced by a combination of climate change and conflict over the next 30 years says a report by the Institute for Economics and Peace (IEP). Changing weather patterns will cause more severe droughts in some areas and more extreme flooding in others. In addition, the world population is expected to increase from seven billion to nearly ten billion by 2050, which will increase food demand by 50 percent and water stress by even more. This will make potable water and food production much more strategic in the future, and a potential source of international conflict.[12]

Food insecurity has increased due to COVID-19, which could also increase population displacement and mass migration. Last year, the World Food Program (WFP) estimated that 135 million persons faced food insecurity, and because of coronavirus that number is expected to increase to 270 million. In addition, the WFP estimates that hunger has a doubling effect on migration, in that for every percentage point increase in severe food insecurity there is a two percent increase in population displacement. The pandemic has also increased food prices, owing to a combination of restricted supply induced by COVID spikes at meat processing centers and reduced production as a result of mass restaurant closures. These price increases have an outsized effect due to the layoffs and unemployment caused by the pandemic. Coronavirus-induced travel restrictions have also impacted food production, on account of migrant workers' inability to travel to areas in need of manual labor. Across the globe, the pandemic's impact is being felt on nearly every continent. In Asia, food supply chains have been disrupted, and some countries have stopped or slowed food exports. In Africa, climate change has exacerbated existing issues with already stressed and limited food supply chains as drought and insect swarms devastate crops and sources of production. Furthermore, food aid programs have been cut by many countries, and travel restrictions are impeding food distribution. In South America, many countries are seeing increases in government dependency to support food needs, and unemployment surges due to coronavirus. Even the industrialized countries of Europe and North America are seeing increased participation in food banks and other emergency aid.[13]

The World Economic Forum *Global Risk Report 2020* names water crisis and food crisis as the top two long-term societal risks, and two of the top ten overall risks in their 2020 (15th Annual) report. The report also lists five environmental global shapers in their top ten long-term risks: biodiversity loss, climate action failure, human-made environmental disasters, extreme weather, and natural disasters. These risks are related to climate change and represent issues that require immediate and multinational attention. However, instead of addressing these issues, multiple actors (including Russia, China, Norway, and the United States) are leveraging new access to previously permanently frozen arctic areas as strategic opportunities for natural resources exploitation of oil, gas, and other mineral deposits. Other countries may also become interested in these regions to support their fishing industries. This competition for resources is another potential source of international conflict.[14]

Global Conflict

In their short book called *The Lessons of History*, historians Will and Ariel Durant wrote a chapter called "History and War," in which they stated (as of 1968), "In the last 3,421 years of recorded history, only 268 have seen no war."[15] Since 1968, the only years with no wars were 1996, 1997, and 2000; so updating the Durant's numbers, we see that through 2020, of 3,473 years of recorded history, there were only 271 with no war. Thus, the percentage of peaceful years in recorded history is only eight percent. The world is hurtling headfirst into a 1930s style environment of totalitarian governments led by leaders-for-life and of populist governments led by cult-of-personality leaders with nationalistic agendas. This is not a good environment for global cooperation and does not bode well for peace in the future.

The next great crisis could come from any number of sources: ideological identity (the struggle of capitalism vs. communism), socio-economics (the haves vs. the have-nots), religious extremism (radical Islam), or climate change, and this is not an exhaustive list. China's growth and need for resources to keep its population from revolting against the current party elites could cause China to alter its economic path and resort to the military option in order to keep hundreds of millions of Chinese from taking up arms against their government. Russia's (meaning Vladimir Putin's) thirst for power and prestige on the world stage could cause more crises such as those associated with Crimea and Ukraine, where his imperialistic vision causes the military option to become more relied upon to fill the need to be feared, if not respected, in the world. North Korea's despotic leader and absolute ruler, Kim Jong Un, could take the rest of the world to the brink of nuclear war with his hysterical rants and threats against the United States, South

Korea, and their allies. Kim has repeatedly threatened to send nuclear tipped missiles "raining down" on North Korea's enemies.

In different scenarios and from different perspectives, the same areas of risk and the same countries seem to top the lists as the most likely hot spots for full-fledged conflict. These lists include those of the Foreign Relations' Center for Preventative Action, which includes Tier 1 trouble spots and instigators of the Korean Peninsula (North Korea), the South China Sea (China and others), the Persian Gulf (Syria, Iran, and Iraq), the Taliban (Afghanistan) and conflict between Russia and Ukraine.[16]

The Crisis Group listed among the top ten locations for potential conflicts in 2020 as: Afghanistan (at number 1), Iran, North Korea, Kashmir (Pakistan/India), and Ukraine – Syria, though not in the top ten, was also mentioned in the piece.[17]

The Ecological Threat Register (ETR) 2020, from the Institute for Economics & Peace, named Afghanistan as the highest ecological threat hot spot, with six threats, and Iran, Syria, Iraq, and Pakistan as not far behind. ETR 2020 measured population growth, water stress, food insecurity, droughts, floods, cyclones, rising temperature, and rising sea levels as threats to stability, and China, North Korea, and Russia were also on the list as medium-to-high exposure.[18]

The following pages highlight some of the recent and historical perspectives with respect to eight countries that are potential sources of conflict or crisis in the future: Afghanistan, China, Iran, Iraq, North Korea, Pakistan, Russia, and Syria. This is by no means an exhaustive list, because there are as many additional potential hot spots in Africa alone. The intent here is only to illuminate some of the more likely areas, and the intractable issues at play.

Afghanistan

Afghanistan is the location of America's longest war, reaching a span of almost two decades, from October 2001 to the present (October 2020) – although there have been recent peace overtures. On September 20, 2001, President Bush addressed Congress and the nation, laying out the identity of the terrorists responsible for 9/11, that they would be held accountable and that the war would be a lengthy campaign. His address came with a warning for the Taliban: "They will hand over the terrorists, or they will share their fate." On October 7, President Bush addressed the American people from the Treaty Room in the White House to announce the beginning of the war in Afghanistan. It started with U. S. cruise missile and air strikes on al-Qaeda and Taliban forces, aided by a coalition of U. S. Special Forces, Pushtun anti-Taliban forces, and elements of the Northern Alliance performing boots-on-the-ground support.[19]

In November 2001, this coalition fought its way through and overcame several Taliban strongholds. Mazar-e-Sharif, the largest city in northern Afghanistan, came under attack by Northern Alliance forces on November 5, and fell within four days. In western Afghanistan, anti-Taliban leader General Ismail Khan captured Herat on November 12. In eastern Afghanistan, Northern Alliance forces captured the capital city of Kabul on November 13. As the anti-Taliban forces pushed eastward, Mohammad Ated, an al-Qaida leader and deputy to bin Laden, was killed in an air strike. Another eastern Afghanistan city, Jalalabad, fell to anti-Taliban forces shortly thereafter. Two more northern cities, Taloqan and Kunduz, fell to Northern Alliance forces by the end of the month.[20]

In early December 2001, the future president of Afghanistan, Hamid Karzai, led a cadre of tribal Pushtun troops against Taliban forces in Kandahar. This southern stronghold of the Taliban fell on December 7, a day marking two months since the beginning of the War on Terror, and 60 years since Pearl Harbor. On December 20, an interim government was established in Afghanistan, with Hamid Karzai installed as its administrative leader. In late December, Afghan militias attacked the remaining al-Qaida forces at Tora Bora, a well-defended complex of caves in the mountains southeast of Kabul. This three-week battle ended with the Afghan forces killing hundreds and capturing 20, but Osama bin Laden, who was suspected to have been among the al-Qaida members hiding in these caves, was not found.[21]

In May 2003, Secretary of Defense Donald Rumsfeld declared an end to combat in Afghanistan. In 2004, Afghanistan got a new constitution, agreed to by over 500 Afghan delegates. A new president was elected in October 2004, and Hamid Karzai became Afghanistan's first democratically elected leader. In May 2005, Karzai and President Bush committed to a strategic partnership to fight the war on terror and strengthen international ties. The year 2006 saw an increase in violence and suicide attacks, while NATO allies withheld sending in more troops and pushed for Afghan security forces to shoulder the risk. In 2007, Mullah Dadullah, a major Taliban leader, was killed by joint operations of Afghan, U. S. and NATO troops.[22]

In 2009, new U. S. president Barack Obama committed to a new strategy and more troops in Afghanistan. In 2011, Obama announced a planned reduction in troop levels, which had reached over 100,000 during the past two years as the war reached the 10-year mark. In 2014, Obama announced a drawdown of U. S. forces in Afghanistan, with a plan to reduce troop levels by up to 90 percent by 2016. In 2017, new U. S. president Donald Trump announced a potential increase in troops and prolonged conflict in Afghanistan if the Taliban could not be brought to the bargaining table for negotiations. In 2018, U. S. troops are deployed across Afghanistan to assist in eradication of opium labs and drug lords in rural areas, and as a means to cut off Taliban sources of revenue. In 2019, Trump called off peace talks with Taliban leaders, after a Taliban attack killed a U. S. soldier. In 2020, peace talks in Afghanistan were re-started, and both the United States and Taliban sides were hopeful of an agreement.[23]

Afghanistan has been called "the graveyard of empires" because throughout the centuries of recorded history, its critical location in central Asia has been at the crossroads of Far East riches and Western ambitions, and has brought some of the greatest empires in history to their knees. The Greek empire of Alexander the Great stretched from the Mediterranean Sea through Persia, but in 327 BC an Afghan archer nearly killed Alexander during the siege of Massaga, the capital of the Assacenians in what is now Afghanistan. The Mongolian empire of Genghis Khan extended into Afghanistan in the 1200s, but after Khan died, the Mongolians were unable to keep the territory. The "sun never set" on the British Empire in the 1800s, but in 1842, 16,000 British soldiers were decimated in a retreat from Kabul to Jalalabad. The Soviet Union invaded Afghanistan in 1979, and ten years later left the country in total defeat, having been unable to subdue the Afghani mujahideen fighters.[24]

In summary, Afghanistan is a land-locked, mountainous and arid country, surrounded by Iran to the west, Pakistan to the south and east, and three former Soviet bloc countries to the north (Tajikistan, Turkmenistan, and Uzbekistan). It even has a small border with China to the east, in its panhandle region between Pakistan and Tajikistan. Surrounded by potential external threats, Afghanis also have to deal with the internal dangers of civil war, opium trade, religious fanaticism, and warlords. The combination of these effects makes this country a potential hot spot for future conflict.

China

In March 2018, China adopted the "Xi Jinping constitution" of 2018, replacing the "Deng Xiaoping constitution" of 1982 thereby eliminating term limits for the president and vice-president. This effectively means that Xi Jinping is now President for Life. Xi is also the leader (general secretary) of the Chinese Communist Party, and chair of the Central Military

Commission, and will retain those titles for the rest of his life. Xi has consolidated power through the Communist Party, naming it the end-all be-all for government, military, civilian and academic life. This style of totalitarian governance has not been seen in China since Chairman Mao, the leader of communist China from its inception in 1949, until his death in 1976. It is apparent that Xi sees himself as the next Mao.[25]

China is an example of a leader-for-life communist government that is taking the long view with respect to international relations. China is now the number one country providing international aid to the world and is using that aid as leverage to gain access to natural resources within the countries receiving it. In what is referred to as a debt trap, infrastructure investment funded by Chinese loans sometimes come with strings attached, like a requirement to use Chinese companies to perform construction, resulting in opaque bidding, inflated prices, and bloated contracts. For example, the country Myanmar (formerly called Burma) cancelled a Chinese funded $3.6 billion hydroelectric dam project in 2011, and recently reduced investment in a Chinese funded deep-water port from $7.5 billion to $1.3 billion, while doubling ownership to 30%.[26]

China is also building a $900 billion New Silk Road, once called "One Belt, One Road," and now known as the Belt and Road Initiative (BRI). Announced by President Xi in 2013, these massive infrastructure investment projects will create a transportation corridor from China through central Asia and into Europe (the Belt), and port development along a maritime route from China through the South China Sea to the Indian Ocean, and through the Red Sea to the Mediterranean Sea into Europe (the Road). Over 60 countries signed up initially to participate, including Egypt, Indonesia, Iran, Pakistan, the Philippines, and Russia, with Pakistan being one of the largest recipients of development projects, including roads, bridges, wind farms and other projects.[27]

While China insists that the BRI is an economic opportunity to expand trade and promote Asian connectivity, skeptics suspect that it is a Trojan horse for Chinese expansion and militarism. Because of its emphasis on port investment and development throughout the Indian Ocean, and on its heavy investment in both Pakistan and Myanmar infrastructure (countries immediately west and east of India, respectively), the Indian government sees it as a "String of Pearls" intended to cut-off its ties to Western allies.[28] The BRI does appear to provide multiple strategic benefits to China: 1) alternative port access to Middle East oil, 2) land access to neighboring oil-rich Kazakhstan, 3) land access to Turkmenistan, a country with the sixth highest gas resources in the world, 4) land access to gold and other minerals exported by Kyrgyzstan, 5) shipping access to ports throughout the Indian Ocean, and 6) opening new markets and export opportunities to boost Chinese incomes, especially in the poorer western provinces that lack access to shipping and ports enjoyed by the eastern sea-facing provinces.[29]

With new economic wealth, China is also flexing its military might, and has been on a military build-up since Xi Jinping became president in 2012. Xi has been particularly interested in strengthening the Chinese Navy, which is now the largest in the world. At present, China controls the three seas nearest its eastern border: The Yellow Sea, the East China Sea, and the South China Sea. The Chinese Navy has nearly 400 ships, roughly 25 percent more than the U. S. Navy has, and welcomed its second aircraft carrier (the *Nanchang*) to its fleet during fleet exercises celebrating its 70th anniversary. Although the U. S. Navy currently has larger ships with more firepower and 11 aircraft carriers, the Chinese Navy is expected to grow to 530 ships and catch up to the U. S. Navy in firepower by 2030. China is now focusing on developing a "blue water" navy, which will allow it to protect its trade routes and project power throughout the world.[30]

Iran

On November 4, 1979, radical Iranian students seized 52 hostages at the American Embassy in Tehran, held them for 444 days, and released them on January 20, 1981, the day of Ronald Reagan's presidential inauguration. Since the day the hostage crisis started, which coincided with Ayatollah Khomeini's overthrow of the Shah of Iran – Mohammad Reza Pahlavi – the United States has been at odds with Iran's regime. President Jimmy Carter, near the beginning of an election year, put everything on hold to focus on negotiations for the hostages, which was called the Rose Garden strategy. By March, it was obvious the Rose Garden strategy wasn't working, so in April 1980, Carter resorted to a military option to rescue the hostages. The rescue attempt, called Operation Eagle Claw, was a failure – a helicopter crashed into an EC-130 aircraft and eight American soldiers died as a result. Although it did not result in a rescue of the hostages, an outcome of the failed rescue attempt was a reorganization of the American military and the creation of a Special Operations command.[31]

The 1980s were a particularly difficult time for American interests in the Middle East as Iran exported its brand of Islamic revolutionary fervor to other countries in the region. Lebanon was the first recipient of this export as Iran's Islamic Revolutionary Guard Corps (IRGC) poured personnel and funding into the Lebanese civil war, supporting Hezbollah – "the party of God" – a Shia militia formed to oppose the Sunni Muslims and Maronite Christians in the country. Hezbollah was trained by the IRGC in Biqa' Valley and provided with arms, techniques, and millions in cash. The April 1983 bombing at the U. S. Embassy in Beirut that killed 63, the October 1983 suicide bombing of a Marine barracks in Beirut that killed 307 (241 U. S. military personnel), and the October 1984 bombing of the U. S. temporary embassy in Awakr, East Beirut that killed 23 are all examples of Hezbollah terrorist activity. In 1985, Hezbollah produced a manifesto that called for an Iranian style Islamic republic in Lebanon, demanded destruction of Israel, and professed allegiance to the supreme leader of Iran.[32]

Mohsen Razai (Rezaee), the rocket man of Iran, was instrumental in the development of Iran's weapons and missile technologies, including manufacturing facilities in Iran to reduce or eliminate Iran's dependence on foreign sources. As leader of the IRGC from 1980 to 1997, he focused on developing missile technology as a response to Saddam Hussein's SCUD missile launches in the Iran-Iraq war during the "war of the cities" between 1984 and 1988. Due to the arms embargo by the United States, Mohsen struck a secret arms deal with the Soviets in 1981, and by 1982 signed contracts with European suppliers for equipment to build their own arms factories. In 1985, he traveled to China to negotiate a $1.6 billion arms deal in Beijing. Weapons were frequently funneled through North Korea from both Russia and China to Iran in order to avoid international oversight. At the end of 1985, Iran's missile industry was born with the groundbreaking ceremony at Semnan, about 100 miles east of Tehran. By the end of 1986, Iran was launching Oghab missiles at Basra in Iraq. In June 1987, North Korea and Iran signed a half billion-dollar deal for SCUD missiles to be used during the War of the Cities (75 SCUD missiles were launched against Iraq), and missile development program coordination continued between these two renegade states.[33]

By 1998, North Korea, with IGRC missile experts in attendance, flight-tested a new two-stage missile called the Taepo-Dong, which flew over a thousand miles (beyond the range of Japan). Now Iran could clearly target Israel from its missile bases, and, with technological advances, countries even further away. With this missile technology in hand, the next phase of Iran's regime – development of nuclear technology and atomic weapons capability – was the goal. Iran had already engaged Russia in rebuilding an incomplete nuclear reactor in Bushehr that had been demolished in the Iran-Iraq war, and would subsequently engage China in supporting its uranium enrichment goals. By 2005, Iran was openly declaring its intent to continue its nuclear program and obtain nuclear technology.[34]

Iran is currently involved in military action in Syria and supporting Russia in backing the dictatorship of President Bashar al-Assad. Iran is also involved militarily in Iraq by arming Shia militants and militias, also known as the Popular Mobilization Forces (PMF). Iran's involvement in PMF attacks on U. S. and coalition military bases in Iraq caused, in response, the U. S. drone killing of Iranian general Qassem Soleimani in January 2020. Iran is still involved in Lebanon, providing military and financial aid to Hezbollah, and uses the jihadists of Hezbollah in pursuit of regime change in other Arab countries, of which Yemen is the latest target. A press statement dated September 19, 2020, by the U. S. Secretary of State Michael Pompeo declared: "...the greatest threat to peace in the Middle East comes from the Islamic Republic of Iran."[35]

The press release also announced the "snapback" of United Nations sanctions on Iran, pursuant to UN Security Council Resolution 2231. However, it remains unclear how effective these moves will be, as other members of the U. N. Security Council (China, France, Russia, and the United Kingdom, besides the United States) are questioning the validity of the sanctions. Instead, France, Germany, and Britain said they would work to preserve the Joint Comprehensive Plan of Action (JCPOA) agreement between the Security Council members and Germany, from which the United States withdrew in 2018. The JCPOA was agreed to in 2015 and was intended to provide Iran with economic sanctions relief in exchange for limiting Iran's nuclear development program. At a time when Iran's global export of fundamentalist doctrine and terrorism is expanding, it remains to be seen if America's unilateral move towards containment of their nuclear ambitions will be successful.[36]

Iraq

On January 16, 1991, the skies above Baghdad lit up with tracers as Iraqi anti-aircraft guns opened fire, and American and Allied aircraft dropped precision-guided munitions on key communications and radar installations throughout the city. As the only 24/7 news network at the time, Cable News Network (CNN) brought their viewership a first-hand look at war, with live global 24-hour coverage. One of those viewers was U. S. Secretary of Defense Dick Cheney, who admitted to following CNN's coverage of the Baghdad attacks.[37]

The threat of war had been building since Saddam Hussein's unprovoked attack on Kuwait in August 1990, and diplomatic resolutions to the crisis proved elusive. President George H. W. Bush announced the start of the Gulf War and called it Operation Desert Storm. In Iraq, Saddam Hussein was calling it the Mother of All Battles. The Gulf War ended up being a defining moment for President Bush, and it would also define our future relationships with Arab countries in the Middle East.[38]

Before Operation Desert Storm started, President Bush decided that in response to Saddam's attack on Kuwait, America needed support and allies in the region, so a team was sent to the Persian Gulf to coordinate approval for staging aircraft, equipment, men and supplies in the region. Because it was an affront to some of the Islam faith to allow non-believers to even set foot on Arab soil, approval to defend Muslim territory was not a given. Bush's team of advisors first approached King Fahd of Saudi Arabia and told the King that Saudi Arabia's oil fields were also at risk of being overrun and stolen by Saddam Hussein. King Fahd approved the positioning of U. S. forces on Saudi soil but extracted a promise that they would leave when the conflict was over. Bush's field team then negotiated similar agreements with Bahrain, Egypt, Oman, Qatar, and the United Arab Emirates. This effort proved that America could build a coalition of Arab countries to defeat a common Arab foe. The coalition was so effective that Saddam's forces were ousted from Kuwait in six weeks, and fighting ceased on February 28, 1991. A negotiated peace was quickly completed, which allowed armed Iraqi helicopters to remain in operation, and the expected rebellion of Kurds and Shia Muslims was brutally repressed by Saddam's Republican Guard. Lacking any support by U. S. troops or air cover, the rebellion was quickly extinguished, leaving both the Kurds in northern Iraq and the Shia Muslims in southern Iraq with a strong resentment of America.[39]

From the end of the war in 1991 to March 2003, the United States fought a holding action of "containment" in Iraq, as Saddam Hussein continued to harass, intimidate, and murder civilians in his country. There was a northern "no fly zone" called Operation Northern Watch and a similar no fly zone of similar name in southern Iraq intended to restrict Saddam's persecution of Kurds and Shia, respectively. The good news was that in 12 years of operations not a single American pilot was lost. The bad news was that the no-fly zones were ineffective in protecting the Kurd and Shia peoples. Owing to Saddam's intransigence in complying with United Nations resolutions and weapons inspections, recurring military raids occurred in 1994, 1996, and 1998. The 1998 action was caused by Saddam's refusal to allow weapons inspectors at Iraq weapons research and development centers. The four-day bombing of Iraq in December 1998 was called Operation Desert Fox and consisted of over 400 cruise missiles launched from U. S. Navy ships and over 600 smart bombs dropped by B-52 and B-1 Air Force bombers; these proved extremely effective.[40]

In March 2002, the United States shifted its focus on the war on terror from the Taliban in Afghanistan to Saddam Hussein in Iraq. Military preparations and strategy to pivot toward Iraq took another year, and in March 2003 the Iraq War began. This second Iraq war in 2003 was a reaction to 9/11, concerns about Weapons of Mass Destruction (WMD), and a desire to finish the job that was left incomplete by the first Iraq war in 1991 – elimination of Saddam Hussein. The Iraq War ended in 2011, with nearly $800 billion spent and 4,500 American lives lost.[41] In the vacuum of authority after the Americans left, the hardline leader of Iraq (Prime Minister Nouri al-Maliki) eliminated competition political and otherwise, especially Sunni Muslims. An ensuing civil war in Iraq pitted Sunni versus Shia Muslims, and the potential for a Taliban takeover. The civil war became a crucible of concern for the United States, with any hope for Iraqi democracy, the American efforts of 10 long years of war, and political influence in the region potentially going down the drain. By 2013, the brutality of the civil war was prolific, and an Islamic State in Iraq and Syria (ISIS) caliphate developed, which took the United States and a global coalition four years to eliminate.[42]

Since 2018, Iraq has been freed of the clutches of the Islamic State (IS), although remaining IS members continued targeted attacks in Iraq. Adil Abdul al-Mahdi, a 76-year-old economist and Shia politician, became prime minister in October 2018 and was expected to be an agent of positive change. However, in October 2019, Iraqis by the hundreds of thousands took to the streets to demand reform. A new Iraq leader, Mustafa Al-Kadhimi, was appointed the prime minister-delegate in April 2020, and took office in May. His future is uncertain, and he will be walking a tightrope between the United States and Iran as the former attempts to reign in Iran's expansionist desires and the latter looks to Iraq as an economic resource and land link to Syria and Lebanon. With these conflicting forces at play, Iraq is a potential pawn for international strategic moves in the future.[43]

North Korea

The leadership of North Korea should be called the Kim Dynasty rather than a communist regime: The current North

Korean "Supreme Leader," Kim Jong Un, is the son of the second leader of the regime, Kim Jong II, and the grandson of the first leader of North Korea, Kim Il Sung. Kim Il Sung became president of the Democratic Peoples of North Korea (DPNK) when that country was created in 1948 as a result of Soviet occupation lasting from the end of World War II in 1945 to the establishment of the independent communist country once the Soviet withdrew their forces in 1948. Kim Il Sung remained in power until his death of a heart attack in 1994, when his son Kim Jong II took over. Kim Jong II had been identified as his father's successor as early as 1980, then became more increasingly involved in 1992 as his father's health slowly declined.[44]

Kim Jong II declared three years of national mourning after his father's passing (while he consolidated power), then declared himself the new Supreme Leader. During the 1990s, after the fall of the Soviet empire, North Korea struggled economically owing to the loss of Soviet aid. This caused massive famine across North Korea, and estimates of a quarter million to over two million people died. International agencies accused Kim Jong II of crimes against humanity for his economic mismanagement of the country. In the 1990s, Kim Jong II instituted a "military first" policy, which provided focus and clarity on economic priorities. North Korea also exported missile technology to other rogue nations, in particular Iran, in return for economic considerations. In 2002, U. S. President Bush declared North Korea to be part of an "axis of evil" supporting terrorism and nuclear proliferation. Kim Jong II's regime was recognized as one of the most repressive governments in world history, and the judgment was thoroughly deserved.[45]

Kim Jong Un, Kim Jong II's youngest son, took over leadership of North Korea in 2011 after his father's death from a heart attack. Kim Jong Un consolidated power over the next several years, through several purges of leadership, including the execution of his uncle (Jang Song Thaek) in 2013, execution of the minister of defense (Hyon Yong Chol) in 2015, and the assassination of his half-brother (Kim Jong Nam) in 2017. These periodic actions seem to be calculated to provide maximum impact on predictability and stability in order for Kim Jong Un to maintain control over party and military elites. In 2014, Kim was indicted by a United Nations commission for systemic and gross violations of human rights in North Korea. Kim Jong Un has consolidated power in a "reign of terror," and it is reported that Kim had ordered over 300 executions between 2011 and 2016, for grievances as minor as sleeping in a meeting.[46]

For a small country, at 46,000 square miles (97th largest in the world), and having a small population, at 26 million (55th most populous in the world), North Korea has outsized military capabilities. It has the world's fourth largest military, with over 1.2 million active personnel and 8.4 million reservists, 4,300 tanks, 1,300 aircraft, 70 submarines, a range of intercontinental ballistic missiles, and an estimated ten to 60 nuclear weapons. Kim Jong Un has ratcheted up North Korea's missile testing program from less than 20 for both his father and grandfather to over 100 flight tests in the relatively short time he has been in power. In addition, Kim has intensified North Korea's nuclear testing program, doubling the number of his father's tests with four nuclear detonations (in February 2013, January 2016, September 2016, and September 2017). The weapons test in 2017 was estimated at 30-100 kilotons, or about two to six times the size of the weapon dropped on Hiroshima. The larger concern here is nuclear proliferation, because in 2003 North Korea had exited the Non-Proliferation Treaty it had signed in 1985. North Korea also has a history of exporting its missiles and nuclear technology to such countries as Iran, Libya, Syria, and Yemen, among others.[47]

The potential for a worldwide crisis exists if Kim Jong Un's recent health issues were to bring about a power vacuum in North Korea. In April 2020, Kim "disappeared" for three weeks and rumors of his premature death swirled. Since he has a family history of heart issues – both his father and grandfather died of heart failure – rumors abounded about a heart procedure gone wrong. Similar rumors occurred during a disappearance in late 2014, until Kim resurfaced with a cane after an apparent ankle surgery to remove a cyst. Despite Kim Jong Un's young age (36 years old in 2020), the potential for an unexpected early transition of power, with no clear heir apparent, could throw the country into chaos. The largest concern of this scenario would be the disposition of North Korea's nuclear weapons stockpile, which could end up in a number of nightmare scenarios, including being launched at South Korea, Japan, or the United States as a demonstration of power and strength by the new leadership, or being sold to terrorists or other rogue countries for economic benefit.[48]

Pakistan

Pakistan gained its independence (along with India) from England in August 1947 as the British separated the area into Islamic and Hindu regions. Pakistan was the Islamic region originally composed of two areas – East Pakistan, on the eastern edge of the former Indian colony and now an independent country called Bangladesh, and West Pakistan, on the western side of India, and now simply called Pakistan. Immediately after their independence from England, Pakistan and India went to war with each other over the northern region of India called Kashmir. Fighting lasted from 1947 to 1948, and India won.

Despite the military failure in the war with India, the Pakistani Army has had a history of ruling the country over long periods of time. General Ayub Kahn ruled from 1960 to 1969 as president, and then was replaced by General Yahya Kahn. In 1970, General Yahya Kahn granted Pakistan its first national election, and Sheikh Mujibur Rahman and his Awami League party from East Pakistan won the election. Rahman was prohibited from becoming prime minister by the Army, so East Pakistan declared its independence in the ensuing civil war;

with the support of the Indian military, Bangladesh (formerly known as East Pakistan) became a separate country. With a new country and a new constitution, West Pakistan became Pakistan, and in 1973 Zulfikar Ali Bhutto became prime minister. In 1977, General Zia ul-Haq declared martial law, arrested Bhutto, put him in prison, and tried him on trumped up charges. Bhutto was found guilty and hanged in 1979, and General Zia stayed in power until his death in a plane crash, in August 1988.[49]

In November 1988, Zulfikar Bhutto's daughter Benazir was elected prime minister representing the Pakistan People's Party (PPP); she was the first female prime minister of an Islamic country and at 35 years old, one of the youngest world leaders. Two years later, Benazir Bhutto was dismissed by the President Ghulam Khan and the Nation Assembly was dissolved – a feature of the Pakistani constitution, the eighth amendment, provided the executive these powers. In October 1990, Nawaz Sharif was elected and served as prime minister until 1993, when the Pakistani military forced him to resign. In 1993, Benazir Bhutto was reelected prime minister, and served until 1996, when President Sardar Leghari, at the direction of the military, dismissed Bhutto and dissolved the National Assembly. This time, Bhutto's husband, Asif Ali Zardari, was thrown in jail and Bhutto fled the country.[50]

In February 1997, Nawaz Sharif was elected prime minister, and he served until October 1999, when the army seized power and General Pervez Musharraf dissolved parliament (the National Assembly and the Senate). Musharraf ruled the country from 1999 to 2008, having declared himself president in 2001, and was elected by referendum in April 2002. He was reelected as president in October 2007 (each presidential term is five years), and that same month Benazir Bhutto returned to Pakistan to run for prime minister in the upcoming elections. Bhutto's convoy was attacked by a suicide bomber on the way from the airport to Karachi – she survived, but over 100 bystanders were killed. In November, Musharraf declared a national emergency, suspending the constitution, arresting his opponents and dismissing the Supreme Court judges, putting them all under house arrest. In December 2007, Musharraf lifted the state of emergency and reinstated the constitution. In late December while attending an election rally, Benazir Bhutto was assassinated by a suicide bomber, which killed an additional 20 innocent bystanders. Elections were held in February 2008, in which Musharraf's party retained only 17 percent of the seats in parliament, and PPP member Syed Gilain was elected prime minister. Under threat of impeachment, Musharraf resigned in August 2008, and in September Asif Ali Zardari (Bhutto's husband and PPP member) was elected president.[51]

In May 2013, national elections were held, and Nawaz Sharif was elected prime minister. One month later, Sharif declared his intent to charge Musharraf with treason on account of the 2007 suspension of the constitution and dissolution of the Supreme Court (formal charges were handed down in December 2013), and in August 2013, a Pakistani court indicted Musharraf for the assassination of Benazir Bhutto. With multiple delays in the trials, and Musharraf escaping to Dubai to avoid trial, he was finally found guilty of treason in December 2019 in absentia because of his continued delays and evasion of the law. The court sentenced Musharraf to death for his crimes, regardless of his absence and inability to offer a defense in his behalf. Pakistan's military reacted strongly to the verdict and sentence, calling it transgression of Pakistan's values of culture, humanity and religion.[52]

In 2018, Imran Khan was elected prime minister of Pakistan. His administration had several former Musharraf associates in his cabinet, and it was aligned with the military. Khan's attorney general called the Musharraf verdict and sentence unfair, and he would work to support Musharraf's appeals all the way to the Supreme Court. In January 2020, Musharraf's conviction was overturned, and he is now free to return to Pakistan. Khan's leadership ability has been questioned recently, due to his handling of COVID-19 and the economy. The pandemic has struck Pakistan with the third highest test positivity in the world, and Khan initially publicly intimated that the disease was no worse that the flu. In addition, Pakistan's economic performance has been dismal, with a negative GDP growth rate and an emphasis on military spending in the budget. On a rare occasion in front of the National Assembly, Khan said the United States had "martyred" Osama bin Laden in the May 2011 raid on bin Laden's compound in Abbottabad, Pakistan, and that Pakistan's support of the United States in the war on terror was a mistake. What should be obvious to the current administration in Washington is that any dependency or expectation of support from the Khan administration in Pakistan would be a mistake.[53]

While the United States is the primary destination for Pakistan exports, Pakistan receives most of its imports from China. Pakistan is one of the largest participants in the Belt and Road Initiative (BRI) with China, which the Pakistanis hope will provide economic stimulus and much needed investment in their country of some 220 million people. Pakistan is the fifth most populous country in the world, and the fifth most vulnerable to climate change. There are glaciers in the mountainous regions in the northwest that could melt by up to two thirds, releasing thousands of gallons of snowmelt causing massive flooding, bursting dams, and topsoil erosion. In addition, monsoons off the Arabian Sea to the southwest are more severe every year, causing flooding, crop damage, and death, in addition to billions of rupees worth of economic loss.[54]

A nuclear power, Pakistan confronts its greatest enemy India in a struggle over the Kashmir area north of India (both countries claim ownership). Because India is also a nuclear power the potential for catastrophe is immense. Pakistan has a history of harboring terrorists, and Taliban activities in Pakistan as well as Taliban influence on Hindu-Muslim relations with India are major concerns and potential sparks for global war.

Russia

Russia is a country with which we have had a nuanced relationship, both positive and negative, since the 1800s: from support of the Russian czars against European aggression in the 1850s, to the purchase of Alaska in 1867, to an ally during World War II and then an enemy during the Cold War. With the advent of perestroika and glasnost in the late 1980s and the breakup of the Soviet Union, it seemed our two countries were on a path of reconciliation and friendship. That opportunity seems to have passed since the election of Vladimir Putin as Russian president. Putin is following the route of China's Xi, in pursuit of a leader-for-life communist government. From June 25 through July 1, 2020, Putin held a referendum on various constitutional amendments, one of which was a "reset" of his term as president. This reset effectively allows him to stay in power until 2036, which would make him the longest serving president in Russia's history (at which point he would be 84 years old). At that point, what would keep him from resetting his term and serving another 16 years?[55]

Power politics are a part of Putin's character. As a result of the Maiden Revolution in February 2014, which pushed out Ukrainian President Yanukovych, Russian forces invaded and occupied the Ukrainian peninsula of Crimea. On March 16, in an annexation and acquisition of land reminiscent of Hitler's pre-World War II activities in Europe, a Crimean referendum occurred offering two options: become a part of Russia or an independent (non-Ukrainian) state. Within a week, the Russian legislature (Duma) passed a law admitting Crimea into the Russian Federation, and Russian ownership of Crimea was a *fait accompli*. The international community protested, 100 countries of the United Nations declaring the referendum invalid.

Furthermore, economic sanctions were imposed on Russia, and Russia was also suspended from the Group of Eight (G8) – Canada, France, Germany, Italy, Japan, Russia, United Kingdom, and United States – which was subsequently renamed the Group of Seven (G7) when Russia officially left the organization in 2017.[56]

More recently, Russia has been actively supporting the brutal dictatorship in Syria, where more than a half million people have been killed or are missing and presumed dead. In the nine-year civil war that started after the "Arab Spring" in March 2011, over half of the population of the country has been displaced, with nearly six million refugees fleeing to other countries and an additional six million removed from their homes and living in other areas within the country. In 2015, Syrian President Bashar al-Assad asked Russia President Putin for support in suppressing the uprising and civil strife, and Russia responded with air strikes in support of the Syrian government. This escalation in the war, both on the part of the Syrian/Russian/Iranian forces and the coalition of rebel forces consisting of the Syrian Democratic Forces (SDF) supported by the United States, Saudi Arabia, and Turkey caused a spike in refugee movement whereby approximately one million of the six million displaced Syrians sought refuge in countries across Europe. This European migration became a political football and a flash point of controversy, as immigration became a serious issue in several countries of the European Union.[57]

In addition to the overt influence Putin is exerting in Ukraine and Syria, Russian operatives are also attempting to surreptitiously subvert democratic processes within the United States and other countries. Russia was recently sanctioned by the United States Treasury Department for election interference in the 2020 election, based upon a Treasury Department press release dated September 10, 2020 that identified Andrii Derkach, Artem Lifshits, Anton Andreyev, and Darya Aslanova as Kremlin- and/or Internet Research Agency (IRA)-linked actors seeking to undermine the U. S. democratic process.[58]

As opposed to the mass hacking and public distribution of private documents during the 2016 presidential campaign, Russian operatives are performing more sophisticated techniques to modify voter behavior, including fomenting conspiracy theories, echoing claims of mail-in voter fraud, and distributing doctored audio and video files via social media. They are also spreading misinformation, fear, and hate by stirring up emotions on both sides of the issues from anti-Israeli causes to Black Lives Matter issues, leveraging racism and hate as a means to impact voter participation and sow seeds of discontent.[59]

Syria

As Syria's President Bashar al-Assad winds down his nine-year civil war against the rebel Syrian Democratic Forces (SDF), many challenges face this war-torn nation. Fighting continues against the insurgent Islamic State (IS) extremists, 98 percent of whose once-claimed lands are now occupied by either SDF or Iraqi security forces. Active military elements from multiple external organizations (Iran, Russia, Turkey, Saudi Arabia, and the United States) raise the potential for escalation in military activities because they work toward cross-purposes. On August 25, 2020, near Dayrick in northeast Syria, an incident occurred between the Russian and U. S. military — a Russian military vehicle deliberately rammed a U. S. Mine-Resistant Ambush Protected (MRAP) vehicle causing minor injuries to the MRAP occupants. The United States deescalated the conflict by leaving the area, but the potential for escalation of conflict between major military powers is a significant risk.[60]

Syria's civil war has also caused a humanitarian and civilian refugee crisis in the region, as 12 million displaced Syrians – 55 percent of the pre-war population of the country – are now either in refugee camps within the country or have fled to neighboring nations in search of peace. The majority of the refugees – 3.6 million Syrians – crossed their northern border into Turkey. Another 949,000 refugees flooded Lebanon, a small (~4,000 square miles) and densely populated (~1,500 per sq. mi.) country on the Mediterranean Sea. Jordan has absorbed another 672,000, while Iraq has received 250,000. This large influx of refugees will tax and weaken the services and economies of these countries and put further strain on an already fragile region of the world.[61]

Syria also teeters towards economic collapse as inflation has skyrocketed and its currency has devalued. Syria's economy has been reduced by about two thirds (67 percent) since before the war, and the value of the Syrian pound – worth about two cents ($0.02) before the war – has fallen by 98.6 percent and is now worth $0.0003. On social media platform posts, Syrians have started using their currency as cigarette paper and smoking it. As poverty and joblessness increase, so does the risk of further civil unrest, and protests about the economic situation have already occurred in the southeast. Government security forces are also imprisoning citizens who document their dissatisfaction on social media. Even the Syrian government is cash strapped and is arm-twisting Syrian tycoons and business leaders for financial assistance in paying for government services. When Rami Makhlouf, a Syrian telecommunications tycoon, openly complained about the practice on Facebook, the Syrian government froze his assets, fined him $180 million, and barred him from future government contracts.[62]

In June 2020, new sanctions went into effect in the United States that target anyone who does business with the Syrian government. These sanctions have been extremely effective in cutting off the flow of funding and export to Syria, especially for aircraft parts and oil industry, engineering, and construction services. The sanctions have been so effective, that Yuri Borisov, the Russia Deputy Prime Minister, said it was "strangling" Syria, and that it was effectively a blockade. Borisov also said that in December 2020, he would be signing a trade agreement in Damascus to provide new economic relationships between the two countries.[63]

Any of the above-mentioned areas of potential conflict could be the spark that ignites the next global conflict, and the United States needs to be militarily, economically, and politically prepared to handle this potential eventuality.

CHAPTER 16

The Next Great Legacy

As highlighted in the previous chapter, the United States is facing many threats and challenges, any one of which (or even more likely multiple numbers of them) may occur. Such events will provide a crucible in which will be forged the next great leader of our country, just as the prior great presidents experienced their own trials by fire. This experience will provide an extreme test of the mettle of that president, and by proving his or her worth, the next great president will go down in history as one of the greatest in our country's history, to be compared to George Washington, Abraham Lincoln, and Franklin Roosevelt. By guiding us through the next national tragedy or major world conflict, our next great leader will help us believe in ourselves and our mission and will deliver us into our next epoch of world leadership. The legacy this leader will leave is that the United States can be counted on in times of worldwide crisis, as the world expects and as we as a nation have delivered for the last 100 years (since World War I).

The myriad global issues presented to the next great president are going to require global solutions. The next great president should not "go it alone" with respect to the positions he takes on these issues but rather should work with other nation's leaders to effect mutually agreeable implementations. The word most apt to be used for this situation is "coalition" — one taken from the multi-nation stance that President George H. W. Bush took against Iraq's invasion of Kuwait. The global effects of climate change will require truly global solutions, and the two largest contributors to carbon dioxide emissions, China and the United States, are going to need to work together to determine cooperative ways for reducing their carbon footprints. In the current environment of Chinese-American relations it is difficult to envision our two countries working together to solve global issues, but that is what will be necessary to tackle the most significant issues facing our future.

While global issues may seem paramount, domestic issues will also need to be addressed, because this country is currently going through the most divisive time in our history since the Civil War. A means of addressing the social contract between our government and its people should be at least as important as battling international issues like climate change. Civil rights, economic opportunity, and education should be common rights for all citizens, but before that can be an objective, basic needs such as healthcare, housing, food and water need to be addressed. While not a cause of the issue, the coronavirus has illuminated the fact that basic food needs are not being met for 12 percent of the people in this country.[1] If that can occur here in the richest, most powerful country in the world, imagine what it says about hunger globally.

A new social contract will be necessary to redress the issues currently being protested in the streets of cities across America. A critical component of this contract will be to employ a new civil rights act to expand existing legislation, to provide expression thereof and resolve the grievances involved. In addition, new economic opportunities for the disenfranchised should be provided in order to open a path for all to achieve the fulfillment of their highest purpose. Education is often the means to that end, but college tuition has spiraled so high that a college degree has ceased to be a realizable goal for many, and to that end some necessary and long overdue reforms are inevitable. Political reforms are also long overdue, and to achieve the national unity that is the hopeful outcome of the coming crisis, these reforms will also be necessary and inevitable.

Climate Agreements

Climate discussions on the part of the United Nations (UN) occurred in May 1992 at a historic summit in Rio de Janeiro, Brazil (called the Rio Earth Summit). One of the results of the summit was a set of agreements called the UN Framework Convention on Climate Change (UNFCCC), which documents that human activities resulting in greenhouse gases are contributing to climate change, and that changes in the earth's climate are a concern for all of mankind. The framework went into effect in 1994, 90 days after the 50th country ratified the agreement, and the ratifiers of the agreement would thence be named the Conference of the Parties (COP). Although the agreement did not require the signatories to meet specific emission reduction targets, it did require (at a minimum) annual meetings of the COP members and exchange of information between the parties.[2]

In December 1997, the third meeting of the COP took place in Kyoto, Japan. The agreements reached in this conference were codified in a multi-national treaty called the Kyoto Protocol. Article 3 of the agreement states that the parties involved will reduce their greenhouse gas emissions per the amounts determined in the appendix, with a goal of reducing emissions to five percent below their 1990 levels by 2012. The agreement also provides provisions for multiple countries to combine their emission totals and reduction amounts to meet their combined goals, or transfer or acquire reductions in order to meet their reduction goals (which would later be referred to as "cap and trade" of emissions). With a change of presidential administrations, the United States withdrew from the Kyoto Protocol in March 2001, on account of economic considerations.[3]

Between 1998 and 2015, there were 17 more meetings of the Conference of the Parties (COP), without significant progress or agreements. During that time, worldwide temperatures increased, and the decade of the 2000s went down in history as the warmest ever recorded. At COP21 in Paris, held from November 30 to December 11, 2015, over 190 countries committed to emission reduction goals. The agreement allows countries to set their own emission reduction targets, and for the first time includes developing countries in the emission reduction goals. The overarching goal of this summit was to limit the global temperature increase to below two degrees Celsius over the historical average. The agreement was set to become effective in November 2016, and that progress towards its goals (called the global stocktake) was to be evaluated every five years starting no later than 2023. With a change of presidential administrations in 2017, the United States withdrew from the Paris accords, once again citing economic considerations.[4]

With such limited progress in meeting emission reduction targets, and the whipsaw effect of the largest contributor of greenhouse gasses (the United States) alternating between joining and withdrawing from these agreements as the political winds favor one political party or the other, a more effective approach to addressing the climate change issue is necessary. It will take the political leadership of the next great president, combined with a global alliance of its largest contributors to the problem (United States, China, India, and other developed nations), to agree to and enforce more stringent and effective agreements toward reductions in greenhouse gas emissions, and new technologies and methodologies for eliminating or arresting carbon dioxide and methane gasses in the air. This would be an incredible legacy and a gift to future generations of Americans and the world.

Global Environmentalism

America's environmentalist movement in the 1960s and 1970s that drove the creation of the National Environmental Policy Act, the Clean Air Act, the Clean Water Act, and the Endangered Species Act, was in part driven by the 1962 book *Silent Spring* by Rachel Carson. This non-fiction book describes and documents the adverse environmental and human health effects of the over-use of pesticides, especially in agricultural use. The book described how pesticides permeate the land, water, and air, and how they are absorbed into the foods we eat, with possible harmful effects (such as cancer – many herbicides are known carcinogens, and Carson herself died of breast cancer at age 56, less than two years after her book was published). The book's chapter on DDT (dichlorodiphenyltrichloroethane), which was a well-known and overly used pesticide for elimination of mosquitoes and other insects, led to the national ban of its use in the United States. Carson's book is also credited with the creation of an environmental movement in the United States, which led to the Congressional acts named above.[5]

More recently, researchers have been investigating the link between biodiversity loss and pathogens like COVID-19. A new study discussed in the periodical *Nature* states that there is growing evidence that deforestation and species extinction can lead to infectious disease outbreaks, because the species that tend to survive (rats and bats) are mammals that are more likely to transmit pathogens to humans. Research has shown that cross-over diseases like SARS (severe acute respiratory syndrome), avian flu, and swine flu are occurring more frequently owing to the conversion of rain forest and other wilderness areas to domesticated and populated regions, thus increasing the contact and interaction between humans and animals. An essay published in *Science* called for action by governments and the international community to control deforestation and eliminate the wildlife trade (the illegal sale of wild and typically rare animals) in order to limit or minimize the risk of future coronavirus-like global diseases. The group of interdisciplinary scientists who published that essay previously worked to track transmission of the Ebola virus in Africa to determine risk areas for potential outbreaks, which accurately predicted where future transmissions would occur.[6]

Pollution and pandemics are only two of the problems that neglect of the environment has on local, national, and global levels. Reduction in biodiversity also affects food supply, specifically that related to the fishing industry, as ocean temperatures rise causing coral "bleaching" and the death of marine habitats around the world. Coral reefs are extremely biodiverse, with thousands of marine animals dependent upon them for shelter, protection, and spawning. Different types of fish, turtles, crab, shrimp, starfish, jellyfish, and other species are dependent upon this ecosystem. In an effect that is similar to deforestation, elimination of coral reefs and their ecosystems causes a domino effect of mass marine species extinction. The National Oceanic and Atmospheric Association (NOAA) estimates that between 2014 and 2017, 30 percent of the world's coral reefs died due to bleaching caused by heat stress. These types of bleaching events put the food security and livelihoods of over 500 million people at risk.[7]

The future is not yet written, but the path we are currently on leads us to an uninhabitable planet. Unless things drastically change, future Americans and human civilization itself could be in for dire consequences. We simply cannot keep consuming millions of acres of nature and replacing it with concrete jungles, or even farmland – that is an unstainable future. We also cannot allow the continued rise in greenhouse gas emissions to continue to raise ocean water temperatures, causing coral whiteout – that is an unsustainable future also.

Global Democratization

Over the past 200 years, democracy has been on the rise. From a minor fraction of the world population in the early 1800s, the worldwide number of people currently living in democracies now exceeds over 50 percent of the global population.[8] With the exception of a dip in the 1940s when the overall percentage dropped to as low as ten percent due to the Axis powers conquering democratic countries during World War II, the democratic form of government has been on a steady rise. The flip side of that coin is that there are still billions of people living under autocratic or totalitarian regimes. And there is no guarantee that the trend towards democratization will continue. As presented in a previous chapter on the coming crisis, several countries have embraced totalitarianism and the "leader for life" approach to political organization.

In her 2018 book *Fascism, A Warning*, former U. S. Secretary of State Madeleine Albright expresses concern that the world is affected by these changes, as other world leaders copy what works and what other leaders can invoke without reprisal. In what she terms a "herd mentality," this could lead a global trend to an anti-democratic direction. She believes that: "Fascism and Fascist policies pose a more virulent threat to international freedom, prosperity, and peace than at any time since World War II."[9]

The most populous democratic nation in the world is India. It has maintained this democracy since it separated from British colonial oversight in 1947. Its politics, like America's, is messy, local, and argumentative. Its society is in some ways reflective of American society – with a fascination of Hollywood (with their own version called Bollywood), consumerism (second in consumption only to America), and an emphasis on capitalism. Like America, India is a country of many different nationalities and cultures; its diversity reflects the global community so that it should be natural to embrace multinational solutions to global issues. Unlike other countries, India also has a positive view of America, according to the Pew Global Attitudes Survey. In addition, many Indians have either visited America or have relatives in America (or both), and we share a common language and worldview. For all these reasons, the United States should have an active partnership with India relative to addressing global issues, from climate change to pandemics to national and international defense (particularly concerning shipping lanes).[10]

The United States should be promoting democratic governments, because democracy promotes stability. Stability should be a long-term goal, because stable governments don't present the type of international issues described in the prior chapter such as civil war, refugee crises, and nuclear proliferation. In addition to promoting democratic governance throughout the world, the United States should promote strategic collaboration with our existing partnerships with Japan, Europe, and the Commonwealth nations as a means of promoting stability and economic growth globally. By joining with Canada, the U. K, the European Union, India, Australia, New Zealand, South Korea and Japan, the United States has nearly contiguous coverage of the globe in terms of defense and force projection in addition to unity with the majority of the democratic industrialized countries of the world. With those relationships in the fold, America should be better suited to handling potential global conflicts in the future – and to deal with the imperialistic actions of Russia or China attempting to subjugate Ukraine or Taiwan, respectively (theoretically, of course). Finally, the United States also needs to do a better job of improving relationships with its next-door neighbors in Central America. By improving our relationships and providing a more reasoned and balanced approach to the immigration and refugee issues that currently exist, the United States could effectively manage the risks associated with these issues before they become full-blown crises.[11]

Industrial Evolution

The Fourth Industrial Revolution (4IR) is coming, or may well be already here, and we all need to be prepared to adapt and evolve to the coming changes in productivity, jobs, skills needed, and pay inequality. As described by Klaus Schwab, founder and chairman of the World Economic Forum, the three previous industrial revolutions were based on steam power (1IR), electrical power (2IR), and computer power (3IR) to mechanize, distribute, and automate production. Schwab also states that 4IR will impact business, government and people in new and profound ways. The impact on business will be in its disruption of value chains, squeezing out middle players and providing a more direct interface between producers and consumers. The impact on government will also be to provide a more direct engagement between citizens and their governments, with a need for governments to become more responsive to demands for change. The impact on people will be to their employment and employability, with an emphasis on highly educated/highly skilled workers, while low-skill positions will continue to be automated and eliminated.[12]

The coronavirus pandemic has emphasized how digitization and the Fourth Industrial Revolution will affect our present and future lives. Instead of decades to process and adapt to 4IR changes, people, business, and governments are being driven to accelerate their conversion in the space of less than a year. People with high-skill positions have been able to work virtually from the safety of their homes during the shutdown, while those who worked with their hands or directly with customers have been either unable to work or had to risk their health to work. Companies and organizations that were prepared for the digital era have been able to thrive, while taking advantage of lower overhead costs, including passing along certain costs (electricity, water, consumables, etc.) to their virtual employees. The future will be more data-driven, with a need for more scientists, engineers and software developers to create and take advantage of new technologies. The key will be expanding and maintaining the computing infrastructure to handle the demand created by increasing numbers of data consumers and interfaces to that infrastructure.[13]

The Fourth Industrial Revolution will require industrial evolution on the part of the United States to meet the challenges of its disruptions and to take advantage of the economic opportunities it presents. This will necessitate a highly educated workforce, a need that will require changes in our education system. There will also be a need for legislative changes and budget priorities to facilitate this change; otherwise there will be a missed opportunity to capture the momentum of the driving force for change and adaptation to the realities of 4IR.

Civil Rights Act Redux

Jim Crow laws mandated racially segregated public facilities (white and black) throughout the South after the Civil War. The Supreme Court upheld these laws with its "separate but equal" ruling in 1896. These laws stayed in effect until the Civil Rights Act of 1964 overruled them, outlawing discrimination on the basis of race, color, religion, sex or national origin. This meant that segregation in businesses (e.g., hotels, restaurants, and theatres) or public places (e.g., public schools, swimming pools, and libraries) was illegal. The act also promoted equal employment opportunities by making it illegal to discriminate when making hiring decisions. Although inequality issues and race relations have improved since the days of separate white and black bathrooms, bars, and restaurants, to quote former President Barack Obama, "Better isn't good enough."[14]

The thousands of protests in cities throughout this country since the death of George Floyd represents the latest chapter of African-American struggle for equality in America. This struggle has been marked by several generationally repeated conflicts, as pressure builds until it is eventually released by violence and protest. Let's look back over the past 100 years for common threads through these events.

As a result of the Great Migration, six million blacks from rural areas in the South moved to northern and western states in search of opportunity and relief from oppression. This migration took place in multiple waves over several decades (between 1916 and 1970) and was associated with the availability of manufacturing jobs or other work during wartime (World War I, World War II, and the Vietnam War). As blacks moved into majority white areas in the North and competed for jobs, whites predictably reacted with violence. In 1919, with the country recovering from World War I, veterans looking for work and the Spanish flu pandemic being in full swing, the heat of the summer season saw an explosion of tempers as racial violence broke out in 25 cities and towns throughout the country. The second wave of migration started in the 1940s, as booming military production for World War II provided opportunities that attracted additional movement to industrial areas in the North and West. By 1943, housing and employment scarcity induced another wave of race riots, with mobs of angry white men roaming black neighborhoods and clashes occurring in over 240 cities nationwide that year. In the 1960s, an economic boom reduced unemployment to four percent and additional demand for labor in the industrialized North. The 1960s were also a time of civil rights activism, anti-war protests, and government repression. The summer of July 1967 exploded into race riots across the country – 163 cities burned and were looted, and police and military troops beat and killed dozens of protestors and rioters in many of these cities.[15]

Voting rights were strengthened in 1964 by the 24th Amendment to the Constitution, which eliminated poll taxes or the payment of any other tax as a requirement to vote. Similar to the Civil Rights Act, the Voting Rights Act of 1965 prohibited discrimination on the basis of race or color; it eliminated illegal literacy tests or other impediments intended to block or nullify minorities' ability to vote and was intended to enforce the Fifteenth Amendment of the Constitution. The Voting Rights Act came about as a direct result of television coverage of the nonviolent protests and marches between Selma and Montgomery, Alabama. The country was outraged by the violent use of force by Alabama state police against protestors who were peacefully demonstrating in what would later be called "Bloody Sunday."[16]

The Civil Rights Act of 1964 needs to be strengthened to eliminate systemic discrimination in the judicial system and provide more equitable treatment of minorities by the local police forces of our country. Police forces throughout the nation need to be equipped with non-lethal methods for handling conflict, but there also needs to be the ability for peace officers to protect themselves. One of the biggest issues confronting society today is the level of distrust and fear on both sides of the line. In an effort to reduce that level of distrust, it may be appropriate to require representation of the ethnic groups being policed in a specific area by a proportional number of people of that ethnic group. The states' rights versus federal rights debate would contest this concept, as funding for local police forces comes from the individual communities themselves. Another area appropriate for review with respect to an amended or new civil rights law would be voter rights.

The Voter Rights Act of 1965 was landmark legislation for civil rights in that it prohibited discrimination on the basis of race at the ballot box, but challenges to this act in Supreme Court rulings recently and in the future could significantly impact its effectiveness. This is another area ripe for contention, because voter registration and polling management has typically been a local responsibility. However, voter suppression and marginalization of minorities is effectively achieved by tactics aiming at these goals, for representation is power – a power only achieved through the ballot box. An amendment to the Voter Rights Act is currently working its way through Congress. House Resolution 4 (HR4), the Voting Rights Advancement Act of 2019, was approved by the House, and is currently working its way through the Senate. The intent of this bill is to strengthen judicial oversight of areas in the country that have been repeat offenders of voter rights. It remains to be seen if this bill will pass the Republican dominated Senate.

A New Social Contract

The existing social contract between our government and its people is currently broken for some, and this breakage certainly needs to be addressed on a national scale. The thousands of people marching in the streets with Black Lives Matter placards are complaining about decades of persistent and systemic bias and attitudes that marginalize and discount the needs and social station of minorities. Healthcare, education, and economic opportunity are three areas where minorities don't get a fair shake owing to historical migration of minorities from farming activities in the South to manufacturing jobs in the North, and owing to the redlining of those minorities in poorer neighborhoods that eliminated the opportunity to receive guaranteed government mortgages. The "redlining" term comes from Federal Housing Administration (FHA) officials drawing red lines around minority areas as too risky to guarantee loans. This is admittedly a historical issue, but over decades those prior practices could amount to significant loss of accumulated capital and inheritable wealth. These days, when it comes to potential clients, real estate agents are taught to only recognize the color green – as in the color of and opportunity to make money.[17]

Another aspect of the social contract between a government and its people is that the people have conferred their consent to be governed and will abide by the government's laws. In this agreement, the right balance must be struck between individual rights and the needs and rights of the many. If there is enough common ground, then common-sense rules should apply. If it has been proven that wearing masks in public can reduce the mass transmission of pandemic diseases like coronavirus, then requiring masks to be worn in public should be viewed as a necessary and appropriate requirement for the greater good.

For some reason, a significant proportion of the population in America has viewed compulsory mask-wearing as an infringement on their personal freedoms. Be that as it may, there are reasons why laws are on the books – to maintain order and provide rules that all should abide by. As it is, the pandemic is disproportionally affecting the black community at a rate more than double that of the white and Asian ethnic groups, and almost double that of the Hispanic and Native American groups with respect to number of deaths per 100,000 people. These statistics point to the reality that minorities, and especially African-American people, have less access to healthcare and live in poorer neighborhoods with poorer air quality.[18]

A new social contract needs to be written between the government and the governed. This new contract needs to fulfill the basic needs of all its citizens, including housing, food, water, healthcare, and clothing. A well-known psychology theory proposed by Abraham Maslow states that there is a pyramid of needs to self-fulfillment. At the bottom of this pyramid are the basic physical and safety needs of humans that must be met before they are motivated to reach for the higher levels. These basic needs are food, water, shelter, safety and security. By providing these basic necessities, the people of the United States will be able to further their pursuits of life, liberty and happiness in the manner that best suits their goals and desires.

Beyond the basic necessities, the country would benefit from two additional goals on the national agenda: education and economic opportunity. These goals go hand in hand, because furthering a person's education usually results in more and better economic opportunities or at least the capability to achieve a better result when it comes to pursuing those opportunities. America needs an educated workforce to compete in the global marketplace, and by providing better educational foundations and opportunities for learning, our country will receive the economic benefit of an improved offering of goods and services and an increase in economic output (GDP).

Affordable Housing

Housing is a basic element in Maslow's hierarchy of needs – without housing, it is very difficult for a person to become a functioning, useful member of society. The United States Department of Housing and Urban Development (HUD) provides funding to states and building owners for facilitating low-income housing opportunities to those in need. It has three types of programs to provide these services: privately owned subsidized housing, public housing projects, and voucher programs for housing. Subsidized housing provides housing to tenants at reduced rents for low-income individuals and families – landlords are paid directly by the government to make up the difference. Public housing is apartments or rental houses that are state-owned and provide housing to people with disabilities, senior citizens, and low-income families. The Housing Choice Voucher Program (formerly known as Section 8) is a program that provides assistance to low-income families, seniors, and people with disabilities by paying part or all of the rent, based on need.[19]

The coronavirus pandemic is exacerbating an already stressed housing system in need of additional supply. There was already a national shortage of seven million homes for low-income families a year ago, before the pandemic started, and now as state-mandated eviction moratoriums expire, even more families are in need of subsidized housing due to loss of income and hospitalizations. This crisis hits at a time when housing projects are stalled on account of a multitude of factors as builders, state and local budgets and local planning departments are not able to get new deals done because of the pandemic and its resulting uncertainty. Although this does not impact existing projects in the pipeline or nearly competed, the outlook doesn't look good beyond 2021. The irony is that 2019 was the first year city budgets had fully recovered from the Great Recession, and 2020 and beyond are looking like there will be significant shortfalls in tax revenue nationwide.[20]

The National League of Cities (NLC) Fiscal Conditions report for 2020, a survey of 485 cities, towns, and villages across the nation, provides insight into how the pandemic is affecting the financial health of America's cities, and the results of the report are shocking. Nearly 80 percent of the respondents believe their tax base will be less able to meet the financial needs of their cities in 2020, compared to 24 percent in 2019. In 2021, that number jumps to 90 percent of the finance officers indicating that their revenues will be less able to meet the fiscal needs of their communities. The responses for this 2020 survey are the highest values recorded since the Great Recession of 2008-2009. Large cities across the country are projecting budget shortfalls in the hundreds of millions of dollars in 2021, as both short-term (sales tax) and long-term (property tax) revenues will be impacted. Overall, city finance officers are expecting general fund revenues to decrease by 13 percent on average. These shortfalls will significantly impact state and local governments' ability to support affordable housing projects, and it will be up to the federal government, which is not restricted by the balanced budget requirements most local governments must meet, to make up the difference.[21]

Eliminating Hunger

As a primary element of Maslow's hierarchy of needs, access to water and affordable food has to exist before citizens are able to meaningfully pursue higher goals. Eliminating hunger throughout the United States should be an objective of government, and part of the overarching commitment between a government and its people (its social contract). As the number one exporter of food in the world, we should have the ability to feed our own people, and that should be an explicit goal. Another explicit goal should be reducing greenhouse gas (GHG) emissions created in the production of the food we do consume. The United States has been effective over the last 20 years in productivity, managing to increase production 30 percent while only increasing GHG by seven percent. But with the worldwide demand for food expected to increase over 50 percent by 2050, the ultimate challenge will be to further increase productivity and food output while *reducing* emissions. Is this even possible?[22]

There are a number of actions that U. S. farmers could take to both boost productivity and reduce emissions. Investments in education, technology, and methodologies have increased productivity for over four decades, and that investment should continue. In the future, the key will be to increase output while reducing footprint. Doing so will rely on the ability to provide the same or higher amounts of food and livestock while reducing land use acreage and then converting the unused agricultural land to forests by planting more trees.

Forests in the United States removed nearly 800 million tons of carbon dioxide in 2018 alone, enough to offset 12 percent of America's emissions. Another means of reducing farmland GHG emissions would be conversion of farm energy sources to solar and wind power. This would save on energy costs while helping to save the planet. One possibility would be to use the existing wind breaks of planted trees, or planting new rows, to channel wind for a Venturi effect that would increase wind speed delivered to a wind mill at the channel's end. Finally, one of the most significant opportunities to provide food to the hungry while still increasing production efficiency is to reduce food waste. By finding effective means to converting imperfect but edible foods from being thrown away by grocery stores and distribution centers to food which can feed the hungry, American farmers and the agriculture industry could continue to provide that overabundance the nation and the world expects.[23]

Government agricultural subsidies already provide over a half trillion dollars in the countries that provide over 65 percent of the global food and livestock, and half of that amount is currently being spent on price supports (in the form of duties on imports or domestic price minimums). Because the subsidies already exist, there is an opportunity to redirect the price support funds to more efficient applications. One would be enhancing efficiency by rewarding farmers who are able to produce the same or more food using fewer hectares of land; this would reward those who are being energy efficient and producing fewer emissions. Another would be providing clean energy sources such as wind farms or solar farms, or a direct investment in local solar panels on buildings and wind turbines on farmland. A third would be using a portion to pay for fallow land in order to keep the carbon dioxide locked up in that land and vegetation.[24]

Universal Healthcare

If your health is compromised, it is difficult to get much enjoyment out of life. Health affects all aspects of your life: your ability to work, to be a good parent, and to contribute to society. All of the industrialized countries of the world provide national health care to their citizens with one exception – the United States. Why is that objective so difficult to achieve in America?

Dr. Bruce Vladeck provided an often-cited article in the *American Journal of Public Health* that discussed these difficulties. In this article he explains five historical-cultural reasons and five political-structural reasons for this condition. Historically, Americans have been anti-government – many of the original colonialists arrived here to escape religious prosecution and later immigrants came here as a result of political upheaval and failed revolts. Americans do not have a history of any aristocracy, and the founding fathers were decidedly against the establishment of one, so America produced a culture of individuality and independence. There is no established labor party in the United States, and so there is no driving force to establish a national health insurance policy. Dr. Vladeck theorizes that the reason for the lack of a labor party is that there has been a history of free land in our nation, which has led to more property ownership and upward mobility. The final historical-cultural reason for no national health care in America is the historical racial divide in our country, which has inhibited a combined movement for universal coverage. The political-structural reasons for the lack of universal health care are: 1) our form of government, which divides power between the executive, legislative, and judicial branches; 2) the diversity of our geographically dispersed country, which localizes politics; 3) the weakness of our political parties owing to the division of power stated above; 4) the economic distribution of power in politics and how money drives policy; and 5) our political system that is designed to find the middle ground, which tends to make policy change difficult.[25]

Throughout the industrialized world, some countries have implemented successful universal health care, with equivalent and, in some areas, better results than the current American mixture of private and government-run (Medicare, Medicaid, and VA) insurance. Australia, Canada, France, Germany, Singapore, Switzerland, and the United Kingdom all provide lower-cost care and with a lower infant mortality rate than the United States. The only measure by which the United States provides better service is wait times for specialist care. The advantages of universal health care are: decreased overall health care costs; decreased administrative costs; service standardization; improved workforce health; improved child-care (preventing future costs); and fostering healthier choices through regulation. The disadvantages are: healthy people pay more than they otherwise would have; decreased incentive to stay healthy; longer wait time for specialist care; increased cost pressure on government budgets; and potential limitations on services for rare diseases.[26]

In these days of the coronavirus pandemic, the time has come to make the case for universal health care. With a precipitous drop in employment and loss of health coverage for millions of Americans just when they need it most, universal health care just makes sense. And with a history of health care costs rising faster than nearly any other indicator in the American economy, the probability of further cost increases due to the reduction in health care participants is almost a certainty.[27]

As more and more Americans lose their jobs, and with the possibility of a recession or sustained economic malaise on the horizon, millions of jobless workers may be forced to take that leap into entrepreneurial enterprises of self-employment just to make ends meet. Wouldn't it be a boon to the economy and personal industry to free those new businesses of the need to buy or provide health insurance, thus giving these new companies a competitive edge on par with the rest of the global industrialized countries?

Education Reform

Attempts at education reform over the past 20 years have failed. From "No Child Left Behind," "Race to the Top," and common core state standards to school choice, the billions of dollars spent on these programs have had minimal effect. Over the past ten years, the report card on education both domestically and internationally is flat from both the National Assessment of Educational Progress (NAEP) and the Program in International Student Assessment (PISA), the latter of which ranks the United States at or near the bottom of 30 industrialized countries. Education in the United States has been key for our economic development, and free primary and secondary education has been a given for decades. However, the education system in the United States is flawed. It is outdated and needs to change to provide the type of education necessary for students to excel and succeed in the 21st century.[28]

The reset needed at the primary (elementary school, grades K-6) and secondary (middle and high school, grades 7-12) education levels include changes to curriculum, better-trained teachers, and better pay for teachers in order to attract the best and brightest. In order to provide these improvements, changes need to be made to the teaching profession itself, in terms of qualification requirements and certifications, and merit-based pay for teachers throughout the country. In addition, the administration systems need a major overhaul, because the bloated bureaucracy of school administrations reduces the funding available to invest in the training and pay of the primary effective tool in increasing the performance of the students, namely the teachers. Finally, the recognized truth regarding the failure in the U. S. education system is that poor students get left behind. Poverty is the number one correlation to standardized test performance, as reflected in a bell curve of test scores versus family income. Wealth, or lack thereof (poverty), is the primary inhibitor to performance. This is reflected by correlation of performance and neighborhood, the lowest performances coming from neighborhoods of low property values, which are also the means (property taxes) by which local schools are typically funded. Accordingly, poorer neighborhoods should get supplementary federal funding for primary and secondary education in order to make up for funding differences.[29]

With respect to universities, there also needs to be a shakeup of the status quo. You might ask, why change a university system traditionally rated best in the world? The answer is that college has become is too expensive. Students are graduating from college with higher and higher debt loads, which is making it impossible for newly employed degreed professionals to make ends meet, even if they are fortunate enough to have a high paying job. There is a movement in leadership circles focusing on strengths-based approaches to management – people are happiest and most fulfilled when the tasks they are asked to complete or are assigned to are within their wheelhouse of ability and skill. This concept should be applied to education in order to provide free education to students who meet criteria for a certain ability in their nature, and then it would be up to the education system to maximize that ability. The other routes to a degree – student-athlete, scholarship, parental funding – should remain available to those who meet those criteria. One other avenue for reducing college costs should also be considered – low cost community college education that can serve as a conduit to state colleges or that are part of cooperative arrangements with specific universities to provide a pipeline of students.

By providing a resolution to our education crisis, the next great president would provide an education legacy in the manner of Washington, Lincoln, and Roosevelt and would earn the title of "the education president" – a moniker long sought by numerous preceding presidents.

Economic Opportunity

The Economic Opportunity Act (EOA) of 1964 spawned a myriad of programs for job creation, education, and training, and it also created the Office of Economic Opportunity (OEO) in the executive branch to be overseen and managed by the president. The EOA was a key element of President Johnson's War on Poverty, and it was effective in reducing poverty in the United States from over 19 percent of the population in 1964 to about 11 percent by the early 1973, its historic low. Considering the period from the approval of EOA in August 1964 to the ending of Johnson's term in January 1969, Johnson oversaw a reduction in poverty in America by nearly one third, which is a significant accomplishment by any measure. Its success should be a next great president's model for a similar program to reduce American poverty and inequality.[30]

Economic opportunity needs to be a centerpiece of any domestic agenda the next great president puts forth. Like President Johnson's "Great Society," this domestic agenda should address civil rights, housing, hunger, healthcare, education and poverty, providing a new social contract between the government and the American people. It should be a means for providing an environment in which everyone can be all that they can be, can strive to embody their goals and aspirations. There is an existing divide between the haves and the have-nots in this country, and there needs to be a way to provide a vision of the future in which every member of society can share in the success of the American economy. This vision, and the strategy to implement it, should be preloaded and ready to implement the day after the election, with expected impediments and their tactical solutions already resolved to push forward.[31]

America, once the land of opportunity, is no longer so for those who do not have the economic advantages of access to and familiarity with technology. This country has been the source of innovation in the Gig economy, and without the education necessary to be successful in this new economy, economic opportunities will be limited. There needs to be an equalizer and an ability to give everyone a chance to succeed so that "the land of opportunity" phrase can be understood to mean "the land of equal opportunity" until the economic success of every citizen can be achieved in our country. This is as important for the nation as it is for its people, because we must make the most of our human capital to compete in the 21st century.

Infrastructure Investment

Following in the footsteps of the last great president, Franklin Roosevelt, the United States should embark on a new program of infrastructure investment, both as a means to rebuild our crumbling infrastructure and as a way to employ inner city youths and other at-risk members of society to provide structure, teamwork, and skills development. This New Civilian Conservation Corps (NCCC) could perform valuable work in planting trees, clearing brush, and renovating dilapidated structures at existing National Parks, some of which have stood since the original CCC teams built them almost 90 years ago. Clearing brush in existing forests throughout the western United States would reduce the probability of additional massive wildfires that have recently hit California, Oregon, and Washington due to drought conditions. In addition, areas that have been impacted will need replanting and refurbishment, and burnt communities rebuilt.

America needs to put itself on the path to renewable energy sources and energy independence. One method of doing so is to create a New Work Projects Administration (NWPA) that would provide employment opportunities to people in need and an infusion of federal funds to states struggling with impacts of the coronavirus pandemic. These projects could include massive wind farms, solar energy fields, and improved hydroelectric facilities. Another area that needs to be addressed is a reinvestment in the massive projects that are still standing from the past: The Grand Coulee Dam, the Hoover Dam, and many others that are in need of refurbishment, maintenance or major overhauls.

Mass transit will help reduce our carbon footprint. An investment in bullet trains between major cities could reduce traffic on the major interstate highways in addition to reducing noise, pollution, and carbon dioxide emissions. Transition to renewable energy sources for all modes of transportation would also be a good step. California Governor Gavin Newsome recently established dramatic new requirements for the state's auto industry – zero emission vehicles (ZEV) for all new passenger cars sold in 2035 and thereafter. This path forward will not be possible unless there is a massive infusion of infrastructure investment that provides electrical chargers, compressed hydrogen, and/or recharging stations throughout the country, because the current limiting factor in any emission-free vehicle is its range. Electric or other emission-free vehicles will never be as readily accepted as an alternative to gasoline or diesel fueled vehicles until there are as many recharging stations on the streets and highways as there are the currently ubiquitous gas stations.[32]

Infrastructure investment is an important and useful tool that has been implemented by all of the progressive presidents, and particularly well by the greatest presidents. Washington invested in shipbuilding, from the ten original revenue cutters for the Coast Guard to the six frigates that were used to protect the United States and help defeat the British in the War of 1812. Lincoln invested in intercontinental railroads and other rail infrastructure, providing free land to homesteading families throughout the Midwestern plains, and in agricultural and engineering colleges throughout the country. Roosevelt invested in hydroelectric dams, airports, hospitals, schools, and other civic and government buildings throughout America, all to the benefit of existing and future generations of Americans.

Political Reform

Political engagement on social media is growing rapidly to the point where a majority of Americans (53 percent) are now civically active via social media platforms. Millennials are now a larger percentage of the American population than Baby Boomers, a fact that will have political implications, assuming the Millennials vote. Millennials will also soon overtake Boomers in the total number of voter-eligible members, assuming they register and vote. Democrats are more than twice as likely as Republicans to look up political information on social media. A majority of Americans (69 percent) also say that social media is an important tool for getting politicians to pay attention to the issues that are important, that social media is an important tool for creating sustained movements for social change (67 percent), and that these tools are vital to influencing policy decisions (58 percent). Will these trends translate to different political outcomes and a shift in political power in the future?[33]

Former President Barack Obama wrote *The Audacity of Hope*, published in 2006, that discussed, among other things, his experiences as a first-term Senator from Illinois. In a chapter called "Politics" he talks about the challenges facing Congressmen as they go about performing their duties and campaigning for votes. He addresses the issues facing today's legislators, and how they could potentially be addressed. According to Obama, the significant issues facing Congressional candidates are: gerrymandering, big money donors, special interest groups, and the media. Gerrymandering is the political practice by which the party in power manipulates district boundaries to obtain a distribution of voters that will ensure the incumbent party's power. Big money donors are the top 1 percent who procure outsized influence on account of their large campaign finance donations. Because it costs $15-20 million to buy the advertising it takes to win a Senate seat, the big money donors are able to put their candidates in a position to win. Special interests are the large organizations working to convince their members that one candidate or the other is an ally to their cause. These groups can represent labor unions, environmental causes, pro-choice, religious sects, gun rights activists, and anti-taxation causes. The media is the fourth and last of Obama's list. Positive press coverage is like free advertising in that it has the potential of reaching millions of viewers or readers. However, the media generally feels there is little to be gained by positive puff pieces, because controversy sells and controversy is what keeps ratings up, advertising revenue coming in, and viewer numbers or subscriptions growing.[34]

To address these issues, Obama recommended a list of political reforms that could — if there was enough resolve in Congress to change (and risk what they already have) — provide a more robust and fair political process. In order to increase election competitiveness and participation he recommended nonpartisan districting, weekend elections, and same-day voter registration. To reduce the effects of special interest groups and the involvement of big money donors, he recommended public campaign funding and free television and radio ads. To address the combative and negative media outlets, he recommended legislative process transparency; Congressional rules changes that provide minority legislative members more of a say in the process; and investigative reporting both on the details of the legislative process and on proposed laws as the proposed laws move through that process.[35]

National Unity

The country is currently more divided than at any other time in our history, with the possible exception of the Civil War period. At a time when there seems to be an exponential rise in the divisions and tensions throughout our nation, there also seems to be a vacuum of leadership and forces trying to bring the country together and help heal those divisions. One of the most visible divisions in our country is the racial divide — witness the demonstrations persisting on both sides of that debate — and it would be a point of greatest leverage to restore some semblance of a united front in the United States. The combination of topics previously discussed on civil rights, education, and economic opportunity provides solutions to help heal the divide, but an attack on the systemic issues associated with poverty (affordable housing, eliminating hunger, and providing healthcare) is also needed. If we could bridge the racial divide, then we will be able to move together as a country united in both culture and politics.[36]

It happened before, so it could happen again. A coalition of forces came together in the 1850s to create the Republican Party and provided a presidential candidate who would eventually reunite the country. Abraham Lincoln was able to unite us and refused to allow the country to break into two separate nations. He did this through his commitment to the Union, and through the just cause that was emancipation and the end of slavery. There is now that same opportunity to end the divisiveness that is roiling our cities and communities throughout the nation and to unite the country through inclusion and a common goal. We must come together to save our democracy, and that must be our common goal. This objective will require political, community, and business leaders throughout our nation to devote themselves to this singular goal. Without this leadership, the opportunity to unite America and fulfil its democratic ideals may fail, and we may no longer be viewed as the beacon of liberty and equality espoused in the Declaration of Independence.[37]

It will take the type of leadership that can provide a counterbalance to the divisiveness that is fraying America's social fabric to bring back that cohesiveness which will "bind up the nation's wounds" and provide a national unity. Who will be the person who could bring us back together? This is obviously a rhetorical question, because only time will tell when the next major crisis will hit and who will be in charge for better or worse to lead our country through that difficult time. It is up to us then, living in a democratic country that elects its leaders, to make sure that we put the right candidates in positions of authority, because it will take the right person in the right place at the right time to meet that crisis head on and successfully guide our country through to its subsequent resolution.

Epilogue

One may notice that a lot of the accomplishments necessary for the Next Great Legacy are similar to those of President Johnson's Great Society program. This is no coincidence. The Next Great President will be challenged by domestic issues similar in scope to the issues that confronted President Johnson as he took over leadership of our country following the assassination of President Kennedy. Johnson successfully pushed through Congress Kennedy's New Frontier agenda as a means to heal our country's emotional scars following the shocking death of a beloved president. Johnson's vision of a War on Poverty to fulfill the promise of America for the nation's poorest is a master blueprint of how the Next Great President could fulfill his destiny and ensure a lasting legacy.

Where President Johnson failed was in his international agenda, which sunk the United States deeper into a quagmire called the Vietnam War, a subject of many books, movies, and documentaries, and will not be discussed here. While there is no existing blueprint for how to define an international agenda to address our next international conflict, the chapter on The Next Great Crisis attempts to lay out potential sources of conflict, and the chapter on Parallel Lines, Pressures and Problems attempts to discuss potential approaches for handling both international and domestic issues, at least those that had some thread of commonality to the prior three Great Presidents.

As previously discussed, the Crisis of 2020 (or the 2020s) is nearly upon us. Let us pray that the person in the White House is up to the challenge when that time comes, and leads our country successfully into the next American epoch of global leadership and respect as the Next Great President of the United States.

Acknowledgements

I would like to thank my family and friends for their love and support. I would also like to thank Brooke C. Stoddard for his editing work and the insight and encouragement he has provided. Finally, I would like to thank Dave at JD&J Designs for the beautiful cover design and layout work.

About the Author

Edward Thomas
(at LOC in WDC)

Edward Thomas received a Master of Business Administration from the University of California in Irvine, California and was a National Merit Scholar at the University of Michigan in Ann Arbor, Michigan. This is his second in a planned trilogy of books about historical cycles. You can read his blog at www.EdwardThomasAuthor.com

Bibliography

Albright, Madeleine. *Fascism, A Warning*, 2018, HarperCollins Publishers, New York, New York

Allen, W. B. *George Washington, A collection*, 1988, LibertyClassics, a publishing imprint of Liberty Fund, Inc., Indianapolis, Indiana

Alter, Jonathan. *The Defining Moment, FDR's Hundred Days and the Triumph of Hope*, by 2006, Simon & Schuster, New York, New York

Angle, Paul M. and Miers, Earl Schenck. *The Living Lincoln, The Man, His Mind, His Times, and the War He Fought, Reconstructed from His Own Writings*, 1955, 1992, Marboro Books Corp., a division of Barnes & Noble, Inc., by arrangement with Rutgers University Press

Beard, Mary. *SPQR, A History of Ancient Rome*, 2015, Liveright Publishing Corporation, a Division of W.W. Norton & Company, New York, New York

Beschloss, Michael. *Presidential Courage, Brave Leaders and How They Changed America, 1789-1989*, 2007, Simon & Schuster, New York, New York

Blinder, Alan S. *After The Music Stopped, The Financial Crisis, the Response, and the Work Ahead*, by 2013, Penguin Press, New York, New York

Brands, H. W. T*raitor to his Class, The Privileged Life and Radical Presidency of Franklin Delano Roosevelt*, 2008, First Anchor Books, a division of Random House, Inc., New York, New York

Brookhiser, Richard. *Founding Father, Rediscovering George Washington*, 1996, The Free Press, a Division of Simon & Schuster, New York, New York

Bush, George W. *Decision Points*, 2010, Crown Publishers, a division of Random House, Inc., New York, New York

Caddick-Adams, Peter. *Monte Cassino, Ten Armies in Hell*, 2013, Oxford University Press, New York, New York

Catton, Bruce. *Never Call Retreat*, 1965, Doubleday & Company, Inc., Garden City New York

Catton, Bruce. *The Army of the Potomac: Mr. Lincoln's Army*, 1951, 1962, Doubleday & Company, Inc., Garden City, New York

Chernow, Ron. *Alexander Hamilton*, 2004, The Penguin Group, New York, New York

Chernow, Ron. *Washington, A Life*, 2010, The Penguin Press, New York, New York

Churchill, Winston S. Memoirs of the Second World War (abridged version of six volumes of The Second World War), 1959, Houghton Mifflin Company, Boston, Massachusetts

Clarke, Richard A. *Against All Enemies, Inside America's War on Terror*, 2004, Free Press, a division of Simon & Schuster, New York, New York

Clayton, Tim and Craig, Phil. *The End of the Beginning, From the Siege of Malta to the Allied Victory at El Alamein*, 2002, The Free Press, a division of Simon & Schuster, New York, New York

Collier, Peter with Horowitz, David. *The Roosevelts, An American Saga*, 1994, Simon & Schuster, New York, New York

Corsi, Jerome. *No Greater Valor, The Siege of Bastogne and the Miracle that Sealed Allied Victory*, 2014, Nelson Books, an imprint of Thomas Nelson, Nashville, Tennessee

Cuomo, Mario M. *Why Lincoln Matters, Today More Than Ever*, 2004, Harcourt, Inc., New York, New York

Davis, Kenneth S. *FDR, Into the Storm, 1937 – 1940*, 1993, Random House, New York, New York

Davis, Kenneth S. *FDR, The Beckoning of Destiny, 1882 – 1928*, 1971, 1972, G. P. Putnam's Sons, New York, New York

Davis, Kenneth S. *FDR, The New Deal Years, 1933 – 1937*, 1979, 1983, 1986, Random House, New York, New York

Davis, Kenneth S. *FDR, The New York Years, 1928 – 1933*, 1979, 1980, 1983, 1985, Random House, New York, New York

Davis, Kenneth S. *FDR, The War President, 1940 – 1943*, 2000, Random House, New York, New York

Davis, William C. *Stand in the Day of Battle*, 1983, Doubleday & Company, Inc., Garden City, New York

Detzer, David. *Dissonance, The Turbulent Days Between Fort Sumter and Bull Run*, 2006, Harcourt, Inc., Orlando, Florida

Donald, David Herbert. *Lincoln*, 1995, Simon & Schuster, New York, New York

Doolittle, James H. with Glines, Carroll V. *I Could Never Be So Lucky Again, An Autobiography*, 1991, Bantam Books, New York, New York

Durant, Will & Ariel. *The Age of Napoleon, A History of European Civilization from 1789 to 1815*, 1975, MJF Books, by arrangement with Simon & Schuster, Inc., New York, New York

Durant, Will and Ariel. *The Lessons of History*, 1968, Simon & Schuster, New York, New York

Eisenhower, Dwight D. *Crusade in Europe*, 1948, Doubleday & Company, John Hopkins Paperback edition, 1997, John Hopkins University Press, Baltimore, Maryland

Ellis, Joseph J. *American Creation, Triumphs and Tragedies at the Founding of the Republic*, 2007, Alfred A. Knopf, a division of Random House, Inc., New York, New York

Ellis, Joseph J. *His Excellency, George Washington*, 2004, Alfred A. Knopf, New York, New York

Fehrenbacher, Don E. *Lincoln, Speeches and Writings 1832 – 1858*, 1989, Library Classics of the United States, Inc., New York, New York

Flexner, James Thomas. *George Washington, And the New Nation (1793-1799)*, 1969, Little, Brown and Company, New York, New York

Flexner, James Thomas. *George Washington, Anguish and Farewell (1793-1799)*, 1969, Little, Brown and Company, New York, New York

Flexner, James Thomas. *George Washington, In The American Revolution (1775-1783)*, 1967-1968, Little, Brown and Company, New York, New York

Flexner, James Thomas. *George Washington, The Forge of Experience (1732-1755)*, 1965, Little, Brown and Company, New York, New York

Foner, Eric. *The Fiery Trial*, 2010, W.W. Norton & Company, Inc., New York, New York

Freehling, William W. *The Road to Disunion, Secessionists at Bay 1776-1854*, 1990, Oxford University Press, New York, New York

Gailey, Harry A. *The War in the Pacific, From Pearl Harbor to Tokyo Bay*, 1995, Presidio Press, Novato, California

Galbraith, John Kenneth. *The Great Crash 1929*, 1954, 1955, 1961, 1972, 1979, 1988, 1997, 2009, Mariner Books, Houghton Mifflin Harcourt, New York, New York

Garrary, John A. *The Great Depression: An Inquiry into the Causes, Course, and Consequences of the Worldwide Depression of the Nineteen-Thirties, as Seen by Comparison and in the Light of History*, 1986, Harcourt Brace Jovanovich Publishers, Orlando, Florida

Goleman, Daniel. *Emotional Intelligence, Why it can matter more than IQ*, 1995, Bantam Books, New York, New York

Goleman, Daniel. *Social Intelligence, The New Science of Human Relationships*, 2006, Bantam Books, New York, New York

Goodwin, Doris Kearns. *Leadership In Turbulent Times*, 2018, Simon & Schuster, New York, New York

Goodwin, Doris Kearns. *No Ordinary Time, Franklin and Elanor Roosevelt: The Home Front in World War II*, 1994, Schuster & Schuster, New York, New York

Goodwin, Doris Kearns. *Team of Rivals, The Political Genius of Abraham Lincoln*, 2005, Simon & Schuster, New York, New York

Gould, Lewis L. *Grand Old Party, A History of the Republicans*, 2003, Random House, Inc, New York, New York

Grant, Ulysses S. *The Personal Memoirs of Ulysses S. Grant*, 1885, Konecky & Konecky, Old Saybrook, Connecticut

Groom, Winston. *Shiloh, 1862*, 2012, National Geographic, Washington, D. C.

Guelzo, Allen C. *Lincoln and Douglas, The Debates that Defined America*, 2008, Simon & Schuster, New York, New York

Hachigian, Nina and Sutphen, Mona. *The Next American Century, How the U.S. Can Thrive as Other Powers Rise*, 2008, Simon & Schuster, Inc., New York, New York

Hagen, Jerome T. *War in the Pacific*, 1996, Hawaii Pacific University, Honolulu, Hawaii

Hamby, Alonzo. *Man of Destiny, FDR and the Making of the American Century*, 2015, Basic Books, a member of the Perseus Books Corp., New York, New York

Hillyard, Michael J. *Cincinnatus and the Citizen-Servant Ideal, The Roman Legend's Life, Times, and Legacy*, 2001, Xlibris Corporation, USA

Johnson, Clint. *Pursuit, The Chase, Capture, Persecution & Surprising Release of Confederate President Jefferson Davis*, 2008, Citadel Press Books, published by Kensington Publishing Corp., New York, New York

Jordan, Jonathan W. *American Warlords, How Roosevelt's High Command Led America to Victory in World War II*, 2015, NAL Caliber, published by the Penguin Group, New York, New York

Kershaw, Alex. *The First Wave, The D-Day Warriors Who Led the Way to Victory in World War II*, 2019, Dutton Caliber, an imprint of Penguin Random House LLC, New York, New York

Klein, Maury. *Days of Defiance: Sumter, Secession, and the Coming of the Civil War*, by 1997, Alfred A. Knopf, New York, New York

Langguth, A. J. *Patriots, The Men Who Started the American Revolution*, 1988, Simon & Schuster, New York, New York

Larson, Edward J. *The Return of George Washington, 1783-1789*, 2014, HarperCollins Publishers, New York, New York

Lee, Robert Edward. *Victory at Guadalcanal*, 1981, Presidio Press, Novato, California

Lincoln, Abraham. *Abraham Lincoln, Selected Writings*, compilation published by Barnes & Noble, Inc., 2013, Barnes & Noble, Inc., New York, New York

Lincoln, Abraham. *Abraham Lincoln, Selected Writings*, 2013, Barnes and Noble, Inc., New York, New York

Lincoln, Abraham. *Abraham Lincoln: Speeches and Writings 1859-1865; Speeches, Letters, Miscellaneous Writings Presidential Messages and Proclamations*, 1989, Volume arrangement, notes, and chronology by Library Classics of the United States, Inc., New York, New York

McCullough, David. *1776*, 2005, Simon & Schuster, New York, New York

McCullough, David. *John Adams*, 2001, Simon & Schuster, New York, New York

McCullough, David. *Mornings on Horseback, The Story of an Extraordinary Family, a Vanished Way of Life, and the Unique Child Who Became Theodore Roosevelt*, 1981, 2001, Simon & Schuster, Inc., New York, New York

McElvaine, Robert S. *The Great Depression, America, 1929-1941*, 1984, 1993, 2009, Three Rivers Press, an imprint of the Crown Publishing Group, a division of Random House, Inc., New York, New York

McPherson, James M. *Tried by War, Abraham Lincoln as Commander In Chief*, 2008, The Penguin Press, New York, New York

Meacham, Jon. *Thomas Jefferson, The Art of Power*, 2012, Random House, New York, New York

Moore, Kathryn. *The American President, A Complete History*, by 2007, Fall River Press, New York, New York

Morgan, Ted. *FDR, A Biography*, 1985, Simon & Schuster, New York, New York

Morris, Edmund. *The Rise of Theodore Roosevelt*, 1979, Random House, New York, New York

Morris, Edmund. *Theodore Rex*, 2001, Random House, New York, New York

Myers, Minor Jr. *Liberty Without Anarchy, A History of the Society of the Cincinnati*, 1983, University of Virginia Press, Charlottesville, Virginia

Neely, Mark E. Jr. *The Abraham Lincoln Encyclopedia*, 1982, Da Capo Press, Inc, New York, New York

Nelson, James L. *Reign of Iron*, 2004, HarperCollins Publishers, New York, New York

O'Connell, Robert L. *Fierce Patriot, The Tangled Lives of William Tecumseh Sherman*, 2014, 2015, Random House, New York, New York

Obama, Barack. *The Audacity of Hope, Thoughts on Reclaiming the American Dream*, 2006, Crown Publishers, an imprint of Crown Publishing Group, a division of Random House, Inc., New York, New York

Perrett, Geoffrey. *Days of Sadness, Years of Triumph, The American People 1939-1945*, 1973, Coware, McCann & Geoghegan, Inc., New York, New York

Peterson, Merrill D. *Lincoln in American Memory*, 1994, Oxford University Press, New York, New York

Prados, John. *Islands of Destiny, The Solomons Campaign and the Eclipse of the Rising Sun*, by 2012, New American Library, a division of Penguin Group (USA), Inc., New York, New York

Prados, John. *Storm over Leyte, The Philippine Invasion and the Destruction of the Japanese Navy*, 2016, NAL Caliber, published by New American Library, an imprint of Penguin Random House LLC, New York, New York

Remini, Robert V. *A Short History of the United States*, 2008, Harper Collins Publishers, New York, New York

Richards, Leonard L. *Who Freed the Slaves? The Fight Over the Thirteenth Amendment*, 2015, The University of Chicago Press, Chicago, Illinois

Ricks, Thomas E. *Fiasco, The American Military Adventure In Iraq*, 2006, The Penguin Press, New York, New York

Roosevelt, Theodore. *The Autobiography of Theodore Roosevelt*, 2009, Seven Treasures Publications, prepared from the 1920 edition published by Charles Scribner's Sons, this autobiography was first published in 1913

Roosevelt, Theodore. *The Naval War of 1812*, 1999, Modern Library, a trademark of Random House, Inc., New York, New York

Rumsfeld, Donald. *Known and Unknown, A Memoir*, 2011, Sentinel, a member of Penguin Group (USA), Inc., New York, New York

Salmaggi Cesare and Pallavisini, Alfredo. *2194 Days of War, An Illustrated Chronology of the Second World War*, 1977. Translated by Hug Young, Gallery Books, New York, New York

Sandburg, Carl. *Abraham Lincoln, The Prairie Years and the War Years*, by Carl Sandburg, 1954, Harcourt, Brace & World, Inc., New York, New York

Sandburg, Carl. *Abraham Lincoln, The Prairie Years and the War Years, Illustrated Edition*, by Carl Sandburg, 1954, 1970, The Reader's Digest Association, Pleasantville, New York

Sandburg, Carl. *Abraham Lincoln, The Prairie Years and the War Years, One-Volume Edition*, 1954, Harcourt, Brace & World, Inc., New York, New York

Schlesinger, Arthur M. Jr. *The Almanac of American History*, 1983, Bramhall House, New York, New York

Sears, Stephen W. *Gettysburg*, 2003, 2004, First Mariner Books, Houghton Mifflin Company, New York, New York

Shaarah, Jeff. *Jeff Shaarah's Civil War Battlefields*, 2006, Ballentine Books, an imprint of Random House Publishing Group, New York, New York

Shesol, Jeff. *Supreme Power, Franklin Roosevelt vs. The Supreme Court*, 2010, W. W. Norton & Company, New York, New York

Shlaes, Amity. *The Forgotten Man, A New History of the Great Depression*, 2007, Harper Collins Publishers, New York, New York

Smith, Andrew F. *Starving the South,* 2011, St. Martin's Press, New York, New York

Smith, Jean Edward. *FDR*, 2007, Random House, Inc., New York, New York

Smith, Richard Norton. *Patriarch, George Washington and the New American Nation*, 1993, Houghton Mifflin Company, New York, New York

Stahr, Walter. *Seward, Lincoln's Indispensable Man*, 2012, Simon & Schuster, New York, New York

Strauss William and Howe, Neil. *Generations, The History of America's Future, 1584 to 2069*, 1991, William Morrow and Company, Inc., New York, New York

Streiner, Richard. *Lincoln's Way, How Six Great Presidents Created American Power*, 2010, Rowman & Littlefield Publishers, Inc., Lanham, Maryland

Symonds, Craig L. *The Battle of Midway*, by 2011, Oxford University Press, New York, New York

Symonds, Craig L. *World War II at Sea, A Global History*, 2017, Oxford University Press, New York, New York

Tertius de Kay, James. *Roosevelt's Navy, The Education of a Warrior President, 1882-1920*, 2012, Pegasus Books LLC, New York, New York

Thomas, Benjamin P. *Abraham Lincoln, A Biography*, 1952, Barnes & Noble, Inc., by arrangement with Alfred A. Knopf, Inc., New York, New York

Thomas, Edward. *What's Next for the Economy, Using the Power of Cycles to Predict "What's Next" for Inflation, the Stock Market, Real Estate, and Business*, 2017, ACCE Publishing LLC, Irvine, California

Thomas, Evan. *The War Lovers, Roosevelt, Lodge, Hearst, and the Rush to Empire, 1898*, 2010, Little, Brown, and Company, a division of Hachette Book Group, Inc., New York, New York

Timmerman, Kenneth R. *Countdown to Crisis, The Coming Nuclear Showdown With Iran*, 2005, Crown Forum, an imprint of Crown Publishing Group, a division of Random House, Inc., New York, New York

Von Drehle, David. *Rise to Greatness, Abraham Lincoln and America's Most Perilous Year*, 2012, Henry Holt and Company, New York, New York

Wert, Jeffry D. *The Sword of Lincoln, The Army of the Potomac*, 2005, Simon & Schuster Paperbacks, New York, New York

Wheeler, Richard. *A Rising Thunder, From Lincoln's Election to the Battle of Bull Run: An Eyewitness History*, 1994, HarperCollins Publishers, Inc., New York, New York

White, Ronald C. Jr. *A. Lincoln, A Biography*, 2009, Random House, New York, New York

Wills, Gary. *Cincinnatus, George Washington and the Enlightenment*, 1984, Doubleday & Company, Inc., Garden City, New York

Zakaria, Fareed. *The Post-American World*, 2008, W. W. Norton & Company, Inc., New York, New York

Zaloga, Steven J. *Battle of the Bulge*, 2010, Osprey Publishing Ltd, Oxford, UK, and Long Island City, New York

Zenger, John H. & Folkman, Joseph. *The Extraordinary Leader, Turning Good Managers Into Great Leaders*, 2002, McGraw-Hill, New York, New York

Index

Notes

Below are the references I used to create this book. As others have often stated when discussing their notes and references, "I stand on the shoulders of giants." There is so much amazing documentation and writing out there for public consumption, it is hard not to be overwhelmed; however, I have tried to err on the side of too much documentation, to provide readers references for the purposes of their own investigations.

CHAPTER 1

[1] *Cincinnatus and the Citizen-Servant Ideal, The Roman Legend's Life, Times, and Legacy,* by Michael J. Hillyard, 2001, Xlibris Corporation, USA, page 107

[2] Ibid, pp 72-78

[3] Ibid, pp 122-123

[4] *Cincinnatus, George Washington and the Enlightenment,* by Gary Wills, 1984, Doubleday & Company, Inc., Garden City, New York, page xxxvi

[5] *George Washington, The Forge of Experience (1732-1755),* by James Thomas Flexner, 1965, Little, Brown and Company, New York, New York, page 66

[6] Ibid, pp 55-56

[7] Ibid, pp 59-69

[8] Ibid, pp 76-80

[9] Ibid, page 82

[10] *His Excellency, George Washington,* by Joseph J. Ellis, 2004, Alfred A. Knopf, New York, New York, page 5

[11] *Washington, A Life,* by Ron Chernow, 2010, The Penguin Press, New York, New York, pp 4 and 34

[12] *George Washington, The Forge of Experience (1732-1755),* by James Thomas Flexner, 1965, Little, Brown and Company, New York, New York, pp 88-90

[13] Ibid, pp 102-109

[14] *Washington, A Life,* by Ron Chernow, 2010, The Penguin Press, New York, New York, pp 50-54

[15] *George Washington, The Forge of Experience (1732-1755),* by James Thomas Flexner, 1965, Little, Brown and Company, New York, New York, pp 115-117

[16] *Washington, A Life,* by Ron Chernow, 2010, The Penguin Press, New York, New York, pp 54-57

[17] Ibid, pp 57-58

[18] Ibid, pp 59-60

[19] *George Washington, The Forge of Experience (1732-1755),* by James Thomas Flexner, 1965, Little, Brown and Company, New York, New York, page 138

[20] *Washington, A Life,* by Ron Chernow, 2010, The Penguin Press, New York, New York, pp 67-68

[21] *George Washington, The Forge of Experience (1732-1755),* by James Thomas Flexner, 1965, Little, Brown and Company, New York, New York, pp 193-194

[22] Ibid, page 222 and Appendix A

[23] Ibid, page 227

[24] Ibid, pp 210-211

[25] Ibid, page 250

[26] *His Excellency, George Washington*, by Joseph J. Ellis, 2004, Alfred A. Knopf, New York, New York, pp 61-63

[27] *George Washington, The Forge of Experience (1732-1755)*, by James Thomas Flexner, 1965, Little, Brown and Company, New York, New York, page 322

[28] Ibid, pp 234-238

[29] Ibid, pp 234-235 and 252-259

[30] *Cincinnatus and the Citizen-Servant Ideal, The Roman Legend's Life, Times, and Legacy*, by Michael J. Hillyard, 2001, Xlibris Corporation, USA, page 79

[31] Ibid, pp 80-81

[32] Ibid, pp 84-85

[33] Ibid, pp 85-86

[34] *George Washington, The Forge of Experience (1732-1755)*, by James Thomas Flexner, 1965, Little, Brown and Company, New York, New York, pp 310-314

[35] Ibid, pp 320-322

[36] *Washington, A Life*, by Ron Chernow, 2010, The Penguin Press, New York, New York, pp 171-174

[37] Ibid, pp 181-184

[38] *George Washington, In the American Revolution (1775-1783)*, by James Thomas Flexner, 1969, Little, Brown and Company, New York, New York, page 511

[39] *Cincinnatus, George Washington and the Enlightenment*, by Gary Wills, 1984, Doubleday & Company, Inc., Garden City, New York, pp 87-89

[40] *George Washington, In the American Revolution (1775-1783)*, by James Thomas Flexner, 1969, Little, Brown and Company, New York, New York, page 522-524

[41] Ibid, pp 511-514

[42] *Washington, A Life*, by Ron Chernow, 2010, The Penguin Press, New York, New York, page 454-456

[43] *George Washington, In the American Revolution (1775-1783)*, by James Thomas Flexner, 1969, Little, Brown and Company, New York, New York, page 526

[44] *His Excellency, George Washington*, by Joseph J. Ellis, 2004, Alfred A. Knopf, New York, New York, pp 147

[45] *George Washington, And the New Nation (1793-1799)*, by James Thomas Flexner, 1969, Little, Brown and Company, New York, New York, page 8

[46] *Cincinnatus and the Citizen-Servant Ideal, The Roman Legend's Life, Times, and Legacy*, by Michael J. Hillyard, 2001, Xlibris Corporation, USA, pp 90-91

[47] Ibid, pp 92-93

[48] Ibid, pp 93-94

[49] Ibid, pp 94-99

[50] *Liberty Without Anarchy, A History of the Society of the Cincinnati*, by Minor Myers, Jr., 1983, University of Virginia Press, Charlottesville, Virginia, pp 15-17

[51] Ibid, pp 19-26

[52] *Washington, A Life*, by Ron Chernow, 2010, The Penguin Press, New York, New York, page 444

[53] *Liberty Without Anarchy, A History of the Society of the Cincinnati*, by Minor Myers, Jr., 1983, University of Virginia Press, Charlottesville, Virginia, pp 49-51

[54] Ibid, pp 52-58

[55] Ibid, pp 58-62

[56] *George Washington, And the New Nation (1793-1799)*, by James Thomas Flexner, 1969, Little, Brown and Company, New York, New York, pp 42-45

[57] *The Return of George Washington, 1783-1789*, by Edward J. Larson, 2014, HarperCollins Publishers, New York, New York, page 85

[58] *Cincinnatus, George Washington and the Enlightenment*, by Gary Wills, 1984, Doubleday & Company, Inc., Garden City, New York, pp 151-156

[59] *The Return of George Washington, 1783-1789*, by Edward J. Larson, 2014, HarperCollins Publishers, New York, New York, pp 85-88

[60] Ibid, pp 92-97

[61] *Cincinnatus and the Citizen-Servant Ideal, The Roman Legend's Life, Times, and Legacy*, by Michael J. Hillyard, 2001, Xlibris Corporation, USA, pp 102-103

[62] Ibid, pp 103-104

[63] Ibid, pp 104-105

[64] Ibid, 105-106

[65] *Washington, A Life*, by Ron Chernow, 2010, The Penguin Press, New York, New York, pp 540-541

[66] Ibid, pp 545-551

[67] *Thomas Jefferson, The Art of Power*, by Jon Meacham, 2012, Random House, New York, New York, pp 261-268

[68] *Washington, A Life*, by Ron Chernow, 2010, The Penguin Press, New York, New York, pp 678-682

[69] Ibid, pp 753-754

[70] *George Washington, Anguish and Farewell (1793-1799)*, by James Thomas Flexner, 1969, Little, Brown and Company, New York, New York, pp 298-302

[71] *Cincinnatus, George Washington and the Enlightenment*, by Gary Wills, 1984, Doubleday & Company, Inc., Garden City, New York, pp 87-90

[72] *George Washington, Anguish and Farewell (1793-1799)*, by James Thomas Flexner, 1969, Little, Brown and Company, New York, New York, pp 450-454

CHAPTER 2

[1] *1776*, by David McCullough, 2005, Simon & Schuster, New York, New York, page 47

[2] *SPQR, A History of Ancient Rome*, by Mary Beard, 2015, Liveright Publishing Corporation, a Division of W.W. Norton & Company, New York, New York, page 289

[3] *Founding Father, Rediscovering George Washington*, by Richard Brookhiser, 1996, The Free Press, a Division of Simon & Schuster, New York, New York, pp 123-127

[4] *George Washington, The Forge of Experience (1732-1755)*, by James Thomas Flexner, 1965, Little, Brown and Company, New York, New York, page 335

[5] *Founding Father, Rediscovering George Washington*, by Richard Brookhiser, 1996, The Free Press, a Division of Simon & Schuster, New York, New York, pp 20-24

[6] *Washington, A Life*, by Ron Chernow, 2010, The Penguin Press, New York, New York, pp 184-189

[7] *George Washington, In The American Revolution (1775-1783)*, by James Thomas Flexner, 1967-1968, Little, Brown and Company, New York, New York, pp 29-33

[8] *Washington, A Life*, by Ron Chernow, 2010, The Penguin Press, New York, New York, pp 197-198

[9] Ibid, page 223

[10] Ibid, page 225

[11] Ibid, pp 226-227

[12] Ibid, page 229

[13] *1776*, by David McCullough, 2005, Simon & Schuster, New York, New York, pp 117-121

[14] *George Washington, In The American Revolution (1775-1783)*, by James Thomas Flexner, 1967-1968, Little, Brown and Company, New York, New York, pp 87, 90, and 95

[15] Ibid, page 95

[16] *Washington, A Life*, by Ron Chernow, 2010, The Penguin Press, New York, New York, page 237

[17] *His Excellency, George Washington*, by Joseph J. Ellis, 2004, Alfred A. Knopf, New York, New York, page 93

[18] *George Washington, In The American Revolution (1775-1783)*, by James Thomas Flexner, 1967-1968, Little, Brown and Company, New York, New York, page 110

[19] Ibid, page 112

[20] Ibid, pp 114-115

[21] Ibid, pp 115-121

[22] *Washington, A Life*, by Ron Chernow, 2010, The Penguin Press, New York, New York, page 253

[23] *George Washington, In The American Revolution (1775-1783)*, by James Thomas Flexner, 1967-1968, Little, Brown and Company, New York, New York, page 123

[24] *1776*, by David McCullough, 2005, Simon & Schuster, New York, New York, pp 214-216

[25] *George Washington, In The American Revolution (1775-1783)*, by James Thomas Flexner, 1967-1968, Little, Brown and Company, New York, New York, pp 128-130

[26] *Washington, A Life*, by Ron Chernow, 2010, The Penguin Press, New York, New York, pp 257-259

[27] *George Washington, In The American Revolution (1775-1783)*, by James Thomas Flexner, 1967-1968, Little, Brown and Company, New York, New York, pp 141-142

[28] *1776*, by David McCullough, 2005, Simon & Schuster, New York, New York, pp 234-236

[29] *George Washington, In The American Revolution (1775-1783)*, by James Thomas Flexner, 1967-1968, Little, Brown and Company, New York, New York, pp 144-148

[30] *Washington, A Life*, by Ron Chernow, 2010, The Penguin Press, New York, New York, page 262

[31] Ibid, page 264

[32] Ibid, pp 269-271

[33] Ibid, pp 271-272

[34] Ibid, page 276

[35] *George Washington, In The American Revolution (1775-1783)*, by James Thomas Flexner, 1967-1968, Little, Brown and Company, New York, New York, page 181

[36] *Washington, A Life*, by Ron Chernow, 2010, The Penguin Press, New York, New York, page 280

[37] Ibid, pp 280-281

[38] *George Washington, In The American Revolution (1775-1783)*, by James Thomas Flexner, 1967-1968, Little, Brown and Company, New York, New York, pp 187-191

[39] Ibid, page 195

[40] *Washington, A Life*, by Ron Chernow, 2010, The Penguin Press, New York, New York, pp 298-299

[41] Ibid, pp 301-302

[42] *George Washington, In The American Revolution (1775-1783)*, by James Thomas Flexner, 1967-1968, Little, Brown and Company, New York, New York, pp 221-224

[43] *Washington, A Life*, by Ron Chernow, 2010, The Penguin Press, New York, New York, pp 308-311

[44] *George Washington, In The American Revolution (1775-1783)*, by James Thomas Flexner, 1967-1968, Little, Brown and Company, New York, New York, page 237

[45] Ibid, pp 246-250

[46] *Patriots, The Men Who Started the American Revolution*, by A. J. Langguth, 1988, Simon & Schuster, New York, New York, page 442

[47] Ibid, pp 439-441

[48] Ibid, pp 442-443

[49] Ibid, pp 444-450

[50] Ibid, pp 452-457

[51] *Washington, A Life*, by Ron Chernow, 2010, The Penguin Press, New York, New York, pp 317-320

[52] Ibid, pp 315-316

[53] *George Washington, In The American Revolution (1775-1783)*, by James Thomas Flexner, 1967-1968, Little, Brown and Company, New York, New York, page 250

[54] *Washington, A Life*, by Ron Chernow, 2010, The Penguin Press, New York, New York, pp 323-324

[55] Ibid, pp 325-327

[56] Ibid, page 328

[57] Ibid, pp 329-331

[58] *George Washington, In The American Revolution (1775-1783)*, by James Thomas Flexner, 1967-1968, Little, Brown and Company, New York, New York, page 290

[59] Ibid, pp 290-291

[60] Ibid, page 286

[61] Ibid, pp 297-299

[62] Ibid, page 305

[63] *Washington, A Life*, by Ron Chernow, 2010, The Penguin Press, New York, New York, pp 342-344

[64] Ibid, page 345

[65] Ibid, pp 347 and 405

[66] *George Washington, In The American Revolution (1775-1783)*, by James Thomas Flexner, 1967-1968, Little, Brown and Company, New York, New York, pp 360-362 and 369-370

[67] *Washington, A Life*, by Ron Chernow, 2010, The Penguin Press, New York, New York, page 401

[68] *George Washington, In The American Revolution (1775-1783)*, by James Thomas Flexner, 1967-1968, Little, Brown and Company, New York, New York, page 431

[69] Ibid, page 455

[70] *Washington, A Life*, by Ron Chernow, 2010, The Penguin Press, New York, New York, pp 413-418

[71] Ibid, pp 419-426

[72] Ibid, page 429

[73] *George Washington, In The American Revolution (1775-1783)*, by James Thomas Flexner, 1967-1968, Little, Brown and Company, New York, New York, pp 476 and 488

[74] Ibid, page 486

[75] *Washington, A Life*, by Ron Chernow, 2010, The Penguin Press, New York, New York, pp 433-434

[76] Ibid, pp 435-436

[77] *George Washington, In The American Revolution (1775-1783)*, by James Thomas Flexner, 1967-1968, Little, Brown and Company, New York, New York, page 508

CHAPTER 3

[1] *Washington, A Life*, by Ron Chernow, 2010, The Penguin Press, New York, New York, pp 575-576

[2] *George Washington, And the New Nation (1793-1799)*, by James Thomas Flexner, 1969, Little, Brown and Company, New York, New York, pp 195-196

[3] Ibid, page 190

[4] *His Excellency, George Washington*, by Joseph J. Ellis, 2004, Alfred A. Knopf, New York, New York, pp 189-190

[5] *Washington, A Life*, by Ron Chernow, 2010, The Penguin Press, New York, New York, pp 608-609

[6] *Founding Father, Rediscovering George Washington*, by Richard Brookhiser, 1996, The Free Press, a Division of Simon & Schuster, New York, New York, page 79

[7] *George Washington, And the New Nation (1793-1799)*, by James Thomas Flexner, 1969, Little, Brown and Company, New York, New York, pp 228-229

[8] *Washington, A Life*, by Ron Chernow, 2010, The Penguin Press, New York, New York, page 610

[9] Ibid, page 615

[10] Ibid, page 609

[11] *Patriarch, George Washington and the New American Nation*, by Richard Norton Smith, 1993, Houghton Mifflin Company, New York, New York, pp 41-42

[12] *Washington, A Life*, by Ron Chernow, 2010, The Penguin Press, New York, New York, pp 630-631

[13] *Patriarch, George Washington and the New American Nation*, by Richard Norton Smith, 1993, Houghton Mifflin Company, New York, New York, pp 47-53

[14] *Washington, A Life*, by Ron Chernow, 2010, The Penguin Press, New York, New York, page 607

[15] Wright, J. Leitch. "Creek-American Treaty of 1790: Alexander McGillivray and The Diplomacy of The Old Southwest." *The Georgia Historical Quarterly* 51, no. 4 (1967): 379-400. Accessed April 28, 2020. www.jstor.org/stable/40578728

[16] *American Creation, Triumphs and Tragedies at the Founding of the Republic*, by Joseph J. Ellis, 2007, Alfred A. Knopf, a division of Random House, Inc., New York, New York, pp 151-157

[17] *Washington, A Life*, by Ron Chernow, 2010, The Penguin Press, New York, New York, page 633

[18] Ibid, pp 644-647

[19] *Patriarch, George Washington and the New American Nation*, by Richard Norton Smith, 1993, Houghton Mifflin Company, New York, New York, pp 88-90

[20] *George Washington, And the New Nation (1793-1799)*, by James Thomas Flexner, 1969, Little, Brown and Company, New York, New York, pp 287-291

[21] Ibid, pp 293 and 301

[22] Ibid, page 297

[23] *Patriarch, George Washington and the New American Nation*, by Richard Norton Smith, 1993, Houghton Mifflin Company, New York, New York, pp 123-125

[24] *George Washington, And the New Nation (1793-1799)*, by James Thomas Flexner, 1969, Little, Brown and Company, New York, New York, page 302

[25] Ibid, pp 304-306

[26] *Patriarch, George Washington and the New American Nation*, by Richard Norton Smith, 1993, Houghton Mifflin Company, New York, New York, pp 130-137

[27] *George Washington, And the New Nation (1793-1799)*, by James Thomas Flexner, 1969, Little, Brown and Company, New York, New York, pp 375-380

[28] Ibid, pp 388-392

[29] *Patriarch, George Washington and the New American Nation*, by Richard Norton Smith, 1993, Houghton Mifflin Company, New York, New York, pp 160-163

[30] *George Washington, Anguish and Farewell (1793-1799)*, by James Thomas Flexner, 1969, Little, Brown and Company, New York, New York, page 34

[31] *Washington, A Life*, by Ron Chernow, 2010, The Penguin Press, New York, New York, page 696

[32] *George Washington, Anguish and Farewell (1793-1799)*, by James Thomas Flexner, 1969, Little, Brown and Company, New York, New York, pp 39-41

[33] Ibid, pp 42-45

[34] *His Excellency, George Washington*, by Joseph J. Ellis, 2004, Alfred A. Knopf, New York, New York, pp 222-223

[35] *The Age of Napoleon, A History of European Civilization from 1789 to 1815*, by Will & Ariel Durant, 1975, MJF Books, by arrangement with Simon & Schuster, Inc., New York, New York, page 71

[36] *Patriarch, George Washington and the New American Nation*, by Richard Norton Smith, 1993, Houghton Mifflin Company, New York, New York, pp 177 and 194

[37] *George Washington, Anguish and Farewell (1793-1799)*, by James Thomas Flexner, 1969, Little, Brown and Company, New York, New York, page 52

[38] Ibid, page 57

[39] Ibid, page 61

[40] Ibid, page 63

[41] Ibid, page 67

[42] Ibid, page 71

[43] *Patriarch, George Washington and the New American Nation*, by Richard Norton Smith, 1993, Houghton Mifflin Company, New York, New York, pp 175-176

[44] *Washington, A Life*, by Ron Chernow, 2010, The Penguin Press, New York, New York, page 701

[45] Ibid, page 701

[46] *George Washington, Anguish and Farewell (1793-1799)*, by James Thomas Flexner, 1969, Little, Brown and Company, New York, New York, page 102

[47] Ibid, page 131

[48] *Washington, A Life*, by Ron Chernow, 2010, The Penguin Press, New York, New York, pp 713-715

[49] *Alexander Hamilton*, by Ron Chernow, 2004, The Penguin Group, New York, New York, pp 341-342

[50] *Hamilton, Writings*, Report on Public Credit, New York Historical Society, 2001, Literary Classics of the United States, Inc., distributed by Penguin Putnam, Inc., page 566

[51] https://www.loc.gov/law/help/statutes-at-large/1st-congress/c1.pdf (pp 199-214)

[52] *George Washington, A collection*, Compiled and Edited by W. B. Allen, 1988, LibertyClassics, a publishing imprint of Liberty Fund, Inc., Indianapolis, Indiana, page 483

[53] *George Washington, Anguish and Farewell (1793-1799)*, by James Thomas Flexner, 1969, Little, Brown and Company, New York, New York, pp 163-165

[54] *Washington, A Life*, by Ron Chernow, 2010, The Penguin Press, New York, New York, page 719

[55] *George Washington, Anguish and Farewell (1793-1799)*, by James Thomas Flexner, 1969, Little, Brown and Company, New York, New York, pp 167-169

[56] *Washington, A Life*, by Ron Chernow, 2010, The Penguin Press, New York, New York, pp 719-721

[57] Ibid, page 723

[58] *Patriarch, George Washington and the New American Nation*, by Richard Norton Smith, 1993, Houghton Mifflin Company, New York, New York, page 222

[59] *George Washington, Anguish and Farewell (1793-1799)*, by James Thomas Flexner, 1969, Little, Brown and Company, New York, New York, pp 177-180

[60] Ibid, pp 188-189

[61] *George Washington, A collection*, Compiled and Edited by W. B. Allen, 1988, LibertyClassics, a publishing imprint of Liberty Fund, Inc., Indianapolis, Indiana, pp 492-499

[62] *George Washington, Anguish and Farewell (1793-1799)*, by James Thomas Flexner, 1969, Little, Brown and Company, New York, New York, pp 183-186

[63] *Washington, A Life*, by Ron Chernow, 2010, The Penguin Press, New York, New York, pp 727-728

[64] Ibid, pp 729-730

[65] *George Washington, Anguish and Farewell (1793-1799)*, by James Thomas Flexner, 1969, Little, Brown and Company, New York, New York, pp 208-210

[66] Ibid, page 233

[67] https://history.state.gov/milestones/1784-1800/pickney-treaty (US Department of State website)

[68] *Washington, A Life*, by Ron Chernow, 2010, The Penguin Press, New York, New York, page 740

[69] https://history.state.gov/milestones/1784-1800/pickney-treaty (US Department of State website)

[70] *George Washington, Anguish and Farewell (1793-1799)*, by James Thomas Flexner, 1969, Little, Brown and Company, New York, New York, pp 252-253

[71] *George Washington, A collection*, Compiled and Edited by W. B. Allen, 1988, LibertyClassics, a publishing imprint of Liberty Fund, Inc., Indianapolis, Indiana, page 501

[72] *George Washington, Anguish and Farewell (1793-1799)*, by James Thomas Flexner, 1969, Little, Brown and Company, New York, New York, page 292

[73] Ibid, pp 294-296

[74] Ibid, pp 296-297

[75] *George Washington, A collection*, Compiled and Edited by W. B. Allen, 1988, LibertyClassics, a publishing imprint of Liberty Fund, Inc., Indianapolis, Indiana, pp 512-519

[76] Ibid, pp 522-527

CHAPTER 4

[1] *George Washington, Anguish and Farewell (1793-1799)*, by James Thomas Flexner, 1969, Little, Brown and Company, New York, New York, page 25

[2] *Washington, A Life*, by Ron Chernow, 2010, The Penguin Press, New York, New York, pp 565-566 and 609

[3] *George Washington, and the New Nation (1793-1799)*, by James Thomas Flexner, 1969, Little, Brown and Company, New York, New York, page 137

[4] *Washington, A Life*, by Ron Chernow, 2010, The Penguin Press, New York, New York, pp 590-591

[5] *George Washington, and the New Nation (1793-1799)*, by James Thomas Flexner, 1969, Little, Brown and Company, New York, New York, page 399

[6] *George Washington, and the New Nation (1793-1799)*, by James Thomas Flexner, 1969, Little, Brown and Company, New York, New York, pp 400-402

[7] https://www.senate.gov/civics/constitution_item/constitution.htm

[8] *His Excellency, George Washington*, by Joseph J. Ellis, 2004, Alfred A. Knopf, New York, New York, page 195

[9] *Washington, A Life*, by Ron Chernow, 2010, The Penguin Press, New York, New York, pp 592-593

[10] https://www.senate.gov/civics/constitution_item/constitution.htm

[11] https://history.house.gov/Institution/SOTU/State-of-the-Union/

[12] Ibid

[13] George Washington, First Annual Address to Congress Online by Gerhard Peters and John T. Woolley, The American Presidency Project https://www.presidency.ucsb.edu/node/203158

[14]https://www.presidency.ucsb.edu/documents/presidential-documents-archive-guidebook/annual-messages-congress-the-state-the-union

[15] *George Washington, A collection*, Compiled and Edited by W. B. Allen, 1988, LibertyClassics, a publishing imprint of Liberty Fund, Inc., Indianapolis, Indiana, page 470

[16] George Washington, First Annual Address to Congress Online by Gerhard Peters and John T. Woolley, The American Presidency Project https://www.presidency.ucsb.edu/node/203158

[17] https://www.senate.gov/civics/constitution_item/constitution.htm

18 Ibid

19 *Washington, A Life*, by Ron Chernow, 2010, The Penguin Press, New York, New York, pp 721-725

20 *George Washington, A collection*, Compiled and Edited by W. B. Allen, 1988, LibertyClassics, a publishing imprint of Liberty Fund, Inc., Indianapolis, Indiana, pp 492-497

21 *Founding Father, Rediscovering George Washington*, by Richard Brookhiser, 1996, The Free Press, A Division of Simon & Schuster, Inc., New York, New York, pages 31-41

22 *George Washington, In the American Revolution (1775-1783)*, by James Thomas Flexner, 1967-1968, Little, Brown and Company, New York, New York, pp 132-134

23 *George Washington, A collection*, Compiled and Edited by W. B. Allen, 1988, LibertyClassics, a publishing imprint of Liberty Fund, Inc., Indianapolis, Indiana, pp 77-78

24 Ibid, page 82

25 The American Presidency Project at UC Santa Barbara, http://www.presidency.ucsb.edu/sou.php

26 George Washington, Eighth Annual Address to Congress Online by Gerhard Peters and John T. Woolley, The American Presidency Project https://www.presidency.ucsb.edu/node/200398

27 https://www.cbp.gov/about/history/timeline

28 https://www.loc.gov/law/help/statutes-at-large/1st-congress/c1.pdf (pp 53-54)

29 *Alexander Hamilton*, by Ron Chernow, 2004, The Penguin Group, New York, NY, pp 288-300

30 https://www.history.uscg.mil/home/history-program/

31 https://www.loc.gov/law/help/statutes-at-large/1st-congress/c1.pdf (pp 145-178)

[32] *Alexander Hamilton*, by Ron Chernow, 2004, The Penguin Group, New York, NY, page 340

[33] Ibid, pp339-341

[34] *John Adams*, by David McCullough, 2001, Simon & Schuster, New York, NY, page 477

[35] *Washington, A Life*, by Ron Chernow, 2010, The Penguin Press, New York, New York, pp 630-631

[36] Ibid, pp 662-663

[37] Ibid, page 663

[38] Ibid, pp 703-704

[39] George Washington, Second Annual Address to Congress Online by Gerhard Peters and John T. Woolley, The American Presidency Project https://www.presidency.ucsb.edu/node/203719

[40] https://www.senate.gov/civics/constitution_item/constitution.htm

[41] "Final Version of the Report on the Establishment of a Mint, [28 January 1791]," Founders Online, National Archives, https://founders.archives.gov/documents/Hamilton/01-07-02-0334-0004. [Original source: The Papers of Alexander Hamilton, vol. 7, September 1790–January 1791, ed. Harold C. Syrett. New York: Columbia University Press, 1963, pp. 570–607.]

[42] https://www.usmint.gov/learn/history/historical-documents/coinage-act-of-april-2-1792

[43] https://www.usmint.gov/learn/history/overview

[44] https://www.usmint.gov/learn/history/timeline-of-the-united-states-mint

[45] https://www.history.navy.mil/browse-by-topic/commemorations-toolkits/navy-birthday/OriginsNavy/the-birth-of-the-navy-of-the-united-states.html

[46] *Washington, A Life*, by Ron Chernow, 2010, The Penguin Press, New York, New York, pp 713-714

[47] https://www.archives.gov/education/lessons/new-us-navy

[48] *The Naval War of 1812*, by Theodore Roosevelt, 1999, Modern Library, a trademark of Random House, Inc., New York, New York, page 28

[49] https://www.westpoint.edu/about/history-of-west-point

[50] *Thomas Jefferson, The Art of Power*, by Jon Meacham, 2012, Random House, New York, New York, page 368

[51] George Washington, Eighth Annual Address to Congress Online by Gerhard Peters and John T. Woolley, The American Presidency Project https://www.presidency.ucsb.edu/node/200398

[52] https://penelope.uchicago.edu/Thayer/E/Gazetteer/Places/America/United_States/Army/USMA/PARHAT/2*.html

[53] Ibid

[54] https://home.army.mil/westpoint/index.php/about/history

[55] Ibid

[56] *Washington, A Life*, by Ron Chernow, 2010, The Penguin Press, New York, New York, pp 661 and 688

[57] Ibid, page 661

[58] *George Washington, Anguish and Farewell (1793-1799)*, by James Thomas Flexner, 1969, Little, Brown and Company, New York, New York, pp 261-264

[59] *George Washington, and the New Nation (1793-1799)*, by James Thomas Flexner, 1969, Little, Brown and Company, New York, New York, pp 171 and 383

[60] *His Excellency, George Washington*, by Joseph J. Ellis, 2004, Alfred A. Knopf, New York, New York, pp 274-275

[61] *George Washington, Anguish and Farewell (1793-1799)*, by James Thomas Flexner, 1969, Little, Brown and Company, New York, New York, pp 332-333

[62] *Washington, A Life*, by Ron Chernow, 2010, The Penguin Press, New York, New York, page 689

[63] *Founding Father, Rediscovering George Washington*, by Richard Brookhiser, 1996, The Free Press, a Division of Simon & Schuster, New York, New York, page 199

CHAPTER 5

[1] *Abraham Lincoln, The Prairie Years and the War Years*, One-Volume Edition, by Carl Sandburg, 1954, Harcourt, Brace & World, Inc., New York, New York, page 3

[2] Ibid, pp 9-21

[3] *Abraham Lincoln, A Biography*, by Benjamin P. Thomas, 1952, Barnes & Noble, Inc., by arrangement with Alfred A. Knopf, Inc., New York, New York, pp 21-27

[4] Ibid, pp 31-34

[5] Ibid, pp 37-40

[6] Ibid, pp 42-43

[7] Ibid, pp 47-48

[8] *Lincoln*, by David Herbert Donald, 1995, Simon & Schuster, New York, New York, pp 55-56

[9] Ibid, pp 56-58

[10] *Abraham Lincoln, A Biography*, by Benjamin P. Thomas, 1952, Barnes & Noble, Inc., by arrangement with Alfred A. Knopf, Inc., New York, New York, pp 54-57

[11] Ibid, pp 58 and 62

[12] Ibid, pp 62-63

[13] Ibid, page 64

[14] Ibid, pp 61-64

[15] Ibid, page 67

[16] *A. Lincoln, A Biography*, by Ronald C. White, Jr., 2009, Random House, New York, New York, pp 81-82

[17] *Lincoln*, by David Herbert Donald, 1995, Simon & Schuster, New York, New York, pp 75-76

[18] Ibid, page 77

[19] *Abraham Lincoln, A Biography*, by Benjamin P. Thomas, 1952, Barnes & Noble, Inc., by arrangement with Alfred A. Knopf, Inc., New York, New York, page 95

[20] *Abraham Lincoln, The Prairie Years and the War Years*, One-Volume Edition, by Carl Sandburg, 1954, Harcourt, Brace & World, Inc., New York, New York, page 70

[21] Ibid, pp 71-73

[22] Ibid, pp 76-77

[23] *Lincoln*, by David Herbert Donald, 1995, Simon & Schuster, New York, New York, pp 91-92

[24] Ibid, pp 92-93

[25] *Abraham Lincoln, The Prairie Years and the War Years*, One-Volume Edition, by Carl Sandburg, 1954, Harcourt, Brace & World, Inc., New York, New York, pp 77-78

[26] *Abraham Lincoln, A Biography*, by Benjamin P. Thomas, 1952, Barnes & Noble, Inc., by arrangement with Alfred A. Knopf, Inc., New York, New York, pp 95-96

[27] *Lincoln*, by David Herbert Donald, 1995, Simon & Schuster, New York, New York, pp 95-96

[28] Ibid, page 97

[29] *A. Lincoln, A Biography*, by Ronald C. White, Jr., 2009, Random House, New York, New York, pp 81-119

[30] Ibid, pp 122-124

[31] Ibid, pp 125-127

[32] Ibid, pp 131-133

[33] *Abraham Lincoln, A Biography*, by Benjamin P. Thomas, 1952, Barnes & Noble, Inc., by arrangement with Alfred A. Knopf, Inc., New York, New York, pp 116-117

[34] Ibid, pp 118-122

[35] *A. Lincoln, A Biography*, by Ronald C. White, Jr., 2009, Random House, New York, New York, pp 158-161

[36] Ibid, pp 161-163

[37] *Abraham Lincoln, A Biography*, by Benjamin P. Thomas, 1952, Barnes & Noble, Inc., by arrangement with Alfred A. Knopf, Inc., New York, New York, pp 132-135

[38] *A. Lincoln, A Biography*, by Ronald C. White, Jr., 2009, Random House, New York, New York, pp 176-178

[39] *Abraham Lincoln, A Biography*, by Benjamin P. Thomas, 1952, Barnes & Noble, Inc., by arrangement with Alfred A. Knopf, Inc., New York, New York, page 133

[40] *Lincoln*, by David Herbert Donald, 1995, Simon & Schuster, New York, New York, pp 153-154

[41] *Abraham Lincoln, A Biography*, by Benjamin P. Thomas, 1952, Barnes & Noble, Inc., by arrangement with Alfred A. Knopf, Inc., New York, New York, page 131

[42] *Lincoln*, by David Herbert Donald, 1995, Simon & Schuster, New York, New York, pp 152-154

[43] *Abraham Lincoln, The Prairie Years and the War Years*, Illustrated Edition, by Carl Sandburg, 1954, 1970, The Reader's Digest Association, Pleasantville, New York, pp 105-106

[44] *Lincoln*, by David Herbert Donald, 1995, Simon & Schuster, New York, New York, page 163

[45] *A. Lincoln, A Biography*, by Ronald C. White, Jr., 2009, Random House, New York, New York, pp 184-185

[46] *Abraham Lincoln, A Biography*, by Benjamin P. Thomas, 1952, Barnes & Noble, Inc., by arrangement with Alfred A. Knopf, Inc., New York, New York, pp 134-139

[47] *A. Lincoln, A Biography*, by Ronald C. White, Jr., 2009, Random House, New York, New York, pp 187-190

[48] *Abraham Lincoln, A Biography*, by Benjamin P. Thomas, 1952, Barnes & Noble, Inc., by arrangement with Alfred A. Knopf, Inc., New York, New York, page 146

[49] Ibid, page 153

[50] *A. Lincoln, A Biography*, by Ronald C. White, Jr., 2009, Random House, New York, New York, pp 206-208

[51] *Abraham Lincoln, A Biography*, by Benjamin P. Thomas, 1952, Barnes & Noble, Inc., by arrangement with Alfred A. Knopf, Inc., New York, New York, pp 155-157

[52] *A. Lincoln, A Biography*, by Ronald C. White, Jr., 2009, Random House, New York, New York, page 218

[53] Ibid, page 220

[54] *Grand Old Party, A History of the Republicans*, by Lewis L. Gould, 2003, Random House, Inc, New York, New York, page 18

[55] *A. Lincoln, A Biography*, by Ronald C. White, Jr., 2009, Random House, New York, New York, pp 227-229

[56] *Abraham Lincoln, A Biography*, by Benjamin P. Thomas, 1952, Barnes & Noble, Inc., by arrangement with Alfred A. Knopf, Inc., New York, New York, page 172

[57] *Lincoln*, by David Herbert Donald, 1995, Simon & Schuster, New York, New York, page 200

[58] *Abraham Lincoln, A Biography*, by Benjamin P. Thomas, 1952, Barnes & Noble, Inc., by arrangement with Alfred A. Knopf, Inc., New York, New York, page 175

[59] *Abraham Lincoln, Selected Writings*, Abraham Lincoln, compilation published by Barnes & Noble, Inc., 2013, Barnes & Noble, Inc., New York, New York, page 134

[60] *A. Lincoln, A Biography*, by Ronald C. White, Jr., 2009, Random House, New York, New York, pp 250-251

[61] Ibid, pp 258-260

[62] *Abraham Lincoln, A Biography*, by Benjamin P. Thomas, 1952, Barnes & Noble, Inc., by arrangement with Alfred A. Knopf, Inc., New York, New York, pp 183-193

[63] *A. Lincoln, A Biography*, by Ronald C. White, Jr., 2009, Random House, New York, New York, pp 287-288

[64] Ibid, page 305

[65] Ibid, page 303

[66] *Abraham Lincoln, Selected Writings*, Abraham Lincoln, compilation published by Barnes & Noble, Inc., 2013, Barnes & Noble, Inc., New York, New York, page 594

[67] *A. Lincoln, A Biography*, by Ronald C. White, Jr., 2009, Random House, New York, New York, pp 309-314

[68] Ibid, pp 317-320

[69] *Team of Rivals, The Political Genius of Abraham Lincoln*, by Doris Kearns Goodwin, 2005, Simon & Schuster, New York, New York, pp 239-241 and 248-249

[70] *A. Lincoln, A Biography*, by Ronald C. White, Jr., 2009, Random House, New York, New York, pp 344-346

[71] *Abraham Lincoln, A Biography*, by Benjamin P. Thomas, 1952, Barnes & Noble, Inc., by arrangement with Alfred A. Knopf, Inc., New York, New York, pp 229-235

CHAPTER 6

[1] *Days of Defiance: Sumter, Secession, and the Coming of the Civil War*, by Maury Klein, 1997, Alfred A. Knopf, New York, New York, pp 415-416

[2] Ibid, pp 417-418

[3] *Dissonance, The Turbulent Days Between Fort Sumter and Bull Run*, by David Detzer, 2006, Harcourt, Inc., Orlando, Florida, page 27

[4] *A. Lincoln, A Biography*, by Ronald C. White, Jr., 2009, Random House, New York, New York, pp 416-417

[5] *A Rising Thunder, From Lincoln's Election to the Battle of Bull Run: An Eyewitness History*, by Richard Wheeler, 1994, HarperCollins Publishers, Inc., New York, New York, page 111

[6] Ibid, page 119

[7] *Team of Rivals, The Political Genius of Abraham Lincoln*, by Doris Kearns Goodwin, 2005, Simon & Schuster, New York, New York, page 355

[8] *A. Lincoln, A Biography*, by Ronald C. White, Jr., 2009, Random House, New York, New York, page 427

[9] *The Sword of Lincoln, The Army of the Potomac*, by Jeffry D. Wert, 2005, Simon & Schuster Paperbacks, New York, New York, pp 7-8

[10] Ibid, pp 8-16

[11] Ibid, pp 16-19

[12] *A Rising Thunder, From Lincoln's Election to the Battle of Bull Run: An Eyewitness History*, by Richard Wheeler, 1994, HarperCollins Publishers, Inc., New York, New York, pp 388-389

[13] Ibid, pp 390-391

[14] *Abraham Lincoln, A Biography*, by Benjamin P. Thomas, 1952, Barnes & Noble, Inc., by arrangement with Alfred A. Knopf, Inc., New York, New York, page 274

[15] Ibid, pp 287-289

[16] *The Sword of Lincoln, The Army of the Potomac*, by Jeffry D. Wert, 2005, Simon & Schuster Paperbacks, New York, New York, pp 29-33

[17] *A. Lincoln, A Biography*, by Ronald C. White, Jr., 2009, Random House, New York, New York, pp 447 and 471

[18] *Abraham Lincoln, A Biography*, by Benjamin P. Thomas, 1952, Barnes & Noble, Inc., by arrangement with Alfred A. Knopf, Inc., New York, New York, pp 305-308

[19] *Starving the South*, by Andrew F. Smith, 2011, St. Martin's Press, New York, New York, page 26

[20] *Reign of Iron*, by James L. Nelson, 2004, HarperCollins Publishers, New York, New York, page 18

[21] Ibid, page 151

[22] Ibid, page 286

[23] *The Personal Memoirs of Ulysses S. Grant*, by Ulysses S. Grant, 1885, Konecky & Konecky, Old Saybrook, Connecticut, page 196

[24] *Rise to Greatness, Abraham Lincoln and America's Most Perilous Year*, by David Von Drehle, 2012, Henry Holt and Company, New York, New York, page 122

[25] *Shiloh, 1862*, by Winston Groom, 2012, National Geographic, Washington, D. C., page 142

[26] *The Personal Memoirs of Ulysses S. Grant*, by Ulysses S. Grant, 1885, Konecky & Konecky, Old Saybrook, Connecticut, pp 199-203

[27] *Fierce Patriot, The Tangled Lives of William Tecumseh Sherman*, by Robert L. O'Connell, 2014, 2015, Random House, New York, New York, pp 99-100

[28] Ibid, pp 100-101

[29] *Tried by War, Abraham Lincoln as Commander In Chief*, by James M. McPherson, 2008, The Penguin Press, New York, New York, pp 81-83

[30] Ibid, page 89

[31] *The Army of the Potomac: Mr. Lincoln's Army*, by Bruce Catton, 1951, 1962, Doubleday & Company, Inc., Garden City, New York, page 125

[32] *Rise to Greatness, Abraham Lincoln and America's Most Perilous Year*, by David Von Drehle, 2012, Henry Holt and Company, New York, New York, pp 180-181

[33] *The Army of the Potomac: Mr. Lincoln's Army*, by Bruce Catton, 1951, 1962, Doubleday & Company, Inc., Garden City, New York, page 128

[34] *Tried by War, Abraham Lincoln as Commander In Chief*, by James M. McPherson, 2008, The Penguin Press, New York, New York, pp 98-99

[35] *The Sword of Lincoln, The Army of the Potomac,* by Jeffry D. Wert, 2005, Simon & Schuster Paperbacks, New York, New York, pp 134-139

[36] *Rise to Greatness, Abraham Lincoln and America's Most Perilous Year,* by David Von Drehle, 2012, Henry Holt and Company, New York, New York, pp 284-286

[37] *The Sword of Lincoln, The Army of the Potomac,* by Jeffry D. Wert, 2005, Simon & Schuster Paperbacks, New York, New York, page 173

[38] *Abraham Lincoln, A Biography,* by Benjamin P. Thomas, 1952, Barnes & Noble, Inc., by arrangement with Alfred A. Knopf, Inc., New York, New York, pp 340-344

[39] *The Sword of Lincoln, The Army of the Potomac,* by Jeffry D. Wert, 2005, Simon & Schuster Paperbacks, New York, New York, pp 174-175

[40] *Rise to Greatness, Abraham Lincoln and America's Most Perilous Year,* by David Von Drehle, 2012, Henry Holt and Company, New York, New York, pp 345-347

[41] *Never Call Retreat,* by Bruce Catton, 1965, Doubleday & Company, Inc., Garden City New York, pp 66-69

[42] *The Sword of Lincoln, The Army of the Potomac,* by Jeffry D. Wert, 2005, Simon & Schuster Paperbacks, New York, New York, pp 231-234

[43] Ibid, pp 235-244

[44] *Never Call Retreat,* by Bruce Catton, 1965, Doubleday & Company, Inc., Garden City New York, page 179

[45] *Stand in the Day of Battle,* by William C. Davis, 1983, Doubleday & Company, Inc., Garden City, New York, page 110

[46] Ibid, page 112

[47] *The Sword of Lincoln, The Army of the Potomac,* by Jeffry D. Wert, 2005, Simon & Schuster Paperbacks, New York, New York, pp 274-277 and 303

[48] *Gettysburg*, by Stephen W. Sears, 2003, 2004, First Mariner Books, Houghton Mifflin Company, New York, New York, pp 249-250, 262, 269-271, 278, and 295-296

[49] Ibid, pp 325-330, 383, 396 and 409

[50] Ibid, pp 376, 409, 417-429, 441-442, and 457

[51] *Stand in the Day of Battle*, by William C. Davis, 1983, Doubleday & Company, Inc., Garden City, New York, page 152

[52] *Fierce Patriot, The Tangled Lives of William Tecumseh Sherman*, by Robert L. O'Connell, 2014, 2015, Random House, New York, New York, page 119

[53] *The Personal Memoirs of Ulysses S. Grant*, by Ulysses S. Grant, 1885, Konecky & Konecky, Old Saybrook, Connecticut, pp 312-313

[54] Ibid, pp 315-320

[55] Ibid, pp 327-333

[56] *A. Lincoln, A Biography*, by Ronald C. White, Jr., 2009, Random House, New York, New York, page 593

[57] Ibid, page 595

[58] *Fierce Patriot, The Tangled Lives of William Tecumseh Sherman*, by Robert L. O'Connell, 2014, 2015, Random House, New York, New York, pp 123-125

[59] *A. Lincoln, A Biography*, by Ronald C. White, Jr., 2009, Random House, New York, New York, pp 597-601

[60] *Never Call Retreat*, by Bruce Catton, 1965, Doubleday & Company, Inc., Garden City New York, pp 262-263

[61] Ibid, pp 263-264

[62] Ibid, pp 264-265

[63] *Abraham Lincoln, The Prairie Years and the War Years*, Illustrated Edition, by Carl Sandburg, 1954, 1970, The Reader's Digest Association, Pleasantville, New York, pp 384-387

[64] *Jeff Shaarah's Civil War Battlefields*, by Jeff Shaarah, 2006, Ballentine Books, an imprint of Random House Publishing Group, New York, New York, pp 182-183

[65] *The Sword of Lincoln, The Army of the Potomac*, by Jeffry D. Wert, 2005, Simon & Schuster Paperbacks, New York, New York, pp 336-341

[66] *Never Call Retreat*, by Bruce Catton, 1965, Doubleday & Company, Inc., Garden City New York, pp 362-364

[67] Ibid, pp 317-329

[68] Ibid, pp 383-387

[69] *Abraham Lincoln, The Prairie Years and the War Years*, One-Volume Edition, by Carl Sandburg, 1954, Harcourt, Brace & World, Inc., New York, New York, pp 617-618

[70] *Abraham Lincoln, The Prairie Years and the War Years*, Illustrated Edition, by Carl Sandburg, 1954, 1970, The Reader's Digest Association, Pleasantville, New York, pp 510-515

[71] *The Sword of Lincoln, The Army of the Potomac*, by Jeffry D. Wert, 2005, Simon & Schuster Paperbacks, New York, New York, pp 361-375

[72] *Fierce Patriot, The Tangled Lives of William Tecumseh Sherman*, by Robert L. O'Connell, 2014, 2015, Random House, New York, New York, pp 172-178

[73] *Never Call Retreat*, by Bruce Catton, 1965, Doubleday & Company, Inc., Garden City New York, pp 441-444

[74] *Pursuit, The Chase, Capture, Persecution & Surprising Release of Confederate President Jefferson Davis*, by Clint Johnson, 2008, Citadel Press Books, published by Kensington Publishing Corp., New York, New York, pp 18-20

[75] *Never Call Retreat*, by Bruce Catton, 1965, Doubleday & Company, Inc., Garden City New York, pp 445-447

[76] *Abraham Lincoln, A Biography*, by Benjamin P. Thomas, 1952, Barnes & Noble, Inc., by arrangement with Alfred A. Knopf, Inc., New York, New York, pp 513-514

CHAPTER 7

[1] Ibid, pp 17-18 and 23-24

[2] *A. Lincoln, A Biography*, by Ronald C. White, Jr., 2009, Random House, New York, New York, pp 201, 214, 227, 240, 271, 276 and 458

[3] Ibid, pp 161-162, 175-185, and 492

[4] *Lincoln, Speeches and Writings 1832 – 1858*, notes by Don E. Fehrenbacher, 1989, Library Classics of the United States, Inc., New York, New York, pp 426-434

[5] *Lincoln and Douglas, The Debates that Defined America*, by Allen C. Guelzo, 2008, Simon & Schuster, New York, New York, page 292

[6] *A. Lincoln, A Biography*, by Ronald C. White, Jr., 2009, Random House, New York, New York, pp 263-264

[7] Ibid, pp 265-266

[8] Ibid, page 267

[9] *Lincoln*, by David Herbert Donald, 1995, Simon & Schuster, New York, New York, page 218

[10] *Lincoln and Douglas, The Debates that Defined America*, by Allen C. Guelzo, 2008, Simon & Schuster, New York, New York, page 152

[11] *Lincoln, Speeches and Writings 1832 – 1858*, notes by Don E. Fehrenbacher, 1989, Library Classics of the United States, Inc., New York, New York, pp 538-539

[12] Ibid, pp 550-569

[13] *Abraham Lincoln, Selected Writings*, 2013, Barnes and Noble, Inc., New York, New York, pp 304-317

[14] *The Road to Disunion, Secessionists at Bay 1776-1854*, by William W. Freehling, 1990, Oxford University Press, New York, New York, page 154

[15] *Abraham Lincoln, Selected Writings*, 2013, Barnes and Noble, Inc., New York, New York, pp 317-322

[16] *Lincoln and Douglas, The Debates that Defined America*, by Allen C. Guelzo, 2008, Simon & Schuster, New York, New York, pp 132-133

[17] *A. Lincoln, A Biography*, by Ronald C. White, Jr., 2009, Random House, New York, New York, pp 270-271

[18] *The Living Lincoln, The Man, His Mind, His Times, and the War He Fought, Reconstructed from His Own Writings*, edited by Paul M. Angle and Earl Schenck Miers, 1955, 1992, Marboro Books Corp., a division of Barnes & Noble, Inc., by arrangement with Rutgers University Press, page 260

[19] Ibid, page 265

[20] *Lincoln and Douglas, The Debates that Defined America*, by Allen C. Guelzo, 2008, Simon & Schuster, New York, New York, pp 193-194

[21] *Abraham Lincoln: Speeches and Writings 1859-1865; Speeches, Letters, Miscellaneous Writings Presidential Messages and Proclamations*, 1989, Volume arrangement, notes, and chronology by Library Classics of the United States, Inc., New York, New York, page 650

[22] Ibid, pp 657-670

[23] Ibid, pp 675-682

[24] *Lincoln and Douglas, The Debates that Defined America*, by Allen C. Guelzo, 2008, Simon & Schuster, New York, New York, pp 201-202

[25] *A. Lincoln, A Biography*, by Ronald C. White, Jr., 2009, Random House, New York, New York, pp 279-280

[26] *Lincoln and Douglas, The Debates that Defined America*, by Allen C. Guelzo, 2008, Simon & Schuster, New York, New York, pp 221-224

[27] *The Living Lincoln, The Man, His Mind, His Times, and the War He Fought, Reconstructed from His Own Writings*, edited by Paul M. Angle and Earl Schenck Miers, 1955, 1992, Marboro Books Corp., a division of Barnes & Noble, Inc., by arrangement with Rutgers University Press, page 269

[28] *Abraham Lincoln: Speeches and Writings 1859-1865; Speeches, Letters, Miscellaneous Writings Presidential Messages and Proclamations*, 1989, Volume arrangement, notes, and chronology by Library Classics of the United States, Inc., New York, New York, page 704

[29] *Abraham Lincoln, Selected Writings*, 2013, Barnes and Noble, Inc., New York, New York, page 416

[30] Ibid, page 417

[31] *Abraham Lincoln: Speeches and Writings 1859-1865; Speeches, Letters, Miscellaneous Writings Presidential Messages and Proclamations*, 1989, Volume arrangement, notes, and chronology by Library Classics of the United States, Inc., New York, New York, page 729

[32] *Lincoln and Douglas, The Debates that Defined America*, by Allen C. Guelzo, 2008, Simon & Schuster, New York, New York, page 242

[33] *Abraham Lincoln: Speeches and Writings 1859-1865; Speeches, Letters, Miscellaneous Writings Presidential Messages and Proclamations*, 1989, Volume arrangement, notes, and chronology by Library Classics of the United States, Inc., New York, New York, pp 731-732

[34] *Abraham Lincoln, Selected Writings*, 2013, Barnes and Noble, Inc., New York, New York, pp 433-436

[35] *Abraham Lincoln: Speeches and Writings 1859-1865; Speeches, Letters, Miscellaneous Writings Presidential Messages and Proclamations*, 1989, Volume arrangement, notes, and chronology by Library Classics of the United States, Inc., New York, New York, page 740

[36] *Lincoln and Douglas, The Debates that Defined America*, by Allen C. Guelzo, 2008, Simon & Schuster, New York, New York, page 246

[37] *Abraham Lincoln: Speeches and Writings 1859-1865; Speeches, Letters, Miscellaneous Writings Presidential Messages and Proclamations,* 1989, Volume arrangement, notes, and chronology by Library Classics of the United States, Inc., New York, New York, pp 243-247

[38] Ibid, pp 753-763

[39] *The Abraham Lincoln Encyclopedia*, by Mark E. Neely, Jr., 1982, Da Capo Press, Inc, New York, New York, found at: https://www.nps.gov/liho/learn/historyculture/debate6.htm, accessed June 29, 2020

[40] *Abraham Lincoln: Speeches and Writings 1859-1865; Speeches, Letters, Miscellaneous Writings Presidential Messages and Proclamations,* 1989, Volume arrangement, notes, and chronology by Library Classics of the United States, Inc., New York, New York, pp 765-766

[41] *Lincoln and Douglas, The Debates that Defined America*, by Allen C. Guelzo, 2008, Simon & Schuster, New York, New York, pp 254-255

[42] *The Living Lincoln, The Man, His Mind, His Times, and the War He Fought, Reconstructed from His Own Writings*, edited by Paul M. Angle and Earl Schenck Miers, 1955, 1992, Marboro Books Corp., a division of Barnes & Noble, Inc., by arrangement with Rutgers University Press, page 277

[43] *Lincoln and Douglas, The Debates that Defined America*, by Allen C. Guelzo, 2008, Simon & Schuster, New York, New York, page 259

[44] *The Abraham Lincoln Encyclopedia*, by Mark E. Neely, Jr., 1982, Da Capo Press, Inc, New York, New York, found at: https://www.nps.gov/liho/learn/historyculture/debate7.htm, accessed June 29, 2020

[45] *Abraham Lincoln: Speeches and Writings 1859-1865; Speeches, Letters, Miscellaneous Writings Presidential Messages and Proclamations,* 1989, Volume arrangement, notes, and chronology by Library Classics of the United States, Inc., New York, New York, page 776

[46] Ibid, pp 781 and 789

[47] *Lincoln and Douglas, The Debates that Defined America*, by Allen C. Guelzo, 2008, Simon & Schuster, New York, New York, page 261

[48] *The Abraham Lincoln Encyclopedia*, by Mark E. Neely, Jr., 1982, Da Capo Press, Inc, New York, New York, found at: https://www.nps.gov/liho/learn/historyculture/debate7.htm, accessed June 29, 2020

[49] Ibid

[50] *The Living Lincoln, The Man, His Mind, His Times, and the War He Fought, Reconstructed from His Own Writings*, edited by Paul M. Angle and Earl Schenck Miers, 1955, 1992, Marboro Books Corp., a division of Barnes & Noble, Inc., by arrangement with Rutgers University Press, page 279

[51] Ibid, page 281

[52] *The Fiery Trial*, by Eric Foner, 2010, W.W. Norton & Company, Inc., New York, New York, page 152

[53] *The Living Lincoln, The Man, His Mind, His Times, and the War He Fought, Reconstructed from His Own Writings*, edited by Paul M. Angle and Earl Schenck Miers, 1955, 1992, Marboro Books Corp., a division of Barnes & Noble, Inc., by arrangement with Rutgers University Press, pp 383-385

[54] *The Fiery Trial*, by Eric Foner, 2010, W.W. Norton & Company, Inc., New York, New York, page 160

[55] Ibid, pp 176-179

[56] *Lincoln*, by David Herbert Donald, 1995, Simon & Schuster, New York, New York, page 345

[57] *The Fiery Trial*, by Eric Foner, 2010, W.W. Norton & Company, Inc., New York, New York, pp 195-200, 204 and 215

[58] Ibid, page 218

[59] *Team of Rivals, The Political Genius of Abraham Lincoln*, by Doris Kearns Goodwin, 2005, Simon & Schuster, New York, New York, page 468

[60] Ibid, page 481

[61] Ibid, page 482

[62] *Who Freed the Slaves? The Fight Over the Thirteenth Amendment*, by Leonard L. Richards, 2015, The University of Chicago Press, Chicago, Illinois, page 14

[63] Ibid, page 7

[64] *Abraham Lincoln, A Biography*, by Benjamin P. Thomas, 1952, Barnes & Noble, Inc., by arrangement with Alfred A. Knopf, Inc., New York, New York, page 493

[65] *Abraham Lincoln, The Prairie Years and the War Years*, by Carl Sandburg, 1954, Harcourt, Brace & World, Inc., New York, New York, pp 644-646

CHAPTER 8

[1] *A. Lincoln, A Biography*, by Ronald C. White, Jr., 2009, Random House, New York, New York, pp 606-607

[2] *Lincoln in American Memory,* by Merrill D. Peterson, 1994, Oxford University Press, New York, New York, page 201

[3] *Team of Rivals, The Political Genius of Abraham Lincoln*, by Doris Kearns Goodwin, 2005, Simon & Schuster, New York, New York, page 747

[4] Ibid, page 748

[5] *A. Lincoln, A Biography*, by Ronald C. White, Jr., 2009, Random House, New York, New York, page 675

[6] *Team of Rivals, The Political Genius of Abraham Lincoln*, by Doris Kearns Goodwin, 2005, Simon & Schuster, New York, New York, page 570

[7] Collected Works of Abraham Lincoln. Volume 3. Lincoln, Abraham, 1809-1865, Address before the Wisconsin State Agricultural Society, Milwaukee, Wisconsin, September 30, 1859. https://quod.lib.umich.edu/l/lincoln/lincoln3/1:144?cite1=lincoln;cite1restrict=author;rgn=div1;singlegenre=All;sort=occur;subview=detail;type=simple;view=fulltext;q1=education

[8] *Lincoln's Way, How Six Great Presidents Created American Power*, by Richard Streiner, 2010, Rowman & Littlefield Publishers, Inc., Lanham, Maryland, page 41

[9] *Grand Old Party, A History of the Republicans*, by Lewis L. Gould, 2003, Random House, Inc, New York, New York, page 11

[10] *A. Lincoln, A Biography*, by Ronald C. White, Jr., 2009, Random House, New York, New York, pp 204-208

[11] *Abraham Lincoln, A Biography*, by Benjamin P. Thomas, 1952, Barnes & Noble, Inc., by arrangement with Alfred A. Knopf, Inc., New York, New York, pp 122-123

[12] *A. Lincoln, A Biography*, by Ronald C. White, Jr., 2009, Random House, New York, New York, pp 212-216

[13] Ibid, pp 216-220

[14] *Team of Rivals, The Political Genius of Abraham Lincoln*, by Doris Kearns Goodwin, 2005, Simon & Schuster, New York, New York, pp 245-246

[15] Ibid, page 487

[16] Ibid, pp 489-490

[17] Ibid, pp 491-492

[18] Ibid, page 495

[19] https://www.senate.gov/civics/constitution_item/constitution.htm

[20] *The Sword of Lincoln, The Army of the Potomac*, by Jeffry D. Wert, 2005, Simon & Schuster Paperbacks, New York, New York, pp 2-3

[21] Abraham Lincoln, First Annual Message Online by Gerhard Peters and John T. Woolley, The American Presidency Project https://www.presidency.ucsb.edu/node/202175

[22] *Rise to Greatness, Abraham Lincoln and America's Most Perilous Year*, by David Von Drehle, 2012, Henry Holt and Company, New York, New York, pp 4-6

[23] *Team of Rivals, The Political Genius of Abraham Lincoln*, by Doris Kearns Goodwin, 2005, Simon & Schuster, New York, New York, page 356

[24] *Dissonance, The Turbulent Days Between Fort Sumter and Bull Run*, by David Detzer, 2006, Harcourt, Inc., Orlando, Florida, page 271

[25] *Rise to Greatness, Abraham Lincoln and America's Most Perilous Year*, by David Von Drehle, 2012, Henry Holt and Company, New York, New York, pp 34-35

[26] *Lincoln in American Memory*, by Merrill D. Peterson, 1994, Oxford University Press, New York, New York, pp 204-205

[27] *Rise to Greatness, Abraham Lincoln and America's Most Perilous Year*, by David Von Drehle, 2012, Henry Holt and Company, New York, New York, pp 108-109

[28] *Why Lincoln Matters, Today More Than Ever*, by Mario M. Cuomo, 2004, Harcourt, Inc., New York, New York, page 90

[29] Congressional Record, Thirty-seventh Congress, Session II, Chapter 33, 1862, Library of Congress, found at: https://fraser.stlouisfed.org/title/legal-tender-act-1107

[30] Congressional Record, Thirty-seventh Congress, Session III, Chapter 53, 1863, Library of Congress, found at: https://fraser.stlouisfed.org/title/national-bank-act-1863-1111

[31] Abraham Lincoln, Fourth Annual Message Online by Gerhard Peters and John T. Woolley, The American Presidency Project https://www.presidency.ucsb.edu/node/202188

[32] https://www.occ.treas.gov/about/who-we-are/history/founding-occ-national-bank-system/index-founding-occ-national-banking-system.html

[33] *Lincoln's Way, How Six Great Presidents Created American Power*, by Richard Streiner, 2010, Rowman & Littlefield Publishers, Inc., Lanham, Maryland, page 38

[34] https://www.loc.gov/rr/program/bib/ourdocs/homestead.html

[35] https://www.nps.gov/home/learn/historyculture/lincolnandwest.htm

[36] https://www.loc.gov/item/today-in-history/may-20/

[37]
https://www.nps.gov/home/learn/historyculture/creationhomesteadmonu
ment.htm

[38] Lincoln, Abraham. Abraham Lincoln papers: Series 1. General Correspondence. -1916: Abraham Lincoln, May-June 1860 Autobiographical Notes; copy in hand of John G. Nicolay. May, 1860. Manuscript/Mixed Material. https://www.loc.gov/item/mal0323000/

[39] *A. Lincoln, A Biography*, by Ronald C. White, Jr., 2009, Random House, New York, New York, page 155

[40] Congressional Record, Thirty-seventh Congress, Session II, Chapter 130, 1862, Library of Congress, found at: http://memory.loc.gov/cgi-bin/ampage?collId=llsl&fileName=012/llsl012.db&recNum=534

[41] https://mitadmissions.org/discover/about-mit/a-brief-history-of-mit/

[42] National Research Council 1995. Colleges of Agriculture at the Land Grant Universities: A Profile. Washington, DC: The National Academies Press. https://doi.org/10.17226/4980.

[43] Ibid

[44] *Starving the South* by Andrew F. Smith, 2011, St. Martin's Press, New York, New York, page 208

[45] *A Short History of the United States*, by Robert V. Remini, 2008, Harper Collins Publishers, New York, New York, pp 122-123

[46] Ibid, pp 122-125

[47]   https://www.loc.gov/collections/railroad-maps-1828-to-1900/articles-and-essays/history-of-railroads-and-maps/the-transcontinental-railroad/

[48] *A. Lincoln, A Biography*, by Ronald C. White, Jr., 2009, Random House, New York, New York, page 606

[49] Ibid, page 135

[50] *Why Lincoln Matters, Today More Than Ever*, by Mario M. Cuomo, 2004, Harcourt, Inc., New York, New York, page 128

[51] *Lincoln in American Memory*, by Merrill D. Peterson, 1994, Oxford University Press, New York, New York, pp 7-12

[52] *Why Lincoln Matters, Today More Than Ever*, by Mario M. Cuomo, 2004, Harcourt, Inc., New York, New York, page 133

[53] *Abraham Lincoln, Selected Writings*, 2013, Barnes and Noble, Inc., New York, New York, page 243

[54] *Team of Rivals, The Political Genius of Abraham Lincoln*, by Doris Kearns Goodwin, 2005, Simon & Schuster, New York, New York, page 207

[55] *Fierce Patriot, The Tangled Lives of William Tecumseh Sherman*, by Robert L. O'Connell, 2014, 2015, Random House, New York, New York, page xiii

[56] *Abraham Lincoln, Selected Writings*, 2013, Barnes and Noble, Inc., New York, New York, page 727

CHAPTER 9

[1] *Mornings on Horseback, The Story of an Extraordinary Family, a Vanished Way of Life, and the Unique Child Who Became Theodore Roosevelt*, by David McCullough, 1981, 2001, Simon & Schuster, Inc., New York, New York, pp 171-180

[2] *The Rise of Theodore Roosevelt*, by Edmund Morris, 1979, Random House, New York, New York, pp 89, 124 and 139

[3] *FDR*, by Jean Edward Smith, 2007, Random House, Inc., New York, New York, pp 49 and 59

[4] *The Rise of Theodore Roosevelt*, by Edmund Morris, 1979, Random House, New York, New York, pp 24-25

[5] Ibid, pp 34, 36, 40, and 43

[6] *FDR, The Beckoning of Destiny, 1882 – 1928*, A History by Kenneth S. Davis, G. P. Putnam's Sons, New York, New York, pp 48-49 and 60

[7] Ibid, page 62

[8] Ibid, pp 79-80

[9] Ibid, pp 155-156

[10] *Mornings on Horseback, The Story of an Extraordinary Family, a Vanished Way of Life, and the Unique Child Who Became Theodore Roosevelt*, by David McCullough, 1981, 2001, Simon & Schuster, Inc., New York, New York, page 177

[11] *FDR, The Beckoning of Destiny, 1882 – 1928*, A History by Kenneth S. Davis, G. P. Putnam's Sons, New York, New York, pp 78 and 156-157

[12] *The Rise of Theodore Roosevelt*, by Edmund Morris, 1979, Random House, New York, New York, pp 101 and 135-136

[13] *FDR, The Beckoning of Destiny, 1882 – 1928*, A History by Kenneth S. Davis, G. P. Putnam's Sons, New York, New York, pp 144, 146, 158-159 and 163

[14] *The Roosevelts, An American Saga*, by Peter Collier with David Horowitz, 1994, Simon & Schuster, New York, New York, page 47

[15] *Mornings on Horseback, The Story of an Extraordinary Family, a Vanished Way of Life, and the Unique Child Who Became Theodore Roosevelt*, by David McCullough, 1981, 2001, Simon & Schuster, Inc., New York, New York, pp 183-188

[16] *The Rise of Theodore Roosevelt*, by Edmund Morris, 1979, Random House, New York, New York, pp 73-76

[17] *FDR, The Beckoning of Destiny, 1882 – 1928*, A History by Kenneth S. Davis, G. P. Putnam's Sons, New York, New York, pp 141-143

[18] *The Rise of Theodore Roosevelt*, by Edmund Morris, 1979, Random House, New York, New York, pp 106-116

[19] *FDR, The Beckoning of Destiny, 1882 – 1928*, A History by Kenneth S. Davis, G. P. Putnam's Sons, New York, New York, pp 191-194

[20] *The Rise of Theodore Roosevelt*, by Edmund Morris, 1979, Random House, New York, New York, pp 102 and 104-108

[21] *Mornings on Horseback, The Story of an Extraordinary Family, a Vanished Way of Life, and the Unique Child Who Became Theodore Roosevelt*, by David McCullough, 1981, 2001, Simon & Schuster, Inc., New York, New York, pp 228-230

[22] *FDR, The Beckoning of Destiny, 1882 – 1928*, A History by Kenneth S. Davis, G. P. Putnam's Sons, New York, New York, pp 188-190

[23] *FDR*, by Jean Edward Smith, 2007, Random House, Inc., New York, New York, pp 48-49 and 51

[24] *The Rise of Theodore Roosevelt*, by Edmund Morris, 1979, Random House, New York, New York, pp 117-119

[25] Ibid, pp 119-121

[26] Ibid, pp 129-131

[27] *FDR, The Beckoning of Destiny, 1882 – 1928*, A History by Kenneth S. Davis, G. P. Putnam's Sons, New York, New York, pp 191-193

[28] *FDR*, by Jean Edward Smith, 2007, Random House, Inc., New York, New York, pp 52-56

[29] *The Rise of Theodore Roosevelt*, by Edmund Morris, 1979, Random House, New York, New York, pp 131-135

[30] *Mornings on Horseback, The Story of an Extraordinary Family, a Vanished Way of Life, and the Unique Child Who Became Theodore Roosevelt*, by David McCullough, 1981, 2001, Simon & Schuster, Inc., New York, New York, pp 252-266

[31] *The Rise of Theodore Roosevelt*, by Edmund Morris, 1979, Random House, New York, New York, pp 220-223 and 227-230

[32] *FDR*, by Jean Edward Smith, 2007, Random House, Inc., New York, New York, pp 65-69

[33] Ibid, pp 70-75

[34] Ibid, pp 92-95

[35] *The Autobiography of Theodore Roosevelt*, by Theodore Roosevelt, 2009, Seven Treasures Publications, prepared from the 1920 edition published by Charles Scribner's Sons, this autobiography was first published in 1913, pp 114-115

[36] *The Rise of Theodore Roosevelt*, by Edmund Morris, 1979, Random House, New York, New York, pp 590-595

[37] *The Autobiography of Theodore Roosevelt*, by Theodore Roosevelt, 2009, Seven Treasures Publications, prepared from the 1920 edition published by Charles Scribner's Sons, this autobiography was first published in 1913, pp 116-119

[38] *Roosevelt's Navy, The Education of a Warrior President, 1882-1920*, by James Tertius de Kay, 2012, Pegasus Books LLC, New York, New York, pp 85-86

[39] Ibid, pp 89-92

[40] Ibid, pp 131-136

[41] *The Autobiography of Theodore Roosevelt*, by Theodore Roosevelt, 2009, Seven Treasures Publications, prepared from the 1920 edition published by Charles Scribner's Sons, this autobiography was first published in 1913, pp 121-122

[42] *The Rise of Theodore Roosevelt*, by Edmund Morris, 1979, Random House, New York, New York, pp 653-664

[43] *The War Lovers, Roosevelt, Lodge, Hearst, and the Rush to Empire, 1898*, by Evan Thomas, 2010, Little, Brown, and Company, a division of Hachette Book Group, Inc., New York, New York, pp 317-327

[44] *FDR*, by Jean Edward Smith, 2007, Random House, Inc., New York, New York, pp 139-140

[45] Ibid, pp 141-142

[46] Ibid, pp 143-144

[47] *The Rise of Theodore Roosevelt*, by Edmund Morris, 1979, Random House, New York, New York, pp 753-755

[48] Ibid, pp 746-751

[49] *FDR*, by Jean Edward Smith, 2007, Random House, Inc., New York, New York, pp 165-168

[50] Ibid, pp 171-177

[51] Ibid, pp 179-182

[52] *The Rise of Theodore Roosevelt*, by Edmund Morris, 1979, Random House, New York, New York, pp 227-229

[53] *Mornings on Horseback, The Story of an Extraordinary Family, a Vanished Way of Life, and the Unique Child Who Became Theodore Roosevelt*, by David McCullough, 1981, 2001, Simon & Schuster, Inc., New York, New York, pp 282-283

[54] *The Rise of Theodore Roosevelt*, by Edmund Morris, 1979, Random House, New York, New York, pp 235-238 and 261-267

[55] *FDR*, by Jean Edward Smith, 2007, Random House, Inc., New York, New York, pp 188-191

[56] Ibid, pp 192-194

[57] *Man of Destiny, FDR and the Making of the American Century*, by Alonzo Hamby, 2015, Basic Books, a member of the Perseus Books Corp., New York, New York, pp 103-106; see also note on page 221 of *FDR*, by Jean Edward Smith, 2007, Random House, Inc., New York, New York

[58] *FDR*, by Jean Edward Smith, 2007, Random House, Inc., New York, New York, pp 209-212

[59] *Mornings on Horseback, The Story of an Extraordinary Family, a Vanished Way of Life, and the Unique Child Who Became Theodore Roosevelt*, by David McCullough, 1981, 2001, Simon & Schuster, Inc., New York, New York, pp 150-151

[60] *The Rise of Theodore Roosevelt*, by Edmund Morris, 1979, Random House, New York, New York, pp 711-721 and 728-738

[61] *Traitor to his Class, The Privileged Life and Radical Presidency of Franklin Delano Roosevelt*, by H. W. Brands, First Anchor Books, a division of Random House, Inc., New York, New York, pp 174-182

[62] *FDR*, by Jean Edward Smith, 2007, Random House, Inc., New York, New York, pp 221-228

[63] *Mornings on Horseback, The Story of an Extraordinary Family, a Vanished Way of Life, and the Unique Child Who Became Theodore Roosevelt*, by David McCullough, 1981, 2001, Simon & Schuster, Inc., New York, New York, pp 193-194

[64] *Theodore Rex*, by Edmund Morris, 2001, Random House, New York, New York, pp 111-116, 182-191, 215-216, 493-495, and 509-510

[65] *FDR*, by Jean Edward Smith, 2007, Random House, Inc., New York, New York, pp 229, 237-238, 242, 244-245 and 263

[66] Ibid, pp 274, 277, 282-283, and 286-287

CHAPTER 10

[1] *The Great Depression: America, 1929-1941*, by Robert S. McElvaine, 1984, 1993, 2009, Three Rivers Press, in imprint of Crown Publishing Group, a Division of Random House, Inc., New York, New York, page xxiii

[2] http://www.u-s-history.com/pages/h1569.html

[3] *What's Next for the Economy, Using the Power of Cycles to Predict "What's Next" for Inflation, the Stock Market, Real Estate, and Business*, by Edward Thomas, 2017, ACCE Publishing LLC, Irvine, California, pp 15-16

[4] *The Forgotten Man, A New History of the Great Depression*, by Amity Shlaes, 2007, Harper Collins Publishers, New York, New York, pp 109-111

[5] *The Great Depression: An Inquiry into the Causes, Course, and Consequences of the Worldwide Depression of the Nineteen-Thirties, as Seen by Comparison and in the Light of History*, by John A Garrary, 1986, Harcourt Brace Jovanovich Publishers, Orlando Florida, page 245

[6] *The Forgotten Man, A New History of the Great Depression*, by Amity Shlaes, 2007, Harper Collins Publishers, New York, New York, page 112

[7] *What's Next for the Economy, Using the Power of Cycles to Predict "What's Next" for Inflation, the Stock Market, Real Estate, and Business*, by Edward Thomas, 2017, ACCE Publishing LLC, Irvine, California, page 14

[8] Ibid, pp 14-15

[9] *The Forgotten Man, A New History of the Great Depression*, by Amity Shlaes, 2007, Harper Collins Publishers, New York, New York, pp 95-97

[10] *The Defining Moment, FDR's Hundred Days and the Triumph of Hope*, by Jonathan Alter, 2006, Simon & Schuster, New York, New York, pp 189-191

[11] *FDR*, by Jean Edward Smith, 2007, Random House, Inc., New York, New York, page 287

[12] *Man of Destiny, FDR and the Making of the American Century*, by Alonzo Hamby, 2015, Basic Books, a member of the Perseus Books Corp., New York, New York, pp 161-164

[13] *FDR, The New York Years, 1928 – 1933*, A History by Kenneth S. Davis, 1979, 1980, 1983, 1985, Random House, New York, New York, page 421

[14] *FDR*, by Jean Edward Smith, 2007, Random House, Inc., New York, New York, pp 298-299

[15] *FDR, The New York Years, 1928 – 1933*, A History by Kenneth S. Davis, 1979, 1980, 1983, 1985, Random House, New York, New York, pp 428-435

[16] *The Defining Moment, FDR's Hundred Days and the Triumph of Hope*, by Jonathan Alter, 2006, Simon & Schuster, New York, New York, pp 216-219

[17] *FDR, The New York Years, 1928 – 1933*, A History by Kenneth S. Davis, 1979, 1980, 1983, 1985, Random House, New York, New York, pp 443-445

[18] *The Defining Moment, FDR's Hundred Days and the Triumph of Hope*, by Jonathan Alter, 2006, Simon & Schuster, New York, New York, pp 229-230

[19] *FDR*, by Jean Edward Smith, 2007, Random House, Inc., New York, New York, page 307

[20] *The Defining Moment, FDR's Hundred Days and the Triumph of Hope*, by Jonathan Alter, 2006, Simon & Schuster, New York, New York, pp 264 and 268

[21] Ibid, page 269

[22] Ibid, page 271

[23] *FDR*, by Jean Edward Smith, 2007, Random House, Inc., New York, New York, page 304

[24] Ibid, page 332

[25] *The Great Depression, America, 1929-1941*, by Robert S. McElvaine, 1984, 1993, 2009, Three Rivers Press, an imprint of the Crown Publishing Group, a division of Random House, Inc., New York, New York, pp 154-163

[26] *FDR*, by Jean Edward Smith, 2007, Random House, Inc., New York, New York, page 321

[27] Ibid, pp 319-320

[28] Ibid, page 322

[29] *The Great Depression, America, 1929-1941*, by Robert S. McElvaine, 1984, 1993, 2009, Three Rivers Press, an imprint of the Crown Publishing Group, a division of Random House, Inc., New York, New York, pp 154 and 178

[30] *FDR*, by Jean Edward Smith, 2007, Random House, Inc., New York, New York, page 326

[31] *The Great Depression, America, 1929-1941*, by Robert S. McElvaine, 1984, 1993, 2009, Three Rivers Press, an imprint of the Crown Publishing Group, a division of Random House, Inc., New York, New York, pp 162 and 175

[32] *FDR*, by Jean Edward Smith, 2007, Random House, Inc., New York, New York, pp 324-325

[33] *The Great Depression, America, 1929-1941*, by Robert S. McElvaine, 1984, 1993, 2009, Three Rivers Press, an imprint of the Crown Publishing Group, a division of Random House, Inc., New York, New York, page 155

[34] *FDR, The New Deal Years, 1933 – 1937*, A History by Kenneth S. Davis, 1979, 1983, 1986, Random House, New York, New York, page 273

[35] Ibid, pp 280-281

[36] *FDR*, by Jean Edward Smith, 2007, Random House, Inc., New York, New York, pp 330-331

[37] *The Great Depression, America, 1929-1941*, by Robert S. McElvaine, 1984, 1993, 2009, Three Rivers Press, an imprint of the Crown Publishing Group, a division of Random House, Inc., New York, New York, page 152

[38] *FDR, The New Deal Years, 1933 – 1937*, A History by Kenneth S. Davis, 1979, 1983, 1986, Random House, New York, New York, page 149

[39] Ibid, pp 148-150

[40] Ibid, page 83

[41] Ibid, pp 82, 364, 365, and 369

[42] *FDR*, by Jean Edward Smith, 2007, Random House, Inc., New York, New York, page 349

[43] Ibid, page 359

[44] *FDR, A Biography*, by Ted Morgan, 1985, Simon & Schuster, New York, New York, pp 417-418

[45] *FDR*, by Jean Edward Smith, 2007, Random House, Inc., New York, New York, page 357

[46] Ibid, pp 351-352

[47] *The Great Depression, America, 1929-1941*, by Robert S. McElvaine, 1984, 1993, 2009, Three Rivers Press, an imprint of the Crown Publishing Group, a division of Random House, Inc., New York, New York, pp 258-259

[48] *Man of Destiny, FDR and the Making of the American Century*, by Alonzo Hamby, 2015, Basic Books, a member of the Perseus Books Corp., New York, New York, pp 247-248

[49] *FDR*, by Jean Edward Smith, 2007, Random House, Inc., New York, New York, page 360

[50] *The Great Depression, America, 1929-1941*, by Robert S. McElvaine, 1984, 1993, 2009, Three Rivers Press, an imprint of the Crown Publishing Group, a division of Random House, Inc., New York, New York, page 277

[51] *FDR*, by Jean Edward Smith, 2007, Random House, Inc., New York, New York, page 361

[52] *The Great Depression, America, 1929-1941*, by Robert S. McElvaine, 1984, 1993, 2009, Three Rivers Press, an imprint of the Crown Publishing Group, a division of Random House, Inc., New York, New York, page 276

[53] Ibid, page 281

[54] *FDR*, by Jean Edward Smith, 2007, Random House, Inc., New York, New York, page 373-374

[55] *The American President, A Complete History*, by Kathryn Moore, 2007, Fall River Press, New York, New York, page 749

[56] *Man of Destiny, FDR and the Making of the American Century*, by Alonzo Hamby, 2015, Basic Books, a member of the Perseus Books Corp., New York, New York, pp 233-236

[57] *Supreme Power, Franklin Roosevelt vs. The Supreme Court*, by Jeff Shesol, 2010, W. W. Norton & Company, New York, New York, pp 150-152

[58] Ibid, page 97

[59] *FDR, Into the Storm, 1937 – 1940*, A History by Kenneth S. Davis, 1993, Random House, New York, New York, pp 48-50

[60] *Supreme Power, Franklin Roosevelt vs. The Supreme Court*, by Jeff Shesol, 2010, W. W. Norton & Company, New York, New York, pp 249, 500, 502 and 525

[61] *Traitor to his Class, The Privileged Life and Radical Presidency of Franklin Delano Roosevelt*, by H. W. Brands, First Anchor Books, a division of Random House, Inc., New York, New York, pp 521-522

[62] *FDR, A Biography*, by Ted Morgan, 1985, Simon & Schuster, New York, New York, pp 486-490

[63] *FDR*, by Jean Edward Smith, 2007, Random House, Inc., New York, New York, pp 411-415

[64] *Man of Destiny, FDR and the Making of the American Century*, by Alonzo Hamby, 2015, Basic Books, a member of the Perseus Books Corp., New York, New York, page 284

[65] *FDR*, by Jean Edward Smith, 2007, Random House, Inc., New York, New York, page 437

[66] *FDR, Into the Storm, 1937 – 1940*, A History by Kenneth S. Davis, 1993, Random House, New York, New York, pp 533-534

[67] *No Ordinary Time, Franklin and Elanor Roosevelt: The Home Front in World War II*, by Doris Kearns Goodwin, 1994, Schuster & Schuster, New York, New York, page 68

[68] *FDR, Into the Storm, 1937 – 1940*, A History by Kenneth S. Davis, 1993, Random House, New York, New York, pp 597-601

[69] *No Ordinary Time, Franklin and Elanor Roosevelt: The Home Front in World War II*, by Doris Kearns Goodwin, 1994, Schuster & Schuster, New York, New York, pp 182-183

[70] *FDR, Into the Storm, 1937 – 1940*, A History by Kenneth S. Davis, 1993, Random House, New York, New York, pp 613, 615, 619, 620, and 625

CHAPTER 11

[1] *FDR*, by Jean Edward Smith, 2007, Random House, Inc., New York, New York, page 446

[2] *Memoirs of the Second World War*, by Winston Churchill, 1959, 1987, Houghton Mifflin Company, Boston, Massachusetts, page 283

[3] *FDR*, by Jean Edward Smith, 2007, Random House, Inc., New York, New York, page 447

[4] *FDR, Into the Storm, 1937 – 1940*, A History by Kenneth S. Davis, 1993, Random House, New York, New York, pp 609-611

[5] *FDR*, by Jean Edward Smith, 2007, Random House, Inc., New York, New York, page 486

[6] Ibid, pp 510-519

[7] *War in the Pacific*, by Jerome T. Hagen, 1996, Hawaii Pacific University, Honolulu, Hawaii, pp 26-29

[8] Ibid, page 30

[9] *I Could Never Be So Lucky Again, An Autobiography by General James H. "Jimmy" Doolittle*, with Carroll V. Glines, 1991, Bantam Books, New York, New York, page 243

[10] Ibid, pp 235-250

[11] Ibid, pp 262-275

[12] Ibid, page 9

[13] *The War in the Pacific, From Pearl Harbor to Tokyo Bay*, by Harry A. Gailey, 1995, Presidio Press, Novato, California, pp 147 and 152

[14] *World War II at Sea, A Global History*, by Craig L. Symonds, 2017, Oxford University Press, New York, New York, pp 276-278

[15] Ibid, pp 279-280

[16] Ibid, pp 280-282

[17] *The War in the Pacific, From Pearl Harbor to Tokyo Bay*, by Harry A. Gailey, 1995, Presidio Press, Novato, California, pp 152-153

[18] *The Battle of Midway*, by Craig L. Symonds, 2011, Oxford University Press, New York, New York, pp 189-191 and 195-197

[19] Ibid, pp 219, 225, and 232

[20] Ibid, pp 253-287 and 301-307

[21] *The War in the Pacific, From Pearl Harbor to Tokyo Bay*, by Harry A. Gailey, 1995, Presidio Press, Novato, California, pp 165-167

[22] *Islands of Destiny, The Solomons Campaign and the Eclipse of the Rising Sun*, by John Prados, 2012, New American Library, a division of Penguin Group (USA), Inc., New York, New York, pp 18-19

[23] *The War in the Pacific, From Pearl Harbor to Tokyo Bay*, by Harry A. Gailey, 1995, Presidio Press, Novato, California, pp 184-186

[24] *Islands of Destiny, The Solomons Campaign and the Eclipse of the Rising Sun*, by John Prados, 2012, New American Library, a division of Penguin Group (USA), Inc., New York, New York, pp 98-99

[25] *Victory at Guadalcanal*, by Robert Edward Lee, 1981, Presidio Press, Novato, California, page 152

[26] Ibid, pp 192-195

[27] *The War in the Pacific, From Pearl Harbor to Tokyo Bay*, by Harry A. Gailey, 1995, Presidio Press, Novato, California, pp 195-196

[28] *Islands of Destiny, The Solomons Campaign and the Eclipse of the Rising Sun*, by John Prados, 2012, New American Library, a division of Penguin Group (USA), Inc., New York, New York, pp 139-153

[29] *The War in the Pacific, From Pearl Harbor to Tokyo Bay*, by Harry A. Gailey, 1995, Presidio Press, Novato, California, pp 198-207

[30] *Man of Destiny, FDR and the Making of the American Century*, by Alonzo Hamby, 2015, Basic Books, a member of the Perseus Books Corp., New York, New York, pp 348-352

[31] *The End of the Beginning, From the Siege of Malta to the Allied Victory at El Alamein*, by Tim Clayton and Phil Craig, 2002, The Free Press, a division of Simon & Schuster, New York, New York, pp 325-326

[32] *FDR, The War President, 1940 – 1943*, A History by Kenneth S. Davis, 2000, Random House, New York, New York, pp 756-757

[33] *No Ordinary Time, Franklin and Elanor Roosevelt: The Home Front in World War II*, by Doris Kearns Goodwin, 1994, Schuster & Schuster, New York, New York, page 407

[34] *Crusade in Europe*, by Dwight D. Eisenhower, 1948, Doubleday & Company, John Hopkins Paperback edition, 1997, John Hopkins University Press, Baltimore, Maryland, pp 147-150

[35] Ibid, pp 154-156

[36] *Memoirs of the Second World War* (abridged version of six volumes of *The Second World War*), by Winston S. Churchill, 1959, Houghton Mifflin Company, Boston, Massachusetts, pp 688-691

[37] Ibid, pp 706 708

[38] *Crusade in Europe*, by Dwight D. Eisenhower, 1948, Doubleday & Company, John Hopkins Paperback edition, 1997, John Hopkins University Press, Baltimore, Maryland, pp 173-175

[39] Ibid, pp 176-181

[40] *No Ordinary Time, Franklin and Elanor Roosevelt: The Home Front in World War II*, by Doris Kearns Goodwin, 1994, Schuster & Schuster, New York, New York, pp 457-461

[41] *Memoirs of the Second World War* (abridged version of six volumes of *The Second World War*), by Winston S. Churchill, 1959, Houghton Mifflin Company, Boston, Massachusetts, pp 727-729

[42] Ibid, pp 738-739

[43] *Monte Cassino, Ten Armies in Hell*, by Peter Caddick-Adams, 2013, Oxford University Press, New York, New York, pp 14-16

[44] Ibid, pp 61-62

[45] *Memoirs of the Second World War* (abridged version of six volumes of *The Second World War*), by Winston S. Churchill, 1959, Houghton Mifflin Company, Boston, Massachusetts, pp 797-799

[46] *Monte Cassino, Ten Armies in Hell*, by Peter Caddick-Adams, 2013, Oxford University Press, New York, New York, pp 147-153, 189-196 and 201

[47] Ibid, pp 211-220, 234-240 and 276-177

[48] Ibid, pp 278-282

[49] *American Warlords, How Roosevelt's High Command Led America to Victory in World War II*, by Jonathan W. Jordan, 2015, NAL Caliber, published by the Penguin Group, New York, New York, pp 307-315

[50] *Crusade in Europe*, by Dwight D. Eisenhower, 1948, Doubleday & Company, John Hopkins Paperback edition, 1997, John Hopkins University Press, Baltimore, Maryland, pp 223-225 and 238

[51] *The First Wave, The D-Day Warriors Who Led the Way to Victory in World War II*, by Alex Kershaw, 2019, Dutton Caliber, an imprint of Penguin Random House LLC, New York, New York, pp 6-10

[52] https://www.archives.gov/historical-docs/todays-doc/?dod-date=606

[53] *Crusade in Europe*, by Dwight D. Eisenhower, 1948, Doubleday & Company, John Hopkins Paperback edition, 1997, John Hopkins University Press, Baltimore, Maryland, pp 253 and 266-270

[54] *World War II at Sea, A Global History*, by Craig L. Symonds, 2017, Oxford University Press, New York, New York, pp 554-555

[55] *The War in the Pacific, From Pearl Harbor to Tokyo Bay*, by Harry A. Gailey, 1995, Presidio Press, Novato, California, pp 352-353

[56] *Storm over Leyte, The Philippine Invasion and the Destruction of the Japanese Navy*, by John Prados, 2016, NAL Caliber, published by New American Library, an imprint of Penguin Random House LLC, New York, New York, pp 165-177

[57] Ibid, pp 185-215

[58] Ibid, pp 232-234

[59] *World War II at Sea, A Global History*, by Craig L. Symonds, 2017, Oxford University Press, New York, New York, pp 575-578

[60] Ibid, pp 578-587

[61] *No Ordinary Time, Franklin and Elanor Roosevelt: The Home Front in World War II*, by Doris Kearns Goodwin, 1994, Schuster & Schuster, New York, New York, page 552

[62] *2194 Days of War, An Illustrated Chronology of the Second World War*, by Cesare Salmaggi and Alfredo Pallavisini, 1977. Translated by Hug Young, Gallery Books, New York, New York, page 581

[63] *Battle of the Bulge*, by Steven J. Zaloga, 2010, Osprey Publishing Ltd, Oxford, UK, and Long Island City, New York, page 106

[64] *2194 Days of War, An Illustrated Chronology of the Second World War*, by Cesare Salmaggi and Alfredo Pallavisini, 1977. Translated by Hug Young, Gallery Books, New York, New York, page 634

[65] *No Greater Valor, The Siege of Bastogne and the Miracle that Sealed Allied Victory*, by Jerome Corsi, 2014, Nelson Books, an imprint of Thomas Nelson, Nashville, Tennessee, pp 202-208

[66] Ibid, page 210

[67] Ibid, pp 280-281

[68] Ibid, pp 282-286

[69] *Memoirs of the Second World War* (abridged version of six volumes of *The Second World War*), by Winston S. Churchill, 1959, Houghton Mifflin Company, Boston, Massachusetts, pp 912-913

[70] *No Ordinary Time, Franklin and Elanor Roosevelt: The Home Front in World War II*, by Doris Kearns Goodwin, 1994, Schuster & Schuster, New York, New York, pp 586, 587 and 598

[71] Ibid, pp 601-602

[72] *Memoirs of the Second World War* (abridged version of six volumes of *The Second World War*), by Winston S. Churchill, 1959, Houghton Mifflin Company, Boston, Massachusetts, pp 955 and 962-964

[73] *World War II at Sea, A Global History*, by Craig L. Symonds, 2017, Oxford University Press, New York, New York, pp 605-609

[74] *The War in the Pacific, From Pearl Harbor to Tokyo Bay*, by Harry A. Gailey, 1995, Presidio Press, Novato, California, pp 426 and 444

[75] *Memoirs of the Second World War* (abridged version of six volumes of *The Second World War*), by Winston S. Churchill, 1959, Houghton Mifflin Company, Boston, Massachusetts, pp 982 and 995

[76] *The War in the Pacific, From Pearl Harbor to Tokyo Bay*, by Harry A. Gailey, 1995, Presidio Press, Novato, California, pp 488-490

[77] Ibid, page 494

CHAPTER 12

[1] *Man of Destiny, FDR and the Making of the American Century*, by Alonzo Hamby, 2015, Basic Books, a member of the Perseus Books Corp., New York, New York, pp 104-105

[2] "These are the top 25 US presidents, according to historians and biographers (and why you won't find Trump on the list)," by Allana Akhtar and Laura Casado, *Business Insider*, Jul 2, 2020, found at: https://www.businessinsider.com/the-top-20-presidents-in-us-history-according-to-historians-2017-2

[3] *Man of Destiny, FDR and the Making of the American Century*, by Alonzo Hamby, 2015, Basic Books, a member of the Perseus Books Corp., New York, New York, page 160

4 *The Defining Moment, FDR's Hundred Days and the Triumph of Hope*, by Jonathan Alter, 2006, Simon & Schuster, New York, New York, page 271

5 *FDR*, by Jean Edward Smith, 2007, Random House, Inc., New York, New York, page 316

6 *FDR, The New Deal Years, 1933 – 1937*, A History by Kenneth S. Davis, 1979, 1983, 1986, Random House, New York, New York, pp 385-386

7 Ibid, pp 387-392

8 Ibid, page 383

9 *The Defining Moment, FDR's Hundred Days and the Triumph of Hope*, by Jonathan Alter, 2006, Simon & Schuster, New York, New York, page 299

10 Ibid, pp 294-297

11 "The Correspondence Files of the Federal Emergency Relief Administration, 1933–1936," by John P. Deeben, *Prologue* magazine, Fall 2012, Vol. 44, No. 2, National Archives and Records Administration (NARA), found   at: https://www.archives.gov/publications/prologue/2012/fall/fera.html

12 *FDR, The New Deal Years, 1933 – 1937*, A History by Kenneth S. Davis, 1979, 1983, 1986, Random House, New York, New York, page 80

13 *The Great Depression, America, 1929-1941*, by Robert S. McElvaine, 1984, 1993, 2009, Three Rivers Press, an imprint of the Crown Publishing Group, a division of Random House, Inc., New York, New York, pp 151-152

14   https://livingnewdeal.org/glossary/civil-works-administration-cwa-1933/

15 *The Great Depression, America, 1929-1941*, by Robert S. McElvaine, 1984, 1993, 2009, Three Rivers Press, an imprint of the Crown Publishing Group, a division of Random House, Inc., New York, New York, pp 254-255

16 Ibid, pp 270-273

17 *FDR*, by Jean Edward Smith, 2007, Random House, Inc., New York, New York, pp 343-345

[18] "Public Works: The Legacy of the New Deal," by Howard Rosen, Managing Director of Program Development and Director of the Public Works Historical Society for the American Public Works Association in Kansas City, Mo., found at: http://www.socialstudies.org/sites/default/files/publications/se/6005/600 506.html

[19] "The Battle Of Midway Was Won With Stimulus Money," by Daniel Gouré, Ph.D., April 12, 2010, found at: https://www.lexingtoninstitute.org/the-battle-of-midway-was-won-with-stimulus-money/

[20] https://livingnewdeal.org/new-deal-agencies/public-works-administration-pwa/

[21] National Research Council 1995. Colleges of Agriculture at the Land Grant Universities: A Profile. Washington, DC: The National Academies Press. https://doi.org/10.17226/4980.

[22] *The Defining Moment, FDR's Hundred Days and the Triumph of Hope*, by Jonathan Alter, 2006, Simon & Schuster, New York, New York, pp 280-281

[23] "Farm Bills and Farmers: The effects of subsidies over time." By Edward Lotterman, December 1, 1996, Minneapolis Federal Reserve, found at https://www.minneapolisfed.org/article/1996/farm-bills-and-farmers-the-effects-of-subsidies-over-time

[23] https://www.fca.gov/about/history-of-fca

[25] *FDR, The New Deal Years, 1933 – 1937*, A History by Kenneth S. Davis, 1979, 1983, 1986, Random House, New York, New York, pp 91-92

[26] Ibid, pp 92-93

[27] Executive Order 7037 Establishing the Rural Electrification Administration, May 11, 1935, President Franklin D. Roosevelt, Online by Gerhard Peters and John T. Woolley, The American Presidency Project https://www.presidency.ucsb.edu/node/208659

[28] *FDR, The New Deal Years, 1933 – 1937*, A History by Kenneth S. Davis, 1979, 1983, 1986, Random House, New York, New York, pp 490-491

[29] https://www.nps.gov/home/learn/historyculture/ruralelect.htm

[30] "Emergency Banking Act of 1933," by Stephen Greene, Federal Reserve Bank of St. Louis, found at: https://www.federalreservehistory.org/essays/emergency_banking_act_of_1933

[31] "Banking Act of 1933 (Glass-Steagall)," by Julia Maues, Federal Reserve Bank of St. Louis, found at: https://www.federalreservehistory.org/essays/glass_steagall_act

[32] *After The Music Stopped, The Financial Crisis, the Response, and the Work Ahead*, by Alan S. Blinder, 2013, Penguin Press, New York, New York, page 266

[33] https://www.fdic.gov/about/what-we-do/

[34] https://www.senate.gov/about/powers-procedures/investigations/pecora.htm

[35] *FDR, The New Deal Years, 1933 – 1937*, A History by Kenneth S. Davis, 1979, 1983, 1986, Random House, New York, New York, pp 362-365

[36] Ibid, pp 370-372

[37] Ibid, page 101

[38] https://rooseveltinstitute.org/home-owners-loan-corporation/

[39] *Man of Destiny, FDR and the Making of the American Century*, by Alonzo Hamby, 2015, Basic Books, a member of the Perseus Books Corp., New York, New York, page 182

[40] https://livingnewdeal.org/glossary/national-housing-act-1934/

[41] *No Ordinary Time, Franklin and Elanor Roosevelt: The Home Front in World War II*, by Doris Kearns Goodwin, 1994, Schuster & Schuster, New York, New York, page 469

[42] https://www.benefits.va.gov/gibill/history.asp

[43] https://www.hud.gov/program_offices/housing/fhahistory

[44] *The Great Depression, America, 1929-1941*, by Robert S. McElvaine, 1984, 1993, 2009, Three Rivers Press, an imprint of the Crown Publishing Group, a division of Random House, Inc., New York, New York, pp 237-240

[45] Ibid, pp 241-242

[46] Ibid, pp 243-247

[47] *Traitor to his Class, The Privileged Life and Radical Presidency of Franklin Delano Roosevelt*, by H. W. Brands, First Anchor Books, a division of Random House, Inc., New York, New York, pp 412-417

[48] *The Great Depression, America, 1929-1941*, by Robert S. McElvaine, 1984, 1993, 2009, Three Rivers Press, an imprint of the Crown Publishing Group, a division of Random House, Inc., New York, New York, pp 225-228

[49] Ibid, pp 258-259

[50] Ibid, pp 303-304

[51] *FDR*, by Jean Edward Smith, 2007, Random House, Inc., New York, New York, pp 446-448, 484 and 500-502

[52] https://www.fdrlibrary.org/documents

[53] *FDR*, by Jean Edward Smith, 2007, Random House, Inc., New York, New York, page 595

[54] Ibid, page 636

[55] https://www.fdrlibrary.org/library-history

[56] Ibid

[57] https://fdr.blogs.archives.gov/2016/06/22/an-act-of-faith-the-75th-anniversary-of-the-fdr-library-and-museum/

[58] https://www.fdrlibrary.org/dedication

[59] https://www.fdrlibrary.org/library-history

[60] "How the 22nd Amendment came into existence," by Scott Bomboy, dated April 8, 2019, found at: https://constitutioncenter.org/blog/how-the-22nd-amendment-came-into-existence

[61] Stathis, Stephen W., "The Twenty-Second Amendment: A Practical Remedy or Partisan Maneuver?" (1990). Constitutional Commentary. 1018. https://scholarship.law.umn.edu/concomm/1018

[62] https://www.senate.gov/civics/constitution_item/constitution.htm

CHAPTER 13

[1] *Lincoln in American Memory,* by Merrill D. Peterson, 1994, Oxford University Press, New York, New York, page 218

[2] *George Washington, The Forge of Experience (1732-1755)*, by James Thomas Flexner, 1965, Little, Brown and Company, New York, New York, page 80

[3] *Leadership In Turbulent Times*, by Doris Kearns Goodwin, 2018, Simon & Schuster, New York, New York, pp 3, 10, 12, 13 and 14

[4] *FDR, The Beckoning of Destiny, 1882 – 1928*, Λ History by Kenneth S. Davis, G. P. Putnam's Sons, New York, New York, pp 48-49

[5] *FDR*, by Jean Edward Smith, 2007, Random House, Inc., New York, New York, pp 58-59

[6] *George Washington, The Forge of Experience (1732-1755)*, by James Thomas Flexner, 1965, Little, Brown and Company, New York, New York, pp 81, 86, 90, 93, 99, 104, 113 and 134

[7] *Abraham Lincoln, A Biography*, by Benjamin P. Thomas, 1952, Barnes & Noble, Inc., by arrangement with Alfred A. Knopf, Inc., New York, New York, pp 58 and 62

[8] *Leadership In Turbulent Times*, by Doris Kearns Goodwin, 2018, Simon & Schuster, New York, New York, pp 98-101

⁹ *FDR, The Beckoning of Destiny, 1882 – 1928*, A History by Kenneth S. Davis, G. P. Putnam's Sons, New York, New York, pp 648-650, 654, 658, 754, and 756

¹⁰ *Washington, A Life*, by Ron Chernow, 2010, The Penguin Press, New York, New York, pp 290-291

¹¹ *Leadership In Turbulent Times*, by Doris Kearns Goodwin, 2018, Simon & Schuster, New York, New York, pp 6-7, 10-11, and 15

¹² *FDR*, by Jean Edward Smith, 2007, Random House, Inc., New York, New York, pp 238 and 315

¹³ *Presidential Courage, Brave Leaders and How They Changed America, 1789-1989*, by Michael Beschloss, 2007, Simon & Schuster, New York, New York, page 324

¹⁴ *Washington, A Life*, by Ron Chernow, 2010, The Penguin Press, New York, New York, pp 13, 49, 59, 281, 329, and 343

¹⁵ *A. Lincoln, A Biography*, by Ronald C. White, Jr., 2009, Random House, New York, New York, pp 46-51

¹⁶ *Leadership In Turbulent Times*, by Doris Kearns Goodwin, 2018, Simon & Schuster, New York, New York, pp 164-166 and 169-171

¹⁷ *Emotional Intelligence, Why it can matter more than IQ*, by Daniel Goleman, 1995, Bantam Books, New York, New York, page 43 (embedded quotation marks per original text)

¹⁸ *Social Intelligence, The New Science of Human Relationships*, by Daniel Goleman, 2006, Bantam Books, New York, New York, page 58 (italics per original text)

¹⁹ *George Washington, and the New Nation (1793-1799)*, by James Thomas Flexner, 1969, Little, Brown and Company, New York, New York, page 260

²⁰ *American Creation, Triumphs and Tragedies at the Founding of the Republic*, by Joseph J. Ellis, 2007, Alfred A. Knopf, a division of Random House, Inc., New York, New York, pp 158-159

[21] *Lincoln*, by David Herbert Donald, 1995, Simon & Schuster, New York, New York, page 27

[22] *Leadership In Turbulent Times*, by Doris Kearns Goodwin, 2018, Simon & Schuster, New York, New York, pp 7-8

[23] *Traitor to his Class, The Privileged Life and Radical Presidency of Franklin Delano Roosevelt*, by H. W. Brands, First Anchor Books, a division of Random House, Inc., New York, New York, pp 174-178

[24] *George Washington, The Forge of Experience (1732-1755)*, by James Thomas Flexner, 1965, Little, Brown and Company, New York, New York, pp 94-100

[25] *Leadership In Turbulent Times*, by Doris Kearns Goodwin, 2018, Simon & Schuster, New York, New York, pp 105-108

[26] Ibid, pp 174-177

[27] *Founding Father, Rediscovering George Washington*, by Richard Brookhiser, 1996, The Free Press, a Division of Simon & Schuster, New York, New York, pp 137-141

[28] *Leadership In Turbulent Times*, by Doris Kearns Goodwin, 2018, Simon & Schuster, New York, New York, pp 5, 6, 15, 107 and 109

[29] *FDR*, by Jean Edward Smith, 2007, Random House, Inc., New York, New York, pp 22-31

[30] *The Extraordinary Leader, Turning Good Managers Into Great Leaders*, by John H. Zenger & Joseph Folkman, 2002, McGraw-Hill, New York, New York, page 231

[31] *Presidential Courage, Brave Leaders and How They Changed America, 1789-1989*, by Michael Beschloss, 2007, Simon & Schuster, New York, New York, pp 2, 6-12, 18 and 32

[32] *Leadership In Turbulent Times*, by Doris Kearns Goodwin, 2018, Simon & Schuster, New York, New York, pp 211-217, 219, 220, 227, 231, and 232

[33] *The American President, A Complete History*, by Kathryn Moore, 2007, Fall River Press, New York, New York, page 748

[34] *Founding Father, Rediscovering George Washington*, by Richard Brookhiser, 1996, The Free Press, a Division of Simon & Schuster, New York, New York, page 123

[35] Ibid, pp 108-111 and 114-119

[36] *Leadership In Turbulent Times*, by Doris Kearns Goodwin, 2018, Simon & Schuster, New York, New York, page 9

[37] Ibid, page 100

[38] Ibid, pp 3, 213, and 366

[39] *Man of Destiny, FDR and the Making of the American Century*, by Alonzo Hamby, 2015, Basic Books, a member of the Perseus Books Corp., New York, New York, page 176

[40] Ibid, pp 12, 19, 21, 57, and 214

[41] *Washington, A Life*, by Ron Chernow, 2010, The Penguin Press, New York, New York, pp 620 and 670

[42] *Team of Rivals, The Political Genius of Abraham Lincoln*, by Doris Kearns Goodwin, 2005, Simon & Schuster, New York, New York, pp 280 and 287-289

[43] Ibid, pp 299-300, 341-342, and 491-492

[44] *The Defining Moment, FDR's Hundred Days and the Triumph of Hope*, by Jonathan Alter, 2006, Simon & Schuster, New York, New York, pp 67-70 and 80

[45] Ibid, pp 80-84

CHAPTER 14

[1] *Washington, A Life*, by Ron Chernow, 2010, The Penguin Press, New York, New York, pp 648-650

[2] Ibid, pp 619 and 630

[3] *A Short History of the United States*, by Robert V. Remini, 2008, Harper Collins Publishers, New York, New York, page 145

[4] https://www.occ.treas.gov/about/who-we-are/history/founding-occ-national-bank-system/index-founding-occ-national-banking-system.html

[5] *The Defining Moment, FDR's Hundred Days and the Triumph of Hope*, by Jonathan Alter, 2006, Simon & Schuster, New York, New York, pp 2, 75, 82, and 155

[6] Ibid, pp 186, 226, and 305

[7] *The Great Crash 1929*, by John Kenneth Galbraith, 1954, 1955, 1961, 1972, 1979, 1988, 1997, 2009, Mariner Books, Houghton Mifflin Harcourt, New York, New York, pp 177-183

[8] *George Washington, A collection*, Compiled and Edited by W. B. Allen, 1988, LibertyClassics, a publishing imprint of Liberty Fund, Inc., Indianapolis, Indiana, pp 509, 605-609, 649, and 668-671

[9] *Leadership In Turbulent Times*, by Doris Kearns Goodwin, 2018, Simon & Schuster, New York, New York, page 9

[10] *The Living Lincoln, The Man, His Mind, His Times, and the War He Fought, Reconstructed from His Own Writings*, edited by Paul M. Angle and Earl Schenck Miers, 1955, 1992, Marboro Books Corp., a division of Barnes & Noble, Inc., by arrangement with Rutgers University Press, pp 9, 301-302, and 335-336

[11] https://www.benefits.va.gov/gibill/history.asp

[12] *Days of Sadness, Years of Triumph, The American People 1939-1945*, by Geoffrey Perrett, 1973, Coware, McCann & Geoghegan, Inc., New York, New York, pp 337-342

[13] "California Wants to Pay For Your College," by Zack Friedman, Sep. 3, 2019, 08:32am EDT, Forbes Magazine, accessed Aug 30, 2020 at 07:47pm PDT

[14] *George Washington, and the New Nation (1793-1799)*, by James Thomas Flexner, 1969, Little, Brown and Company, New York, New York, page 239

[15] "What is the National Debt Year By Year From 1790 to 2019?", by Eric Reed, Feb. 26, 2019, 6:06pm EST, https://www.thestreet.com/politics/national-debt-year-by-year-14876008, accessed Sep. 4, 2020 at 5:06pm PDT

[16] Ibid

[17] Ibid

[18] *FDR*, by Jean Edward Smith, 2007, Random House, Inc., New York, New York, pp 320-322 and 359

[19] https://history.state.gov/milestones/1937-1945/lend-lease, accessed Sep. 5, 2020 at 4:02pm PDT

[20] "The Financial Facts You Never Learned About World War II", by Doug Whiteman, Jul. 30, 2020, https://moneywise.com/a/financial-facts-about-world-war-ii, accessed Sep. 5, 2020 at 3:51pm PDT

[21] "The National Debt, Visualized. How big is this thing anyway?", by Brian McGill, Published Aug. 3, 2019 at 5:39am EDT, https://www.wsj.com/graphics/us-national-debt-visualized/, accessed Sep. 5, 2020 at 3:14pm PDT

[22] *His Excellency, George Washington*, by Joseph J. Ellis, 2004, Alfred A. Knopf, New York, New York, pp 29 and 107

[23] Ibid, pp 214-217

[24] *Team of Rivals, The Political Genius of Abraham Lincoln*, by Doris Kearns Goodwin, 2005, Simon & Schuster, New York, New York, pp 239-249, 280, and 487-495

[25] *Presidential Courage, Brave Leaders and How They Changed America, 1789-1989*, by Michael BE Schloss, 2007, Simon & Schuster, New York, New York, page 170

[26] Ibid, page 177

[27] Ibid, pp 181-188

[28] *George Washington, Anguish and Farewell (1793-1799)*, by James Thomas Flexner, 1969, Little, Brown and Company, New York, New York, pp 23-32

[29] *Seward, Lincoln's Indispensable Man*, by Walter Stahr, 2012, Simon & Schuster, New York, New York, pp 290-293

[30] Ibid, pp 348-350

[31] *FDR, Into the Storm, 1937 – 1940*, A History by Kenneth S. Davis, 1993, Random House, New York, New York, pp 543, 549 and 610

[32] *FDR, The War President, 1940 – 1943*, A History by Kenneth S. Davis, 2000, Random House, New York, New York, pp 75 and 271

[33] Ibid, pate 371

[34] *The Age of Napoleon, A History of European Civilization from 1789 to 1815*, by Will & Ariel Durant, 1975, MJF Books, by arrangement with Simon & Schuster, Inc., New York, New York, pp 177 and 189

[35] *George Washington, Anguish and Farewell (1793-1799)*, by James Thomas Flexner, 1969, Little, Brown and Company, New York, New York, pp 204-206

[36] https://history.state.gov/milestones/1784-1800/pickney-treaty (US Department of State website)

[37] *Seward, Lincoln's Indispensable Man*, by Walter Stahr, 2012, Simon & Schuster, New York, New York, pp 266 and 307

[38] Ibid, pp 308-313

[39] Ibid, pp 313-318

[40] Ibid, pp 318-323

[41] *A Short History of the United States*, by Robert V. Remini, 2008, Harper Collins Publishers, New York, New York, pp 231-233

[42] Ibid, pp 233-235

[43] *Alexander Hamilton*, by Ron Chernow, 2004, The Penguin Group, New York, New York, pp 339 and 341

[44] *Washington, A Life*, by Ron Chernow, 2010, The Penguin Press, New York, New York, pp 110 and 140

[45] "Historical Aspects of U. S. Trade Policy," by Douglas A. Irwin, NBER Reporter, Summer 2006, found at https://www.nber.org/reporter/summer06/irwin.html, accessed Sep. 8, 2020 at 3:43pm PDT

[46] *A. Lincoln, A Biography*, by Ronald C. White, Jr., 2009, Random House, New York, New York, pp 371-372

[47] TO PASS H.R. 338. (P. 1065-2), Senate Vote #512 in 1861 (36th Congress), https://www.govtrack.us/congress/votes/36-2/s512

[48] U.S. TARIFF RATES - RATIO OF IMPORT DUTIES TO VALUES: 1821-1996 (percent), http://www.econdataus.com/tariffs.html

[49] "Economic Report of the President," Transmitted to the Congress, 109th Congress, 2nd Session, February 2006, together with, THE ANNUAL REPORT of the COUNCIL OF ECONOMIC ADVISERS, UNITED STATES GOVERNMENT PRINTING OFFICE, WASHINGTON, DC, pp 149-152, found at: https://www.govinfo.gov/content/pkg/ERP-2006/pdf/ERP-2006.pdf, accessed Sep 9, 2020 at 2:45pm PDT

[50] Ibid

[51] *Founding Father, Rediscovering George Washington*, by Richard Brookhiser, 1996, The Free Press, a Division of Simon & Schuster, New York, New York, pp 24-32

[52] Ibid, pp 32-41

[53] *Jeff Shaarah's Civil War Battlefields*, by Jeff Shaarah, 2006, Ballentine Books, an imprint of Random House Publishing Group, New York, New York, pp 3-5

[54] *The Almanac of American History*, by Arthur M. Schlesinger, Jr., General Editor, 1983, Bramhall House, New York, New York, pp 472-477

⁵⁵ "What is the National Debt Year By Year From 1790 to 2019?", by Eric Reed, Feb. 26, 2019, *The Street*, https://www.thestreet.com/politics/national-debt-year-by-year-14876008, accessed Sep. 4, 2020 at 5:06pm PDT

CHAPTER 15

¹ *Generations, The History of America's Future, 1584 to 2069*, by William Strauss and Neil Howe, 1991, William Morrow and Company, Inc., New York, New York, page 35

² Ibid, page 382

³ *The Naval War of 1812*, by Theodore Roosevelt, series introduction and editor Caleb Carr, 1999 Modern Library Paperback Edition, published by Random House, Inc., New York, New York, page xxvii

⁴ Gross Domestic Product, 2nd Quarter 2020 (Second Estimate); Corporate Profits, 2nd Quarter 2020 (Preliminary Estimate), Bureau of Economic Analysis (BEA), found at: https://www.bea.gov/index.php/news/2020/gross-domestic-product-2nd-quarter-2020-second-estimate-corporate-profits-2nd-quarter, accessed on Sep. 10, 2020

⁵ "2010-2019: A landmark decade of U. S. billion-dollar weather and climate disasters," by Adam B. Smith, January 8, 2020, https://www.climate.gov/news-features/blogs/beyond-data/2010-2019-landmark-decade-us-billion-dollar-weather-and-climate, accessed Sep 10, 2020

⁶ NOAA National Centers for Environmental Information (NCEI) U.S. Billion-Dollar Weather and Climate Disasters (2020). https://www.ncdc.noaa.gov/billions/ DOI: 10.25921/stkw-7w73

⁷ Institute for Economics & Peace. Ecological Threat Register 2020: Understanding Ecological Threats, Resilience and Peace, Sydney, September 2020. Available from: http://visionofhumanity.org/reports, (accessed 11 September 2020).

⁸ *The Lessons of History*, by Will and Ariel Durant, 1968, Simon & Schuster, New York, New York, pp 79-80

[9] "How people in 14 countries view the state of the world in 2020," by Jacob Poushter and J.J. Moncus, Sep 23, 2020, Pew Research Center, found at: https://www.pewresearch.org/fact-tank/2020/09/23/how-people-in-14-countries-view-the-state-of-the-world-in-2020/, accessed Sep 30, 2020

[10] "The Changing Racial and Ethnic Composition of the U.S. Electorate," by BY Ruth Igielnik and Abby Budiman, Sep 23, 2020, Pew Research Center, found at: https://www.pewresearch.org/2020/09/23/the-changing-racial-and-ethnic-composition-of-the-u-s-electorate/, accessed Sep 30, 2020

[11] "North Korea's Military Capabilities," by Eleanor Albert, Last updated December 20, 2019, the Council on Foreign Relations, found at: https://www.cfr.org/backgrounder/north-koreas-military-capabilities, accessed Sep 27, 2020

[12] "Climate crisis could displace 1.2 billion people by 2050, report warns," By Jessie Yeung, CNN, September 10, 2020, found at: https://www.cnn.com/2020/09/10/world/climate-global-displacement-report-intl-hnk-scli-scn/index.html, accessed Sep 11, 2020

[13] "Rising Hunger: Facing a Food-Insecure World," by Amelia Cheatham, Author, Claire Felter, Author, and Sabine Baumgartner, Photo Editor, Sep 21, 2020, Center for Preventive Action, found at: https://www.cfr.org/article/rising-hunger-facing-food-insecure-world, accessed Sep 27, 2020

[14] "The Global Risks Report 2020," World Economic Forum, Strategic Partners: Marsh & McLennan, Zurich Insurance Group, Academic Advisers: National University of Singapore, Oxford Martin School, University of Oxford, Wharton Risk Management and Decision Processes Center, University of Pennsylvania, found at: https://www.weforum.org/reports/the-global-risks-report-2020, accessed Sep 10, 2020

[15] *The Lessons of History*, by Will and Ariel Durant, 1968, Simon & Schuster, New York, New York, page 81

[16] "Preventive Priorities Survey 2020," Paul B. Stares, General Director, John W. Vessey Senior Fellow for Conflict Prevention, Center for Preventive Action, found at: https://www.cfr.ogr/report/conflicts-watch-2020/, accessed Sep 26, 2020

[17] "10 Conflicts to Watch in 2020," by Robert Malley, President & CO, the Crisis Group, Dec 27, 2019, found at: https://www.crisisgroup.org/global/10-conflicts-waaatach-2020/, accessed sep 10, 2020

[18] Institute for Economics & Peace. Ecological Threat Register 2020: Understanding Ecological Threats, Resilience and Peace, Sydney, September 2020. Available from: http://visionofhumanity.org/reports, (accessed 11 September 2020).

[19] *Decision Points*, by George W. Bush, 2010, Crown Publishers, a division of Random House, Inc., New York, New York, pp 183-193

[20] *Known and Unknown, A Memoir*, by Donald Rumsfeld, 2011, Sentinel, a member of Penguin Group (USA), Inc., New York, New York, pp 395-400

[21] Ibid, pp 400-405

[22] "The U. S. War in Afghanistan, 1999-2020," a timeline by the Council on Foreign Relations, found at: https://www.cfr.org/timeline/us-war-afghanistan/, accessed Sep 17, 2020

[23] Ibid

[24] *Known and Unknown, A Memoir*, by Donald Rumsfeld, 2011, Sentinel, a member of Penguin Group (USA), Inc., New York, New York, pp 365-367 and 398

[25] "China's New "Xi Jinping Constitution": The Road to Totalitarianism," by Suzuki Ken, *Nippon News*,
Nov 27, 2018, found at: https://www.nippon.com/en/in-depth/a05803/, accessed on Sep 11, 2020

[26] "The China-Myanmar Economic Corridor and China's Determination to See It Through," by Lucas Myers, May 26, 2020, the Wilson Center, found at: https://www.wilsoncenter.org/blog-post/china-myanmar-economic-corridor-and-chinas-determination-see-it-through, accessed Sep 13, 2020

[27] "China's $900 billion New Silk Road. What you need to know," by Anna Bruce-Lockhart, Lead, Editorial and Visual Content, World Economic Forum, Jun 26, 2017, found at https://www.weforum.org/agenda/2017/06/china-new-silk-road-explainer/, accessed Sep 12, 2020

[28] "Here Is All You Should Know About 'String Of Pearls', China's Policy To Encircle India," Maninder Dabas, Updated on Jun 23, 2017, *India Times*, found at: https://www.indiatimes.com/news/india/here-is-all-you-should-know-about-string-of-pearls-china-s-policy-to-encircle-india-324315, accessed on Sep 13, 2020

[29] "China's Massive Belt and Road Initiative," by Andrew Chatzky and James McBride, Last updated January 28, 2020, Council on Foreign Relations, found at: https://www.cfr.org/backgrounder/chinas-massive-belt-and-road-initiative, accessed Sep 12, 2020

[30] "Special Report: China's vast fleet is tipping the balance in the Pacific," by David Lague and Benjamin Kang Lim, Apr 30,2019, Reuters, found at: https://www.msn.com/en-us/news/world/special-report-chinas-vast-fleet-is-tipping-the-balance-in-the-pacific/, accessed Apr 30, 2019

[31] "The Iranian hostage crisis and its effect on American politics," by Elaine Kamarck, November 4, 2019, Brookings Institute, found at: https://www.brookings.edu/blog/order-from-chaos/2019/11/04/the-iranian-hostage-crisis-and-its-effect-on-american-politics/, accessed Sep 24, 2020

[32] "Hezbollah: Revolutionary Iran's most successful export" by Jeffrey Feltman, January 17, 2019, Brookings Institute, found at: https://www.brookings.edu/opinions/hezbollah-revolutionary-irans-most-successful-export/, accessed Sep 24, 2020

[33] *Countdown to Crisis, The Coming Nuclear Showdown With Iran*, by Kenneth R. Timmerman, 2005, Crown Forum, an imprint of Crown Publishing Group, a division of Random House, Inc., New York, New York, pp 58-65

[34] Ibid, pp 152, 154, 158, 207, and 300-303

[35] "The Return of UN Sanctions on the Islamic Republic of Iran," Press Statement, Michael R. Pompeo, United States Secretary of State, September 19, 2020, found at: https://www.state.gov/the-return-of-un-sanctions-on-the-islamic-republic-of-iran/, accessed Sep 26, 2020

[36] "U.S. Reimposes U.N. Sanctions on Iran Over Objections of World Powers," By Lara Jakes and David E. Sanger, Sept. 19, 2020, *The New York Times*, found at: https://www.nytimes.com/2020/09/19/us/politics/us-iran-un-sanctions.html, accessed Sep 26, 2020

[37] "The Media Business: CNN Takes an Early Lead In Coverage of the Gulf War," by Bill Carter, Jan 17, 1991, *The New York Times*, found at: https://www.nytimes.com/1991/01/17/business/the-media-business-cnn-takes-an-early-lead-in-coverage-of-the-gulf-war.html, accessed Sep 21, 2020

[38] "Operation Desert Storm: 25 years on," by Ingrid Formanek, January 19, 2016, CNN, found at: https://www.cnn.com/2016/01/19/middleeast/operation-desert-storm-25-years-later/index.html, accessed Sep 16, 2020

[39] *Against All Enemies, Inside America's War on Terror*, by Richard A. Clarke, 2004, Free Press, a division of Simon & Schuster, New York, New York, pp 57-66

[40] *Fiasco, The American Military Adventure In Iraq*, by Thomas E. Ricks, 2006, The Penguin Press, New York, New York, pp 12-19

[41] "The Iraq War, 2003-2011," a timeline by the Council on Foreign Relations, found at: https://www.cfr.org/timeline/us-war-afghanistan/, accessed Sep 17, 2020

[42] "The Iraq War is not yet over," by Andrew Milburn, March 18, 2020, *Military Times*, found at: https://www.militarytimes.com/opinion/commentary/2020/03/18/the-iraq-war-is-not-yet-over/, accessed Sep 16, 2020

[43] "Iraq Timeline: Since the 2003 War," by Sarhang Hamasaeed and Garrett Nada, May 29, 2020, found at: https://www.usip.org/publications/2020/05/iraq-timeline-2003-war, accessed Sep 24, 2020

[44] "North Korea's Power Structure," by Eleanor Albert, Last updated June 17, 2020, the Council on Foreign Relations, found at: https://www.cfr.org/backgrounder/north-koreas-power-structure, accessed Sep 27, 2020

[45] "Kim Jong Il: Revered at home; remembered outside as repressive," by the CNN Wire Staff, December 19, 2011, found at: https://www.cnn.com/2011/12/18/world/asia/kim-jong-il-obit/index.html, accessed Sep 27, 2020

[46] "The Education of Kim Jong-Un," by Jung H. Pak, February, 2018, the Brookings Institute, found at: https://www.brookings.edu/essay/the-education-of-kim-jong-un/, accessed Sep 27, 2020

[47] "North Korea's Military Capabilities," by Eleanor Albert, Last updated December 20, 2019, the Council on Foreign Relations, found at: https://www.cfr.org/backgrounder/north-koreas-military-capabilities, accessed Sep 27, 2020

[48] "After Kim Jong Un, It Is Time to Plan for North Korea's Inevitable Succession Crisis," by Katrin Fraser Katz and Victor Cha, May 14, 2020, *Foreign Affairs*, found at: https://www.foreignaffairs.com/articles/north-korea/2020-05-14/after-kim-jong-un, accessed Sep 27, 2020

[49] "Pakistan : History," from The Commonwealth - a voluntary association of 54 independent and equal countries, found at: https://thecommonwealth.org/our-member-countries/pakistan/history, accessed Sep 28, 2020

[50] "Benazir Bhutto, Former Prime Minister of Pakistan," Biography — Academy of Achievement, found at: https://achievement.org/achiever/benazir-bhutto/, accessed Sep 28, 2020

[51] "Pakistan : Constitution and politics," from The Commonwealth - a voluntary association of 54 independent and equal countries, found at: https://thecommonwealth.org/our-member-countries/pakistan/constitution-politics, accessed Sep 28, 2020

[52] "Why Pakistan's former ruler Musharraf was sentenced to death, and what it means," Madiha Afzal, Brookings Institute, Thursday, December 19, 2019, found at: https://www.brookings.edu/blog/order-from-chaos/2019/12/19/why-pakistans-former-ruler-musharraf-was-sentenced-to-death-and-what-it-means/, accessed Sep 28, 2020

[53] "The Unraveling of Imran Khan: How Pakistan's Prime Minister Fumbled," by Tilak Devasher, July 05, 2020, *The Diplomat*, found at: https://thediplomat.com/2020/07/the-unraveling-of-imran-khan-how-pakistans-prime-minister-fumbled/, accessed Sep 28, 2020

[54] "Pakistan's Most Terrifying Adversary Is Climate Change," by Fatima Bhutto, Sept. 27, 2020, *The New York Times*, found at: https://www.nytimes.com/2020/09/27/opinion/pakistan-climate-change.html, accessed Sep 27, 2020

[55] "Putin Is Ruling Russia Like a Central Asian Dictator," by Sergey Radchenko and Baurzhan Rakhmetov, Aug 6, 2020, ForeignPolicy.com, found at: https://foreignpolicy.com/2020/08/06/putin-ruling-russia-like-a-kazakhstan-kyrgyzstan-uzbekistan-tajikistan-belarus-central-asian-dictator/, accessed Sep 12, 2020

[56] "Crimea: Six years after illegal annexation," by Steven Pifer, Brookings Institute, Tuesday, March 17, 2020, found at: https://www.brookings.edu/blog/order-from-chaos/2020/03/17/crimea-six-years-after-illegal-annexation/, accessed Sep 14, 2020

[57] "Why is there a war in Syria?" February 25, 2019, BBC News, found at: https://www.bbc.com/news/world-middle-east-35806229, accessed Sep 15, 2020

[58] "Treasury Sanctions Russia-Linked Election Interference Actors," Treasury Department press release dated September 10, 2020, found at: https://home.treasury.gov/news/press-releases/sm1118, accessed Sep 14, 2020

[59] "Russia is back, wilier than ever — and it's not alone," by Mark Scott, Politico, Sep 14, 2020, found at: https://www.politico.com/news/2020/09/14/russia-cyberattacks-election-413757, accessed Sep 14, 2020

[60] "Syria war: American troops hurt as Russian and US military vehicles collide," August 27, 2020, BBC News, found at: https://www.bbc.com/news/world-middle-east-53930795, accessed Sep 15, 2020

[61] "Why is there a war in Syria?" February 25, 2019, BBC News, found at: https://www.bbc.com/news/world-middle-east-35806229, accessed Sep 15, 2020

[62] "Syria's Economy Collapses Even as Civil War Winds to a Close," By Ben Hubbard, the New York Times, June 15, 2020, found at: https://www.nytimes.com/2020/06/15/world/middleeast/syria-economy-assad-makhlouf.html, accessed Sep 15, 2020

[63] "Russia vows to help Syria "break through" crippling U.S. sanctions," by George Baghdadi, September 9, 2020, CBS NEWS, found at: https://www.cbsnews.com/news/russia-vows-to-help-syria-break-through-united-states-sanctions-as-war-wrecks-syrian-economy/, accessed Sep 15, 2020

CHAPTER 16

[1] "Rising Hunger: Facing a Food-Insecure World," by Amelia Cheatham, Author, Claire Felter, Author, and Sabine Baumgartner, Photo Editor, Sep 21, 2020, Center for Preventive Action, found at: https://www.cfr.org/article/rising-hunger-facing-food-insecure-world, accessed Sep 27, 2020

[2] "UNITED NATIONS FRAMEWORK CONVENTION ON CLIMATE CHANGE," United Nations, 1992, found at: https://unfccc.int/files/essential_background/background_publications_html/pdf/application/pdf/conveng.pdf, accessed Oct 3, 2020

[3] "UN Climate Talks, 1992 – 2020," a timeline by the Council on Foreign Relations, found at: https://www.cfr.org/timeline/un-climate-talks, accessed Oct 3, 2020

[4] Ibid

[5] "Environmentalism Was Once a Social-Justice Movement, It can be again," by Jedediah Britton-Purdy, Dec 7, 2016, *The Atlantic*, found at: https://www.theatlantic.com/science/archive/2016/12/how-the-environmental-movement-can-recover-its-soul/509831/, accessed Oct 11, 2020

[6] "Why deforestation and extinctions make pandemics more likely," by Jeff Tollefson, August 7, 2020, *Nature* 584, 175-176 (2020), found at: https://www.nature.com/articles/d41586-020-02341-1, accessed Oct 11, 2020

[7] "Everything You Need to Know about Coral Bleaching—And How We Can Stop It," by Lorin Hancock, World Wildlife Fund, found at: https://www.worldwildlife.org/pages/everything-you-need-to-know-about-coral-bleaching-and-how-we-can-stop-it, accessed Oct 11, 2010

[8] "2019 Positive News: Seven Charts Show How the World Is Getting Better," by Julius Probst, January 8, 2019, *Newsweek*, found at: https://www.newsweek.com/positive-news-2019-charts-world-improving-trump-brexit-life-expectancy-child-1283256, accessed Jan 9, 2019

[9] *Fascism, A Warning*, by Madeleine Albright, 2018, HarperCollins Publishers, New York, New York, pp 245-246

[10] *The Post-American World*, by Fareed Zakaria, 2008, W. W. Norton & Company, Inc., New York, New York, pp 136-152

[11] *The Next American Century, How the U.S. Can Thrive as Other Powers Rise*, by Nina Hachigian and Mona Sutphen, 2008, Simon & Schuster, Inc., New York, New York, pp 171-181

[12] "The Fourth Industrial Revolution: what it means, how to respond," by Klaus Schwab, Jan 14, 2016, World Economic Forum, found at: https://www.weforum.org/agenda/2016/01/the-fourth-industrial-revolution-what-it-means-and-how-to-respond/, accessed Oct 17, 2020

[13] "The Fourth Industrial Revolution has begun: Now's the time to join," by Laurel Ruma, director of Insights, the custom publishing division of *MIT Technology Review*, Oct 15, 2020, found at: https://www.technologyreview.com/2020/10/15/1010365/the-fourth-industrial-revolution-has-begun-nows-the-time-to-join/, accessed Oct 17, 2020

[14] *The Audacity of Hope, Thoughts on Reclaiming the American Dream*, by Barack Obama, 2006, Crown Publishers, an imprint of Crown Publishing Group, a division of Random House, Inc., New York, New York, page 233

[15] "2020 is not 1968: To understand today's protests, you must look further back," by Thomas J. Sugrue, June 11, 2020, *National Geographic*, found at: https://www.nationalgeographic.com/history/2020/06/2020-not-1968/, accessed Oct 11, 2020

[16] "Congress and the Voting Rights Act of 1965," Legislative Archives, National Archives and Records Administration, found at: https://www.archives.gov/legislative/features/voting-rights-1965, accessed Oct 13, 2020

[17] "Our social contract is tearing at the seams. What will emerge?" by Ayooshee Dookhee and Abhinav Chugh, Sep 3, 2020, World Economic Forum, found at: https://www.weforum.org/agenda/2020/09/our-social-contract-is-tearing-at-the-seams/, accessed Sep 30, 2020

[18] "COVID-19 has hit Black Americans hardest. Healing this divide would lift the nation," by Nick Noel, Jason Wright, and Shelley Stewart III, Aug 17, 2020, World Economic Forum, found at: https://www.weforum.org/agenda/2020/08/covid19-racial-wealth-gap-black-americans/, accessed: Sep 30, 2020

[19] "Find Affordable Rental Housing," U. S. Department of Housing and Urban Development (HUD), found at: https://www.usa.gov/finding-home, accessed Oct 14, 2020

[20] "The Pandemic Threatens The Already Vulnerable Affordable Housing Crisis," by Jennifer Castenson, Oct 12, 2020, *Forbes*, found at: https://www.forbes.com/sites/jennifercastenson/2020/10/12/the-pandemic-threatens-the-already-vulnerable-affordable-housing-crisis/, accessed Oct 14, 2020

[21] "City Fiscal Conditions 2020," by Christiana K. McFarland and Michael A. Pagano, National League of Cities (NLC), found at: https://www.nlc.org/wp-content/uploads/2020/08/City_Fiscal_Conditions_2020_FINAL.pdf, accessed Oct 15, 2020

[22] "6 Ways the US Can Curb Climate Change and Grow More Food," by Richard Waite and Alex Rudee, August 20, 2020, World Resources Institute, found at: https://www.wri.org/blog/2020/08/us-agriculture-emissions-food, accessed Oct 2, 2020

[23] Ibid

[24] "Redirecting Agricultural Subsidies for a Sustainable Food Future," by Tim Searchinger, July 21, 2020, World Resources Institute, found at: https://www.wri.org/blog/2020/07/redirecting-agricultural-subsidies-sustainable-food-future, accessed Oct 2, 2020

[25] "Universal health insurance in the United States: reflections on the past, the present, and the future." By Bruce Vladeck, *American journal of public health* vol. 93,1 (2003): 16-9. doi:10.2105/ajph.93.1.16, found at: https://www.ncbi.nlm.nih.gov/pmc/articles/PMC1447684/, accessed Oct 15, 2020

[26] "Universal Health Care in Different Countries, Pros and Cons of Each," by Kimberly Amadeo, March 13, 2020, *The Balance*, found at: https://www.thebalance.com/universal-health-care-4156211, accessed Oct 15, 2020

[27] "Point Turning Point: the Case for Universal Health Care," by Lorie A. Sousa, Vicki Lindblade, and Charlotte Markey, May 13, 2020, *U.S. News & World Report*, found at: https://health.usnews.com/health-care/for-better/articles/the-case-for-universal-health-care, accessed Oct 15, 2020

[28] "The Education Reform Movement Has Failed America. We Need Common Sense Solutions That Work," by Diane Ravitch, Feb 1, 2020, *Time*, found at: https://time.com/5775795/education-reform-failed-america/, accessed Oct 18, 2020

[29] "How 20 Years of Education Reform Has Created Greater Inequality," by Michael A. Seelig, June 18, 2020, *Stanford Social Innovation Review*, found at: https://ssir.org/articles/entry/how_20_years_of_education_reform_has_created_greater_inequality, accessed Oct 18, 2020

[30] "How Johnson Fought the War on Poverty: The Economics and Politics of Funding at the Office of Economic Opportunity," by Martha J. Bailey and Nicolas J. Duquette, found at: https://www.ncbi.nlm.nih.gov/pmc/articles/PMC4266933/, accessed Oct 16, 2020

[31] *Leadership In Turbulent Times*, by Doris Kearns Goodwin, 2018, Simon & Schuster, New York, New York, pp 326-329

[32] "Governor Newsom Announces California Will Phase Out Gasoline-Powered Cars & Drastically Reduce Demand for Fossil Fuel in California's Fight Against Climate Change," Office of the Governor, press release dated Sep 23, 2020, found at: https://www.gov.ca.gov/2020/09/23/governor-newsom-announces-california-will-phase-out-gasoline-powered-cars-drastically-reduce-demand-for-fossil-fuel-in-californias-fight-against-climate-change/, accessed Oct 11, 2020

[33] "Public attitudes toward political engagement on social media," by Monica Anderson, Skye Toor, Lee Rainie, and Aaron Smith, July 11, 2018, Pew Research Center, Internet & Technology, found at: https://www.pewresearch.org/internet/2018/07/11/public-attitudes-toward-political-engagement-on-social-media/, accessed Sep 30, 2020

[34] *The Audacity of Hope, Thoughts on Reclaiming the American Dream*, by Barack Obama, 2006, Crown Publishers, an imprint of Crown Publishing Group, a division of Random House, Inc., New York, New York, pp 103-127

[35] Ibid, pp 133-135

[36] "Pursuing Unity: Race and the American Story," by S. Adam Seagrave, August 16, 2017, *Public Discourse*, found at: https://www.thepublicdiscourse.com/2017/08/19898/, accessed Oct 18, 2020

[37] "One Week to Save Democracy," by David w. Blight, June 5, 2020, *The Atlantic*, found at: https://www.theatlantic.com/ideas/archive/2020/06/one-week-save-democracy/612718/, accessed Oct 11, 2020

www.ingramcontent.com/pod-product-compliance
Lightning Source LLC
Chambersburg PA
CBHW071845090426
42811CB00035B/2332/J